Small Nations,
Giant Firms

WITHDRAWN

Small Nations, Giant Firms

LOUIS W. GOODMAN

Holmes & Meier
NEW YORK | LONDON

Holmes & Meier Publishers, Inc.
30 Irving Place
New York, NY 10003

Great Britain:
1–3 Winton Close
Letchworth, Hertfordshire SG61 1BA
England

Book design by Mark O'Connor

Library of Congress Cataloging-in-Publication Data

Goodman, Louis Wolf.
  Small nations, giant firms.

  Bibliography: p.
  Includes index.
  1. International business enterprises.
2. International business enterprises—Latin America.
3. States, Small. I. Title.
HD2755.5.G66 1987   338.8'888   87-42
ISBN 0-8419-0996-2
ISBN 0-8419-1112-6 (pbk.)

Manufactured in the United States of America

Contents

Preface

What is a small nation to do? Involvement in the international economy is an ever-increasing necessity if leaders hope to provide citizens with desirable choices. Yet the international economy is so complex and so volatile that it strains the administrative capacity of many small states to try to understand it, let alone use it for national benefit. Furthermore, small nations are disadvantaged. Most lack qualities that would cause other nations or transnational actors to seek them out or to strike bargains on their terms. Few have large markets, diversified economies, varied and valuable natural resources, state-of-the-art skilled populations, or strategic locations. What is a small nation—one the World Bank and the United Nations euphemistically call "low income"—to do?

This question is too important to go unanswered. Small nations may have few easy options that are realistic, but the increasing dependence of a low-income nation's welfare and prospects on effectively relating to the international economy makes an answer imperative. While it is unlikely that Ecuador or Bolivia[1] will ever again rival Brazil for international economic attention, there are steps that such small nations can take to improve their contemporary positions.

This book focuses on what a small nation can do to effectively relate to a particularly important set of actors within the international economic system—giant firms—more commonly known as transnational corporations (TNCs).[2] In doing so, this study attempts to develop tools for minimizing lost opportunities for *both* small nations and giant firms.

Chapter 1 presents an overview of the results of the field study on which this book is based and discusses the perspectives of both small nations and giant firms on the subject of direct foreign investment. To create a context for the discussion that follows, the text also briefly discusses some of the dynamics of the international economic order.

Chapter 2 presents and tests eight formal hypotheses about the determinants of foreign investment decision making in TNCs. These hypotheses are tested by systematically comparing investment decisions made for Andean and Brazilian subsidiaries of six U.S.-based TNCs in 1973 and 1974. Therefore, Chapter 2 discusses the different circumstances and foreign investment policies of Brazil and the nations of the Andean Common Market (ANCOM) in the mid-1970s. Using rigorous case study methodology based on detailed interviews in the home offices and subsidiaries of these firms, eight different investment criteria are compared for their Brazilian and Andean operations. Implications of the paradoxical results of these comparisons are then examined in subsequent chapters.

Chapter 3 uses these results to clarify how TNC managers evaluate business environments in developing nations.[3] As a first step, third-world environments are distinguished from first- and second-world environments as locales for transnational business. Next, aspects of third-world business environments important to TNC managers are identified and discussed. These include the host country's receptiveness to TNCs; host country's ability to structure a favorable environment for international business; the ability of the host country's market to generate adequate revenue flows; the cost and availability of production inputs that correspond with the TNC's global strategy; perceived ease of doing business in the host country (referred to as "the freedom to manage"); and the time horizon for business prospects. The result is a significant clarification of what constitutes an investment opportunity in a developing country for a TNC manager.

Chapter 4 directly analyzes differences between decision processes affecting marginal parts of complex organizations and those affecting the organizations' core. The key difference uncovered in the field study is that the efficient use of executive time is the primary concern in marginal decisions and revenue implications are primary in central decisions. The chapter argues that this finding has important implications for sociological and microeconomic decision-making theory. Since traditional theory explains only how core decisions are made, substantial revision is needed to account for the dynamics of marginal decisions. A number of revisions are discussed in Chapter 4, as are the implications of time-efficiency concerns for both host country officials and transnational corporate managers. Particular attention is given to why incentives that stimulate investment in central areas of corporate activity may not necessarily work in the same way in more marginal areas, such as small developing nations.

Chapter 5 discusses how the complexity of contemporary international business relationships has augmented transnational corporate managers' concern about the efficient use of executive time to manage investments in marginal areas. A brief review of the evolution of business negotiations between third-world nations and TNCs underscores this increased complexity. Particular attention is paid to the growing importance for foreign investment of a few third-world nations and the growing marginality of the remainder. Stress is placed on identifying new dimensions in the bargaining context within which international investment decision processes take place. Because field study findings suggest that growing complexity will increase the marginality of small developing nations for TNCs, the chapter concludes with a discussion of mechanisms for simplifying this context and clarifying situations of mutual interest to both giant firms and small nations.

Chapter 6 summarizes the implications of the argument both for the development of third-world nations and for decision making in large complex organizations. The chapter highlights the difficulty that officials of small third-world nations encounter in attempting to advance development objectives through collaboration with TNCs despite the clear-cut existence of opportunities for mutual benefit. By identifying how the structure of decision making in these firms and the goals of individual managers diminish chances for fruitful collaboration between small nations and giant firms, it is hoped that steps can be taken by both parties to benefit from new opportunities. Possibilities for such constructive action are illustrated by examples of time-efficient intra-TNC communication strategies for identifying business opportunities in small nations and by successful efforts of a small number of developing countries to attract foreign investment by targeting and streamlining inputs into TNC decision processes. On the level of theory, Chapter 6 aims at assisting the integration of social scientific approaches into the study of the social organization of economic life. Efforts to this end focus on relating individual motivations, organizational constraints, and the larger economic limits on decision making in firms.

The field research on which this book is based was carried out principally in the international headquarters and Latin American subsidiaries of six U.S.-based TNCs engaged in manufacturing.[4] The research was designed to ascertain how proposals for capital expenditures for business opportunities in Latin America were acted on positively or negatively by the corporations involved. Firms with subsidiaries in both Brazil and the Andean region were selected for study so that judgments could be made regarding differences in reactions to different investment climates, holding constant the reacting organization.

Detailed questions were posed during both home office and subsidiary interviews to obtain insight into the impacts of different aspects of these investment climates. Managers at both the home office and subsidiary levels were asked to evaluate the importance for the decision process of such factors as the host government's policies toward foreign corporations, host country's economic and political stability, the size of the domestic market, the availability and cost of factors of production, expected profit levels, and the use of executive time for managing the investment.

Lengthy open-ended interviews were carried out at both sites with key individuals involved in decisions to commit resources to business opportunities in Latin America. In the home office, such individuals included corporate presidents and other officers serving on the board of directors, corporate officers responsible for reporting to the board on activities of Latin American subsidiaries on both a product line and a regional basis, and headquarters executives to whom Latin American subsidiary managers reported. Interviews in the subsidiaries were carried out with subsidiary managers as well as other executives involved in proposing or evaluating possibilities for future commitment of corporate resources.

In these interviews, the nature of the research was explained, and respondents were asked to discuss their international business experience. Based on the first few interviews, a set of questions was developed to ensure comprehensive coverage of the research objectives. These questions were presented at the end of the interview if they had not been addressed by the respondents themselves. In addition to asking respondents to evaluate the importance of such factors as those just mentioned for the resource allocation decision process, questions were posed regarding how business opportunities in Latin America are brought to the attention of management; the nature of the formal organization and reporting hierarchy; formal limits on resource commitment at different levels of the reporting hierarchy; the importance of informal decision-making channels in resource allocation decisions; the type of information available at each stage of the decision process; the nature of costs associated with collecting additional information; and how such information was used in reporting prospects for new business opportunities. In this fashion, the researcher was able to gain an understanding of the capital allocation decision process as it proceeded through the hierarchy of the firm, especially from the level of the subsidiary to the home office and the board of directors. Special attention was given to understanding bases for recommendations made by management at different stages in the decision process, with an emphasis on how the impact of host country policy was evaluated at each stage. In this way, it was hoped to identify aspects of both corporate structure and practice as well as government policy that act as practical deterrents to achieving the host country's development objectives and impediments to the TNC's perceptions of business opportunities.

The six corporations intensively studied were chosen from a list of more than a hundred firms known to have direct foreign investments in both Brazil and one of the ANCOM countries in 1973. Portfolio investments were excluded from consideration, as were licensing agreements and ongoing negotiations for the initial establishment of a subsidiary. Manufacturing firms were chosen because of projected growth of that sector and the importance of manufacturing for national development plans.[5] The focus on capital expenditure decision processes in already-established subsidiaries centered research on the interaction of decision processes within the firm and host country's development processes, since the operating subsidiaries were already involved there. Furthermore, by the early 1970s, decisions made by firms with already-existing subsidiaries far outnumbered and involved the commitment of more annual expenditure than decisions by firms to make an initial investment in Latin America. The number of large firms considering initial investments in Latin America in 1973 was small simply because so many firms had established transnational networks and Latin American affiliates by that time.[6] Therefore, in 1973, the study of capital expenditure decision processes in corporations with already-established affiliates seemed much more germane to future host country development processes than the study of capital allocation in corporations without existing subsidiaries.[7]

Interviews were carried out in the home offices of the six firms and in offices of twenty-three of their subsidiaries, nine located in Brazil and fourteen in the Andean countries (Bolivia, Colombia,

Chile, Ecuador, and Peru).[8] To ensure a variety of experience within the region, four of the firms were selected because they had relatively long experience in the region (subsidiaries established before World War II) and the remaining two because they had established their first subsidiary since 1960. To ensure variety in the type of manufacturing firm, two were selected because of their attention to marketing, advertising, and establishing sales networks, with the remaining four largely basing their international competitive advantage on technology. Three of the firms were technology oriented and had long experience; one was technology oriented with short experience; one was market oriented with short experience; and one market oriented with long experience. Because the size of the sample of firms and subsidiaries was extremely small, this variety was important so that findings could be generalized across a range of manufacturing TNCs.

In all, ninety-six interviews were carried out in the six companies intensively studied—twenty-five with managers located in home offices and seventy-one in subsidiaries. Nearly one hundred additional interviews were carried out in the United States and Latin America with officers of thirty-seven other U.S. corporations involved in agriculture, mining, and services, as well as in manufacturing, with managers of corporations based in Canada, Japan, Western Europe, and Eastern Europe; and with staff of the Council of the Americas (an organization established by U.S.-based TNCs with investments in Latin America for the stated purpose of promoting discussion of international business issues). Finally, interviews were carried out with host government officials responsible for regulating the activities of TNCs in Brazil, Colombia, and Peru, as well as with staff of ANCOM involved in regulations affecting TNCs.

This field research was buttressed by publicly available statistics on international business, scholarly literature in international business, and publications produced by TNCs doing business in Latin America. Corporate publications ranged from public information, such as annual reports to stockholders and 10-K forms on file with the U.S. Securities and Exchange Commission to restricted corporate documents. This statistical, scholarly, and business material is referenced in notes except where proscribed by confidentiality.

Any project conceived and executed under such circumstances accumulates many debts, and this one is no exception. A number of corporate executives and Brazilian and Andean officials contributed to this book by providing information and commentary. None are acknowledged by name, since complete confidentiality was one of the guarantees I offered when setting out to gather data.

Remembering the individuals and institutions in the world of scholarship who made this book possible is one of the pleasures of acknowledgment writing. The initial fieldwork, carried out when I was on leave from Yale University, was made possible by support from the Council on Foreign Relations, the Carnegie Endowment for International Peace, the Joint Committee on Latin American Studies of the American Council on Learned Societies and the Social Science Research Council, and Yale's Concilium on International Studies. The Rockefeller Foundation's International Affairs Fellowship Program made it possible for me to distill thousands of pages of material into the few hundred of this book, while offering classes on international business in the third world at Yale's School of Organization and Management. Final revisions were made possible through a leave of absence provided by the Woodrow Wilson International Center for Scholars. Appointment to The American University's School of International Service gave me the incentive to stop revising and surrender the manuscript to my editors at Holmes & Meier.

Many of my colleagues at Yale, the Social Science Research Council, the Wilson Center, and the American University offered encouragement as I struggled to link the findings of my fieldwork with both social science theory and issues of national development. Properly explaining the contribution of each would require another full chapter, and inclusion in a long alphabetical list would not do justice to the quality of their support. I will therefore trust that each knows how invaluable his or her assistance was. I hope that the contents of this book and my continuing friendship will be recompense for their help.

Finally, I would like to thank Nancy, Liz, and Jenny Goodman—the three women who have endured this project while living with me as wife and daughters. The pages of this book are spiced with their encouragements and loving admonitions.

Bethesda, Maryland   L. W. G.
May 1986

NOTES

1. The fact that Ecuador and Brazil have been important within the international economic system is a reminder of the difficulty of prediction.

Ecuador has experienced a number of commodities booms, including a nineteenth-century cacao craze; Bolivia was the main source of silver for Spain and the rest of Europe during the sixteenth century.

2. The adjective transnational is used here in preference to such alternatives as multinational or international because the corporate activities examined in this book are coordinated across nations in accord with global strategies rather than merely operating in many countries.

3. Throughout this book the terms third-world nations, developing nations, and less-developed countries will be used interchangeably, despite the obvious differences in their denotative meanings. All three terms refer to a broad set of nations with low levels of per capita income and little industrial development. The term third-world nations stresses these nations' attempts to find development paths necessarily different from North America, Western Europe, and Japan (the first world), on the one hand; and the Soviet Union and Eastern Europe (the second world), on the other. The term developing nations suggests that real output per capita is rising in these countries. The term less-developed countries indicates lower levels of per capita product in these countries than in more-developed countries. These three terms are used interchangeably in the hope of communicating all of these meanings with each of the terms.

4. Manufacturing firms were chosen as the focus for this study because they replaced extractive industries in the 1970s as the most dynamic sector of TNC expansion and because of the centrality of manufacturing in the development plans of Latin American nations.

5. United Nations Centre on Transnational Corporations, *Transnational Corporations in World Development: Third Survey* (New York: United Nations, 1983), pp. 23–24, shows that manufacturing was the most important sector for direct foreign investment through the 1970s and early 1980s.

6. For data on affiliate establishment, see Joan P. Curhan, William Davidson, and Rajan Suri, *Tracing the Multinationals* (Cambridge, Mass.: Ballinger, 1977).

7. Yair Aharoni's *The Foreign Investment Decision Process* (Boston: Harvard School of Business Administration, 1966) focuses on initial investment decisions. This research was launched in 1960, a date much nearer to the initiation of foreign investments in the host country he studied (Israel). His sample included twenty-seven companies with existing investments and 11 companies considering initial investments.

8. After the conclusion of the initial field research phase of this study Venezuela joined ANCOM (1973) and Chile dropped out (1976).

Small Nations,
Giant Firms

1:
Introduction

Making huge profits is not my bottom line. If I have a terrific year I worry whether I can manage a repeat performance. . . . This is a small subsidiary. Even doubling or tripling last year's profits would have little impact at headquarters. My bottom line is to make a satisfactory showing and, most important, not to waste my boss's time worrying about my territory . . . or too much of my own time on projects that should be well on their way.

(LIMA, 1973)

The excerpt cited above was taken from an interview with the manager of a world-renowned transnational corporation (TNC). This was my first encounter with an executive who was more worried about saving time than making money.

I had arrived in Lima to begin the second stage of a field study on transnational corporate investment strategies in the newly formed Andean Common Market (ANCOM). Stage one, which had taken nearly half a year, consisted of interviews in U.S. home offices of more than twenty TNCs with subsidiaries in both the ANCOM and Brazil. Stage two would take me to the capital cities of the then three largest ANCOM countries—Bogota, Colombia, Lima, Peru, and Santiago, Chile—and for a non-Andean contrast, to Rio de Janeiro and São Paulo, Brazil. There I met with TNC executives and discussed their plans for the subsidiaries they were managing. I also met with host country government officials and heard their views on how these giant firms could best advance the economic development of these Latin American nations. I would later return to the home offices and subsidiaries of six of these corporations to learn how proposals for new investment in their South American operations had been handled during a specific six-month period. By the end of the field study, I had gathered comprehensive information on the reasons behind the approval or disapproval of all of these investment proposals and had used it to develop explanations for how managers of giant firms make decisions about investments in the third world.

Results of this field study have been used as the basis for a number of articles and are fully presented for the first time in the pages of this book.[1] Their focus on the determinants of direct foreign investment decisions in small third-world nations could not be more relevant for the late 1980s. These countries are facing development crises with enormous implications for their own economies and the future economic health of the United States and other developed nations. Except for East Asia, economic growth has stagnated in all developing regions since the 1970s, and prospects for rapid rebound are highly unlikely. Most small developing nations are mired in international indebtedness accumulated during the inflation-wracked 1970s and face low export commodity prices, slowed developed-nation demand, proliferating protectionist threats, and excess domestic capacity. This situation is critical because the unmet needs of third-world people both carry a huge human cost and weaken the underpinnings of developing nations' democracies. Furthermore, they impact on the economic health of the industrialized world. For example, dependent on expanding markets, from 1970 to 1984, the United States lost $18.5 billion in real export earnings and 1.4 million export-generated jobs due to reductions in exports to developing countries.[2] The main strategy now being pursued by developing nations to revive their economies is the promotion of new investment by the private sector, including direct foreign investment. Because this book examines, from the perspective of giant TNC investors, the criteria for investing in different business environments, it bears directly on such strategies.

DIRECT IMPLICATIONS OF THE FIELD STUDY

The fact that making money was not uppermost in the minds of many of the executives I met came as a surprise. The notion that free enterprise managers are profit maximizers had been drummed into me first as a young consumer of the folklore of capitalism and later as reader of economics texts. Furthermore, my research on the investment promotion programs of both developed and developing countries had led me to believe that the primary motivation for direct foreign investment by TNCs was the pursuit of profit. Andean Common Market planners held this view. Central to their organization's foreign investment rules were profit incentives for corporate practices that they thought would promote regional integration and economic development. However, they were also concerned lest new opportunities for profit created by the region's economic integration be missed by local companies and exploited by foreign firms. As a result, their rules also included provisions designed to help smaller domestic firms compete effectively with foreign companies, many of which were subsidiaries of giant TNCs. These planners felt that they had designed regulations that provided a counterweight to the huge power of the foreign firms while offering them clear profit incentives for expanding their operations in the region.

Reflecting on my talks with Andean officials and earlier interviews at the headquarters of these giant firms made me wonder if I should take this Lima interview seriously. In print and interviews, home office managers had complained that strict interpretation of ANCOM rules might impede earning a fair return on the capital their firms had invested in the region. They had said they were worried about how the new rules would affect their firms' ability to make money. Andean and host country representatives had gone to great lengths to devise investment rules permitting what they saw as "fair" profits. I wondered if the manager of the Lima subsidiary was merely a cynic, or if he was trying to create barriers between himself and his home office. The tension between headquarters' desire for control and the subsidiary manager's desire for autonomy was, after all, a classic theme in business organization literature. On the other hand, if making money were not the primary concern of certain managers, opportunities for both countries and firms were being lost to the extent that host country officials and corporate executives were "talking past" one another.

As my research progressed, I found more executives who shared the Lima manager's point of view, many in corporate headquarters. I also discovered that a growing number of host country officials had concluded that incentives for earning profits would be ignored unless transnational corporate managers first judged that their investments could be managed in a time-efficient manner. As evidence piled up that the Lima manager was not merely a cynic, I concluded that I had to take his point of view seriously.

Developing a satisfactory understanding of the implications of an executive concerned primarily with time efficiency required more field research and more interviews with managers of giant firms. A major difficulty was that not all corporate managers and host country officials shared the Lima manager's viewpoint. Managers involved with Brazilian operations—operations almost always of central concern to headquarters' global strategy—were not sanguine on this point. Managers of Andean subsidiaries—subsidiaries that were characteristically small and of marginal interest to global strategists—were much more concerned about time efficiency. This pattern exemplified what I came to see as an important difference between small-nation and large-nation foreign investment decision making: The efficient use of management time is a primary consideration for small-nation investment decisions and of secondary concern in large nations. Profit rates, while always important, are of secondary consideration for small-nation investments and of primary concern in large nations.

But discovering this pattern did not explain why so many home office and subsidiary managers of Andean operations were primarily concerned with time efficiency. Uncovering the explanation through my interviews was arduous. In the end, I was helped by an insight from the work of economist Edith T. Penrose. In *The Growth of the Firm*, she hypothesized that "the rate of growth of firms can usefully be analyzed with reference to the ratio between the managerial services available for expansion and the managerial services required per dollar of expansion."[3] Penrose was discussing determinants of the expansion of firms, and I was investigating the basis of such expansion—corporate investment. This link between corporate expansion, managerial services, and the size of expansion helped me combine in a single statement the management concerns with which I had been grappling. My statement became a mathematical equation that explained the desirability of a given investment as a function of perceptions of executive time efficiency involved in its management and perceptions of resulting profits. The equation was

$$i = f(p, 1/t)$$

Where
i = investment desirability
p = profits perceived resulting from the investment
t = time perceived needed to manage the investment

Thus, investment desirability is positively affected by perceived profits and negatively by the amount of managerial time required. To grow, a well-managed firm should seek investments requiring the least amount of managerial services and the most profit.

It therefore made eminent sense for the Lima manager to be concerned about time efficiency, since this was the element of the investment desirability equation over which he had most control. Managers involved in Brazilian operations, on the other hand, stressed profits because the size of Brazil's market permitted them to emphasize that substantial revenue growth might result from a given investment. Minimizing the use of executive time can thus be seen as the other side of the coin of the profit-maximizing free enterprise manager myth. Furthermore, it is the "head," or most important side of the coin, in situations of marginal importance to the main corporate strategy.

Having found a way of discussing transnational corporate managers' concerns with both managerial time efficiency and profits from potential investments, the question remained: Whose time efficiency—the subsidiary manager or the superiors at headquarters? This was answered straightforwardly in interview after interview: Time efficiency meant both the amount of time spent by the subsidiary manager and the headquarters staff. If an executive could manage an investment using little time, it would free him or her for other productive tasks, and the same was true of the headquarters staff to whom he or she reported. The worst situation would be a troublesome investment that fully occupied a subsidiary manager and also required his or her superiors to involve extra headquarters staff to solve problems. Worse still for the subsidiary manager's career was having recommended spending both time and money on such an investment.

BROADER IMPLICATIONS

As discussed in the chapters that follow, this finding has implications beyond the circumstances of small-nation economic planners and international business managers. Such findings shed light on the wider role of TNCs in national development and, in broader context, on certain types of decision processes involving centralized decisions in complex organizations that largely affect marginal components of these organizations.

Far from being unusual, decision processes affecting the margins are routine occurrences in most complex organizations. A well-managed organization has the ability to anticipate which marginal decision will have important future implications; a poorly managed one misses opportunities for growth or neglects functions that later become critical. For example, some consumer products firms have largely focused on product development, while others, such as General Electric and IBM, decided years ago to also develop expertise in servicing and distributing their products. These two prosaic functions, seemingly marginal to manufacturing, have consistently given these two firms competitive edges in markets with little real product differentiation. Similarly, the marginal and routinized handling of toxic waste disposal by chemical companies in the 1950s and 1960s had disastrous consequences for Hooker Chemical's Love Canal and other locales when forgotten dump sites were transformed into suburban developments.

Less dramatic, but equally marginal, are decisions to expand or close one production facility rather than another; promote one employee while passing over another; and to use or not use a particular supplier. In all of these, and in parallel circumstances in complex public sector organizations, executives are involved in decision processes of varying importance to both their own primary concerns and their interpretation of their organizations' missions. Bad decisions, of course, produce dire consequences and lead to lost opportunities whether such decisions are made in areas of central or marginal concern. However, errors in marginal areas are more likely to go unnoticed, with lost opportunities there chalked up to extraneous factors and no resultant learning and a high probability of repeating the error.

Decision processes involving small nations and subsidiaries of giant firms located far from their headquarters perhaps provide unparalleled opportunities for marginality-induced bad decision making. Officials of small developing nations generally believe that foreign firms can make important contributions to improving their economies. Giant firms, however, are likely to expand operations in such locales only if their managers view the investment process as streamlined, fair, easy to understand, and generating benefits that advance their firms' global strategies. Difficulty understanding a small nation's investment climate, especially if few corporate managers are familiar with it, can easily result in losses due to excessive optimism or, more likely, missed opportunities due to excessive caution. Increasingly, intensive global economic competition will push the best-managed firms to incorporate dealing with the complexities of doing business in small nations into their corporate strategies. Less well-managed firms will miss opportunities in marginal areas, these opportunities will also be lost to the economies of potential host nations, and their loss will weaken the global positions of the firms involved.

THE TNCs' PERSPECTIVE

This study is an analysis of decision making and business activities of TNCs operating in Latin America. It is an analysis from two perspectives—that of corporations attempting to follow global strategies and that of Latin American nations trying to advance national objectives. Differences between these two perspectives have sometimes been the cause of bitter conflicts; complementarity of objectives has sometimes resulted in agreements promising mutual benefit. Often, however, mutual misperceptions have resulted in confusion, unintended hostility, or mere inaction.

The perspective of the TNC is based on a desire to enhance a firm's business through the international exploitation of one or more perceived advantages. These may include a special technology, a strong trade name, an economy of scale, an efficient distribution system, or the capacity for using low-cost factors of production. The resultant TNC is a set of affiliated firms located in different countries that: (1) are linked by common ownership ties; (2) have use of a common resource pool, including managerial services, finance, information, trade names, and patents; and (3) respond to a common strategy normally monitored by a headquarters or home office.

It has been estimated that TNCs produce between one-third to one-half of the gross world product.[4] For 1981, the U.S. Department of Commerce reported that the total stock of direct foreign investment held by developed-market economies was more than $528 billion.[5] This $528 billion represented only the equity portions of overseas investments and ignored both home country equity controlled by TNCs and assets controlled by means other than direct ownership. Taking these into account is likely to increase the total assets controlled by TNCs throughout the world to over two trillion dollars in 1981 and to close to three trillion in 1985.

While TNCs continue to play vital roles in the world's economy, the nature of these roles changed in the 1970s and early 1980s. Even though U.S. foreign direct investment has consistently grown

from the 1950s through the early 1980s, the pace of foreign investment by other nations—especially Germany, Japan, and
Switzerland—increased even more rapidly. As a result, the U.S. share
of total direct investment abroad declined from 48.5 percent in 1960
to 41.5 percent in 1981. During the same period, Germany's share
increased from 1.2 percent to 8.3 percent; Japan's from 0.8 percent to
8.3 percent, and Switzerland's from 3.0 percent to 6.7 percent. This
shift is due to a decline in the competitive advantage held by U.S.
firms at the end of World War II, so that firms in nations other than
the United States now possess sufficient capital, technology, and
managerial skills to build competitive global networks.

In addition to rivaling U.S. TNCs throughout the world, foreign
individuals and firms have increased their pace of direct foreign
investment in the United States. In the 1970s and 1980s rates
reached twice those of the 1950s and 1960s, increasing at more than
15 percent per year.[6] Despite this increase, U.S. assets abroad were
still, in 1978, more than four times as large as the value of foreign-
controlled assets in the United States, with only 7 percent of U.S.
manufacturing assets foreign owned, compared with 14 percent in
the United Kingdom and 25 percent in West Germany.[7] These shifts
demonstrate what has become an obvious fact in the 1980s: U.S.
TNCs are no longer solely dominant in global trade and production
and now share controlling positions with firms from a range of other
nations.

In addition to the increased importance of European, Japanese,
and even a few third-world-nation-based TNCs, other aspects of the
international business environment have changed in the 1970s and
1980s. A number of basic changes in the international environment
currently confronting TNCs are:

1. Economic growth in the major industrialized nations declined,
largely due to dramatic increases in energy costs in 1974 and 1978.
From 1960 to 1970, industrial production grew at average annual rates
of 13.0, 4.3, and 4.6 percent in Japan, Western Europe, and the United
States respectively. From 1970 to 1982, these rates fell to 5.6, 2.0, and
1.9 percent.[8] Since 1982, economic growth in Japan and the United
States has rebounded but remained sluggish in Western Europe.

2. Those nations experiencing the most rapid economic growth
since the mid-1970s are a few relatively advanced third-world nations.
Brazil and Mexico grew at rates exceeding 5 percent a year until 1980
but then slumped in the face of worldwide recession. A small number
of Asian countries, including South Korea, Taiwan, Thailand, Singapore, and Hong Kong, sustained growth rates in excess of 5 percent
throughout the period.[9]

3. With the collapse of the Bretton Woods system of fixed exchange rates and its replacement by a regime of floating rates, the relative values of national currencies have become unstable. The decline of the U.S. dollar, through the mid-1980s, relative to the Swiss and French francs, Japanese yen, Dutch guilder, German mark, and British pound was a key factor in shifting global investment patterns and rendering investment in the United States increasingly attractive. Although general business climate factors sustained flows of foreign investment to the United States after the dollar rebounded in 1980, the slumping British pound and short-term fluctuations in other currencies continued to make foreign exchange instability a factor, increasing uncertainties associated with international business.

4. Prices of basic commodities, including goods as diverse as cocoa and corn, and minerals as varied as petroleum and copper, have turned downward.[10] This has resulted in substantial imbalances in international payments, accompanied by steep and abrupt changes in the terms of trade between groups of countries. This downturn, however, has been abrupt rather than gradual, thus adding to the economic uncertainties of both commodity producers (especially small monoproduct developing nations) and such commodity consumers as TNCs.

5. In addition to exchange rates and commodity prices, a third key economic variable affecting trade and investment patterns is interest rates. Interest rates have been especially volatile since the 1970s, rising markedly in the early 1980s. The high level of real interest rates in the mid-1980s economic recovery distinguishes it from previous recoveries. This anomaly has had a further impact on international business uncertainty. Explanations range from the combined effect of tight monetary and expansionary fiscal policies and resultant budget deficits in the United States, to the increased international integration of capital markets, to the deregulation-induced removal of financial interest rate ceilings in several major developed countries, to demand–supply imbalances in world savings.[11] This difficult-to-predict and increased cost of money has changed capital allocation calculations for both giant-firm money managers and small-nation policy makers.

6. Changes in government policies, in both developed and developing nations, have increased caution among TNC managers regarding conditions for international business. In the former, threats of protectionism and inconsistencies between fiscal and monetary policies inhibit trade expansion and encourage TNCs to adjust strategically their operating policies.[12] In the latter, political instability, as in Iran in 1978 and South Africa in the 1980s, and a new openness to direct foreign investment, in countries as diverse as China and Mexico, have caused reassessments of both the forms and locales for direct foreign investments.

The impact of these changes has been increased uncertainty for managers of TNCs, as choices are made among a vast array of possible business strategies. This uncertainty has resulted in a slowed growth of overseas investment to rates roughly equaling annual rates of growth of the global product, but below that of world trade. As a result, TNCs will continue to play major roles in shaping world economic power, but they will not totally dominate global economics, as was the prediction of some TNC-watchers in the late 1960s.[13]

Although patterns of international business will continue to change in the future, developing nations will generally be less important in the business plans of TNCs than these will be for achieving certain national development objectives of developing nations. The reason for this lies in the overall structure of international business. The major activities of TNCs, despite changes already mentioned, are located in the developed-market economies of North America, Europe, and Japan. When business attention turns to developing nations, it usually focuses on the thirteen OPEC countries;[14] six small tax havens;[15] and a few advanced developing nations, including Mexico, Brazil, Argentina, India, Malaysia, Singapore, South Korea, Taiwan, Hong Kong, and the Philippines. In 1981, 19 percent of direct foreign investment by Organization for Economic Cooperation and Development (OECD) countries was located in these twenty-nine developing countries, and 74 percent in other developed-market countries, leaving some eighty-eight small, poor nations with roughly 7 percent of the overseas assets of TNCs.[16]

This pattern of concentration continued through the early 1980s[17] and is repeated worldwide in the distribution of foreign investments by TNCs. Of $545 billion direct foreign investment held by TNCs in 1982, 73.4 percent was located in developed-market economies; 13.5 percent in rapidly growing third-world countries, known as "newly industrializing countries" (NICs)—Brazil, Mexico, Venezuela, Nigeria, India, Malaysia, Argentina, Singapore, and Peru—with the remaining 13.1 percent distributed among one hundred other countries.[18]

The fact that developing nations do not represent a major investment interest for TNCs is illustrated by the business activities of these firms. Of the 150 largest U.S.-based TNCs in terms of foreign-generated revenue, only twenty-five had 50 percent or more of their revenue generated by foreign sources,[19] and most TNCs had one-third or less.

The operations of a large U.S.-based TNC, the Continental Group, ranked in 1980 as the world's one hundred and twenty-eight largest industrial TNC, with 29.8 percent of its $5.7 billion world-wide sales generated outside the United States,[20] are in many ways typical of the pattern of the largest manufacturing TNCs.[21]

Incorporated in New York in 1913 as the Continental Can Corporation, by 1976, when it changed its name to the Continental Group, it had become a diversified packaging, natural resources, and financial services company. In 1977, Continental held $702 million of its $2004 million total assets abroad; of this $702 million, $660 million was held in developed-market economies. Worldwide, $1302 million of its assets were located in the United States, $478 million in Europe, $182 million in Canada, and $42 million in the rest of the world.[22] In terms of assets, revenue, and earnings for Continental and most other large TNCs, the economy of a given third-world nation was less important than the smallest state in the United States.

Certain third-world countries did, of course, hold particular interest for Continental and other TNCs. By 1977, Continental was well on its way to evolving "beyond its can-maker origins and its more recent packaging-company image." Its Continental Can Company division maintained its preeminent place in the fast-growing world rigid-can market through the operation of eighty-two plants in the United States and thirty-five in other nations, forty-five technical licensees, and equity interests in twenty-three companies operating in twenty-one countries. Its Continental Diversified Industries manufactured plastic containers in twenty-five plants in North America, South America, and Europe, reaching markets in some ninety countries. Its integrated forest products company, Continental Forest Industries, operated timberlands, mills, and manufacturing facilities in the United States, Canada, West Germany, and Brazil. Its financial services organization, Richmond Company, operated in more than 700 communities in the United States, Canada, and the Bahamas. Included among Continental's top operating-group executives listed in its *Annual Report for 1977* were ninety-six located in the United States and Europe, two in Brazil, one in Mexico, one in Colombia, and one in Kuwait.[23]

In 1984, Continental was taken over by the Kiewit–Murdock Investment Corporation and transformed into a holding company, KMI Continental Inc. To finance the merger, the buyers borrowed $2.17 billion from a syndicate of banks. Following the takeover, as part of the credit agreement with the banks, the new KMI Continental sold a number of its holdings to reduce its borrowings to $1.15 billion. These included a title insurance business, pipeline, and oil and gas operations acquired during the previous five years in an effort to move beyond its initial mid-1970s diversification. Although the purpose of the merger was to transform Continental into a privately held holding company, as 1985 began, its ongoing businesses were the packaging, forest products, and financial services it had operated for more than ten years. Continental continued to be the world's leading packaging manufacturer, producing metal and plastic containers, closures, and packaging equipment in eighty-two US facilities, thirty-four in the European Common Market, four in Canada, three in Mexico, and one in the Netherlands Antilles. Elsewhere, including Argentina, Brazil, Bolivia, Hong Kong, Indonesia, South Korea, Kuwait, Nigeria, Peru, Saudi Arabia, Uruguay, and Venezuela, Continental stated that it "maintains a minority interest in foreign packaging companies, receiving income in the form of dividends, license and service fees, and from machinery sales."[24] Its assets continued to be concentrated in developed-market economies—$3,134 million in the United States, $462 million in Europe, $88 million in Canada, and $42 million in Latin America and other areas.

The history and operations of this giant firm are in many ways typical. Continental's base is in the United States and other developed-market economies; in the past ten years, top management has been involved in dealings that have significantly restructured the corporation not once, but twice. Although Continental has substantial holdings in Mexico and Brazil, these and its other operations in developing nations were not an issue for either the firm's massive internal struggles or its overall earnings picture. On the other hand, within the more than twenty developing nations in which Continental held investments and the more than one hundred in which it has marketed its technology or sold its products, its profile as "the world's leading diversified packager"[25] is quite visible, and its operations can be important for the progress of economic development. We now turn to the perspective of the developing nation.

THE PERSPECTIVE OF LATIN AMERICAN NATIONS

The perspective of Latin American nations is influenced by the desire to accelerate national development, taking into account existing resources and the nation's role in the international order. Latin American leaders have long cherished the ideal of national autonomy, but awareness of their reliance on foreign markets and foreign sources of technology and capital has caused them to view their national situation as one of *externally conditioned development.* Development, or the "rapid and sustained rise in real output per head and attendant shifts in the technological, economic, and demographic characteristics of a society,"[26] for Latin American nations is regarded as "conditioned by" the development and expansion of other economies.[27] While all nations, including industrialized ones, consider their development prospects as, in part, affected by the world economic and political systems, Latin American and other third-world nations are more vulnerable to external forces than are more industrialized countries. The economic aspect of this external conditioning has three powerful bases: (1) the nature of international trade; (2) financial indebtedness of developing nations to foreign private and public sources; and (3) foreign ownership of important components of the productive apparatuses of developing nations.

Most Latin American nations have traditionally involved themselves in international trade by exporting a limited number of agricultural or mineral products and importing a wide variety of consumer, intermediate, and capital goods. Thus, in 1982, coffee accounted for 56 percent of Colombia's official exports; copper was 45 percent of Chile's exports; tin, 46 percent of Bolivia's; cotton, 37 percent of Paraguay's; coffee and bananas, 58 percent of Honduras's; copper, fishmeal, and zinc, 28 percent of Peru's; and wool, meat, and hides, 50 percent of Uruguay's.[28] Most of these exports are purchased by nations in North America and Western Europe. These exports are crucial to Latin American countries for generating foreign exchange used to promote development projects as well as service hard currency debts and purchase consumer goods from abroad. Development planning in third-world nations can be drastically affected by changes in the prices of these products in international markets or by changes in patterns of commodity purchase by more *developed* nations. On the other hand, more developed countries can often choose among a number of commodity suppliers. Thus, an economic downturn in more developed nations or mere changes in their purchasing patterns can have severe economic repercussions for third-world nations. Although economic declines in third-world nations do have negative impacts on more developed nations' trade and employment, these are relatively limited in scope. In this way, the nature of international trade makes economic development in third-world nations more conditioned by the expansion and development of first- and second-world nations than vice versa.

A second source of external conditioning derives from the financial indebtedness of developing nations to foreign sources. In 1984 the total foreign debt of Latin American nations was $360 billion, with amounts owed to financial agencies of foreign governments, to international lending agencies, and private entities— largely commercial banks.[29] This indebtedness increased markedly during the 1970s, not always due to events under the control of the borrowing nations. Substantial amounts of private foreign funds first became available when Eurodollar interest rates plummeted during the 1971 to 1972 economic recession. The recession that began in 1974 and the need for newly cash-rich oil-producing nations to place surplus funds facilitated the roll-over of previously accumulated debt and provided new sources of credits. This trend continued through the 1970s and into the 1980s, albeit with different intensity in different national contexts. At the end of 1984, Brazil's total foreign debt amounted to $102 billion. Brazilian planners estimated that interest payments on this debt alone would amount to $9.8 billion in 1984, or 36.5 percent of Brazil's expected export revenue. Other Latin American nations at that level for 1984 included Bolivia (57.0 percent), Peru (35.5 percent), Mexico (36.5 percent), Costa Rica (32.0 percent), Chile (45.5 percent), Uruguay (31.5 percent), and Argentina (52.0 percent).

Such indebtedness severely limits development prospects in Latin America for two reasons: (1) It consumes substantial portions of a nation's foreign exchange earnings that could otherwise be used for domestic capital formation and the purchase of materials and technologies promoting development projects; and (2) it makes Latin American nations dependent on their creditors. This latter limitation is particularly salient when it becomes difficult for a debtor nation to repay its foreign obligations. New loans and interest levels are granted to such nations only after extensive negotiations, in part involving careful scrutiny of the nation's domestic economic policies. If such policies are judged to put the capital of the creditors at risk, they are questioned and pressure is applied in attempts to change such policies prior to the authorization of new credit.

These sources of external conditioning are complemented by another—the significant foreign ownership of productive facilities. Foreign firms held $118 billion worth of assets in developing nations in 1981.[30] Somewhat less than 25 percent was located in the extractive sector, primarily petroleum, non-fuel minerals, and agriculture;

50 percent in manufacturing; and the balance in the service sector. In the 1970s, a clear trend developed away from extraction investments and toward banking, insurance, and manufacturing.[31] Many of the manufacturing assets are located in growing industries, such as chemicals, machinery, food processing, and transportation equipment. Foreign investments in other sectors are also important sources of dynamism for national economies. Foreign ownership of these assets causes their productive capacity to be conditioned by a force exogenous to local circumstances: the global strategies of their transnational owners. Flows of resources to transnational corporate subsidiaries in third-world nations can be adversely affected by economic crises in other parts of a transnational network or by plans to concentrate corporate growth elsewhere. Conversely, transnational subsidiaries can be expanded or shored up by infusions of resources generated in other parts of the transnational network. Such external effects, be they positive or negative, are part of the external conditioning of the economies of third-world nations—economic dependence due to foreign ownership of productive assets.

Although the development of nations in Latin America may be conditioned by external economic forces, this conditioning does not preclude development there. In the decade of the 1960s, the average annual change in gross domestic product (GDP) for Latin American nations was 5.6 percent while it was 4.3 percent for the United States.[32] In the 1970s, the average rates were 4.5 percent for Latin American nations and 3.0 percent for the United States. Although economic growth in the United States far outdistanced that in Latin America until the 1960s, changed historical circumstances reduced the difference so that, at the end of the 1970s, some Latin American nations were growing more rapidly than a number of more developed nations. This led an OECD study to suggest that the trend would continue for the remainder of the century, with Latin America becoming the fastest growing world area, although continuing to lag far behind the first world in terms of absolute development.[33]

However, the deep recession in industrial countries from 1980 to 1983 and its adverse effect on the export volume and terms of trade of developing nations, the steep rise in international interest rates from 1981 to 1984, and the sharp cutback in international lending since 1982 have combined to produce, in Latin American and other developing nations, the most severe recession since the Great Depression in the 1930s. Beginning in 1981, rates of economic growth plummeted in both developing and developed-market countries. While the impact on developed countries was severe, resulting in GDP changes of only 1.6, −0.2, 2.4, and 4.5 percent in 1981 through 1984,[34] Latin American economies were hit even harder, with GDP changing at rates of 1.7, −1.0, −3.1, and 2.6 percent for the same years.[35] In 1983 the region's per capita product had fallen to its 1976 level, and it was predicted that some countries would not regain their late 1970s living standards until the 1990s. While the 1984 recovery of the world economy, especially that of the United States, buoyed Latin American trade and development, its fragility made prospects for newly sustained growth dim.

Faced by a changing and uncertain global economy, Latin American nations have adopted economic policies that differ substantially from those of the high-growth 1960s and 1970s. These include exchange rate adjustments and import controls to improve payment balances, and public sector expenditure, budget deficit, and money supply adjustments to combat inflation. Although change has been slowed by the necessity of taking into account domestic politics and welfare, and some policies, such as Chile's 1979 to 1983 open and fixed peso–dollar exchange, had disastrous consequences, the overall regional negative growth rates of 1982 and 1983 turned positive in 1984. Patterns, of course, varied from country to country. For example, Argentine GDP growth fell from 3.1 to 2.5 percent from 1981 to 1983 while Peru's GDP rose from −10.8 to 3.5 percent, and Colombia maintained its unbroken positive pace.[36] These trends and differences among countries, as well as year-to-year changes, demonstrate that efforts to increase economic development have been pursued by individual Latin American countries with various degrees of success in a context that, in part, depends on external forces.

While operating as elements of global networks, subsidiaries of TNCs have played prominent roles in the development of Latin American nations. Foreign enterprises accounted for 44 percent of the sales of Brazil's manufacturing sector in 1977, 32 percent of Peru's in 1974, 31 percent of Argentina's in 1972, and 27 percent of Mexico's in 1972.[37] The importance of foreign firms for national development in Latin America is highlighted when these figures are compared with corresponding figures for more developed nations. In 1974, only 16 percent of the United Kingdom's manufacturing sales were produced by foreign firms; in 1972, foreign firms controlled 4 percent of Japan's manufacturing sales; and in 1974, foreign firms controlled 4 percent of U.S. manufacturing sales.[38]

The history of foreign firms in developing mining and petroleum resources in Latin America has been even more prominent than in manufacturing, although many large holdings in bauxite, copper, iron ore, petroleum, and tin had been nationalized by the late 1970s.[39] Foreign participation in service industries, such as banking, insurance, transportation, and tourism, became increasingly important during the 1970s.[40] Bank lending in particular assumed great importance, first as money-center banks followed their TNC clients abroad, and then as they recycled billions of surplus petro-dollars to the region in the late 1970s.

Although the activities of TNCs in the development of Latin American nations have been changing, it is perhaps more important to note changes in the nature of their involvement. With the evolution of national development schemes, the roles to be played by TNCs have come under increasing scrutiny by national governments. Much legislation has been enacted,[41] and there are now regulations prescribing acceptable practices for making initial investments, sharing technology and know-how, using local capital markets, employing local personnel, increasing domestically produced content, remitting profits, expanding existing investments, and many other matters. The purpose of such legislation is to promote development objectives through the participation of TNCs.

Increased regulation has been paralleled by increased state and local private participation in promoting development objectives. In some circumstances this has meant the exclusion of TNCs from banking, natural resources, and such basic services as telephones and power generation. In other instances this has meant the involvement of TNCs with state companies or local private investors. In Brazil joint ventures have been worked out among TNCs, state enterprises, and local private capital in the chemical and machinery industries. In Venezuela the holdings of transnational oil companies have been nationalized, yet they continue to work with state enterprise managers providing technical assistance and selling Venezuelan oil on world markets. In Peru Massey–Ferguson Ltd. and the Perkins Engine Company have entered into partnerships with the Peruvian government to manufacture tractors and diesel engines.[42]

In summary, while Latin American countries continue to look for ways in which TNCs can make additional contributions to fulfilling national development objectives, foreign firms have become involved in a vast array of complicated relationships that are vitally important to advancing economic development there.

THE POTENTIAL FOR MUTUAL INTEREST

Examining the interaction of third-world nations and TNCs raises a host of questions that have not been fully addressed by policy makers or social scientists. In the pursuit of national development goals, developing nations hope that TNCs will make technology and know-how available to local enterprises, enabling a larger range of products to be produced more efficiently. Furthermore, developing nations hope that arrangements worked out with TNCs will enable them to sell goods in markets to which they would not otherwise have access. Transnational corporations, on the other hand, are interested in maintaining and expanding their control in production and marketing areas in which they have expertise and seek to identify and penetrate areas that have the greatest immediate potential for corporate growth. From the standpoint of the developing country, TNCs are one of a number of forces that it is hoped will cooperate in their pursuit of development objectives. Although the importance of domestic business people, farmers, workers, and government employees may each be more important than the cooperation of TNCs, TNCs are seen as playing potentially important roles linking developing nations' economies to the rest of the world and helping them compete effectively in selected market areas.

As illustrated by the example of Continental, the major focus of most transnational corporate activity is developed-market economies. Corporations are also interested in doing business in centrally planned economies and are working out arrangements to do so. The developing nations that hold interest for TNCs typically have large, easily penetrable markets or unusually valuable natural resources. Those developing nations with small domestic markets and few resources generally have contact with TNCs by purchasing their products as imports.

However, every country in Latin America, including the small island nations in the Caribbean, does host subsidiaries of at least a few TNCs.

While total investment in most countries is small, firms with investments in small poor countries are often among the largest TNCs. The existence of such subsidiaries provides an opportunity for learning more about possible future involvement of TNCs in the economies of developing nations. Despite their minor roles in the overall activities of their parent companies, these subsidiaries do exist. Their activities are monitored by their corporations' headquarters, at times, some are expanded, some shrink in size or are shut down, and others are created. Viewed from the perspective of the developing nations, this corporate activity takes place in contexts where constructive TNC involvement is usually welcome and in which measures have been taken to make such involvement both feasible and attractive.

Although this book highlights the marginal role most third-world nations play in international business, it also identifies challenges to be faced by officials of both firms and nations in pursuing undertakings of mutual benefit. By identifying how the decision-making structure of TNCs and the motivations of individual managers affect changes for collaboration, it is hoped that steps can be taken by both small host countries and giant firms to identify and use new opportunities for growth and development.

NOTES

1. See Louis W. Goodman, "Prospects for Investment in the Andean Group," in Council of the Americas, *Andean Pact: Definition, Design, and Analysis* (New York: Council of the Americas, 1973); "The Social Organization of Decision Making in The Multinational Corporation," in David E. Apter and Louis W. Goodman, eds., *The Multinational Corporation and Social Change* (New York: Praeger, 1976); and "The Decision Process in the Firm: Theoretical Underpinnings of How Power Is Exercised in Complex Organizations" (New York: Wenner–Gren Foundation, 1980).

2. See Karen Pennar, Jeffrey Ryser, Ronald Buchanan, Lynne Curry, and Laxmi Nakarni, "Solving the Third World's Growth Crisis," *Business Week*, Aug. 12, 1985, 36–38; and Stuart K. Tucker, "Update: Costs to the United States of the Recession in Developing Countries," Overseas Development Council, Working Paper no. 10, Jan. 1986.

3. Edith T. Penrose, *The Growth of the Firm* (Oxford: Basil Blackwell, 1959), p. 201.

4. See Judd Polk, "The International Corporation," *Hearings before the Subcommittee on Foreign Economic Policy of the Joint Economic Committee, Congress of the United States,* July 27–30, 1970; and Raymond Vernon and Louis T. Wells, Jr., *Manager in the International Economy* (Englewood Cliffs, N.J.: Prentice-Hall, 1981), p. 4.

5. Data on direct foreign investment of developed market economies from 1960 to 1981 is taken from U.S. Department of Commerce, *International Direct Investment: Global Trends and the U.S. Role* (Washington, D.C.: International Trade Administration, Aug. 1984), table 1, p. 45.

6. United Nations Centre on Transnational Corporations, *Transnational Corporations in World Development: Third Survey* (New York: United Nations, 1983), annex table II-2; and *Business Week*, Oct. 8, 1984, 165.

7. United Nations Centre on Transnational Corporations, *Transnational Corporations in World Development: A Reexamination* (New York: United Nations, 1978).

8. International Bank for Reconstruction and Development, *World Development Report 1984* (Washington, D.C.: IBRD, 1984), table 2, p. 221.

9. *Forbes*, June 25, 1979, 54; and *Business Week*, Aug. 12, 1985, 37.

10. United Nations, *World Economic Survey 1985* (New York: United Nations, 1985), figure IV-I, p. 39 and table V-1, p. 51.

11. For a comprehensive discussion that concludes that the major factor behind interest rate increases is the current policy mix in the United States and the responses of other developed nations, see Oliver Blanchard and Lawrence Summers, "Perspective on High World Real Interest Rates," *Brookings Papers on Economic Activity*, no. 2 (1984): 273–324.

12. For example, see "Drastic New Strategies to Keep U.S. Multinationals Competitive," *Business Week*, Oct. 8, 1984, 168–72.

13. See Polk, op. cit., and Howard V. Perlmutter, "Super-Giant Firms in the Future," *Wharton Quarterly* (Winter 1968).

14. The OPEC nations are Algeria, Ecuador, Gabon, Indonesia, Iran, Iraq, Kuwait, Libya, Nigeria, Qatar, Saudi Arabia, the United Arab Emirates, and Venezuela.

15. The six tax haven nations listed in the U.N. *Transnational Corporations in World Development: A Reexamination*, table III-47, p. 254, are the Bahamas, Barbados, Bermuda, the Cayman Islands, the Netherlands Antilles, and Panama.

16. United Nations, *Reexamination*, table III-33, p. 237; and table III-47, p. 254.

17. United Nations, *Third Survey*, pp. 17–20.

18. U.S. Department of Commerce, *International Direct Investment*, p. 8.

19. "The 150 Largest U.S. Multinationals," *Forbes*, June 25, 1979, 56–62.

20. United Nations, *Third Survey*, table II-31, pp. 357–64.

21. Continental's transnational activities are discussed here merely for illustrative purposes. No interviews were carried out with anyone connected with Continental during the field study reported in this book. All Continental group data is from public sources.

22. The Continental Group, Inc., *Annual Report for 1977*.

23. Ibid.

24. KMI Continental, Inc., Form 10-K for the fiscal year ending December 31, 1984, p. 9.

25. Ibid., p. 3.

26. There is much conceptual and terminological disagreement regarding the term development. This definition is taken from Richard A. Easterlin, "Economic Growth," in *Internationial Encyclopedia of the Social Sciences*, Vol. 4, David L. Sills, ed. (New York: Macmillan, 1968), p. 395.

27. This definition of dependence is based in Teotonio Dos Santos, "The Structure of Dependence," *American Economic Review* 60, 5 (1970): 235–46.

28. Export data from United Nations, *Economic Survey of Latin America and the Caribbean*, Vol. 1 (New York: United Nations, 1982).

29. Latin American external indebtedness data are taken from Economic Commission for Latin America and the Caribbean, "Preliminary Overview of the Latin American Economy During 1984," *Notas sobre la economía y el desarollo,* No. 409/410 (Jan. 1985), table 13.

30. United Nations Centre on Transnational Corporations, *Transnational Corporations in World Development: An Update* (New York: United Nations, 1984), p. 31.

31. United Nations Centre on Transnational Corporations, *Third Survey,* p. 23.

32. GDP data for Latin American nations are from Inter-American Development Bank, *Economic and Social Progress in Latin America,* (Washington, D.C.: International Development Bank, 1984); for the United States, data are from the International Bank for Reconstruction and Development, *World Development Report 1984* (Washington, D.C.: IBRD, 1984).

33. OECD, Interfutures (OECD, Paris), *Review* (1979), various issues; reported in *Latin America Economic Report* (July 27, 1979): 226.

34. United Nations, *World Economic Survey, 1985,* table A-1, p. 105.

35. Economic Commission for Latin America and the Caribbean, "Preliminary Overview of the Latin American Economy during 1984," *Notas sobre la economía y el desarollo,* no. 409/410 (Jan. 1985), table 2.

36. Ibid.

37. Foreign-controlled manufacturing data from United Nations Centre on Transnational Corporations, *Reexamination* and *Third Survey,* both op. cit.

38. United Nations, *Reexamination,* table III-54, pp. 263–64.

39. For histories of nationalizations, see Norman Girvan, "Making the Rules of the Game: Country–Company Contracts in the Bauxite Industry," *Social and Economic Studies* 20, no. 4 (Dec. 1971): 378–449; George M. Ingram, *Expropriation of U.S. Property in South America* (New York: Praeger, 1974); Theodore H. Moran, *Multinational Corporations and the Politics of Dependence: Copper in Chile* (Princeton: Princeton University Press, 1974); Franklin Tugwell, *The Politics of Oil in Venezuela* (Stanford: Stanford University Press, 1974); Paul Sigmund, *Multinationals in Latin America* (Madison: University of Wisconsin Press, 1980).

40. United Nations, *Reexamination,* pp. 46–48, and *Third Survey* 1983, pp. 17–31.

41. See United Nations Centre on Transnational Corporations, *National Legislation and Regulations Relating to Transnational Corporations,* Parts I–IV (New York: United Nations, 1978–83).

42. For a good survey of developments through the early 1980s, see Eduardo White, "Evolution and Recent Trends in Host Developing Countries vis-à-vis TNCs" (Buenos Aires: Centro de Estudios Juridicos–Economicos Internationales, Dec. 1982).

2:
The Hypotheses
and
Their Context

This book examines transnational corporate decision processes for Latin American subsidiaries in both a large nation—Brazil—and a number of small nations—members of the Andean Common Market (ANCOM). These processes were studied in order to understand the conditions under which TNCs could be expected to involve themselves in the economies of developing nations. Such an understanding is essential if, as many analysts have predicted, direct foreign investment is to play a catalytic role in advancing the development objectives of these nations.[1] To develop this understanding three types of issues are addressed: (1) issues relating to the impact of different types of business environments on how TNC decision processes are structured (Chapter 3); (2) issues relating to how decisions are made within highly differentiated complex organizations, such as TNCs (Chapter 4); and (3) issues relating to the increasing complexity of the outcomes of these decision processes (Chapter 5).

Chapter 2 tests eight hypotheses that bear on these issues by systematically comparing the bases of investment decisions made for the Andean and Brazilian subsidiaries of six U.S.-based TNCs in 1973 and 1974. To provide a context for understanding these comparisons, the chapter begins with a discussion of the different circumstances and foreign investment policies in Brazil and ANCOM during the mid-1970s.

The comparison is, in itself, of interest to students of national development, since the two approaches are based on substantially different premises: Brazil's on providing incentives to foreign investors who advanced development objectives and ANCOM's on clearly specifying limits for acceptable behavior by foreign in-

	TABLE 2.1 Direct Investments in Manufacturing of U.S. Majority-Owned Affiliates[1]			TABLE 2.2 Sales of U.S. Majority-Owned Manufacturing Affiliates in Selected Markets[2]			TABLE 2.3 Rates of return for U.S.-Owned Manufacturing Affiliates in Selected Countries[3]		
	1966	1973	1974	1966	1973	1974	1967	1973	1974
World	22.058†	44,370	50,915	47.374†	140,878	175,703	8.5††	15.0	12.8
Europe	8,876	20,777	23,765	21,738	75,254	92,437	8.7	16.8	12.6
United Kingdom	3,716	6,611	7,201	8,275	19,559	24,320	8.9	11.8	6.2
France	1,201	2,946	3,411	3,114	11,774	13,756	5.4	17.5	8.9
West Germany	1,839	4,449	4,804	4,795	19,347	22,001	11.1	22.5	16.0
Latin America	3,081	6,456	9,122	5,861	16,220	20,859	7.6	9.1	9.2
Argentina	656	781	772	1,302	2,246	2,835	4.0	4.5	loss
Mexico	802	1,798	2,146	1,548	3,945	4,912	8.7	27.5	12.0
Brazil	846	2,033	2,502	1,283	5,738	7,727	7.7	16.9	11.0
ANCOM	616	1,153	1,287	1,492	3,548	4,331	8.9	14.0	12.7
Chile	51	50	43	94	105	126	14.5	1.0	2.3
Colombia	190	325	375	305	921	1,185	4.2	11.7	16.0
Peru	93	164	159	263	270	231	3.1	7.9	7.5
Venezuela	241	523	609	729	2,010	2,461	14.1	14.7	13.9
Bolivia & Ecuador*	41	91	101	101	242	328	1.1	11.0	5.0

[1] *Survey of Current Business (SCB)* 48, no. 10 (10/68):19–31; 55, no. 10 (10/75):43–63.

[2] *SCB* 55, no. 8 (8/75):22–37; 54, no. 5 (5/76):25–34.

[3] *SCB* 48, no. 10 (10/68):19–31; 55, no. 10 (10/75):43–63.

* *SCB* does not report data separately for Bolivia or Ecuador. The *SCB* data for these countries are estimates taken from the category "other, continental South America."

† Expressed in millions of current U.S. dollars.

†† Rate of return was calculated as the ratio of earnings to book value assets as reported by *SCB*. It is expressed in percentage form.

	TABLE 2.4 Capital Expenditures[4]		TABLE 2.5 Net Capital Outflow from U.S.[5]		TABLE 2.6 Reinvested Earnings[5]		TABLE 2.7 Millions Population[6]	TABLE 2.8 Average Population Growth Rate[6] 1970–1977 (%)
	1973	1974	1973	1974	1973	1974	1973	1970–1977
World	8.915†	11,626	1,863†	2,712	4,107†	3,786		
Europe	3,137	6,374	1,225	1,515	2,071	1,448		
United Kingdom	1,404	1,576	490	399	350	173		
France	748	923	134	141	365	185		
West Germany	1,367	1,593	305	277	499	141		
Latin America	1,035	1,217	360	503	476	534	286.1	2.8
Argentina	89	94	26	14	1	-23	24.3	1.7
Mexico	180	243	19	162	138	185	56.2	3.5
Brazil	563	670	233	221	259	241	101.4	2.8
ANCOM	153	153	47	68	23.5	43	68.8	2.7
Chile	1	3	-2	-7	.5	-1	9.9	1.9
Colombia	51	49	10	14	20	38	22.3	2.7
Peru	6	6	2	5	7	8	14.6	2.9
Venezuela	85	81	35	40	-6	-3	11.3	3.1
Bolivia & Ecuador*	10	14	12	16	2	1	4.4/6.3††	2.3/29††

4 SCB 55 no. 3 (3/75):19–25; 59, no. 9 (9/76):22–28.
5 SCB 55, no. 10 (10/75):54–55.
6 Economic and Social Progress in Latin America (ESP), 1977 Report Inter American Development Bank, Washington, D.C., Table 1, statistical appendix, p. 390.

* SCB does not report data separately for Bolivia or Ecuador. The SCB data for these countries are estimates taken from the category "other, continental South America."
† Expressed in millions of current U.S. dollars
†† Here begins separate reporting of Bolivia and Ecuador.

	TABLE 2.9	TABLE 2.10	TABLE 2.11			TABLE 2.12		
	Percentage of Population Considered Urban[7]	Growth Rate of Urban Population[7] (%)	Gross Domestic Product[8] (expressed in billions of 1976 dollars)			Per Capita GDP[8] (1976 dollars)		
	1973	1960–1977	1960	1973	1974	1960	1973	1974
World								
Europe								
United Kingdom								
France								
West Germany								
Latin America	58.9	4.3	131.2	280.9	310.7	657	982	1,057
Argentina	81.9	2.3	24.0	42.1	44.8	1,207	1,733	1,818
Mexico			23.5	55.2	58.4	672	982	1,005
Brazil	57.9	4.8	35.8	93.1	102.2	506	918	981
ANCOM	61.3	4.4	32.9	63.7	68.0	688	926	965
Chile	76.2	2.9	8.2	13.2	13.9	1,065	1,333	1,376
Colombia	62.6	5.1	6.1	12.5	13.2	398	561	576
Peru	59.3	5.2	6.3	12.5	13.5	630	856	897
Venezuela	72.9	4.1	10.1	20.5	21.7	1,377	1,814	1,860
Bolivia & Ecuador*	29.1/37.9	3.1/4.6	0.9/1.3	1.8/3.2	2.0/3.7	274/310	409/508	451/569

[7] ESP, Table 2, statistical appendix, p. 390.
[8] ESP, Table 3, statistical appendix, p. 395.

* SCB does not report data separately for Bolivia or Ecuador. The SCB data for these countries are estimates taken from the category "other, continental South America."

	TABLE 2.13 Average Annual Inflation Rate[9]		TABLE 2.14 Annual Variations in GDP[10]			TABLE 2.15 Percentage of Merchandise Exports Contributed by Top Two Products[11]
	1960–1970	1970–1978	1966–70	1971–73	1974	1976–77
World						
Europe						
United Kingdom	4.1	14.1				
France	4.1	9.3				
West Germany	3.2	5.9				
Latin America			5.9	6.5	7.3	25.3
Argentina	21.8	120.4	4.3	3.8	6.5	27.2
Mexico	3.5	17.5	6.9	5.7	5.9	12.2
Brazil	46.1	30.3	7.7	10.9	9.8	30.8
ANCOM						
Chile	32.9	242.6	3.9	– 0.3	5.7	66.9
Colombia	11.9	21.7	5.8	6.2	6.0	56.7
Peru	9.9	22.2	4.9	5.2	8.0	39.5
Venezuela	1.3	11.1	4.6	4.8	5.8	65.0
Bolivia & Ecuador*	3.5/n.d.	22.7/14.8	7.1/6.1	6.1/10.3	6.5/14.9	19.5/62.6

9 World Bank Report, 1980 (WBR), Table 1, Basic Indicators, pp. 110–11.
10 ESP, Table 1–2, p. 7.
11 ESP, Table 64, p. 444.

vestors. The comparison cannot, however, evaluate conclusively the appropriateness of either policy. To do this, an evaluation must not only take into account ultimate policy objectives but also national circumstances and administrative capacities for implementing these policies.

INVESTMENT DECISIONS IN BRAZIL AND IN ANCOM

Through the 1970s and into the 1980s, the investment climates of Brazil and the ANCOM countries have been seen by most TNC managers as markedly different. Managers of manufacturing firms saw Brazil as a country of substantial importance for their firms' future. Most saw the ANCOM countries—both individually and collectively—as largely irrelevant for their firms' foreseeable plans. This was, by and large, the view of managers in the six firms whose capital allocation decision processes are discussed in this chapter, although a few—especially managers located in Andean nations— also saw promising business opportunities in the Andean region. These differences in evaluating business opportunities in the two regions powerfully shaped the decision processes in which these TNC managers were involved and consequently conditioned the manner in which TNC activities in those nations have affected both the firms and the countries in question.

BRAZIL AS AN INTERNATIONAL
BUSINESS ENVIRONMENT IN 1974:
THE PERFORMANCE OF U.S. TNCs

Since 1964, when the Brazilian military ousted the government of João Goulart, Brazil had been considered by TNC managers as open and receptive to international business activity, including foreign investment.[2] In 1974, Brazil was seen as an "economic miracle" with GDP growth averaging more than 10 percent a year since 1968,[3] led by the performance of the manufacturing sector.[4] Foreign firms were prominently involved in this process, to the extent that in 1972, Brazil was characterized by *Business Latin-America* as "the Latin American darling of the international business community."[5] In that year, 147 of the 300 largest manufacturing firms in Brazil were foreign owned (forty-seven by U.S. interests). More than 50 percent of assets in the machinery, transport equipment, rubber, and chemical sectors were controlled by foreign firms.[6] All of the top ten and sixteen of Brazil's twenty largest private corporations, ranked in terms of total sales, were foreign owned (five of the top ten and seven of the top twenty were U.S. controlled).[7]

The attractiveness of Brazil as a business environment to U.S. based TNCs can best be seen by reviewing these firms' investments, sales, and profits during the late 1960s and early 1970s. In 1966, Brazil accounted for $846 million (3.8 percent) of the $22.058 billion worth of U.S. investments in manufacturing worldwide. By 1973, U.S. manufacturing investment in Brazil had grown to $2.033 billion or 4.6 percent of $44.370 billion invested worldwide, a rate of growth greater than that of any other major country during that period (see Table 2.1). During a period of massive global expansion by U.S. TNCs, investment in Brazil led the way.

These investment figures are complemented by data for sales by U.S. affiliates in Brazil. In 1966, sales by U.S. majority-owned manufacturing affiliates in Brazil totaled $1.283 billion (2.7 percent) of $47.374 billion worldwide. In 1973, these sales had increased to $5.738 billion (4.1 percent) of $140.878 billion worldwide (see Table 2.2). In 1966, total sales by U.S. affiliates in Brazil were smaller than sales in Argentina or Mexico. By 1973, Brazil was the largest market for U.S. manufacturing affiliates in Latin America and the sixth largest in the world. As with the growth of U.S. investment, these increases came at a time when the U.S. economy was undergoing a fundamental structural transformation: The operations of manufacturing, banking, and other firms based in the United States were becoming globalized. Foreign operations were becoming an increasingly important part of investments, sales, and profits of U.S.-based firms.[8] The country, not only in Latin America but worldwide, in which those operations were growing most rapidly was Brazil.

The earnings of TNC affiliates in Brazil also set them apart from affiliates in other Latin American countries. In 1973, affiliates of U.S. firms located in Brazil earned $303 million of the $759 million earned by affiliates of U.S. TNCs in Latin America (see Table 2.3). This represented a 16.9-percent return on the book value of assets, compared with a Latin American regional return of 9.1 percent. In the late 1960s and early 1970s, rates of return achieved by Brazilian affiliates of U.S. TNCs were consistently higher than the regional average for Latin America. Together with Mexican affiliates, Brazilian subsidiaries outpaced those of all other countries in the region. By 1973, Brazilian affiliates had become absolutely central to the global operations of U.S. TNCs, performing at levels comparable to West Germany and France, the European countries with the highest return on investments (see Table 2.3).

Perhaps the most telling statistics indicating that Brazilian affiliates were viewed as central to the global expenditures for 1973 (the year in which most of my interviews took place) and 1974 (the year for which plans were being developed when I was interviewing), worldwide capital expenditures by U.S. TNCs in 1973 were $8.915 billion, or 20.1 percent of total assets; in 1974, they were $11.626 billion, or 22.8 percent of total assets (see Table 2.4). For the Latin American region, expenditures were equal to only 16 percent of assets for 1973 and to 13.3 percent of assets in 1974. However, Brazilian capital expenditures were equal to 27.7 and 26.8 percent of assets for 1973 and 1974, respectively—roughly twice the regional average and higher than that of any other country worldwide except West Germany. If commitment of capital expenditures can be viewed as a indication of managers' future expectations, in 1973, managers of U.S. TNCs expected their Brazilian affiliates to become increasingly central to their firms' global operations.

TNC MANAGERS' EVALUATIONS

Brazil's importance for the international operations of U.S.-based TNCs was derived from their managers' evaluations of the country in terms of such factors as business climate, potential revenue return, fit with TNC strategy, lack of "red tape" or freedom to manage there, and views of its future as a business locale. The *business climate* was seen as open and receptive to foreign investment. This was the universal view of managers in all of the home offices and subsidiaries in which I conducted interviews. The few doubts expressed focused on the possibility of restrictions if Brazil's high GDP growth rate were to falter. A comment by the manager of the Rio de Janeiro subsidiary of an American transport firm was typical:

> Growth and business here during the last five years have been unbelievable. I do worry, however, about the expectations of much of the foreign business community. Recent growth rates will not be able to be sustained forever—increased oil costs are making that clear—and it is entirely possible that this might cause the growth of foreign business in Brazil to slow [down]. Despite this, I expect my operations to continue expanding.
>
> (MAY 1973)

The aspect of the Brazilian business climate that most gener-ated positive feeling among TNC managers was the sense that they understood the rules of the game for doing business in Brazil. For example, according to a manager of a chemical firm with a number of Brazilian subsidiaries:

> We have been doing business in Brazil for a number of years, and we expect to be here for the foreseeable future . . . to do business here, like anywhere else, we have to keep on top of all too many rules and regulations, and we have to know how to get the right information from the right government officials when we need it. It has taken us some time to get to where we are now, and we will always have to work hard at keeping on top of things, but we do feel comfortable and confident here.
>
> (MAY 1973)

There were many rules of the game to be understood in Brazil in 1974. The Brazilian government had enacted many restrictions of which foreign business people had to be aware, and surveillance of foreign business was keen. Despite the popular impression that Brazil was wide open to foreign investment, its government had promulgated a fairly comprehensive and interlocking set of invest-ment regulations. The basis of these impressions of openness to foreign business was twofold: (1) the extensive and visible involve-ment of TNCs in Brazil's economy, as already described, and (2) the flexible and decentralized manner in which foreign investment ac-tivity was regulated.

The principal institutions regulating foreign investment in Bra-zil in 1973 were the Central Bank, which maintained the Register of Foreign Investment; the National Monetary Council, which set criteria for registration as well as profit repatriation and foreign exchange control; the National Institute of Industrial Property (INPI), which maintained the Register of Licensing and Technical Assistance Contracts; and the Industrial Development Council (CDI), which set industrial development policies, including criteria for investment incentives and the integration of specific investment proposals with national and regional development plans.

These institutions largely regulated foreign investments by of-fering incentives for behavior considered in the national interest. Contrary behavior was not restricted; it was merely not granted often considerable incentives in the form of direct and indirect subsidies. For example, registration of foreign investments was re-quired only if a firm wished to remit profits from Brazil. Adherence to the regional development, sectoral development, and local content investment priorities set by the CDI were not required unless the firm wished to benefit from such incentives as tax and tariff exemptions and preferable treatment by the Central Bank. Since these could amount to 50 percent or more of total costs, firms wishing to be competitive usually adhered to the priorities. Similarly, no limitations were placed on profits or dividends remitted from Brazil. Remitted earnings, however, were subject to a 25 percent withholding tax. Finally, no limitations were placed on percentages of foreign ownership or the form of business in manufacturing, but the CDI had the authority to create investment incentives if it wished to control corporate behavior in these areas.

This openness regarding registration, investment plans, and capital repatriation was, however, complemented by rigid restrictions in other areas. Brazilian law permitted the National Monetary Council to restrict remittances to 10 percent of a firm's registered capital in "times of balance of payment stress," or to increase the withholding tax to 60 percent in the case of excessive remittances. However, as of 1973, these provisions had never been employed.

More serious were restrictions on sectors proscribed for foreign investment, regulations on international loans and interest payments, and regulations on technology and licensing agreements. The Brazilian constitution prohibited foreign participation in communications, electric power generation, shipping, and petroleum exploration and refining. (In 1976, exploration was allowed by foreign firms in certain areas.) Foreign commercial banking was regulated by the Central Bank and allowed on a reciprocity basis. A 1971 law prohibited foreigners from owning rural property in designated "national security zones." Domestic airlines and insurance companies had minimum levels of local ownership requirements.

In the area of international credit, all loans were required to be registered, and Brazil's central bank had the authority to disallow interest payments on loans whose interest rates exceeded those prevailing in the lending country.

The areas of technology and licensing agreements contained the most extensive set of restrictions. All contracts were required to be registered with INPI. Approval of agreements was uncertain and lengthy (up to five years).[9] Royalty payments could not exceed 5 percent of gross sales for patents and were set on an industry basis by the minister of finance. Trademarks were accepted only on a reciprocal basis, and payments for their use could not exceed 1 percent of gross sales. Royalty payments to a TNC subsidiary's parent were treated as an ordinary profit distribution and subjected to the remittance withholding tax. Patents expired within fifteen years and industrial designs and licensing agreements within ten years. Products and processes in the food and pharmaceutical industries were not patentable. Finally, unused patents were quickly forfeited.

The clarity of these rules of the game, despite their complexity, made TNC managers view Brazil's attitude toward TNCs as extremely positive. This was combined with a positive view of the Brazilian government's ability to structure clearly its business environment. Brazil's government, in 1973, was the most stable in continental South America. Its stability had been achieved by a military coup in 1964, followed by severe repression of traditional Brazilian democratic institutions, including labor unions and political parties, and by the institutionalization of the process of presidential succession, controlled by the Brazilian military.[10] Threats to the dominance of the military government were extremely weak, and by 1973, it had succeeded in expanding the Brazilian economy at a pace of over 10 percent a year, reduced annual inflation from over 80 percent in 1964 to less than 14 percent, and increased foreign currency reserves from a low (in 1967) of $157 million to over $6 billion. The major blot on this record of economic achievement was the increased concentration of wealth that had accompanied the macroeconomic successes.[11] Gains were inordinately concentrated in the top 20 percent of the population. The greatly increased purchasing power of the 20 million people in this top 20 percent, plus their geographic concentration in the country's highly developed Southern and Southeastern market areas produced a large, rapidly growing, easily penetrable market, and four-fold growth in the value of sales by affiliates of U.S. TNCs in Brazil between 1966 and 1973, and 35 percent additional growth between 1973 and 1974 (see Table 2.3).

Two clouds did loom on the economic horizon for TNC managers in Brazil. One was the difficulty of sustaining GDP growth rates in excess of 10 percent year after year. Managers hedged this worry with the suspicion that the growth rate decline would be to a lower and more long-term sustainable level. (When the GDP growth rate did fall to 5.7 percent in 1975, this was still nearly double the Latin American regional average of 3.1 percent.)[12]

More serious was concern over the impact of the increased cost of a most important input for *potential revenue return:* energy. In 1973, Brazil consumed 281.6 million barrels of oil, of which 252.8 million, or 90 percent, were imported.[13] However, the diversification of Brazil's economy and its "miraculous" growth trend so impressed important TNC managers that the impact of oil price increases was largely seen as "one more bottleneck to eliminate," and as giving Brazilian industry an excuse to catch up with itself after eight years of explosive growth. In the words of the manager of a foreign bank branch in Rio de Janeiro:

> Brazil's economic planners must reckon with soaring petroleum prices as well as with economic slowdown in nations that are Brazil's best customers . . . However, pauses in some economic sectors will be compensated by surges in others, and slowdowns are needed in many sectors to make needed adjustments in inventories and capital investment . . . A slower pace of expansion will probably turn out to be more of a pause for breath than cause for pessimism about Brazil's economy . . . It is fortunate for Brazil that the oil crisis has come at a time when it is advantageous for other reasons to slow industrial growth and when its external economic position is strong.
>
> (MAY 1974)

This optimism was reinforced by Brazil's increasing importance in the global strategies of TNCs. Brazil was already the sixth largest market and the sixth largest recipient of capital expenditures (after Canada, the United Kingdom, West Germany, France, and Australia—ahead of Japan, Italy, the Netherlands, and Mexico) for subsidiaries of U.S. TNCs.[14] Doing business in a big way in Brazil was essential for major members of global oligopolies. Firms that had not entered the Brazilian market by 1973 were carefully evaluating their strategies in terms of that fact. Furthermore, many firms saw Brazil as an extremely attractive locale from which to integrate their overall marketing and productive activities. Its location in South America, propinquity to West Africa, and equidistance from the eastern coast of North America and the western coast of Europe caused some managers to think of Brazil as a potential sourcing locale for markets on four continents in addition to a rapidly growing domestic market. Furthermore, the CDI's export incentives made such global-sourcing export schemes additionally attractive for many manufacturers.

Concerning the critical dimension of the freedom to manage, Brazil's program of regulation had been explicitly designed to encourage managers to take the initiative in areas related to national development objectives that effectively included the entire manufacturing sector. Despite delays by Brazilian agencies in responding to requests, firms learned how to communicate with host country nationals and to extract approvals needed in carrying out their business activities. By 1973, there were many large U.S. TNCs doing business in Brazil, and most had been there for ten years or more, with the result that knowledge of how to pursue corporate objectives within the context of the Brazilian economy and/or government bureaucracy had been substantially expanded by both time and experience. In the words of an executive in the São Paulo branch of a U.S. pharmaceutical manufacturer.

> We first incorporated here nearly thirty years ago and have been growing with the market ever since. Perhaps if we were just starting up today, we would have some trouble getting things done . . . but then maybe not . . . we would hire locals who know the ropes . . . The government here is interested in a fast pace of economic expansion. We share that objective, and since we have been here so long, we and people in the government have come to know what to expect from one another . . . If someone in the government surprises me with an objection, I usually know who to get to to get around him. More important, I like to think I have learned how to keep my ear to the ground, to know what is possible and what is not.
>
> (MAY 1973)

By 1974, TNC managers and Brazilian government officials had so much experience working together that managers generally felt they knew what kinds of initiatives would be favorably received and which ones were impossible. Furthermore, foreign firm–host country relations had reached the point where the Brazilians who headed affiliates of TNCs had often had important prior government experience and TNCs, the Brazilian state, and local Brazilian firms were often competing to employ the same upper- and middle-level managers. The best known example of this is ex-General Golberry da Cuato de Silva, who served as president of Dow Chemical's Brazilian subsidiary from 1968 to 1972 and has been variously described as the "eminence grise" and "chief of the cabinet" for all Brazilian presidents from 1964 through the early 1980s, with the exception of the 1968–1972 Costa y Silva presidency.

The result of this long-term experience and circulation of personnel was that managers knew what types of projects policy boards, such as the CDI or the INPI, would favor. Managers felt they knew what types of TNC activities would not meet with support. This did not mean that there were no disappointments. Transnational corporations often competed against each other for projects; for example, Bayer, Celanese, Dow, Dupont, Grace, Hoechst, ICI, and Rhone

Poulenc all had chemical plants in Brazil in 1973 and bid against each other for new projects. A similarly broad panorama could be drawn for any other industry. The major point is that Brazilian operations were so central to the global activities of many TNCs in 1973 that the operation of business there was seen as a miniature version of business practices in the home country. There were, of course, different politics, different national priorities, and different people to deal with, but TNC managers expected their Brazilian business operations to be large, profitable, and long term. In the words of the New York based vice president of a large diversified international consumer products manufacturing firm: "We like to think of Brazil and European countries in the same terms" (September 1973).

THE ANDEAN COMMON MARKET AS AN ENVIRONMENT FOR INTERNATIONAL BUSINESS IN 1974

In 1974, the Andean Common Market (ANCOM) had six member countries—Bolivia, Chile, Colombia, Ecuador, Peru, and Venezuela. ANCOM had been created in May 1969 by the Cartagena Agreement on the part of Bolivia, Chile, Colombia, Ecuador, and Peru. Venezuela joined ANCOM in 1973, and Chile dropped out in 1976. ANCOM was officially created as a subregional grouping of the Latin American Free Trade Association (LAFTA)[15] to speed its integration efforts, which ANCOM accomplished in part through an automatic tariff-cutting program. However, from its inception, ANCOM went far beyond the limited integration provisions of LAFTA, in which internal trade barriers for single products would be reduced and a common external tariff was applied to nonmember countries. The long-term intention of ANCOM was to structure a full-blown common market by harmonizing regional economic policies, implementing regional industrial development programs, promoting intraregional investments, forming a regional capital base (the Andean Development Finance Corporation—CAF), and establishing a common code for regulating foreign investments.[16] By moving toward the harmonization of their economic, industrial, and social policies, the six member countries of the ANCOM undertook to form a base for economic development that would put them on an equal footing with the larger nations of Latin America.

In doing so, however, they opted against policies similar to those of Brazil, which would have stressed Andean comparative advantage in international trade. Such policies would have shifted emphasis to promoting labor-intensive exports and increasing production of raw materials (both agricultural and mineral) by rationalizing tariff structures, correcting exchange rate valuations, and eliminating distortions in relative factor prices. This policy option was rejected, in part, because of doubts regarding the possibility of developing a sufficient Andean comparative advantage and, in part, because of the economic and social distortions, especially increased income concentration, which advocates of AN-COM feared would result.

Instead, the framers of ANCOM designed a collective strategy for a broad-based program of development through industrialization in which collective self-reliance was given more weight, and comparative advantage less weight, than in Brazil's development scheme.

Viewed separately, ANCOM consisted of four nations with medium-sized economies and populations—Chile, Colombia, Peru, and Venezuela—and two nations of smaller economic and human dimensions—Bolivia and Ecuador. Taken together, in 1973, ANCOM's population was 68.8 million—nearly three times as large as Argentina's, 20 percent larger than Mexico's, and two-thirds as large as Brazil's (see Table 2.7). The combined GDP of the six ANCOM nations was $63.7 billion—one and one-half times as large as Argentina's, 85 percent as large as Mexico's, and two-thirds the size of Brazil's (see Table 2.11).

By forming ANCOM, the six countries hoped to expand import-substituting industrialization, which they had pursued since the 1930s, and to move further into heavy, technologically sophisticated industries. Regional integration was seen as an important prerequisite to developing industries at economies of scale not achievable within isolated national markets. The overall logic was (1) to promote efficiency and self-sufficiency in traditional industries by establishing a common external tariff and eliminating internal trade barriers (by 1973, tariffs had been lowered 40 percent on half of the items traded among ANCOM members); (2) to spur regional development and the use of economies of scale by granting individual nations exclusive production rights and duty-free regional sales for specified products in some twenty industrial sectors (by 1973, agreements had been worked out for the metalworking and petrochemical sectors, and agreements were under discussion for automotive, iron and steel, and fertilizers); (3) to facilitate intraregional investment by harmonizing national legislation; (4) to pro-

37

vide capital for investments contributing to regional economic integration by creating, in 1970, CAF, which had granted $101.4 million in loans through 1974; and (5) to regulate the role of foreign investment in the development process by establishing a common code that specified areas and procedures for operating foreign business in the region.[17]

In 1974, two aspects of ANCOM's economic policy especially affected TNC decision makers considering actual or potential operations within the region. The first was the group's commitment to a development strategy in which links to the global economy were to be set by local development needs rather than the group's comparative advantage in the worldwide economy. Second, and more important, were aspects of ANCOM's "Common Regime for the Treatment of Foreign Capital Trademarks, Patents, Licensing Agreements, and Royalties," which had been effective throughout the region since June 30, 1971. This common regime (known as Decision 24 because it was the twenty-fourth made by ANCOM's commission) was intended to clarify and stabilize conditions for TNC involvement in the ANCOM nations. However, Decision 24 was depicted in TNC home countries' popular and business presses as so restrictive that it created greater uncertainty due to the improbability of its enforcement.

The actual intent of Decision 24 was to ensure, on the one hand, that Andean interests derive the main benefit from the integration movement and, on the other hand, when foreign interests were involved, that foreign investment and imported technology make strong positive contributions to development within the region. This was to be achieved by both limiting foreign business to activities in which regional firms could not meet local needs and specifying the terms under which allowable foreign business could operate. The actual mechanisms of Decision 24 were quite complex and designed to affect directly the conduct of foreign and domestic firms operating within the Andean group. Lynn K. Mytelka has described Decision 24 as follows:

> Decision 24 contained two broad sets of measures: those governing direct foreign investment and those regulating the transfer of technology. Among the former are provisions that authorize the establishment of national agencies to register and review all direct foreign investment contracts (articles 5, 6); prohibit any new foreign direct investment in utilities, insurance, commercial banking and finance, transport, advertising, and communications sectors (articles 41–44); limit the repatriation of profits to 14 percent of registered capital per

year (article 37); oblige all presently established wholly or majority-owned foreign firms desirous of securing the benefits of tariff liberalization in intraregional trade (articles 27–29) as well as all new foreign firms to divest over a specified term (article 30); limit the access of foreign firms to medium- and long-term local credit (article 17); prohibit reinvestment by foreign firms of more than 5 percent of profits annually without review and approval (article 13); and bind the members to create a network for the exchange of information relevant to direct foreign investment and technology transfer, including data on the pricing of intermediary products (articles 6, 48). Among the latter are provisions that set up national agencies for the registration and review of all technology transfer contracts in order to ensure that such imported technology makes an "effective contribution" (article 18); require the identification of the value of each element in the technology package to be imported (article 19); prohibit restrictive clauses formerly incorporated in technology contracts (articles 20–25); and provide for the development of a program to promote the generation of appropriate technology in the subregion (article 23).[18]

These regulations troubled foreign firms for two reasons: (1) they were viewed by the firms as adding uncertainty to the conditions for conducting foreign business in the region and (2) they contained certain restrictions that ran counter to the global business practices of TNCs.

Transnational corporate managers felt Decision 24 added to uncertainty because it contained numerous provisions allowing a national government to depart from the structures of the code when it judged that circumstances warranted it. Article 44, for example, allowed a government to waive restrictions on the treatment of foreign investors in extractive industries and in sectors closed to foreign investment if it judged that special circumstances existed. This and other loopholes, combined with political differences among the six ANCOM nations, suggested that implementing the ANCOM policies would vary from nation to nation and also within nations as political currents changed. This final point was, in 1974, particularly apparent in the wake of changes in the governments of Bolivia, Chile, and Peru since ratification of Decision 24. In 1970, Bolivia was headed by General Juan Jose Torres, who strongly favored an end to excessive incentives for TNCs; socialist Salvador Allende had just been elected President of Chile; and General Juan Velasco Alvarado had been in power in Peru for two years and had already adopted legislation regulating foreign investment that went beyond the restrictions of Decision 24. By 1974, General Torres had been ousted by the far more conservative General Hugo Banzer, the government of Salvador Allende had been overthrown in September 1973 in a bloody military coup, and the Velasco government's policies were heavily criticized by the Peruvian private sector's National Society of Industries.

Among the restrictions Decision 24 placed on TNCs, managers were most displeased with the requirement that foreign firms divest themselves of majority control if they wished to take advantage of intraregional tariff liberalization.[19] They were also disturbed by restrictions on the remittance of funds, on access to local capital, on the valuation of local assets, on the regulation of technology transfer, and on the paperwork that increased surveillance involved. These restrictions, if implemented would make exceedingly difficult the full integration of Andean operations into the global operations of TNCs. The investment and remittance of funds, the expansion or initiation of operations, and the use of corporate-controlled technology would all be subject to the scrutiny of national agencies whose major objective was to strengthen the position of Andean enterprises.

Despite objections to the terms of Decision 24, few firms that were established in the region anticipated pulling out. Executives polled in a Harvard Business School survey indicated that long-term possibilities for an expanded market were worth the problems of complying with the terms of Decision 24.[20] The manager of a Canadian manufacturing firm in Peru stated it more succinctly: "It's better to have 49 percent of something than 100 percent of nothing" (June 1973).

The restrictions imposed by Decision 24 led some observers to conclude that the code would have a negative effect on TNC involvement in the region. Writing in 1973 for the Bureau of Intelligence and Research of the U.S. Department of State, Andrew B. Wardlaw stated, "The code's provisions, combined with political conditions prevailing in the area, will discourage a significant flow of foreign capital and technology."[21]

The staff of the New York based business association, the Council of the Americas, was so distressed with the content of Decision 24 that, in 1971, it organized a campaign of letter writing and private visits designed to pressure Colombian officials to refuse to ratify Decision 24.[22] John Gallagher, head of Sears Roebuck's Latin American operations in 1971, who participated in the Council of the Americas effort, reported that "we would retaliate by cutting off all new investment" if the code were ratified in its entirety.[23] This effort eventually proved unsuccessful and was publicly exposed and labeled by the Colombian government as improper interference in domestic affairs.

Framers of the code, on the other hand, believed that while foreign investors might not initially find Decision 24 to their liking, they would see ANCOM's rapidly growing market of over 60 million people sufficiently attractive to come forward with capital and technology.

What had taken place in 1974 was neither a concerted movement away from the Andean region by TNCs nor an increased rate of TNC activity. Instead, TNC activity in the region geared itself to the changing political and economic conditions of individual ANCOM nations. Since, in the 1960s, these nations were individually and collectively marginal to the global operation of most TNCs, this condition of relative marginality continued with country-by-country variation (see Tables 2.1–2.6). Between 1966 and 1974, investments and sales of U.S. majority-owned manufacturing TNCs increased at rates equal to the world average in Venezuela and Colombia and declined in Chile and Peru. As indicated in Tables 2.1 and 2.2, this happened at a time when Brazil and Mexico were becoming increasingly important to the global operations of TNCs. The marginality of certain ANCOM nations was also expressed in the level of capital expenditures by U.S.-based TNCs in the region—$153 million in 1974 versus Brazil's $670 million (see Table 2.4)—and level of reinvested earnings—$43 million versus $241 million for Brazil (see Table 2.6). These figures contrasted sharply with profit rates for ANCOM affiliates (see Table 2.3), which were at levels comparable to those of Brazil and to worldwide returns.

This apparent paradox of marginality, despite profits at levels comparable to those of countries important to global operations of TNCs, can be understood by examining ANCOM in 1974 as an environment for international business in terms of the eight business environment characteristics introduced in the previous discussion of 1974 Brazil as a locale for foreign investment. These, discussed in greater depth in Chapter 3, are:

1. Fit of host country's subsidiary with the TNC's global strategy
2. Host country's constraints on TNC executives' freedom to manage
3. TNC-generated constraints on management of host country's subsidiary
4. Host country's market structure
5. Cost and availability of host country's inputs

6. TNC managers' perceptions of host country's attitude toward TNCs
7. Host country's capacity to structure business environments
8. TNC managers' view of future business relationships in host country

Critics of ANCOM have stressed that its "investment code embodies a harsh attitude toward foreign investment."[24] However, a review of the eight characteristics of host country business environments depicted in Figure 3.4 reveals more basic problems with the ANCOM countries as hosts for TNC activities in the early 1970s. With few exceptions, the ANCOM countries correspond to the typical representation of a host country marginal to the global strategies of TNCs. The *attitude* of the ANCOM countries toward TNCs as embodied in Decision 24 was clearly mixed. Transnational corporations were welcome within the region but only if they agreed *ex ante* to a series of restrictions on their activities.

The *ability* of the ANCOM countries to structure a coherent business environment was also mixed. The political complexion of three of the governments changed radically in the early 1970s; inflation rates were high by world standards (see Table 2.13); and although GNP growth was good in all countries except Chile, it was not so impressive as Brazil's (see Table 2.14). Capacity, as measured by performance, was good but not exceptional and was called into question by recent political instability.

ANCOM's regional *market* was large (see Table 2.7) and growing, but the combination of political and geographical barriers to easy commerce made it difficult to think of ANCOM as anything other than a loose federation of six separate medium- and small-sized economies. This was exacerbated by the vulnerability of the ANCOM economies to changes in world prices of the one or two products that comprised the bulk of each country's exports (see Table 2.15). However, the most important barrier to integrated market development of the ANCOM region was its geography. 61 percent of the 68.8 million citizens of the ANCOM countries lived in cities in 1973 (see Table 2.9), but these cities were separated by thousands of miles and cut off from each other by the Andes—the highest and most rugged mountain chain in the western hemisphere. By contrast, more than 60 million of Brazil's 101.4 million people were concentrated in the South and southeastern regions that accounted for over 80 percent of Brazil's national income. These regions comprise only 18 percent of Brazil's national territory, serviced by good harbors and highways, and include the metropolitan areas of Belo Horizonte, Curitaba, Porto Alegre, Rio de Janeiro, Santa Catarina, and São Paulo. While the Andean market contained a population of considerable size, political and geographical factors made it difficult for TNCs to penetrate its market using standard business practices.

The availability and price of physical *inputs* were not an issue of special concern for Andean operations. All six Andean countries were optimistic about their energy reserves, and a variety of raw materials existed in the countries of the region. Transportation costs, however, were a problem due to the region's geography; labor was readily available and docile, although uncertainties remained in the wake of policies of the Popular Unity government in Chile and Peru's Industrial Communities legislation.[25] Capital was a possible problem due to restrictions in Decision 24. Professional and managerial services were available but generally not at levels expected in countries more central to TNC global operations. In short, the availability and costs of inputs also earned mixed marks as affecting potential TNC revenue returns.

Data on investments, sales, and capital allocations shown in Tables 2.1, 2.2, and 2.4 clearly indicate little immediate fit for the ANCOM nations in *TNC global strategies.* ANCOM's location on the eastern edge of the Pacific Ocean made these countries particularly remote from the Atlantic community and a relatively unlikely candidate for adding flexibility to global sourcing. Even within Latin America transport costs necessitated by the Andes mountains and the Amazon jungle made it difficult to integrate Andean operations with those of large markets in Argentina and Brazil. Andean markets were viewed neither as glamorous nor hotbeds of international competition in 1974. Nevertheless, the size of the subregion's population, the steady GDP growth of its member nations, and the promise of economic harmonization represented by ANCOM did make it important for the longer term plans of TNCs. As an executive of the Peruvian subsidiary of a Japanese trading house said:

> Today, my company is concentrating its efforts in Brazil. We see Indonesia as our next "Brazil" and are intensifying operations there . . . Our operations in the Andean region are relatively small, but they do supply Japan with some needed raw materials. More importantly, they are enabling my company to familiarize itself with business conditions in an area that we know will be an important growth region some years ahead.
>
> (LIMA, JULY 1973)

The provisions of Decision 24 made the Andean region appear particularly inauspicious from the standpoint of the *freedom to manage.* TNC managers feared that increased surveillance would result in excessive red tape and lost time. Rather than feeling free to pursue any alternative that made business sense to TNC management, the explicit prohibitions and preferences shown to Andean enterprises in Decision 24 made TNC managers feel hemmed in. This was exacerbated by national variations in interpreting Decision 24 and in the pace of implementation. In 1974, TNC managers were unsure of the implications of Decision 24 and doubted whether ANCOM would be able to follow its schedules for tariff reformulation, sectoral allocation, and phased divestment of foreign ownership. This situation, needless to say, did not create an atmosphere of partnership and understanding among TNC managers and host country regulators. However, few managers of TNC subsidiaries in the region recommended pulling out. This was reflected in a statement by the manager of an American manufacturing firm in Chile in 1973, two months before the overthrow of the Allende government:

> We are not clear on what the government wants from us, in large part because the government is not clear. In the meanwhile, we have kept a low profile—you didn't see a prominent sign at our company gate . . . but we are still doing business and, in terms of returns, we are doing as well as ever . . . there are many opportunities here that we are not able to follow up on—it is very hard to get Chilean requests "past New York" this year . . . I have confidence that we can keep on operating here . . . they need us.
>
> (SANTIAGO, JULY 1973)

The *TNC-generated constraints* were as important as host country constraints for doing business in ANCOM. The small importance of ANCOM operations for most TNCs, the relative lack of familiarity with ANCOM by headquarters staff, and the extreme depictions of difficulties for international business in ANCOM projected by media in headquarters countries combined to make it difficult for headquarters staff to respond sensitively to business opportunities that often required detailed qualified explanations. The importance of TNC-generated constraints was particularly noticeable by its absence in the few firms where an important manager had had substantial recent experience in an Andean country. In those cases, an executive vice president or assistant to the president took special pains to explain ANCOM business conditions to other headquarters staff, with the result that such subsidiaries were able to take advantage of business opportunities that were seen by their competitors as "too problematic." However, the small size of Andean staffs and operations made such circumstances rare, occurring in only four of the forty-three firms in which interviews took place and in none of the six firms studied more intensively.

The Andean Common Market also suffered from TNC managers' assessment of *future TNC–host country relations.* In 1973, Decision 24 had not been implemented with sufficient consistency nor in force long enough to convince TNC managers that it would be a stable guide for the future. Political and economic volatility in the region exacerbated uncertainties about future TNC–host country relations. The net result was concern over future conflicts whose full dimensions could not be satisfactorily anticipated. In summary, despite progress toward regime integration, a large potential market, satisfactory profit levels, and good GDP performance, Andean operations in 1973 were largely marginal to the global strategies of most TNCs.

Strong contrasts can be drawn between environments for international business in Brazil and ANCOM in 1973. Brazil had a booming economy, a large, fast-growing market, a central geographic location, and a regulatory system designed to harness a wide range of foreign business activity. The Andean Common Market's economies were growing at a respectable pace; however, its regional market was difficult to penetrate; it was distant from major economic centers, and its regulations for foreign business appeared to TNC managers both unstable and restrictively selective.

THE TNCs STUDIED

The six firms in which home office and subsidiary interviews took place were all U.S.-based TNCs with manufacturing-sector subsidiaries in ANCOM and Brazil. All sold similar products in both markets, and four of the six manufactured the same products in both regions. The firms varied in size from less than $300 million in assets worldwide, to over $13 billion. Their 1973 sales ranged from approximately $300 million to over $12 billion. Latin American sales and assets ranged from over 30 percent for one of the smaller firms to less than 2 percent for one of the larger firms. All six of the firms had over $150 million worth of sales in Latin America in 1973. The six firms had operations in a wide range of product areas includ-

45

ing chemicals, consumer goods, data processing equipment, electrical equipment, food processing, medical products, and pharmaceuticals. In addition, four of the firms were active in such nonmanufacturing activities as agriculture, data processing and financial services, equipment rental, tourism, and natural resources development. Although some interviews were held with managers with responsibility for nonmanufacturing operations, the following information is based on decision processes involving the manufacturing operations of the six firms.

The six firms were selected for study because they represented a wide range of products, sizes, and dependence on international relations. Furthermore, they had varied experience in the region—four had established subsidiaries in the region before World War II and two only since 1960. Finally, they reflected a mix of marketing and technological concern, with four companies spending roughly twice as much in 1973 on research and development as they did on advertising, and two with advertising and other marketing costs exceeding research and development expenses. This variety should not be taken to imply that the data are representative of any universe of manufacturing TNCs. However, the variety represented by the firms and the clear patterns of responses suggest that conclusions based on these six cases might well be relevant beyond the circumstances under direct discussion in the interviews.

HYPOTHESES: COMPARISONS OF INVESTMENT CRITERIA FOR BRAZIL AND THE ANDEAN COMMON MARKET

The findings were based on interviews with TNC managers for which the focus of discussion was capital allocation requests made by ANCOM or Brazilian subsidiaries during the most recently concluded reporting period prior to the interview—in most cases, a fiscal year's quarter. Table 2.16 shows that twenty-one of the twenty-three subsidiaries made such requests—all nine of the Brazilian subsidiaries in which interviews were conducted and twelve of the fourteen ANCOM subsidiaries. Of these, six of the nine Brazilian requests discussed were approved, as were three of the twelve ANCOM requests.

These requests were made to the home offices because, in all six firms, investment decisions above certain amounts could not be made locally due to internal corporation regulations. In 1973, these limits ranged from $10,000 to $50,000 for the six firms under study.

TABLE 2.16

	ANCOM	Brazil	Total
Number of subsidiaries	14	9	23
Number of capital allocation requests in reporting period	12	9	21
Number approved	3	6	9

Most of the twenty-one requests were for authorization to commit $200,000 or less—three were in the $10,000 to $50,000 range, twelve in the $50,000 to $200,000 range, and the remaining six about $200,000—one in excess of $1 million, involving the construction of a large new facility. The average size of the Brazilian requests was much larger than those for ANCOM—$625,000 as opposed to $160,000—yet two-thirds of the Brazilian requests were approved compared with one-fourth of the ANCOM requests.

Discrepancies in both the size of requests reported and the proportions approved reflect the greater importance accorded Brazilian operations in the firms' global strategies. Equally telling is the fact that not all the ANCOM subsidiaries made capital allocation requests during the reporting period prior to the interviews. The manager of one of the subsidiaries that had not made a request explained, in May 1973, that his firm would make "no guesses about its future in ANCOM because the future [was] clouded by so many unknowns that [the company] has no control over." He explained that he was, in the long run, "eager to set up a basic manufacturing plant to service the entire region" but felt that he could not move ahead on such an idea until the Sectoral Development Plan covering his firm's products was more fully developed. Not only were the ANCOM subsidiaries viewed as less central to their firm's operations, but also as subject to far greater uncertainties. This is more clearly shown in answers to some of the other questions posed in the six firms' home offices.

FIT WITH GLOBAL STRATEGY AS A CRITERION FOR THE DECISION PROCESS

Questions were posed that directly tested hypotheses based on the eight business environment characteristics already discussed in this chapter. These questions and the home office and subsidiary level responses are reported in Tables 2.17 to 2.24 below. Of these,

TABLE 2.17

Hypothesis: TNC managers will be hesitant to commit additional capital to subsidiaries whose operations are not well related to the firm's global objectives. Conversely, they will be favorably disposed to committing new funds to subsidiaries whose operations reinforce those objectives.

Question: Does the capital allocation request fit your company's global strategy?

	ANCOM	Brazil
Yes	3	6
No	9	3
Agreements with request outcomes	12 (100%)	9 (100%)

the hypothesis that was most closely tied to outcomes of capital allocations requests was based on characteristic 1—the fit of the host country environment with the global objectives of TNCs. The question "Does the capital allocation request fit with your company's global strategy?" was posed only to TNC home office managers as they, not the subsidiary managers, were responsible for directly participating in the formulation and implementation of their firms' global strategies. When managers responded that they deemed requests inappropriate, it was for such reasons as that the environment was not yet ripe for additional corporate involvement, that anticipated revenue returns would not be satisfactory, or that too much time would be spent monitoring the project in question.

Inasmuch as the corporate headquarters has the authority to rule on large capital allocations requests, it is not surprising to find fit with global strategy in 100-percent agreement with the request outcomes, since the headquarters also formulates these objectives. Responses of home office managers to this question corresponded perfectly with capital allocation request outcomes. In the three instances where ANCOM subsidiaries' requests had been approved, home office managers stated that they felt the request fit company global strategy. In the nine instances where the ANCOM subsidiaries' requests were turned down, home office managers stated that the request did *not* fit company global strategy. Similarly for the Brazilian requests, home office managers stated that the approved requests fit with corporate global strategy and the disapproved requests deviated from that strategy.

REVENUE AND USE OF MANAGERIAL TIME
AS ALTERNATIVE CRITERIA

Four other questions were posed regarding aspects of the particular capital allocation requests: Whether it was judged that the host country would allow management the freedom to act efficiently according to its best business judgment (characteristic 2); whether TNC-generated constraints would pose difficulties for managing the proposed project (characteristic 3); whether the market's potential return justified the request (characteristic 4); and whether the request made sense in terms of the cost and availability of inputs (characteristic 5). Of these judgments about the freedom to manage, both host country and TNC-generated constraints were most closely linked with the fate of the capital allocation requests. Market potential and input cost judgments were also linked, but less closely. These differences in the predictive capacity of specific characteristics resulted entirely from views regarding capital allocation requests for ANCOM subsidiaries. The four hypotheses were

---

TABLE 2.18

Hypothesis: TNC managers will hesitate to commit additional capital to subsidiaries whose operations are seen to be unreasonably constrained by the host country's business environment. Conversely, they will be favorably disposed to committing new funds to subsidiaries whose TNC managers are not considered to be constrained when acting in their managerial capacities.

Question: Will the host country allow management the freedom to act efficiently according to its best business judgment?

	ANCOM	Brazil
Yes	2	9
No	10	0
Agreement with request outcomes	11 (92%)	6 (67%)
SUBSIDIARY		
Yes	9	9
No	3	0
Agreement with request outcomes	6 (50%)	6 (67%)

equal in their ability to predict the outcome of requests for Brazilian subsidiaries, but the hypotheses regarding the freedom to manage added substantial predictability to the outcome for ANCOM capital allocation requests.

The TNC managers in both home offices and subsidiaries were asked about management's freedom to act according to its best business judgment in each of the requests. The answers are revealing both because they reflect home office and subsidiary judgments about an important issue and because they show differences in points of view at different locations in the firms' organizations.

The opening question put to each manager was, "Did you think that the host country would allow management the freedom to act on its best business judgment regarding the project for which the request was made?" The ensuing discussion was always long and involved, touching on such topics as the amount of red tape involved in doing business in the locale under discussion, the possibility of changes in host country development priorities, whether the company had easy communication with host country regulators, the frustrations involved in obtaining official approvals, and especially in subsidiaries, annoyance at not being able to take advantage of promising opportunities. Typical of home office responses were the following:

> We have been operating in Brazil for more than twenty years. We have hung in during good times and the bad, and we think that we are seen as serious participants in Brazil's economic success. We have clear lines open to the agencies that set economic priorities. If we decide to expand or develop a new area, we expect to be clearly understood and we are. I think that that is one of the reasons why the Brazilian market has become so important for our firm. We feel comfortable there.
>
> (NEW YORK, FEB. 1974)

> We are taking a wait-and-see attitude toward our operations in Colombia and Chile. The political situation in Chile and the regulations of the Andean Common Market have us stymied. We can't be sure that measures like divestment and technology sharing will actually be enforced. If they are, they will have implications for our worldwide operations . . . Things are changing so fast politically that we often don't know who in the government to ask questions of. Since these operations are small, and it would take a lot of digging to feel comfortable taking a big step right now in the Andean region, we are going to stand pat until the dust settles.
>
> (NEW YORK, MAY 1973)

Home office managers felt that they clearly understood which opportunities could be pursued in Brazil and which could not. On the other hand, they felt that good ideas and valuable executive time might be squandered by premature action in the Andean region. Uncertainties about host country policy, combined with the relative unimportance of Andean operations for firms' global activities, substantially dampened headquarters' short-term interest in the region and weakened chances for capital allocation requests. ·

Managers in Andean subsidiaries of these firms felt differently about their ability to act on business opportunities. They felt they understood the business environments in their host countries and could separate feasible business opportunities from unfeasible ones. They often voiced frustration over the lack of understanding of their situation they thought they perceived in their corporate headquarters. As stated by the manager of a subsidiary based in Lima, Peru:

> Things are changing quickly here . . . but we pay attention and we keep up. Our performances, despite all of the changes here since 1968 [the date of the military coup], show that. We could do better if we could expand our plant, but New York still wants to sit tight. It is very frustrating when you think you have worked it all out and you don't get a go-ahead.
>
> (JUNE 1973)

Nine of the twelve Andean managers whose offices had sent capital allocation requests to the home office stated that they felt comfortable about their freedom to manage in their host country's business environment (Table 2.18). The home offices of seven of these nine were unconvinced or unaware of their managers' feelings of confidence. The difficulty these managers faced convincing their superiors to invest in the Andean region was mirrored by the frustration ANCOM and host country officials expressed at the reaction of some sectors of the international business community to the code in the early 1970s. For example, in a May 1973 speech at an American Bar Association Conference on legal aspects of doing business in Latin America, Felipe Salazar Santos, coordinator of the junta of ANCOM, said:

> In some sectors of the international business community complaints have been voiced, sometimes with acrimonious overtones, about some of the provisions of the common code to the effect that it presents an insuperable barrier to foreign investment which will work to the detriment of the same countries which adopt it. I can assure you that this

was not the purpose of the junta in drafting its proposal nor that of the governments approving it. On the contrary, we believe that the code established a set of reasonable rules which are clear and stable with undeniable benefits for the investor and for the host countries. The foreign investor is welcome in so far as he contributes to the economic development of our countries by providing essential scarce resources, especially in the areas of capital and technology, but providing that the purposes of the investor are in harmony with the national interests.

This is not a new policy in the world and there are outstanding cases in which it has had excellent results. Allow me to cite a few of these. In Japan . . . [rules] . . . prohibit foreign investments in certain sectors of economic activity or in certain enterprises, and . . . limit the participation of foreign capital to a certain minority proportion in Japanese enterprises. Despite these rules there has been a highly important flow of foreign investments to Japan and many of the large enterprises which today criticize the rules of the Andean group are knocking at the doors of Japan to obtain access to its market.

In Canada, there are laws which limit foreign investment in banks and other financial institutions and which guarantee that radio communications, newspapers and magazines will be maintained under Canadian control. Also, the government a little more than a year ago presented to the Parliament a bill which would give the Ministry of Industry and Commerce the authority to examine foreign investment projects and to approve only those considered beneficial for Canadian development . . . and I do not hesitate to speculate that in the relatively near future, indeed as is already beginning to occur, large corporations from the so-called capitalist world will begin to explore the possibilities of establishing business relations in the People's Republic of China as international relations with that country are increasingly expanded.

In this context, then, I find it hard to believe that the rules established by the Andean group are conceived as . . . [stricter] than those based on a Marxist philosophy and where the state has an absolute control over all of the productive activities of an economy.[26]

Managers of Brazilian subsidiaries felt quite differently about the support and understanding they obtained from headquarters. Table 2.18 reports that all home office managers share with managers of their Brazilian subsidiaries the impression that they would be free to manage their subsidiaries in ways that made business sense. The fact that only six of the nine capital allocation requests by Brazilian subsidiaries were approved does not detract from this uniform and positive vision. Firmwide requests for capital allocation normally exceed the amount of capital available, and less pressing or promising opportunities or ideas that do not fit with current strategies are routinely denied. One interpretation of the positive views of Brazilian operations was expressed by the head of a Peruvian subsidiary who had recently been transferred from Brazil:

> In Brazil, I felt we were in the middle of the action. Here, I feel more isolated. The business in Brazil has grown so big and so fast that we all assumed that we know what we are doing . . . no one from headquarters ever seriously questioned us as long as we showed bottom-line results. Here in Peru, you also aren't questioned . . . unless you have an idea to do something. Then the assumption is that we are trying to get ourselves noticed and are not being realistic about real opportunities. In Brazil, you didn't have to show continually that you were realistic; you just had to produce.
>
> (LIMA, JUNE 1973)

Thus, for ANCOM subsidiaries marginal to the operations of TNCs, judgments about host country constraints on the freedom to manage were a central part of the capital allocation decision process. Such considerations were paid lip service in the case of Brazilian subsidiaries, but their centrality to the operations of the TNCs made revenue generation considerations much more important.

These views were echoed in responses to the second question TNC managers were asked about their freedom to manage. Answers to the question of whether TNC-generated constraints would pose difficulties for managing the proposed project were very closely linked to the capital-allocation-request outcome for the ANCOM managers and similar to the pattern noted in other answers by Brazilian managers. These results are reported in Table 2.19.

Notable in Table 2.19 is the divergence between the views of home office and subsidiary managers. Although intrafirm communication difficulties were anticipated by managers in both locales, both sets of subsidiary managers judged them more likely to affect the project under discussion. The managers of the nine ANCOM subsidiaries whose requests were turned down, plus one whose request was approved, all anticipated such problems. Their headquarters counterparts voiced less concern, and home office managers for Brazil saw virtually no problem, although four out of nine subsidiary managers anticipated difficulties.

The most important interpretation of the answers reported in Tables 2.18 and 2.19 is that in 1974, managers of TNC subsidiaries in the Andean countries were regarded as doubly disadvantaged. They and their home office superiors anticipated significant difficulty in exercising their best business judgment, because of con-

TABLE 2.19

Hypothesis: TNC managers will hesitate to commit additional capital to subsidiaries with which the home office has difficulty maintaining full communication when necessary. Conversely, they will be favorably disposed to committing new funds to subsidiaries with which future communications are anticipated to be clear and positive.

Question: Would home office-subsidiary communication difficulties present any problems for managing the proposed project?

	ANCOM	Brazil
Yes	5	1
No	7	8
Agreement with request outcomes	8 (67%)	7 (78%)
SUBSIDIARY		
Yes	10	4
No	2	5
Agreement with request outcomes	5 (42%)	6 (67%)

straints imposed both by Andean host countries and communications within the TNCs themselves. Significantly, home office and subsidiary managers placed different emphases on restrictions on their freedom to manage. Ten of the twelve home office managers (none of whom had been stationed in the Andean region) saw host country restrictions as potentially troublesome, but only three of the subsidiary managers shared their opinion. Ten of the Andean subsidiary managers saw firm-generated restrictions as management impediments, and five home office executives agreed.

Managers of Brazilian subsidiaries, on the other hand, reported no concern with host country restrictions and significantly less intrafirm communications difficulties. These results are consistent with the report that TNC managers viewed their Brazilian operations as a "miniaturization of conditions at home," but Andean operations were seen differently, so that anticipated constraints on managerial freedom were used there as a negative criterion for capital allocation decisions.

Answers to questions about revenue generation further clarified the nature of the TNC capital allocation process in the two business environments. Tables 2.20 and 2.21 show that managers' views on

TABLE 2.20

Hypothesis: TNC managers will hesitate to commit new capital to subsidiaries servicing small unorganized markets. Conversely, they will be more favorably disposed to committing new funds to subsidiaries servicing large, expanding, and well-organized markets.

Question: Does the market's potential revenue return justify the request for capital?

	ANCOM	Brazil
Yes	10	9
No	2	0
Agreement with request outcomes	5 (42%)	6 (67%)
SUBSIDIARY		
Yes	12	9
No	0	0
Agreement with request outcomes	3 (25%)	6 (67%)

TABLE 2.21

Hypothesis: TNC managers will hesitate to commit new capital to subsidiaries in host countries where input availability and costs are volatile or expensive. Conversely, they will be favorably disposed to committing new funds to subsidiaries with privileged access to cheap, plentiful inputs.

Question: Are the cost and availability of inputs favorable for revenue returns?

	ANCOM	Brazil
Yes	12	9
No	0	0
Agreement with request outcomes	3 (25%)	6 (67%)
SUBSIDIARY		
Yes	12	9
No	0	0
Agreement with request outcomes	3 (25%)	6 (67%)

potential revenue return and on costs and availability of inputs were weakly associated with positive action on requests for Andean subsidiaries, but closely associated with positive action on Brazilian subsidiary requests, as were questions about the freedom to manage. This mirrors the statement by the Peruvian subsidiary manager previously quoted—that estimations of the freedom to manage were confounded with revenue considerations for Brazilian subsidiaries. For ANCOM operations, they were a separate and additional criterion for evaluating capital allocation requests.

Brazilian subsidiaries were seen in the same positive light as in earlier questions. The revenue–return prospects of ANCOM subsidiaries were viewed much more positively than had been estimates of freedom to manage. No serious doubts were expressed at the home office or subsidiary level regarding cost and availability of inputs (Table 2.21). Concern over dependence on foreign energy suppliers was expressed by some managers—especially those in Brazilian subsidiaries—but input cost data had been tabulated for all of the requests, and both home office and subsidiary managers foresaw no serious problems related to them.

The potential of the market (Table 2.20) was only slightly more of an issue than cost and availability of inputs. The growing importance of the Brazilian market was clear to both home office and subsidiary managers, and both considered the proposals reasonable in light of that growth. The ANCOM subsidiary managers felt they had demonstrated that their requests would put their firms in positions to take advantage of a market that would be of increasing importance. Most home office managers concurred that the market could generate profitable returns on the requested investments. The two home office managers who did not share this view were critical of requests that specifically sought to take advantage of anticipated reduced intraregional tariffs. They both argued that increases in purchasing power would not compensate for added transport and advertising costs.

BUSINESS CLIMATE AS A CRITERION IN THE DECISION PROCESS

Differences between the home office and Andean subsidiaries were stronger when the focus was on the host country's business climate (Table 2.22). Home office and subsidiary managers agreed substantially about the short-term business climate in Brazil, although there was some disagreement about medium-term prospects there.

In light of public criticism over the ANCOM Foreign Investment Code, questions were raised about both the business climate for TNCs in general and for each firm's subsidiaries. This contrast between the home offices' and subsidiary managers' responses in Tables 2.22 and 2.23 corresponded to results reported in a survey conducted by Harvard Business School students in 1971.[27]

In regard to ANCOM, both home office and subsidiary managers were more optimistic about the situations of their firms than about the general climate for TNCs. This disparity offers some insights into both the practice and rhetoric of international business: It makes sense for managers to complain about conditions they consider adverse—if they are heeded, they may spur change. In addition, general complaints may hide resourceful adaptations to seemingly difficult situations. Finally, the interest of home office decision makers is sparked less by resourceful adaptations than by established positive patterns, such as the growth of sales by U.S. TNCs in Brazil from 1966 to 1973.

The problem of sparking interest in decision makers somewhat removed from the business environment is evident when home office and subsidiary views of ANCOM are compared in all five questions on the business climate. Compared with managers in subsidiaries, home office managers viewed host country attitudes as more hostile (Table 2.22), host country governments as less capable of structuring a satisfactory business environment (Table 2.23), and ANCOM environments as less likely to be satisfactory five years into the future (Table 2.24).

There is a number of possible explanations for these disparities. One is that managers in subsidiaries are in closer touch with actual conditions and have a clearer understanding than the more distant headquarters staff. A second is that subsidiary managers are more positive because they want to increase their responsibilities and advance in the corporation. A third is that subsidiary managers' judgments are based on evaluations of only their host country's business climate, while headquarters' views reflect comparisons among host country attitudes and capacities in a number of different locales.

Table 2.22 shows that the attitudes of Brazilian officials toward both TNCs in general and the subsidiaries of the firms studied were viewed as more positive by TNC managers than the attitudes of officials in the ANCOM countries. The correlation of this with the

TABLE 2.22

Hypothesis: TNC managers perceiving a hostile attitude on the part of a host country will be hesitant to commit additional capital there. Conversely, TNC managers perceiving positive attitudes will be favorably disposed to committing additional capital.

Question (to home office managers): Do you see the host country's attitude as hostile to TNCs in general?*

	ANCOM	Brazil
Yes	5	0
No	1	6
Agreement with request outcomes	11 (92%)	6 (67%)

Question (to subsidiary managers): Do you see the host country's attitude as hostile to your subsidiary?*

	ANCOM	Brazil
Yes	4	1
No	10	8
Agreements with request outcomes	5 (42%)	7 (78%)

*When questions are posed about the six TNCs, $n = 6$ for both ANCOM and Brazil; when questions are posed about the host countries or subsidiaries, $n = 14$ for ANCOM and $n = 9$ for Brazil. When questions are posed about capital allocation requests, $n = 12$ for ANCOM and $n = 9$ for Brazil.

greater success of Brazilian subsidiaries in obtaining capital allocation request approvals supports the hypothesis that TNC managers are more likely to approve requests made by subsidiaries in countries whose officials are perceived to have positive attitudes toward TNCs.

Table 2.23 shows that Brazil's capacity for structuring a satisfactory business environment was also viewed more positively than ANCOM's. This supports the hypothesis that managers would be more favorably disposed to committing funds to host countries with a strong capacity to structure a satisfactory business environment.

Table 2.24 shows that home office managers considered Brazil a more satisfactory business environment than ANCOM in the middle term (five years), but ANCOM subsidiary managers were somewhat more favorable about medium-term prospects than Brazilian managers. Since the capital allocation decisions were ultimately

TABLE 2.23

Hypothesis: TNC managers will hesitate to commit new capital to subsidiaries in host countries whose governments are perceived to have little capacity to structure an environment for international business. Conversely, they will be favorably disposed to committing new capital in host countries with strong capacities for structuring such environments.

Question (to home office managers): Do you see the host country as capable of structuring a satisfactory business environment for TNCs in general?*

	ANCOM	Brazil
Yes	2	6
No	4	0
Agreements with request outcomes	10 (83%)	6 (67%)

Question (to subsidiary managers): Do you see the host country as capable of structuring a satisfactory business environment for your subsidiary?*

	ANCOM	Brazil
Yes	10	9
No	4	0
Agreements with request outcomes	5 (42%)	6 (67%)

*For explanation of the number of responses corresponding to each question, see the note to Table 2.22.

made in headquarters, this confirms the hypothesis that managers would be more likely to commit funds to environments where the future is thought to be clear and positive.

However, the negative evaluation of the midterm Brazilian environment by managers in three Brazilian subsidiaries merits comment in light of the uniformly positive evaluation of the 1973 to 1974 environment. Although most of the Brazilian managers saw a midterm positive environment in Brazil, all nine saw problems brewing. They cited difficulties in maintaining "the boom of the last five years." They were also worried about the costs concomitant with Brazil's dependence on foreign energy sources and about the Brazilian government's "ability to keep the lid on"—to squelch political disruption through the repression of trade unions and polit-

TABLE 2.24

Hypothesis: TNC managers will hesitate to commit additional capital to subsidiaries located in host countries with which future relations are unclear. Conversely, they will be favorably disposed to committing new funds to subsidiaries located in host countries with which future relations are seen to be clear and positive.

Question: Will the host country be a satisfactory environment for international business in five years?*

	ANCOM	Brazil
Yes	3	6
No	3	0
Agreements with request outcomes	9 (64%)	6 (56%)
SUBSIDIARY		
Yes	11	6
No	3	3
Agreements with request outcomes	6 (43%)	5 (56%)

*For explanation of the number of responses corresponding to each question, see the note to Table 2.22.

ical parties. What the negative evaluations really meant were anticipation of slower growth.

The positive ANCOM evaluations, on the other hand, reflected subsidiary managers focusing on the stated intention of ANCOM investment regulations rather than on public criticisms of their restrictive nature, on the satisfactory earnings their subsidiaries continued to generate rather than on their marginal role in global TNC operations, and on possible new benefits afforded by a clarified regional environment for foreign investment.

The coincidence of home offices' and subsidiary managers' views bears on the hypothesis that when there is clear communication between home office and subsidiary, management will be more likely to commit funds to subsidiaries making requests. Comparing the nine Brazilian and fourteen ANCOM subsidiaries, home office and subsidiary views coincided on 89.1 percent of the questions regarding Brazilian operations (fifty-seven of sixty-four questions) and on 64.4 percent of the questions regarding the ANCOM operations (fifty-eight of ninety questions).

One interpretation of this result is that it was easier to show Brazil's strengths and weaknesses to headquarters, while information about ANCOM was more mixed and therefore more confusing. Another interpretation was that, because of the small size of AN-COM operations (or due to flawed organization of communication flows), the home office staff was not able to process information about ANCOM adequately. The hypothesis regarding clear communication was directly supported by interviews with the subsidiaries of four firms that had expanded in Chile and Peru from 1970 to 1972, a period when these two countries' business climates were described as especially difficult due to domestic politics. All four of these expansions had been greatly facilitated by the presence, and active intervention in the home office, of a staff member with recent experience in the host country. In none of these cases had intervention been part of overall corporate strategy; it had been spontaneous yet highly beneficial to both the host country and the TNC. It is unlikely that unplanned interventions of this type can take place in many firms due to the small size of TNC operations in small nations, such as those comprising the Andean group, and the resultant small chance that headquarters staff has had recent experience in such locales. Therefore, to minimize lost opportunities for both giant firms and small nations, special attention should be paid to home office-subsidiary relations and stress laid on building up home office sensitivity to business conditions in small nations.

Some companies have adopted practices designed to clarify such home office–subsidiary relations. The simplest mechanism used is adding to corporate headquarters regional coordinators with the responsibility of educating headquarters staff about conditions in specified environments. Another such mechanism has been the establishment, in some companies, of a small internationally oriented staff group reporting directly to the office of the president. The responsibility of such groups is to identify situations where clear opportunities for the firm would not be exploited under normal conditions. More complex are elaborate mechanisms such as that adopted by Westinghouse Electric Corporation in 1971. When Westinghouse changed from an international division to a global product structure, a World Regions Group was formed to coordinate more effectively global activities. The president of the World Regions Group reported to the vice chairman of Westinghouse's board of directors. The group consisted of eleven regional vice presidents—seven from U.S. areas and four from international areas. Each vice president was part of headquarters staff and also served as corporate "eyes, ears and voice" in his or her assigned region, sitting on subsidiary boards of directors, interpreting events in the region for headquarters, and representing the chairman in the region.

Such mechanisms as these provide important coordination for TNC activities that are somewhat central to global operations. However, difficulties in responding to unusual conditions in the unfamiliar Andean region made such mechanisms less sensitive than the unplanned intervention of staff with recent experience in that particular region. This finding dramatizes the difficulties such complex organizations as giant firms experience in responding to unusual opportunities in the unfamiliar environments of small nations.

Some of the reasons for these difficulties will be discussed in the following chapters. Particular attention will be paid to the implications of the finding that executive time is, in an important sense, the firm's scarcest resource and that the basis of corporate response to opportunities in business environments of central concern differs substantially from responses to opportunities in less familiar locales.

NOTES

1. In the mid-1980s, the importance of direct foreign investment for third-world-nation development has been stressed by observers as diverse as U.S. Organization of American States Ambassador J. William Mittendorf, "Free Enterprise: Key to Latin American Economic Revival," *Current Policy,* No. 692 (Washington, D.C.: U.S. Dept. of State, Feb. 22, 1985); the secretary of the Economic Commission in Latin America and the Caribbean (see "Preliminary Overview of the Latin American Economy during 1984," *Notas sobre la Economía y el desarollo,* no. 409/410; and Colombian President Belisario Betancour, "Betancour Gets Serious about Proposals to Ease Foreign Investment Rules," in *Business Latin America,* May 29, 1985, 169 and 175.

2. Through the mid-1980s Brazil, with Malaysia, Singapore, South Korea, Spain, and Taiwan, has been the recipient of the largest and most consistent flows of direct foreign investment from the United States and other countries. Between 1978 and 1983, U.S. direct foreign investment in Brazil increased from $6.96 billion to $9.02 billion (U.S. Dept. of Commerce, *International Direct Investment: Global Trends and U.S. Role,* 1984. Of these six countries, Brazil is the only one whose foreign investment strategy has important restricting elements. Compared with the other countries mentioned, Brazil's large market size, rich natural resources, and relatively advanced industrial structure have drawn investment to Brazil

despite important restrictions on foreign acquisition of local companies, technology transfer restrictions, and the 1983 decision largely to restrict the country's informatics industry to Brazilian ownership.

3. *First National City Bank*, "Brazil," (New York: First National City Bank) 1974, p. 16.

4. Inter-American Development Bank, *Economic and Social Progress in Latin America, 1977 Report* (Washington, D.C.: IADB, 1977), pp. 170–81, 391–404.

5. *Business Latin America*, June 22, 1972, p. 196.

6. Richard S. Newfarmer and Willard F. Mueller, *Multinational Corporations in Brazil and Mexico: Structural Sources of Economic and Noneconomic Power* (Washington, D.C.: GPO, 1975).

7. *Brasil em exame*, Editora Abril, Sao Paulo, Sept. 1974.

8. Ronald Müller discusses this trend in "The Political Economy of Global Corporations and National Stabilization Policy," in David E. Apter and Louis Wolf Goodman, eds., *The Multinational Corporation and Social Change* (New York: Praeger, 1976).

9. See John M. Conner and Willard F. Mueller, *Market Power and Profitability of Multinational Corporations in Brazil and Mexico* (Washington, D.C.: GPO, 1977), p. 19.

10. For the political history of Brazil through 1973, see Octavio Ianni, *A formacão do estado populista na America Latina* (Rio de Janeiro: Editora Civilizacão Brazilien, 1975); Alfred C. Stepan, *The Military in Politics: Changing Patterns in Brazil* (Princeton: Princeton University Press, 1971), and Alfred C. Stepan, ed., *Authoritarian Brazil: Origins, Policies, and Future* (New Haven: Yale University Press, 1973).

11. The impact of the Brazilian "economic miracle" on domestic income distribution is a continuing subject for debate. The terms for discussion were originally set in Alfred Stepan, *Authoritarian Brazil*, especially in Alfred Fishlow's essay, "Some Reflections on Post-1964 Brazilian Economic Policy," and Samuel A. Morley and Gordon W. Smith's essay, "The Effect of Changes in the Distribution of Income on Labor, Foreign Investment, and Growth in Brazil."

12. Inter-American Development Bank, *1977 Report*, table 3, p. 395.

13. Ibid., table 69, p. 450.

14. *Survey of Current Business* 55, no. 3 (Mar. 1975): 19–25.

15. LAFTA was formed in 1960 with an eleven-country membership that included Argentina, Boliva, Brazil, Chile, Colombia, Ecuador, Mexico, Paraguay, Peru, Uruguay, and Venezuela. As a free trade association, its aim is to gradually eliminate internal trade barriers while maintaining existing trade relations with nonmember countries.

16. For detailed discussions of the history of ANCOM, see David Morawetz, *Integration among Developing Countries* (Cambridge, Mass.: MIT Press, 1974); Lynn K. Mytelka, *Regional Development in a Global Economy: The Multinational Corporation, Technology, and Andean Integration* (New Haven: Yale University Press, 1979); and "The Andean Group: Fifteen

Years Later," *Integracion latinoamericana* 10, no. 98 (Jan.–Feb. 1985). For an analysis of ANCOM's prospects, see Augusto Aninat, Ricardo Ffrench–Davis, and Patricio Leiva, "La Integracion andina en el nuevo escenario de los años ochenta," *Apuntes CIEPLAN*, no. 52 (Oct. 1984).

17. Since their inception, the ambitious original objectives of ANCOM have proven difficult to achieve. Initiated at a time when its six member countries had achieved a degree of political consensus and were beginning a period of economic growth, radical regime changes and economic depression have taken a toll on ANCOM's hopes for economic integration. Adjustments were first made in the system to accommodate Venezuela's entry in 1973 and then in an attempt to forestall Chile's departure in 1976. Since then, internal disagreements have made it impossible to achieve the consensus needed for formal implementation of such important mechanisms as the common external tariff and the harmonization of economic policies or for full realization of the benefits of sectoral programs for industrial development, and it has been necessary to revise and amend Decision 24. However, ANCOM officials point to "increased and more diversified intra-subregional trade," numerous bilateral trade agreements, and the Cartagena Agreement Court of Justice, the Andean Council of Ministers of Foreign Affairs, and the Andean Parliament as evidence of "far from negligible material achievements . . . [despite] the adverse setting of the last few years." While not functioning as predicted at the time of the field research reported in this book, ANCOM continues, in the mid-1980s, to have an impact on economic integration and direct foreign investment in the region. Mid-1980s discussions of ANCOM's history and prospects can be found in *Integracion latinoamericana* 10, no. 98 (Jan.–Feb. 1985); and Inter-American Development Bank, "Economic Integration in Latin America," *Economic and Social Progress in Latin America, 1984 Report* (Washington, D.C.: IADB, 1984.)

18. Mytelka, op. cit., p. 62.

19. Based on interviews conducted in 1973 and 1974 as well as a survey of twenty North American TNCs carried out by Harvard Business School students and reported in "How Will Multinational Firms React to the Andean Pact's Decision 24?" *Inter-American Economic Affairs* 25, no. 2 (Autumn 1971): 55–65.

20. Recent econometric evidence further demonstrated that the code caused no significant change in direct foreign investment in the Andean group compared with other nations in Latin America. See Michael C. Aho and José Nuñez del Arco, "U.S. Direct Foreign Investment in Latin America, 1966–1976: An Empirical Analysis of the Impact of the Andean Code (Decision 24)," *Latin American Integration*, Apr. 1981; and Jürgen Riedel, "Attitude of the Federal Republic of Germany toward the Policies of Developing Countries regarding Foreign Investors," *Industry and Development*, no. 13 (1985). For a discussion of how TNCs adjusted their business practices to conform with the policies of Decision 24, see Gabriel Misas

Arango, *Empresas multinacionales y pacto andino* (Bogota: Oveja Negra, 1983).

21. Andrew B. Wardlaw, *The Andean Integration Movement* (Washington, D.C.: U.S. Dept. of State, 1973), p. 33.

22. Described in Miguel S. Wionczek, "U.S. Reaction to the Andean Group System for the Treatment of Foreign Capital," *Comercio exterior* (June 1971): 27–30.

23. Reported in Richard J. Barnet and Ronald E. Müller, *Global Reach* (New York: Simon & Schuster, 1979), p. 86.

24. Wardlaw, op. cit., p. 33.

25. In 1973 to 1974, Peru's Industrial Communities legislation required 13.5 percent of pretax company profits to be set aside to purchase shares in the company for a workers' "community" until the community controlled 51 percent of the company's capital. Through this community, employees could participate in company ownership and board-level decision making.

26. Felipe Salazar Santos, coordinator of the Junta of the Cartagena Agreement, New York, American Bar Association, May 1973.

27. *Inter-American Economic Affairs*, op. cit.

3:
Decision Processes
and
Business Environments

THE CONTEXT OF INTERNATIONAL
BUSINESS RELATIONSHIPS

The significance of an environment for international business is determined by factors both within the physical environment of the potential business locale and by factors outside that environment. A business relationship can be forged and sustained only if a wide range of considerations is taken into account and is evaluated in terms of the opportunity in question. In pursuing the separate objectives described in Chapter 1, the actions of decision makers in TNCs and host countries were conditioned by a wider context. This context affected both the total size of benefits resulting from a given business relationship and how those benefits were divided. The elements in this wider context are shown in Figure 3.1.

Locating the firm's decision process within the broader context of a business environment moves the discussion from how a decision is made by one party acting in relative isolation to a much more complex setting. In pursuing their objectives, decision makers in the firm respond to their own internal constraints (box 4, Figure 3.1), and they also take into account the constraints and objectives of the host country in which they hope to do business (box 5). In the final analysis, the TNC–host country business relationship (box 6) is shaped by the objectives of the two parties involved. These objectives are, in turn, affected by the objectives of other firms in the same industry as the TNC in question (box 3) and by the concerns of the country in which the TNC's home office is located (box 2). All of

Figure 3.1

Factors Affecting a Transnational Corporation (TNC)–Host Country (HC)
Business Relationship

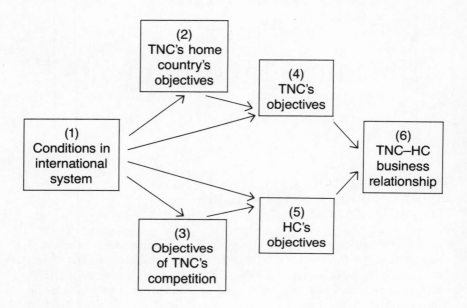

these are affected by other exogenous conditions in the international economic and political systems (box 1).

A workable business relationship results if the benefits from that relationship can satisfy the objectives of both the TNC and the host country. If total possible benefits are less than that required by the sum of the objectives of the potential partners, then new relationships will not form and old relationships will be threatened with dissolution.[1] For example, in 1978 the government of Panama and the Canadian firm Texasgulf could not work out a relationship to develop the Cerro Colorado copper deposit because Texasgulf's objectives required guaranteed earnings levels that exceeded those permissible under the mining code promulgated in Panama to advance its economic development. Rio Tinto Zinc, on the other hand, with different business objectives, after lengthy negotiations, was able to work out an arrangement with the government of Panama. In 1980, the Rio Tinto Zinc–government of Panama agreement satisfied both parties' objectives in terms of revenue potential, managerial discretion, and other business objectives, although one would expect both parties to continue to examine the project carefully as it progresses and to renegotiate when appropriate.[2]

All elements of the business environment, however, do not affect the potential for reaching and sustaining an agreement. These elements can have an impact on (1) the total size of the benefits to be derived from the business relationship or (2) on the way in which benefits from the relationship are divided between the parties involved (the TNC and the host country).

THE SIZE OF BENEFITS FROM BUSINESS RELATIONSHIPS

The total size of potential benefits is primarily shaped by exogenous forces in the international economic and political system (box 1, Figure 3.1). For example, the value of the Cerro Colorado project will be heavily influenced by the world price of copper when consumers sign contracts for its future or spot output. Some historical examples make this case more concretely: More than 90 percent of the world's supply of naturally occurring nitrates are located in northern Chile. When, during World War I, American scientists developed a process for synthesizing nitrates in a chemical laboratory, the potential value to be obtained from nitrate properties by the Chilean state and U.S. investors developing the properties dropped precipitously.[3] When, in 1973, the Organization of Petroleum Exporting Countries (OPEC) successfully negotiated the formation of a petroleum cartel, the total benefit to be obtained from the development of petroleum properties skyrocketed. When, in the 1950s, scientists working for the Mexican firm Syntex S.A. developed a process for producing steroid hormone drugs from the root of the barbasco plant, the world price of steroid hormones fell, and European TNCs saw the value of enterprises designed to extract these drugs from animal by-products plummet.[4] When, in the wake of 1973 oil price increases, an international liquidity glut resulted from recycling petrodollars, TNC banks scrambled to find products to take advantage of the resulting reduced cost of money for many third-world nations through more favorable loan terms and the funding of a number of previously unfinanceable development projects.[5]

A wide range of factors in the international system can dramatically affect the value to be obtained from a given business relationship. New sources of an input or a final product can lower prices for a good; curtailment of traditional sources can raise prices. The development of new technologies can also affect the value to be obtained from a relationship, as can the entry of new competitors into a market. When evaluating the progress of negotiations for a business relationship, all parties normally attempt to keep themselves apprised of details of the arrangement under negotiation, but they must also keep tabs on such exogenous factors as the exhaustion of a mine, bad crop weather, a long strike, or political turmoil in some other part of the world as well as developments in international capital markets and markets for technology. Such vigilance does not end with signatures on dotted lines. It is expected that all parties will continue to monitor such conditions for the life of their business relationship.

When such changes occur, they cause the weights assigned to other aspects of the business environment to shift for all parties. A dramatic increment in the relative value of a commodity may increase home country and TNC concern over adequate supply and the possibility of finding substitutes; it can cause a host country to bargain for an enlarged share of the benefits; or it may spur other firms to expand operations. If and when such exogenous changes occur and when they promise to endure, business relationships are normally renegotiated or dissolve through nationalization by host countries or liquidation by TNCs.

Although negotiations for the formation of business relations normally take as a given the existing nature of the international economic and political systems, the probability of an important change in that order does have an impact on building business relationships. If a major change occurs, such as the devaluation of the currency of a nation in which factors or outputs of production are bought or sold, negotiations often stall until the dust has settled. If it is unclear how often exogenous changes may occur, such as the accumulation or depletion of U.S. stockpiles of a given commodity, special steps may be taken to cover the adjustment costs concomitant with such uncertainty.

A second factor exogenous to the business relationship and the objectives of the parties involved are the concerns of the home country of the TNC involved (box 2, Figure 3.1). In the 1970s and 1980s, the U.S. government has been concerned lest firms incorporated within its borders engage in business practices considered illicit, such as obtaining favors through bribery.[6] Furthermore, national concern for certain foreign policy objectives, such as the preservation of the State of Israel,[7] the world wide promotion of human rights,[8] and not sharing strategic technologies with potential enemies,[9] has limited, to some extent, foreign trade and other international business activities. In addition, a longstanding national concern with the evils of monopoly has prevented U.S.-based firms from openly working together with competitors in many areas.[10]

In other countries, some of the same concerns are voiced, but often the home country is more concerned that its national firms survive and prosper. Thus, many large European firms, such as FIAT (Italy), Peugeot (France), Pegaso (Spain), and BP (United Kingdom) are actually partnerships between the home government and national entrepreneurs.[11] In such cases, the government may be directly concerned with the ability of its standard bearer to achieve its business objectives, or the government may put pressure on the firm because of broader policy interests. At any rate, different pressures will be placed on such firms by their home governments than on firms, such as those in the United States, which do not have such direct state ties.

Firms continually lobby their home governments for greater support and reduced pressure. In the United States, corporate complaints that the antimonopoly provisions of the Clayton and Sherman acts place U.S. firms at a disadvantage with competitors from other nations have been business gospel since the legislation was enacted in the early twentieth century.[12] United States firms also complain about strictures that attempt to remove certain actions from the domain of the strategic business decision and subject them to the rule of law. Most notable has been legislation enacted in 1977 making payments illicit in the United States also illegal if made by U.S.-based firms in other countries.[13] Representatives of firms argue that such legislation, while well intended, is inappropriate to the varied business cultures encountered in international dealings and has the effect of tying decision makers' hands in situations in which they should exercise managerial discretion.[14] United States firms also complain that their home government does not provide them with direct and indirect support comparable to that afforded by other governments. For example, business representatives have complained that the U.S. government's Overseas Private Investment Corporation's (OPIC) protection against extraordinary risks, such as nationalization, devaluation, and so forth, is more costly and provides inferior coverage when compared with support offered by Japan, Germany, and the Netherlands.[15]

Thus, a second exogenous factor that impinges on TNC–host country business relationships is the concerns of the firm's home government. Firms assert that it is easier for them to enter into business relationships with other parties when the hands of their decision makers are not tied by government regulation and their enterprise is generously supported. In addition, firms that are partially owned by their home government may receive special assistance in the face of international competition, but they may also be asked to service the nonbusiness objectives of their part-owner. These considerations, together with those imposed by the nature of the international economic and political systems, may constrain the formation of TNC–host country business relationships due to pressures exogenous to the objectives of either party and to the immediate business environment in which the relationship is being forged.

THE DIVISION OF BENEFITS
FROM BUSINESS RELATIONSHIPS

Most discussions of international business environments focus on how constraints internal to the TNC and the host country affect the nature of their objectives and how a given benefit will be distributed among the parties involved. The objectives of other firms in the international industry of which the TNC is a part can affect this division of benefits in a decisive fashion (box 3, Figure 3.1). If the TNC and other firms have formed a formal or informal cartel, the TNC may be able to bargain with the host country with the assurance that no competitor will put in a rival bid for the arrangement under negotiation.[16] If no such agreement exists, then the host country may try to solicit bids from a number of TNCs, thus increasing its bargaining power. For example, in 1973, the terms the government of Peru were able to extract from the Massey–Ferguson Company and Perkins–Volvo (cobidders for the production of tractors in Peru) were considerably more favorable to Peru once additional bidders showed interest in the project.[17]

On the other hand, competition in some industries is rather tightly controlled by relationships among the principal producers in that industry. The international electronics industry is perhaps most famous for such practices, including the division of markets among major companies.[18] In such cases of cooperation and forbearance among competitors, host countries may experience difficulties improving on existing terms unless they can identify a firm that, for its own internal reasons, is willing to break ranks. Such was the case when Jamaica attempted to renegotiate the terms of its business relationships with international aluminum producers. Negotiations were at a standstill until a relatively minor aluminum producer, Anaconda (a small aluminum producer but a large copper producer), made an offer more favorable to Jamaica than those offered by major producers.[19]

Despite constraints imposed by the international economic and political systems, home countries of TNCs, and other members of the international oligopoly of which the TNC is a part, the possibility of forging a business relationship is, in the end, feasible only when there is a minimum of mutual interest and compatibility of objectives between the TNC and the host country. Figure 3.2 describes the process through which host countries and TNCs attempt to forge business relationships once their individual objectives have been specified. Objectives, initially phrased broadly, can be specified in terms of more specific criteria by both parties and, as TNC-host country interaction proceeds, are eventually stated in terms specific to the relationship at hand. For example, specific tariff levels or tariff exemptions can be stated for inputs to a manufacturing process; exemptions from certain taxes and import restrictions can be negotiated. A specific minimum of the value added resulting from domestic labor can be required—thus aiding the host's balance of payments, ensuring local jobs and/or the development of local ancillary industries. Intracorporate loan interest rates, royalty payment levels, management, and sales and service contracts can all be determined through negotiation at levels mutually acceptable to both parties.

Normally, a business relationship is not worked out overnight, although there have been projects of such obvious mutual interest that they have been negotiated rapidly (path 1, Figure 3.2). However, a potential project may be dropped quickly by one or both parties (path 2). For example, when a large U.S.-based tractor company considered approaching the government of Peru about the previously mentioned tractor production arrangement, its executives decided that potential market size and government support were too unpredictable, so the firm abandoned the project. Business relationships that do develop usually involve lengthy negotiations and trade-offs between the interested parties (path 3). In the tractor negotiations, the Massey–Ferguson Company wanted to locate its plant near Lima, the Peruvian capital. It eventually acceded to government demands to locate its factory in a new industrial area—the northern city of Chimbote. On the other hand, the Massey–Ferguson Company was able to obtain, through bargaining, monopoly rights to tractor manufacture in Peru (and later, with the assistance of the Peruvian government, monopoly rights to the manufacture of

Figure 3.2
Interaction between a TNC and a Host Country about a Possible Business Relationship

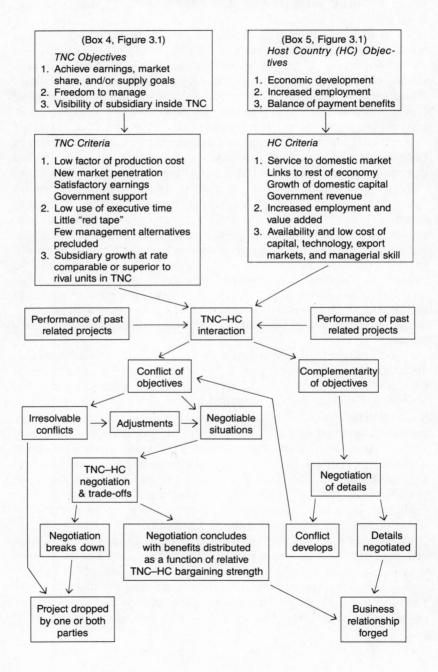

certain size tractors in the entire Andean region) as well as concessions regarding tax levels and tariffs on imported production
inputs. These negotiations continued over a period of more than two
years (and rights to exclusive manufacture in the Andean region
were not allocated until more than eight years after Massey–Ferguson and Peruvian interaction began on the project).[20]

As Figure 3.2 suggests, a number of other paths, in addition to
the three mentioned, can be followed in forging or dropping a possible business relationship. Parties can adjust their positions after
identifying seemingly irresolvable conflicts and reenter negotiations. Negotiations can break down after they have commenced, and
a project can be abandoned; an unforeseen conflict can develop in
late stages of negotiation requiring reentry into basic and time-
consuming bargaining. When entities as large and complex as TNCs
and host countries attempt to pursue mutual interests, it is not
surprising that a lengthy process results. In addition to starting with
differing (but not necessarily conflicting) objectives, each party to
the potential agreement must respond to the diverse interests of the
many parts of which it is composed. For a lasting business relationship, a formula must be developed to establish mutual interests
and allocate the benefits of the relationship in a manner that both
parties regard as equitable and can endure over time, despite changes
in the business environment affecting the size of the benefits or the
pressures to which each party is subject.

TNC EVALUATIONS OF HOST COUNTRY
BUSINESS ENVIRONMENTS

When a TNC considers making a capital allocation, a time-
consuming evaluation of the business climate in the potential host
country is normally carried out. As previously discussed, it is important for the firm to evaluate exogenous factors in the international system that impinge on the host and the TNC, as well as
mutual host country and TNC objectives. A major focus of such an
evaluation is the business environment of the potential host country. Many lists of questions have been proposed to evaluate host
country business environments, but no single list can do more than
suggest the kinds of considerations to be taken into account in a
given situation. On the one hand, the situation of each potential
TNC–host country relationship is different. Acceptable levels of
profit or use of executive time for one year may not be acceptable for

another. On the other hand, no single list is appropriate for all stages of evaluation of the same potential relationship even within the same TNC. At the initial stage of evaluation, it may be appropriate to pose a small number of relatively broad-gauged questions, such as those designed in Robert Stobaugh's eight-item scale for measuring a country's investment climate.[21] Later, when the corporate planning office is conducting its evaluations and a concrete relationship is being negotiated, a wider range of detailed questions must be examined. Finally, when the matter is brought before a decision-making board, answers to these questions must be presented in a concise and understandable form.

Examples of questions raised by decision makers in TNCs about the suitability of business environments in a host country for possible investment are presented in Figure 3.3. How questions are posed, the identities of the individuals making the evaluations, and the precision with which evaluations are specified vary from firm to firm and can undergo marked changes over time in any particular firm. Some firms continually monitor certain countries on specific questions; others carry out evaluations only when the nature of a potential business relationship is under actual consideration. Some firms pose exhaustive batteries of questions and others use a few simple measures. Some firms rely on large in-house planning and evaluating staffs, and others employ outside experts for their evaluations. Some firms evaluate a country's business environment with metrics graded from zero to a hundred or even finer, whereas other firms use more general categories, such as desirable, marginal, undesirable.

The firms in which the interviews reported in Chapter 2 were conducted reflect the variety of approaches to the evaluation of host country business environments. However, decision makers in those firms were generally interested in the five dimensions of a host country's business environment indicated in Figure 3.3: (1) the country's business climate—the general "attitude" of the country toward foreign investment and the capacity of the country to transform that attitude into reality; (2) factors determining the potential return from the business relationship in terms of revenue—especially, in the case of manufacturing firms, market-related factors; and for manufacturing, primary products, and service-related firms, availability and cost of factors of production; (3) how the business relationship would fit with the TNC's global strategy; (4) whether TNC executives will feel free to manage their investment; and (5) whether the evaluation will be valid in the future.

From the neoclassic economic standpoint, articulated in Chapter 4, such an array of considerations may be seen as inelegant at the least, and more critically, a waste of time. Much more to the point would be a straightforward estimation of the potential return on any new capital expenditure, with capital allocation based on revenue flow generated by rate and size of return, and with large, highly profitable investments being irresistible.

The more differentiated evaluation of potential host country business environments, suggested in Figure 3.3, is consistent with the revisions of traditional microeconomics discussed in Chapter 4. The precise questions in Figure 3.3 are derived from field research and are the bases of the hypotheses discussed and tested in Chapter 2.

DIMENSION I: MONITORING HOST COUNTRY BUSINESS CLIMATES

Although the kinds of questions listed in Figure 3.3 were posed by almost all of the firms in which field research interviews were carried out, each had its own way of approaching the matter.[22] The planning office of one firm constantly monitored all countries in the world with respect to such issues as those listed under the heading business climate. When firm managers had to make a decision about a new investment or an additional capital expenditure, this information was used. If the country were rated a desirable place to do business, then the managers evaluated whether the project in question fit with the TNC's overall strategy. If it did, calculations were carried out regarding projected returns and the freedom to manage in the prospective host country. Once all of this information was assembled, the planning office was in a position to make its recommendation and shepherd the information through the firm's complex capital allocation decision process.

In another firm, information was not systematically gathered on a prospective host country unless executives at headquarters decided that a possible business relationship looked promising. At that point, the planning office was instructed to carry out an in-depth analysis of the prospective host country's business climate.

DIMENSION II: REVENUE RETURN—MARKETS AND INPUTS

The TNC's business purposes also determine—the kinds of questions it asks. For example, TNCs operating in primary products industries, such as agriculture, fishing, and mining, would have

Figure 3.3

Questions for TNC Managers
about a Host Country Business Environment

I. Business Climate

A. *Attitude* of Host Country (HC) toward TNCs
1. Is foreign ownership of investment allowed?
2. Is capital allowed to be repatriated freely?
3. Are foreign firms treated on an equal basis with local firms?
4. Is the HC willing to grant tariff and other protections to firms operating within its borders?
5. Is the HC on friendly terms with the government of the country in which the TNC's home office is located?

B. *Capacity* of HC to Structure Business Environment
1. Does the government have long-term prospects for political stability?
2. Is the inflation rate low?
3. Is the rate of per capita economic growth high?
4. Are exchange rates set in a reasonable manner?
5. Are local capital markets developed?

II. Potential Revenue Return

A. *Market Factors*
1. How many people are in positions to buy the TNC's products?
2. Is this number increasing rapidly?
3. Is purchasing power overly sensitive to business cycle fluctuations?
4. Is the TNC's potential market already controlled by a competitor?*
5. Does the transporation system facilitate market penetration?
6. Do any government regulations block TNC market penetration?*

B. *Input-Related Structures*
Are the following inputs available (1) in sufficient quantity and (2) at low cost: raw materials, energy, transportation facilities, labor, capital, professional and management services.

III. Fit with Strategy of TNC
1. Will business in this HC help integrate the TNC's global and/or regional marketing and production operations?
2. Will doing business in this HC enhance the TNC's competitive position worldwide?

3. Will doing business in this HC enhance the TNC's worldwide image?

IV. Freedom to Manage

A. *Host-Country-Generated Constraints*
   1. Is it easy to communicate with HC nationals?
   2. Is it likely that bureaucratic "red tape" or delays in official approvals, construction schedules, and so on, will be at a minimum?*
   3. Will the amount of executive time used by comparable to the financial resources deployed and expected benefits?
   4. Will TNC managers be precluded from pursuing certain business opportunities?*

B. *TNC-Generated Constraints*
   1. Are there efficient communication services between the HC and the TNC's home country?
   2. Is the TNC organized so that it can respond sensitively to requests from its subsidiary in the HC?

V. Future TNC–HC Relations
How will all of this be in the future?

---

*Negative responses are desired for questions followed by an asterisk.

little interest in market-related business structure questions, since markets for their products are often located in countries different from those in which they obtain raw materials. On the other hand, they would be interested in input-related business structure questions, especially the availability and cost of labor and other inputs required to produce and export the raw materials they seek.

The TNCs operating in manufacturing industries place a different emphasis on the first two aspects of the business structure dimension. While expressing concern over the cost and availability of inputs for manufacturing processes, much greater emphasis is placed on market-related factors. Of primary concern to TNCs that establish manufacturing subsidiaries around the world is locating their subsidiaries in host countries with large, fast growing, penetrable markets.

Manufacturing firms are, however, primarily interested in input-related questions if the rationale for establishing a subsidiary is other than servicing the host country's market. Such interests may be stimulated by forces within the firm, such as the desire for fuller integration of its global operations, or by forces within the host country seeking to stimulate exports. Either motivation can result in subsidiaries throughout the world making products for both consumption in their host countries and for export and use by corporate subsidiaries in other nations. For example, the Coca Cola Company uses its Mexican subsidiary both to market its products in Mexico and to oversee production of fruit products that are exported to the United States and elsewhere. As part of its agreement with the government of Peru, the Massey–Ferguson Company must manufacture and export from Peru tractor parts of value equal at least to products it imports for assembly in the country. With mounting balance of payments deficits aggravated by large debt service problems, many third-world countries are now making just such evaluations and demands of TNCs that import intermediate goods for assembly and sale in domestic markets.[23]

Other manufacturing firms set up facilities to take advantage of cheap or easily available inputs. For example, all of the baseballs, footballs, and softballs assembled in the plant that New Jersey based MacGregor Sporting Goods, Inc., established in Haiti are exported. Haiti does not afford MacGregor a domestic market but provides important inputs, especially cheap, docile labor. Similarly, a portion of the recent economic growth in East Asian countries, such as Korea, Taiwan, and Singapore, as well as factories on the U.S.–Mexican border, derives from the export platforms they have provided electronics and other firms whose products are assembled there by local labor.

DIMENSION III: FIT WITH TNC STRATEGY

The fit of the business environment of the prospective host country with the TNC's global strategy can play a decisive role in a firm's decision to establish new facilities or expand existing ones. For example, W. R. Grace & Co.'s 1971 decision to sell most of its holdings in Latin America was largely motivated by its board of directors' fear that being perceived as a company with large third-world interests would cause its stock to become undervalued and thus make it vulnerable to an unfriendly takeover. Today, W. R. Grace & Co., which began in 1864 as a trading and manufacturing concern in Peru, is one of the world's largest transnational chemical concerns, with virtually no remaining commercial interests in Latin America.[24] In 1980, Nestlé Company, the world's largest transnational food processor, announced that its 1979 level of 35 percent of its sales from operations in third-world nations made it too vulnerable to business environmental fluctuations and signaled its intention to slow corporate growth outside of more developed countries, despite high profitability from these operations.[25] These are two examples of firms deciding not to expand business relationships in third-world host countries, not because of expected low returns on such operations, but because such operations were perceived to be damaging to the TNC's worldwide image. While such considerations are central to capital allocation decision processes in only a small number of circumstances, they can redirect the path along which a given TNC's business relationships will develop.

Other aspects of the potential impact of a host country's business environment on a TNC's global strategy are much more likely to be germane to a given capital allocation decision process merely because they are questions arising as a business strategy evolves rather than when a long-term strategy is abruptly changed. Examples of such considerations include whether integrating the TNC's global or regional operations will be affected by a new capital expenditure and whether the TNC's worldwide competitive position will be enhanced. A negative answer to the integration question indicates that investing or expanding in a given locale would result in dispersion of the corporation's resources. For example, in 1976, the International Basic Economy Corporation (IBEC), a diversified U.S.-based conglomerate that promoted joint ventures with Latin American entrepreneurs, concluded that it was spreading its managerial talent too thinly. It moved to divest itself of supermarket and fishing interests and focused on its other existing divisions, which included combining its agribusiness and fertilizer production divisions.[26]

Similarily, Chrysler Corporation's 1979 decision to sell its profitable operations in South America were, in large part, motivated by management's decision that its resources could not, in the short term, be effectively integrated with the operations of its principal (and imperiled) unit in the United States. On the other hand, the Ford Motor Company's decision to build a Pinto engine plant in Brazil in 1973 integrated its worldwide operations. The decision both provided Ford with an alternative source in the event of production disruptions in other Pinto engine plants and strengthened Ford's presence in Latin America, especially facilitating intrafirm sales between Ford's subsidiaries in Brazil and Argentina.

At least as important as the integrative effects of Ford's engine plant in Brazil was the impact on its worldwide competitive position. In the 1970s, Brazil became one of the world's most important markets for automobile sales, and in the early 1970s, Volkswagen dominated the Brazilian market. Ford's sales outside of its U.S. home base became increasingly important during the 1970s as profits in the United States fell and them moved into the red. The establishment of a substantial Ford presence in Brazil was then essential for keeping up with other major automobile producers and for keeping the Ford Motor Company afloat overall. Conversely, situations may easily emerge in which a new capital allocation does not enhance but even damages a firm's worldwide competitive position. A proposal to set up a manufacturing facility in a host country that is already serviced by another TNC subsidiary through exports could be an unneeded drain on corporate resources and might not add to the firm's world sales. Such circumstances do not usually lend themselves to easy analyses because mounting debt burdens and the pursuit of development goals are rapidly persuading planners in third-world countries to insist that wherever possible, TNCs service their markets by establishing production facilities rather than through imports. While not necessarily increasing a firm's worldwide market share, establishing such facilities may preserve existing markets in the face of changing environmental conditions.

DIMENSION IV: THE FREEDOM TO MANAGE

Concern over the freedom of TNC executives to manage their firms as they see fit has been implicit in a number of the preceding questions. On a worldwide scale, advancing a firm's global strategy facilitates pursuit of that strategy. However, TNC managers worrying about the freedom to manage are more often specifically concerned with being able to exercise what they consider sound business judgement in a particular host country. Questions regarding the ease of communication with host country nationals belie deeper worries about complementarity of objectives. Not understanding is often a polite way of describing lack of cooperation in achieving business objectives. This can result from badly organized regulatory organizations and corresponding delays and red tape. It can stem from changing host country policy due to internal politics or clear conflicts between certain objectives of the TNC and the host country. It can also be due to host country personnel that is inadequately trained to respond to the needs of the TNC or TNC executives who have not learned how to work in a given host country's environment.

The bottom line in concerns regarding freedom to manage is the efficient use of executive time. For managers themselves, it is important for the host country to provide a milieu enabling them to pursue alternatives that make business sense and have time to work on ideas that help business grow (not merely survive). From the standpoint of the manager, the host country environment should also pay the level of respect that he or she feels is due and enables him or her to fulfill corporate objectives in a manner that facilitates career development. From the standpoint of the firm, it is important for the host country milieu not be so complicated to deal with that it drains more time from the TNC's store of executive talent than is justified by financial and other rewards expected from the business relationship.

As shown in Chapter 2, some of these questions are more appropriate for certain host country environments than others. Freedom to manage concerns is less important in host country environments that are marginal to a TNC's overall strategy and more important in business relationships that are central to a firm's global plans. For example, the president of a large mining company explained why his firm had undergone years of time-consuming negotiations to develop a large mineral deposit in a middle-sized Latin American country by saying, "The deposit is so valuable that it is simply in our interest to find the time to work out a way to develop it." An executive vice president in a manufacturing firm, commenting on business prospects in the same country during the same year, stated that he could easily see that large profits could be made there but he was afraid to expand his firm's operations because he feared that, in addition to the time of managers working in the host country, all of his time (he had regional responsibility) would be taken up.

DIMENSION V: FUTURE TNC–HOST COUNTRY RELATIONS

Finally, in the very front of most managers' minds is the question, "What will all of this be like in the future?" Managers of firms in host countries in different situations all desire predictability. Certain situations (where outcomes are assured) are naturally preferred over risky situations (where probabilities can be assigned to outcomes), which are in turn preferred over uncertain situations (where not enough is known to assign probabilities).

TNC HOME COUNTRY BUSINESS ENVIRONMENTS

In Figure 3.4, the preceding questions are translated into descriptions of three different kinds of business environments. From

Figure 3.4

Business Environments in TNC Home Countries, Host Countries Central to TNC Strategies, and Host Countries Marginal to TNC Strategies

	TNC HOME COUNTRY	CENTRAL HOST COUNTRY	MARGINAL HOST COUNTRY
Attitude toward TNC	Supportive & desirous of retaining	Supportive & desiring expansion	Ambivalent & evaluating cost & benefits
Capacity to structure business environment	Strong, but increasingly vulnerable	Strong but subject to short-term crisis	Not well organized & vulnerable to short-term crisis
Market structure	Large well-organized market	Market growing in size and organization	Market small & not well organized
Inputs	All inputs available, although cost rising	Most inputs available, some very inexpensive	Input availability and cost volatile
Fit with TNC strategy	Essential but losing absolute centrality	Growing in importance	Essentially unrelated
Country-generated management constraints	Related to country's history and desire to retain centrality for TNC	Few, as TNC activity seen as advancing development objectives	Unclear, related to costs and benefits of TNC activity for development objectives
TNC-generated management constraints	Few due to physical and organizational centrality	Few due to growing organizational centrality	Difficulties of physical distance and marginal organizational role
View of future relations with TNC	Clear but conflicts anticipated due to changes in TNC strategy	Clear, although conflicts anticipated	Unclear, worry about unanticipated conflicts

the standpoint of the TNC manager, the environment in the TNC's home country is likely to be different from environments in third-world host countries. Most large TNCs continue to maintain their international headquarters in the country in which they were established. Texaco, Inc., was established in the United States in 1902 and has its international office in White Plains, New York. Nestlé was established in Switzerland in 1866, and its international offices are in the Swiss town of Vevey. Phillips, the Dutch electrical and electronics TNC, has had its headquarters in Eindhoven, Holland, since it was founded in 1891. The Marubeni Corporation's founding year was 1858, and its home office has always been Osaka, Japan. The General Electric Company, founded in 1878, continuously had its home office in the United States—now in Fairfield, Connecticut. These firms have grown and expanded in environments to which they have continually adapted and that have, in part, been molded by their actions.

The nations, states, and municipalities in which these operations are located desire to retain them and the jobs and tax revenue they provide. The success and growth of each of these TNCs have depended, to a large extent, on the compatibility of the firm's purpose with the needs of the country serving as the locale for its headquarters. Each of these home countries has provided stable and supportive environments for carrying out transnational business, including well-organized home markets and cheap, abundant inputs, or has negotiated trade agreements to facilitate access to markets and inputs. Each of these TNCs has carefully developed its business strategy to take advantage of opportunities offered by its home country, be it access to large markets or exceptional inputs or unusual facilities for trading with other nations. From the standpoint of the home country the long familiarity established between it and a given TNC can be disrupted by efforts by other countries trying to increase their share of the jobs and revenues offered by TNC operations, or by TNC actions, for some reason, seeking more favorable business arrangements outside the home country.

THIRD-WORLD HOST COUNTRIES OF CENTRAL IMPORTANCE TO TNCs

Host countries in which subsidiaries of the home office are located also desire to increase the benefit they obtain from the operations of TNCs within their borders. However, business environments in these countries are generally not so fully compatible with the operations of TNCs. Compared with a TNC's home country, their involvement with the TNC's operations has generally been shorter and more limited. While this difference in compatibility may be slight and have little impact on TNC business relationships in developed-nation host countries, its impact in third-world-nation host countries is usually substantial.

Such lack of established compatibility with host country business environments is most felt in third-world hosts of marginal importance to a TNC's global strategies. It has a lesser impact in such nations as Brazil, Mexico, Thailand, or India that may be more central to the global strategies of particular TNCs. In a third-world host country that has become central to the operations of a TNC, relationships have normally been established that clarify, for both parties, expectations regarding costs and benefits. These expectations are formulated as a result of past business experiences and ongoing discussions in the host country about the role of international business in national development.

Such nations as Brazil and India, while possessing a strong capacity to structure their domestic business environments, are more subject to short-term economic and political crises than are OECD host countries that have more fully diversified economies and more fully institutionalized political systems. The importance of such host countries for TNCs engaged in manufacturing largely derives from domestic markets that are growing in size and organization. Market size, in turn, can also become the basis for a host country gaining additional importance in a TNC's worldwide operations. For example, the large market for Massey–Ferguson tractors in Brazil in the 1970s enabled the firm to purchase important inputs in Brazil and to use Brazil as a source of parts and assembled vehicles for other markets.

Particularly important in such host countries is management's perception that clear understandings exist regarding their freedom to manage. Although TNCs may be prohibited from operating in such economic sectors as public utilities or energy production and may have to share patent rights with domestic enterprises, such infringements on managerial freedom have been enacted even in host countries central to TNC operations in the course of ongoing successful business relationships. Because of such long-standing relationships, business environments in central host countries are generally perceived as less restrictive than less familiar business environments, regardless of the actual number of constraints in those less familiar settings.

THIRD-WORLD HOST COUNTRIES
OF MARGINAL IMPORTANCE TO TNCs

Third-world host countries marginal to the operations of a TNC are often seen by TNC managers as reflecting hostile government attitudes toward foreign business and having little capacity to structure a business environment congenial to substantial international operations. Such perceptions are reinforced by the small contributions to overall corporate earnings afforded by subsidiaries located in such countries as Guatemala, Ghana, Burma, Bolivia, or even in a nation as large as Colombia. Although the ratio of profits to invested capital may be unusually high in such countries (see Table 2.3), the absolute size of sales is usually so small that its operations within the TNC are hardly noticed unless a manager has direct responsibility for that subsidiary.

Although small market size is reason enough to be skeptical of the value of expanding operations in a given host country, a TNC's limited experience doing business in small third-world nations makes the likelihood of expansion in such countries additionally remote. As a consequence, when a capital allocation request is considered for such a subsidiary, its operations may appear to be essentially unrelated to the firm's evolving global strategy. The original reasons for establishing the subsidiary, such as exploiting a hitherto untouched market or complementing operations in other nearby countries, may or may not continue to be as positive for the TNC as reasons for investing in other operations more central to TNC global strategy.

Furthermore, the limited international business experience and precarious economic positions of many third-world nations may generate additional constraints on managerial freedom due to unresolved discussions of the costs and benefits of TNC activity for national development objectives. All of this may make the TNC's view of future business relations with countries hosting small marginal subsidiaries unclear and fraught with worry about unanticipated conflicts.

NOTES

1. The most familiar approach to analyzing the formation of two-party relationships relies on game theory and the concept of bilateral monopoly. Classic works on this topic include: George Stigler, *The Theory of Price* (New York: Macmillan, 1961); Thomas Schelling, *The Strategy of Conflict*

(London: Oxford University Press, 1963); Charles Kindleberger, *Economic Development* (New York: McGraw-Hill, 1965), and *American Business Abroad* (New Haven: Yale University Press, 1969); Raymond Mikesell, ed., *Foreign Investment in the Petroleum and Mineral Industries: Case Studies in Investor–Host Country Relations* (Baltimore: Johns Hopkins Press, 1971).

2. See *Latin American Political Report*, June 1980.

3. See Mira Wilkens, *The Maturing of Multinational Enterprise* (Cambridge: Harvard University Press, 1974), p. 192.

4. Gary Gereffi, *The Pharmaceutical Industry and Dependency in the Third World* (Princeton: Princeton University Press, 1983), chap. 5.

5. Richard Weinert, "Why the Banks Did It," *Foreign Policy*, no. 30 (Spring 1978): 143–48.

6. This resulted in the enactment of the Foreign Corrupt Practices Act on Dec. 19, 1977.

7. Title II (antiboycott provisions) of the Export Administration Amendment of 1977, Public Law 95–52 details U.S. policy toward U.S. firms' responses to the Arab boycott of Israel.

8. In 1974, Congress required that such U.S. government business assistance as Ex-Im Bank financing and OPIC (Overseas Private Investment Corporation) Investment Insurance not be granted for projects in nations judged human rights violators by the U.S. Department of State.

9. The Trading with the Enemy Act prohibits U.S. firms and their subsidiaries from trading with specific enemy countries in a number of defense-related products. In the mid-1970s and early 1980s, this act inhibited some business interaction with the Soviet Union and Cuba despite requests by American firms to rescind its restrictive provisions.

10. The appendix of Willard F. Mueller's *A Primer in Monopoly and Competition* (New York: Random House, 1970) contains an analytic listing of the foundations of U.S. antitrust legislation.

11. This is discussed in Kenneth D. Walters and R. Joseph Monsen, "State-Owned Business Abroad: New Competitive Threat," *Harvard Business Review* 51, no. 2 (Mar.–Apr. 1979): 160–70.

12. For a statement objecting to aspects of U.S. legislation seen as restrictive, see *Toward Realism in Western Hemisphere Relations*, (New York: Council of the Americas, July, 1980), especially pp. 7–9.

13. The Foreign Corrupt Practices Act mentioned above, note 6.

14. For examples of these arguments, see Robert Pear, "Corrupt Practices Dispute," *New York Times International Financial Survey*, Feb. 8, 1981.

15. Such an argument is made in "Toward Realism in Western Hemisphere Relations," p. 8. A comparison of OECD countries' policies toward private direct investment in developing countries may be found in Organization for Economic Cooperation and Development, *Investing in Developing Countries*, 4th rev. ed., Paris: OECD, Sept., 1978).

16. Such arrangements are discussed in Richard S. Newfarmer, *Transnational Conglomerates and the Economics of Dependent Development* (Greenwich, Conn.: JAI Press, 1980).

17. Alfred C. Stepan describes this bargaining process in *The State and Society: Peru in Comparative Perspective* (Princeton: Princeton University Press, 1978), pp. 280–81.

18. This has been most clearly documented in two U.S. government publications: The Federal Trade Commission, *Report on International Electronic Equipment Cartels* (Washington, D.C.: GPO, 1948); and U.S. House of Representatives, Committee on Interstate and Foreign Commerce, *International Electrical Association: A Continuing Cartel* (Washington, D.C.: GPO, 1980).

19. See Isaiah A. Litvak and Christopher J. Maule, "Nationalism in the Caribbean Bauxite Industry," *International Affairs* 51 (June 1975): 43–59.

20. *Latin American Economic Report*, April 12, 1974, 57–58; and May 10, 1974, 69–70.

21. Robert B. Stobaugh, "How to Analyze Foreign Investment Climates," *Harvard Business Review* 47, no. 5 (Sept.–Oct. 1969), 102.

22. The variety of approaches taken by different firms is discussed in R. J. Rummel and David A. Heenen, "How Multinationals Analyze Political Risk," *Harvard Business Review* 57, no. 1 (Jan.–Feb. 1978): 101–9. For a thorough study on the emergence of in-house TNC identification and assessment of key political factors in foreign business environments, see Stephen Blank, John Basek, Stephen J. Kobrin, and Joseph LaPalombara, *Assessing the Political Environment: An Emerging Function in International Companies*, Report no. 794 (N.Y.: Conference Board, 1980).

23. For a discussion of these policies and their impact on North–South trade, see Louis Turner, Colin Bradford, and Neil McMullen, *The Newly Industrializing Countries, Trade and Adjustment* (London: George Allen & Unwin Ltd., 1983).

24. W. R. Grace & Co., internal documents.

25. *Business Week*, Feb. 2, 1981, 56–58.

26. For a history of IBEC, see Wayne Broehl, *The International Basic Economy Corporation* (Washington, D.C.: National Planning Assoc., 1968).

4:
Marginal Decisions
and
Executive Time

How capital allocation decisions are made by TNCs for their operations in third-world nations is an unusual topic[1] for the social science specialty which has most extensively discussed decision making in business enterprises: the microeconomic theory of the firm. The theory of the firm, mainly developed in economics, is a distinct and largely abstract body of literature.[2] The theory discusses general motivations of the behavior of business enterprises but makes little attempt to explain firm conduct in particular circumstances. This focus on the general is necessary for abstraction and theory construction, which have produced elegant and intellectually challenging models of firms and their behavior in abstractly specified markets. This general focus, however, necessarily obscures the variety of decisions made by firms as they pursue their objectives on a day-to-day basis.

The primary function of the firm in traditional or neoclassical microeconomics is that of an allocator of resources. To play this role, each firm is abstracted and treated as if it were atomistic in size, with decisions resulting in the optimal use of inputs and outputs in order to maximize profits. The utility of such an approach becomes questionable when the firms under study do not lend themselves easily to consideration as abstract decision points. Exceedingly complex and differentiated firms, many of which operate transnationally, can be reduced to single decision points through determined abstracting processes aided by aggregative financial accounting. However, there are few issues for which such reductionism does not obfuscate more than it illuminates.

Such abstration is particularly inappropriate for decisions made by TNCs for their operations in developing nations because of the relative marginality of these operations. This marginality means that decisions are often based on different criteria than those pertaining to operations more central to a TNC's global operations, especially decisions regarding operations in the TNC's principal markets.

The marginality of most operations in third-world nations to overall operations is clearly indicated by sales and ownership statistics. Operations in third-world nations account for only approximately 7.5 percent of the sales of the two hundred largest TNCs.[3] Furthermore, like the ownership patterns reported in Chapter 1, nearly two-thirds of this 7.5 percent of business activity is located in the thirteen OPEC nations, six nations labeled tax havens by the United Nations Center on Transnational Corporations, and in ten relatively advanced third-world nations. Less than 3 percent of the business activities of these large and complex firms derive from operations in some eighty-eight relatively small and poor nations, marginal in both the international order and the global strategies of TNCs.[4]

The lack of centrality to overall TNC operations of subsidiaries in third-world nations is brought home by the following comments made by Peter Drucker:

> Data on about forty-five manufacturers, distributors and financial institutions among the world's leading multinationals . . . show that the developed two-thirds of Brazil is an important market for some of these companies . . . [but no other "developing country"] . . . not even India or Mexico ranks for any of the multinational companies in my sample ahead of even a single major sales district in the home country, be it the Hamburg–North Germany district, the English Midlands or Kansas City.[5]

The marginal importance of many third-world nations for TNC global operations is especially critical for decisions involving commitments of sizable quantities of resources or departures from standard operating procedures. This is the case because such decisions must normally be passed on and/or made in a firm's home offices.[6] As we saw in Chapter 2, when the home office becomes involved, it uses different criteria in making decisions for operations in marginal third-world nations than for operations in locales more central to its global operations.

THE DECISION PROCESS IN LARGE FIRMS

Decisions made in TNCs pertaining to subsidiaries in third-world nations reflect the reporting process on which decision making in large corporations is based.[7] The impetus for making a decision may come from a variety of sources. For example, the impetus to decide whether or not to expand a subsidiary can come from the firm's long-term planning office, an officer located in the firm's home office, a corporate officer located in a subsidiary, an official in a host country's government, from a host country businessman, a rival firm looking for a partner, a family member of one of the firm's employees, or from a number of other sources. For the corporation to react favorably to such an idea, however, normally requires a long and painstaking evaluation process. (Figure 4.1)

Depending on the nature and size of the commitment and the internal policies of the firm in question, the final official decision-making body is either the officers of the division in which the subsidiary is located or the board of directors of the entire corporation. Before being presented to the final decision-making body, the idea must be favorably acted on by at least three levels of a complex investigatory process. After being recommended by such sources as those just described (step 1, Figure 4.1), a memorandum proposing the idea is normally drawn up and forwarded to the corporation's planning office (step 2). The planning office evaluates the suggestion using information from the memorandum and economic, political, and social data at its own disposal, then decides on the likelihood of the idea, as opposed to other actual and hypothetical ideas, best advancing corporate objectives.

If the planning office's evaluation is favorable, a field investigation is authorized (step 3). A team from the planning office is sent to the locale where the new activity is being proposed and conducts an on-the-spot investigation. The feasibility of implementing the idea is discussed with appropriate government officials and local businessmen. When considering the expansion of an existing subsidiary, the team from the planning office normally works together with staff from the subsidiary in preparing its report.

The first result of the field investigation is a report to the head of the planning office (step 4). The feasibility report is analyzed by planning office staff in conjunction with the prior evaluation of the suggestion's appropriateness for corporate objectives.

If the planning office's second review is favorable, a formal

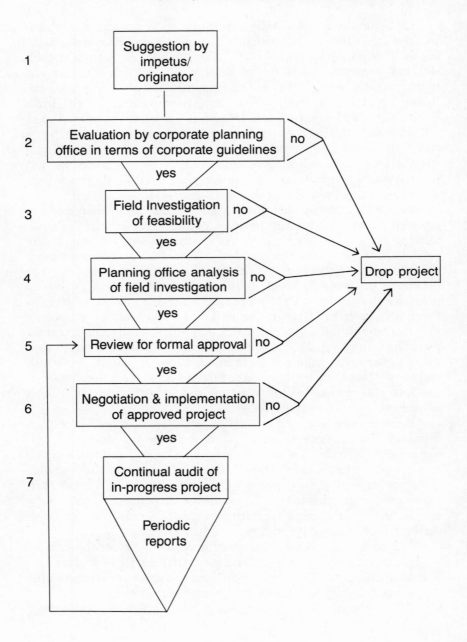

Figure 4.1

Steps in the Capital Expenditure Decision Process

1 — Suggestion by impetus/ originator

2 — Evaluation by corporate planning office in terms of corporate guidelines — no
yes

3 — Field Investigation of feasibility — no
yes

4 — Planning office analysis of field investigation — no
yes

5 — Review for formal approval — no
yes

6 — Negotiation & implementation of approved project — no
yes

7 — Continual audit of in-progress project

Periodic reports

Drop project

proposal is drawn up and then presented for review outside the planning office. Depending on the procedures and size of the corporation involved, the proposal may be immediately considered for formal approval (step 5). In large TNCs, it must usually first be presented to at least one division level body whose favorable endorsement is needed before the final body, such as the firm's board of directors, can decide whether or not to commit resources.

The capital allocation process, however, does not stop with approval by the firm's formal decision-making body. The formal approval is merely a signal for company negotiators to obtain formal guarantees from other parties needed for implementation (step 6). Funds are only disbursed as progress is made on the project. If projections made by the planning board are incorrect or conditions in the host country change or the price or availability of necessary inputs changes beyond specified limits, a project may be reconsidered and scrapped.

Once in operation, a project continues to be evaluated (step 7). If conditions change or faulty evaluations were made earlier, a project can still be scrapped. Thus, a continual audit of a project's performance is important, not only for its own future, but also for the disposition of similar proposals in the same or other host countries.

This seven-step process of suggestion, planning office evaluation, field investigation, planning office feasibility review, division level and/or board of directors authorization, renegotiation during implementation, and continual audit when in progress, is summarized in Figure 4.1. These steps constitute the formal stages of decision making by TNCs for capital expenditure, including those in third-world nations. These steps are, however, merely the skeleton of the decision process. Like any skeleton, they form the structure that supports the muscle driving the decision process. As with the human body, techniques can be employed in decision processes to compensate for the "inevitable" effects of bone structure. Just as cheekbones can be made to appear higher through skillful application of makeup, so proposals can be slanted by data presentation and analysis. Just as locomotion can be speeded up by driving instead of walking, so can stages in the decision-making process be bypassed by the strong action or clever intervention of a committed advocate.

THEORIES OF DECISION MAKING IN THE FIRM

Social scientists, particularly economists, have developed a number of theories of intrafirm decision processes. As suggested in the opening pages of this chapter, such theories sometimes permit discussing only general situations and may cloud understanding of decision processes that diverge from the general pattern—such as those relating to marginal aspects of a firm's global activities. Traditional theory does, however, implicitly or explicitly, touch on all of the important analytic dimensions of decision processes and has provided the basic structure from which other approaches have developed. Therefore, it makes sense first to become familiar with the traditional or neoclassical theory and its best known critiques and then to construct a revised theory of decision making in the firm appropriate for such marginal situations as the operations of subsidiaries of TNCs in small third-world nations.

NEOCLASSICAL THEORY OF THE FIRM

Neoclassical economics focuses on the firm and the consumer as the principal unit of resource allocation within the economy. The firm in neoclassical economics is "a heuristic fiction"[8] that permits us to explore "market relationships and other relationships between firms [but] bears little or no direct relevance to the internal organization of firms."[9]

> [The firm] is assumed to be composed of a single, omniscient economic man, for whom all problems are given and who, aware of all the alternative courses of action and relative consequences, instantly decides on actions to achieve his goal of profit maximization. Each firm is atomistic in size, and the number in the market is infinitely large. Firms cannot grow beyond a certain size because of the indivisibility of management. Each decision maker is faced with a constant "state of the art"; i.e., there are no technological changes.[10]

This view of the firm is based in a set of nine assumptions. Neoclassical economic theory, assumes that, within the firm, (1) instantaneous, (2) centralized, and (3) unitary decisions are (4) based on perfect knowledge of markets, and alternatives (5) are rationally motivated (6) to maximize (7) profits so that (8) property owners (shareholders) will be satisfied, and all of this happens in (9) an environment of perfect competition (an environment composed of many anonymous competitors producing homogenous products with free mobility of resources subject to constraints imposed by a single clearly interpretable force).[11] These nine assumptions of neoclassical theory are presented schematically in Figure 4.2 (column 1), together with important revisions made by contemporary econo-

Figure 4.2
Differences among Neoclassical, Revisionist, and Marginal Decision-Oriented Theories of Decision Making in the Firm

Aspect of Decision	Neoclassical Approach	Revisionist Approach	Theory for Marginal Decisions
Interval	Instant	Process (Aharoni)*	Process*
Locale	Organization center	Organization center	Organization center & periphery†
Structure	Unitary	Complex & consensual (Cyert & March)*	Complex with asymmetric authority vested in the center (home office)†
Information base	Certain—perfect knowledge	Uncertain—imperfect knowledge*	Uncertain—imperfect knowledge*
Impetus		Initiating force (Aharoni)*	Initiating force*
Rule	Rationality	Satisfice (Simon)*	Satisfice*
Criteria	Maximize Profit	Growth with profit constraint (Baumol)* Executive time (Penrose) Share price (Marris)* Managerial discretion, viz. earnings (Williamson)*	Managerial discretion, viz. earnings* Managerial discretion, viz. executive time*
Objectives	Give owners satisfactory income	Give owners satisfactory income* Give managers satisfactory autonomy from owners* Prevent takeovers*	Achieve earnings goals* Give managers satisfactory autonomy* Impress headquarters to advance career†
Environment	Many anonymous competitors regulated by home government	Oligopoly regulated by home government (Bain)*	Oligopoly regulated by home government and host government†

*Changes from neoclassical theory. (Points raised by individuals named within parentheses are discussed in the text.)

†Changes from neoclassical and revisionist theories.

97

mists (column 2), and revisions suited to the problem of capital allocation decisions by TNCs in third-world nations (column 3).

REVISIONS TO NEOCLASSICAL THEORY

While the antiseptic neoclassical vision may be useful as an ideal type for theory construction, it provides little insight into decision processes in actual firms. In business, and most real-life situations, decisions are not made under such circumstances as those described by neoclassical theory; in fact, it is even difficult to say that a decision is actually "made." Instead, most decisions are actions that so called decision makers take by virtue of previous commitments. Furthermore, many decisions are more reactions to situations in which decision makers find themselves than calculated choices based on careful intellectual processes. In a business situation a decision maker often acts and identifies or invents bases for decisions after they have been made.

This view of decisions as relatively nonreflective reactions to past involvement does not negate the importance of analyzing the decision process in a scientific manner. The web of past commitments and organizational and social structures in which they are enmeshed is, in fact, fraught with information about decision processes: Examining results of decision processes can suggest objectives and criteria basic to the choice of one option rather than another. The basis for such an approach is the view that decisions are the outcome of processes in which individuals or organizations follow one course óf action, thereby foregoing alternatives. This places the focus for research on what has been called by Yair Aharoni "decision process" or "the continuous dynamic social process of mutual influences among various members of an organization constrained by the organization's strategy, its resources, and the limited capacity, goals, and needs of its members throughout which choices emerge."[12]

In contrast to the idealized view of an instantaneous decision (assumption 1), the decision process requires taking a wide range of considerations into account in order to understand how a firm follows a particular course of action. The decision process incorporates a sequence of many small actions taken by different individuals in different locales at different points in time (assumption 2).

Viewing decision making as a process rather than an instantaneous act immediately suggests that the structure for decision making is complex rather than unitary (assumption 2). However, this view does not in itself reveal problems with the neoclassical approach for explaining which alternative courses are followed and which are foregone. Neoclassical theory assumes perfect knowledge of market conditions and business alternatives (assumption 4): Only with perfect knowledge can decisions be made that allow managers to pursue corporate objectives optimally. In neoclassical theory, the impetus behind this optimal pursuit of business objectives is rationality (assumption 5), and the criterion or rule for decision making is the maximization of profits (assumptions 6–8). Without perfect knowledge, either additional assumptions must be made about certain business alternatives or decisions must be made under conditions of uncertainty.[13] The complexity of most decision processes within firms as large and differentiated as TNCs is such that individuals involved are usually uncertain about many of the consequences of various alternatives.

This uncertainty results from a lack of knowledge deriving from three possible sources: (1) non-existence of information; (2) inability of a decision maker to make use of existing information; and (3) inability of a decision maker to evaluate complex and seemingly contradictory information. For example, in considering resource allocation to a subsidiary, officers in a TNC may not have commissioned an analysis of investments by competitors in the subsidiary's host country; or such an analysis may have been carried out, but officers may not know of its existence; or the positions of competitors as described in the analysis may be so complex that the officers cannot use the analysis as a basis for their own decision. Although, in every step of a decision process, some information exists that enables managers to make assumptions that partially reduce uncertainty, other important pieces of information cannot be assumed away, such as future reactions by competitors and governments to the selection of one course of action or another. As a result, revisionist theorists attempting to ground the theory of the firm in actual decision processes necessarily saw this task as the study of decision making in the face of uncertainty. By rendering it impossible to assign probabilities to all possible outcomes and their consequences, uncertainty makes maximization impossible as a practical alternative. Since the full range of outcomes, including maximum and minimum values of criteria used to measure realization of decision objectives, is left unspecified, decision makers must fall back on decision rules other than maximization. It is the nature of these decision rules that undermines the utility of the neoclassical approach for predicting outcomes of decision processes.

The decision rules adopted in the face of uncertainty cause decision processes to be governed by what has been referred to as bounded rationality, and "the replacement of the goal of maximizing with the goal of 'satisficing,' of finding a course of action which is 'good enough . . . ' "[14] The notion of satisficing is based on the idea that individuals involved in decision processes have cognitive and other limitations so that they have neither the capacity nor time to identify a best alternative but rather accept the first one that appears satisfactory. The best, or maximized, alternative is thus replaced by a satisficing solution. The rationality of the decision maker is thus bounded as he or she searches for a satisficing rather than an optimal solution and accepts the first satisfactory alternative encountered, without continuing to search for a superior one.

The replacement of decision rules based on maximizing principles with those governed by satisficing principles is part of the conceptualization of the "social man" developed by Herbert Simon. In contrast to the rigid maximizing economic man of neoclassical economic theory, the social man is adaptive and constantly seeks new ways of operating in a complex and uncertain world. The social man's rationality is naturally bounded and seeks satisficing solutions. This approach is seen by Simon as relatively efficient because operating on the basis of maximizing rules would require exploring so many alternatives and collecting so much information that the costs of decision making would usually be greater than the added benefits resulting from choosing a maximizing rather than a satisficing solution.

A basic assumption of the neoclassical theory of the firm is that the firm's objective is to maximize profits (assumptions 7 and 8). Simon's formulation of the social man challenges the decision rule of maximization implicit in this assumption. Several alternatives have also been proposed to the decision criterion of profits. These alternatives are based on dissatisfaction with the two basic assumptions of the profit maximization goal: (1) A firm must maximize profits to survive, since competition in product markets would force down prices to the level of long-run average costs; and (2) more profits are always preferable to fewer profits to the owners of a firm.

The first assumption has been undermined by the many industrial organization studies that have shown product markets to be dominated by a small number of firms earning excessive rates of return. Competition, rather than being perfect, was shown to be oligopolistic (especially in industries in which TNCs actively participate), and the determinants of prices and profit levels were shown to be more complex than the mere forces of supply and demand. Rather than having to maximize profits because of their vulnerability to market forces, most firms examined by students of industrial organization have been large enough to exercise some power in the markets in which they sell their products.

The second assumption has been undermined by a series of studies, beginning with Berle and Means' *The Modern Corporation and Private Property*.[15] This study clearly established that managerial control and shareholder ownership were separate from one another in large firms. Robert Gordon then examined the concerns of managers and concluded that the primary objective of managers, once survival of the firm had been assured, was growth rather than profits.[16] Kenneth Boulding, anticipating Simon's satisficing social man, examined corporate records and concluded that managers specify levels of a wide range of variables, such as sales and profits, as being satisfactory and attempt to arrange firms so that significant deviations above or below the satisfactory range are adjusted by the action of countervailing forces.[17] These three contributions, in themselves, demonstrated that the decision objectives of large firms, rather than satisfying shareholders through profit maximization, are to satisfy both managers and shareholders by achieving satisfactory levels of profits, growth, and other concerns.

The first work that attempted to incorporate into a formal model Gordon's insight, that managers would seek only enough profit to ensure the survival of the firm, was William Baumol's *Business Behavior, Value, and Growth*.[18] This work clarified what was to many a hazy difference between the maximization of profits and the maximization of firm growth (measured by Baumol by growth in sales revenue). Because sales increases impress consumers, creditors, and distributors with a product's success, as well as increase employee morale, job security, and enhance market power, a firm works to expand its market—maximize profits. However, when the cost of expanding marketing efforts begins to exceed the additional revenues generated, profit-maximizing managers curtail attempts at sales expansion. Baumol argued that managers push sales-expanding efforts beyond the point of diminishing returns because of feelings that declining returns would be accelerated if sales expansion were to slow down, Baumol's argument is that business people believe that consumers shun products whose sales appear to be waning, creditors grow apprehensive with reports of sales declining, distributors are concerned when products move slowly, employees become demoralized due to fears of layoffs, and managers' salaries do not increase due to the presumed relationship between executive compensation and the scale of the enterprise.

Like Gordon, Baumol did not argue that managers of firms are concerned with only growth of sales. They are also concerned with profit—in part, to ensure the firm's survival and avoid bankruptcy and, in part, to prevent shareholder revolts against management. Hence, for Baumol, managers strive to increase sales subject to a profit constraint.

A somewhat different criterion for business decisions was put forth by Edith Penrose in *The Theory of the Growth of the Firm*.[19] Penrose argued that managers do strive for the firm's growth and try to earn profits to finance that expansion because of the potential loss of managerial autonomy incurred in the search for capital outside the firm. The main constraint on the growth of the firm according to Penrose is determined by the fundamental ratio of "the relevant managerial services *available* for expansion in relation to the amount of these services *required* per dollar of expansion."[20] Availability of managerial services is essential to firm growth because of the careful planning required for corporate expansion. Difficulties associated with integrating new managers into the existing team preclude hiring managerial services from the outside every time a new opportunity for expansion presents itself. Therefore, new opportunities for the firm are examined by managers for their growth and profit potentials *and* the ease with which they can be taken on by the existing cadre of managers without damaging ongoing operations. As a result, Penrose argues, when firms expand, they grow in areas that employ unused byproducts of existing operations. As we will see, this decision criterion, the use of executive time, is of central importance to decision makers in remote subsidiaries of TNCs.

A fourth decision criterion has been proposed by Oliver Williamson. Williamson argues that when ownership and control are clearly separated and are not pressed by rigorous competition:

> There is no compelling reason to assume that the firm is operated so as to maximize profit. . . . Such behavior would appear to require an unusual variety of rationality—and one not widely found in human affairs—namely, a complete detachment of individual interests from occupational decision making.[21]

Williamson argues that the opportunity to exercise discretion over the allocation of resources is basic in determining which courses of action are selected by firm managers. Precisely how a particular manager allocates resources depends on individual circumstances. Williamson proposes three areas in which, he argues, managers strive to have discretion in resource allocation: (1) staff, (2) personal emoluments, and (3) profits.

Discretion to allocate resources for staff expansion is important to managers for reasons in addition to productivity. Williamson argues that professional survival and advancement can be linked to a manager's demonstration that staff is continuously providing more and better services. This promotes incentives for staff expansion irrespective of impacts on productivity or profit. Furthermore, expansion may increase the morale of existing staff, dampening fear of layoffs and providing opportunities for personal development.

Discretion to allocate resources for personal emoluments, such as lavish office furnishings, expense accounts, salaries, fringe benefits, and on-the-job leisure, can be viewed as part of the pay a manager receives that prevents him or her from seeking alternative employment. It can also be viewed as providing the manager with more than mere earnings—a sense of control over the immediate work environment and the quality and quantity of reward received from work.

Discretion to allocate profits is possible when the firm generates profits in excess of the shareholders' minimum expectations. Once this level is exceeded, decisions can be made to allocate the excess to increase dividends, finance general corporate expansion, provide emoluments, or expand existing departments. Therefore, managers will prefer to choose courses of action in which expected profit levels can easily be attained and additional earnings will not be so closely monitored by shareholders or superiors that the discretion to allocate resources is prevented.

Managers, then, seek to direct their firms to achieve satisfactory levels of (1) growth in order to demonstrate corporate robustness; and (2) profits in order to preserve managerial autonomy in expansion; to (3) use executive time efficiently in order to be able to take advantage of opportunities for growth; and (4) managerial discretion to increase a sense of control and reward from work. These criteria for managerial decision making suggest a tension between shareholders' desires for high dividends and high market value of equity capital, and managers' desires for autonomy in directing the firm and high rewards for carrying out that direction. Berle and Means demonstrated the difference between managers' and owners' interests; Gordon, Baumol, Penrose, and Williamson have argued that managers pursue their own interests subject to minimal satisfaction of the shareholders' interests. Combining these arguments with Simon's concept of satisficing depicts managers as evaluating business alternatives in terms of their impacts on profits, growth, use of executive time, and managerial discretion to achieve satisfactory levels of the separate objectives of shareholders and managers.

However, it should also be noted that shareholders and managers have mutual as well as opposing interests. One important source of mutual interest has been suggested by Robin Marris: the need to keep share prices high to prevent the ever-present possibility of a corporate takeover.[22] Depressed share prices invite takeovers by other firms, threatening both the autonomy and job security of existing management. To prevent takeovers, managers must strive to keep high the market value of equity capital held by shareholders (that is, declare high profits and dividends). By keeping the relation of share prices to asset values high, managers are able to make corporate takeovers expensive, assure the high value of shareholders' equity, and retain control of the firm. A focus on the bases of decision making by managers in the center of firms thus suggests three objectives of managerial decisions: (1) satisfying shareholders' expectations regarding income from dividends and the value of equity capital; (2) satisfying managers' desires for autonomy in directing the firm and for satisfactory reward for such direction; and (3) preventing takeovers by other corporations (assumption 8).

Five criteria used to select courses of action for pursuing these objectives involve prospects for achieving (1) satisfactory profit levels, (2) satisfactory rates of growth, (3) satisfactory use of executive time, (4) satisfactory levels of managerial discretion in allocating resources, and (5) satisfactory levels of the market value of the firm's equity capital (share prices). The determination of what constitutes "satisfactory" is a function of the particular circumstances of each decision-making situation.

Those aspects of the theory of the firm discussed up to this point all treat internal organizational decision processes. Neoclassical theory also makes quite a stringent assumption about the nature of the environment in which the firm operates: perfect competition (assumption 9). The corollary of the profit maximization assumption, that competition would, in the long run, force down profits to the level of absolute costs, went ignored and essentially unchallenged until 1926 when Piero Sraffa pointed out that the existence of increasing returns in a wide range of circumstances indicated the existence of market conditions other than that of many atomistic producers of an homogenous product.[23] Sraffa's work paved the way for descriptions of economic environments that relegated perfect competition to the extreme case.

Oligopolistic competition, or market situations where there are sufficiently few sellers so that they are all mutually conditioned by each other's behavior, assumed a central role for economics in 1933 with the simultaneous publication of Joan Robinson's *The Theory of Imperfect Competition*[24] and Edward Chamberlin's *The Theory of Monopolistic Competition*.[25] Since oligopolistic competition encompasses most existing industrial situations, it has been the subject of substantial attention since the 1930s. Research has focused on the sources of power that enable oligopolists to limit competition and exercise control over the markets in which they operate. Joe S. Bain's pioneering work on advantages existing firms hold over possible new competitors in an industry (conditions of entry) greatly refined understanding of the market environment in which firms operate.[26] Bain identified three main types of barriers to the entry of new competition: (1) absolute cost, or lower production costs for the established firm; (2) product differentiation, or customer preference for established products as opposed to new ones; and (3) economies of scale, or the requirement that a new firm occupy a substantial share of an industry's market in order to compete efficiently. This and subsequent works have rendered the model of "the single-product atomistic firm in a static environment using only production or price as its strategic variable . . . "[27] useful for only the most abstract of theoretical analyses. Contemporary microeconomists, such as Marris, Williamson, and others, have gone far beyond this relatively primitive view to incorporate greater complexity into oligopoly theory and the economic theory of the firm.

While revisionist microeconomics has paid great attention to oligopoly competion, it has virtually ignored another aspect of the environment relevant to the operations of TNCs in third-world nations: the number of regulators of business activity. Most of oligopoly theory assumes that competition takes place in an environment regulated by one governmental authority and thus does not consider consequences of regulation by more than one such authority. This is, of course, the very situation that confronts large firms with subsidiaries operating in many countries controlled by a single headquarters. This topic and other aspects of the theory of the firm and its environment requiring reexamination in light of the operations of TNCs are discussed in the following section.

Revisions of Neoclassical Theory for Marginal Decisions

The neoclassical vision of decision making in the firm as re-vised by modern microeconomists is quite useful for framing issues for the research on which this book is based. However, additional modifications are needed to address properly the central issue—understanding intrafirm decision processes involving TNC subsidiaries located in third-world nations. This is the case because revisions of neoclassical microeconomics previously discussed did not take into account certain elements basic to those decision processes. In terms of the decision processes outlined in Figure 4.2, the revisionists assumed that the decision process (1) took place largely in the center of the firm (aspect 2) and (2) was complex yet consensual (aspect 3). For decision processes involving subsidiaries of TNCs located in small third-world nations, decisions result from an interplay between central and peripheral elements of the firm, with more authority in the center than the periphery. These differences in locale and structure of the decision process, in turn, have serious implications for the objectives underlying such decision processes (aspect 7) and the criteria used to evaluate alternative courses of action (aspect 8). Finally, the implications of these differences for the outcomes of decision process are considerable due to the added complexity of the environment within which the decision is made (aspect 9). As discussed in Chapter 3, in addition to considering the behavior of other oligopolists and the firm's home government, behavior of the host country's government must also be taken into account.

The Locale and Structure of Marginal Decisions

As indicated in Chapter 1, TNC subsidiaries in third-world nations generally account for a very small portion of the firm's global sales or investments. This and the fact that current business trends indicate that TNCs are, if anything, increasingly concentrating their sales and investments in more developed countries[28] make the operations of most TNC subsidiaries in third-world nations of minor consequence for the firm's overall operations. This situation is compounded by the physical distance separating most TNC headquarters from the operations of their third-world subsidiaries, a circumstance that further impedes easy and full communication among these different components of the firm.

Despite this distance, capital expenditure decisions are normally closely controlled by a firm's home office.[29] Control is typically exercised by a combination of the capital budget and the graduated expenditure ceiling. Capital budgets are usually forecast from three to five years in advance; reviewed by headquarters each year; and serve as the basis for operations, with separate approval required for major deviations. Graduated expenditure ceilings are established for each level in the corporate organization. If a capital expenditure, such as the expansion of an existing plant or the construction of new facilities, has been included in the capital budget and falls below a subsidiary's designated expenditure ceiling, then the subsidiary manager has approval authority. If the capital expenditure has not been included in the budget, a separate approval must be requested; if it exceeds the subsidiary's expenditure ceiling, approval must be sought from the appropriate corporate level.

Although expenditure ceilings for subsidiaries in third-world nations vary considerably from country to country and from firm to firm, they are seldom higher than $100,000 and usually less than $50,000. This means that, for positive action to be taken regarding capital expenditures of any significance, a subsidiary manager must include the item in the capital budget forecast, thereby requiring home office approval, *and* also obtain corporate approval when it is time to actually commit funds. Capital expenditures and finance are the two areas in which the home office most closely controls international operations.[30] More control is typically exercised on these functions than on such functions as marketing, personnel, or production because the former govern the scope of corporate commitment in particular locales. Controlling capital expenditures and finances gives headquarters' staff greatest leverage for organizing into a global corporate strategy the activities of otherwise autonomous units.

Balancing the inputs of headquarters and subsidiary staff is a major problem for TNCs. On the one hand, the principal markets of most TNCs are in their home countries and the international experience of headquarters' staff rarely includes long exposure, especially to small third-world subsidiaries. On the other hand, each subsidiary has its own identity, and its managers strain to pursue business opportunities autonomously, using the TNC as a resource base.

The balance, however, is asymmetrical: Headquarters' staff has the power to approve or reject requests made by subsidiary managers. Two strategies employed by some firms to redress this balance are: (1) adding international staff coordinators to corporate headquarters; (2) establishing regional headquarters with substantial decision-making authority. The tasks of international coordinators can range from the educational role of developing international expertise in the home office, to formally reporting to the chief executive officer on each capital expenditure requested by an international subsidiary. Regional headquarters are typically set up when business in a geographic area grows to the point that it becomes unwieldy for all upper level management functions to be located at corporate headquarters. Regional headquarters permit many management decisions to be tailored to the needs of local operations, necessarily within capital budget and graduated expenditure limitations.

Whether or not such strategies successfully balance the concerns of home office and subsidiary, they indicate differences between the complexity of the decision processes with which revisionists of the neoclassical theory of the firm were mainly concerned and international business decisions, especially those involving relatively small subsidiaries. The growth and frequent changes in international business since World War II have been so rapid that decision processes within firms have not had time to catch up with the diversity of business activity. Although many firms have adjusted their internal structures with some frequency, many find it necessary to compensate for the centrality of the authority of global headquarters and for the limited international experience of high-level headquarters staff and make adjustments to help headquarters staff better understand the needs of subsidiaries.

This organization to combat the effects of hierarchy contrasts with the central organizational problem attacked by Richard M. Cyert and James G. March in *A Behavioral Theory of the Firm*.[31] Cyert and March view the firm as a coalition of all individuals affected by the firm (for example, managers, workers, stockholders, suppliers, customers, lawyers, tax collectors, regulatory agencies, and so forth). The firm pursues the collective goal of the coalition as a result of a process of bargaining and learning among members of the coalition. Individuals remain in the coalition despite divergences of their goals because part of the firm's resources are also used to make "side payments" in kind or policy influence in exchange for the coalition's ability to reach a compromise.

Cyert and March's model has a number of additional features, but the one central to this discussion is the consensual nature of coalition formation. Coalitions are formed by individuals and sub-groups with different objectives, bargaining among themselves and learning how to adjust goals by observing the bargaining conduct of others. A critical problem with that view of goal setting is the implicit assumption that all active members of the coalition that constitutes the firm have equal power. No room is left in the model for such forces as leadership or coercion.[32] Bargaining and learning produce consensual coalitions most easily in situations where hierarchy is absent and in institutions where all members understand each other's point of view. While firms do strive to facilitate intra-firm communication, the experiences of headquarters' staff and staff of subsidiaries in third-world nations can differ so that mutual understanding becomes difficult on all issues. In such instances, the coercive power of the firm's hierarchy becomes more important than all of the bargaining and learning that may have taken place between home office and subsidiary in the process of forwarding a proposal and considering it for approval.

Difficulties in understanding are exacerbated because of the time frame within which management must make decisions. This pressure often makes it impossible to have corporate goals based on subsidiary managers' complete understanding of, for example, how expanding or not expanding a plant services global goals, or complete understanding by headquarters staff of, for example, how one or another option proposed by a subsidiary manager would be beneficial for the firm as a whole.

At times, gaps in understanding reach the point that subsidiary managers believe they are pursuing one set of objectives while headquarters staff views their behavior as directed toward different outcomes. In such circumstances, fully understanding each other's position might require needlessly expending costly executive time and reduce commitment of one or both parties by disabusing cherished illusions. For example, the subsidiary's staff may view approval to expand a plant as concurrent with its suggestion to penetrate more fully a host country's market. Headquarters staff may see it as an opportunity to use capacities fully in other segments of the firm to produce intermediate goods consumed by the newly expanded plant.

Whether action is taken as a result of agreement between the view of headquarters and subsidiary or despite differences in objectives, it is an important fact of transnational corporate life that final approval for capital expenditures normally rests with the home office and it is sometimes difficult for the home office to adapt global strategies to rapidly changing idiosyncratic situations in particular subsidiaries. Therefore, in adopting the view of decision making in the firm developed by critics of neoclassical microeconomic theory, special attention must be paid to both the asymmetric power of corporate headquarters in the decision process and mechanisms that facilitate mutual understanding between the subsidiary and home office. In terms of the decision process in Figure 4.2, this means expanding the decision process locale (aspect 2) to include the periphery of the organization as well as its center, and recognizing that the decision process structure (aspect 3) is complex, with greater authority vested in the firm's home office.

Criteria and Objectives for Marginal Decisions

Orienting the decision process to include such marginal elements of the firm as subsidiaries located in small third-world nations also requires reconceptualizing the objectives included in the firm's decision process (aspect 8) and the criteria employed in pursuit of those objectives (aspect 7).

Implicit in the objectives of shareholders and managers discussed by revisionist economists is the assumption that both are striving to enjoy what John R. Hicks called "the best of all monopoly profits"—the quiet life.[33] If satisfactory levels of profits were earned more or less automatically, shareholders could be paid dividends corresponding to their expectations and managers could relax in their autonomy, immune from interference from both corporate raiders and anxious shareholders. Managers could construct a work environment where quiet living was possible by setting staff expenditures at levels that got the work done and kept employees happy and by designing managerial emoluments to finance quiet lives for managers. Since few business situations are such that satisfactory levels of profits flow automatically, managers typically find themselves settling for lives that are less than quiet, yet with enough insulation from worldly noise to be bearable.

Missing from this view of managers' ultimate objectives is the manager who strives to be more central in the firm's decision-making process by participating more fully in decisions that structure the firm's over-all activities. In Williamson's conception of the firm, such managers would be viewed as "staff". From the point of view of managers high in the firm's hierarchy, managers of subsidiaries are staff for whom sufficient revenues must be available so that their career expectations can be satisfactorily met, in addition to the profits needed to satisfy shareholders and the emoluments needed for the high-level managers themselves. From the point of view of the ongoing decision process, however, managers of subsidiaries make contributions that are conditioned heavily by their own views of the objectives of the portion of the firm in which they work. A primary consideration in forming these objectives is how a given course of action will affect the future in the firm or job market for individuals with managerial skills. As a result, managers in subsidiaries pay special attention to achieving the profit levels specified in the annual plan for their subsidiary. In doing so, they attend to concerns similar to those of higher-up managers: They attempt to generate earnings which provide for their own staff needs and their own managerial emoluments, leaving sufficient excess to satisfy the indicated profit objectives of the subsidiary.

In addition to concerns with allocating earnings, these managers (and most likely managers in corporate headquarters) also aim for discretion over the allocation of that scarcest of the firm's resources—their own executive time. Penrose has argued that a firm's ability to grow is limited by its endowment of "managerial resources." It is crucially important for both the firm and the manager's career objectives that managers find time-efficient standard operating procedures for directing the business activities for which they are responsible. If existing responsibilities are efficiently organized, then time can be found to develop new activities for the firm and/or to cope with unforeseen problems in the management of existing activities. This both facilitates realizing the firm's earnings objectives and puts the manager in a position to further his or her own career.

This view combines Penrose's observation of the importance of executive time for the firm with Williamson's view that managers strive for discretionary control over important resources. Williamson focused on discretionary control over earnings. At least when considering the participation of managers of peripheral subsidiaries in the decision process, discretionary control of managerial time must also be taken into account. In brief, these managers evaluate alternative courses of action both in terms of their ability to exercise discretionary control over flows of earnings *and* in terms of their ability to exercise discretionary control over flows of executive time. They strive for discretionary control over the allocation of time among three possibilities: (1) attending to responsibilities indicated in the current annual plan; (2) developing new activities to be proposed to headquarters for inclusion in future plans; and (3) on-the-job leisure.[34] To be able to exercise discretion over the allocation of one's own time and one's staff, careful attention must be paid to the nature of the work load to which a manager is committed. Responsibilities that take little time to dispatch, require little new information to continue dispatching, that yield high rates of return and high absolute returns are preferred to responsibilities that require both time to accomplish and continual infusions of new information, yield low rates of return, and are small in absolute size.

The importance of these considerations for managers of subsidiaries of TNCs located in third-world countries stems from the relatively small importance that these operations have for the overall activities of the corporation. In a situation in which subsidiaries in the United States, Canada, Japan, and four Western European countries each generate more than ten times the sale of a subsidiary in Colombia, headquarters managers spending on a Colombian subsidiary-related decision more than 10 percent of the time on a decision relating to a subsidiary in one of the other countries mentioned, are not using time efficiently.

The Complex Environments of Marginal Decisions

These differences in decision process objectives and criteria are compounded by actual and perceived changes in the business environments in which subsidiaries in third-world countries operate (aspect 9, Figure 4.2). For example, during the course of this research, national politics and the evolution of national development plans in many third-world host countries, especially in Latin America, resulted in dramatic changes in governments and policies toward the operation of foreign firms in these countries. The regulation of foreign business in Chile became much more focused on clearly indicated development objectives with the ratification of ANCOM's Common Regime on the Treatment of Foreign Capital in 1971. The volatility of Chilean politics and the change from past policies caused foreign firms to question the permanence of these laws and to withhold new commitments of funds until the meaning of the new legislation was understood and believed in by the home office. Skepticism was rewarded when, in 1976, the military government withdrew Chile from ANCOM and removed many of the explicit regulations instituted in 1971.

During the 1970s, similar flip-flops occurred at different times in Argentina, Brazil, Bolivia, and Ecuador. During interviews carried out for the research reported in Chapter 2, a number of head office managers stated the belief that volatility in the regulation of foreign business was a permanent condition for Latin America. This perception of an unstable business environment in a host country contrasts sharply with the relatively stable set of constraints imposed by home-country regulators, implicit to the revisions of the neoclassical theory of the firm.

The small importance of subsidiaries in third-world nations to the overall operations of the firm, plus perceptions of volatility in politics and business policy suggest that managers may have to expend considerable amounts of time keeping up with rapidly changing business circumstances just to make relatively unimportant operations viable. Even if rates of return on invested capital or other indicators of profit are high compared with the firm's other worldwide operations,[35] the small size of subsidiaries in third-world countries and the expectation that much time will have to be spent gathering information needed to manage the operations of these subsidiaries are powerful disincentives for the head office.

CONSEQUENCES FOR DECISION PROCESSES INVOLVING SUBSIDIARIES OF TRANSNATIONAL CORPORATIONS IN THIRD-WORLD NATIONS

These differences have consequences both for how managers of subsidiaries located in third-world nations choose among alternative courses of action, and for the overall shape of the decision processes regarding capital expenditures for these subsidiaries in which these managers and the headquarters staff participate.

For a subsidiary manager to expect approval of a proposal for capital expenditure in his subsidiary he must convince both headquarters staff and planning office staff that: (1) operations financed by the expenditure will not require an unusual amount of executive time to start up; (2) once initiated, the time required to manage the operation, including gathering necessary information about the host country business environment, will be reasonable; (3) the size of resultant earnings will justify time spent managing the operation; and (4) the rate of return to invested capital will be at a satisfactory level.

These four considerations correspond to rules of thumb used by the headquarters staff to evaluate proposals for new capital expenditures. Proposals must be for operations (1) not requiring excessive time spent in start-up, and (2) managing ongoing operations. These prospective time commitments are measured against (3) the size of prospective earnings provided that (4) the rate of return to invested capital is above a specified minimum.

In brief, this suggests that, once a minimum rate of return is projected, the "fundamental ratio" determining whether a corporate expenditure is approved is that suggested by Penrose: the amount of executive time expended per amount of earnings realized.

If the projected rate of return falls below a minimum satisfactory level, a home office manager will not consider a proposal, and presumably, a subsidiary manager will not suggest it. If a minimum rate of return is projected, the home office staff may be interested in small expenditures requiring little managerial time. However, the home office staff would be somewhat more interested in large expenditures with large returns requiring correspondingly large amounts of managerial time and greatly interested in small expenditures yielding large returns yet requiring little managerial time. The home office would certainly not be interested in small expenditures requiring vast amounts of managerial time, no matter what the rate of return on invested capital. For example, in explaining why he was proposing liquidation of a highly profitable subsidiary in a small Caribbean island, a vice president in charge of U.S. Western Hemisphere Activities of a large TNC stated:

> When I took over this assignment, the plant required no time to manage and accounted for approximately 0.02 percent of my division's earnings. With its current political turmoil, I am spending one-fourth of my time holding on to that 0.02 percent, and I have taken the time away from . . . [overseeing] operations in Brazil and Canada.
>
> (NEW YORK, JANUARY 1974)

This plant was therefore sold despite an annual return on invested capital in excess of 20 percent, due to the excessive cost in terms of executive time per dollar earned.

Awareness of such rules of thumb constrains the subsidiary manager's choice of proposals for capital expenditures. If a proposal is not executive-time-efficient and lacks potential to generate sufficient earnings, it will not be proposed, no matter what the projected rate of return.

The enormous size of TNCs results in executive-time-intensive proposals being forwarded by managers of subsidiaries in third-world nations in only three circumstances: (1) When the third-world country has a sufficiently large and penetrable internal market so that growth in sales will compensate for expenditures of managerial time. (2) When the third-world country possesses some unusual natural resource that the TNC has the means to exploit; for example, investment in copper mining in Peru by ASARCO, in oil in Angola by Gulf, and in fruit in Mexico by Coca-Cola. (3) When the third-world country can function as a platform for generating earnings in excess of those naturally provided by its domestic market or natural resources; for example, Ford Motor Company's engine plant in Brazil, both to exploit the Brazilian market and to export to Europe or North America in times of production shortfalls there; Texas Instrument's establishment of a computer microchip plant in Singapore for worldwide export; or establishment of corporate subsidiaries in the Bahamas, Liechtenstein, Panama, or other tax havens, affording firms the flexibility of adjusting prices or holding capital without suffering tax consequences.

A few third-world countries have large penetrable markets—for example, Brazil, Mexico, and India—others are large but not necessarily penetrable—for example, China, Indonesia, Nigeria, Pakistan, and Colombia—and most are small. A majority of third-world nations have established some ties with TNCs in order to exploit natural resources, but, with the exception of petroleum, these commodities as a rule neither command high enough prices on world markets nor are sufficiently diverse to withstand short-term price fluctuations in order to provide a solid base for the realization of development objectives. Serving as an export platform requires political stability and docile, cheap, high-quality labor, currently available in only a few third-world nations, such as Hong Kong, Singapore, Taiwan, South Korea, and Malaysia. Serving as a platform for large corporations' transnational financial dealings is attractive only to countries with little indigenous business activity, since low tax rates and financial flexibility afforded by such arrangements erode the host government's ability to collect tax revenues and give firms the power to ignore national development objectives.

Despite the fact that some third-world nations may present more attractive opportunities for TNCs, all managers of subsidiaries of TNCs located in third-world countries are anxious to impress headquarters in order to advance their careers. But impressing headquarters requires fulfilling goals set forth in annual plans. In addition, it is often necessary for managers to request capital expenditures in excess of their graduated limit just to expand subsidiary activities at the pace maintained by the corporation as a whole. Finally, the identification and development of local business opportunities resulting in increased subsidiary earnings and increased responsibilities for the subsidiary manager can speed advancement within the firm. Therefore, despite the limited opportunities available for most TNCs in most small third-world nations, where subsidiaries are in place, subsidiary managers do periodically make routine requests for new capital expenditures. Furthermore, some managers may attempt to make extraordinary requests in the hope of generating increased corporate earnings and advancing their careers.

NOTES

1. See Sanjaya Lall, "Less-Developed Countries and Private Foreign Direct Investment: A Review Article," *World Development* 2, Nos. 4 and 5 (Apr.–May 1974): 43–48, for a succinct summary of the more general literature on transnational corporations and development.

2. For clear presentations of traditional microeconomic theory, including the theory of the firm, see James Henderson and Richard Quandt, *Microeconomic Theory* (New York: McGraw Hill, 1971) and Edwin Mansfield, *Principles of Microeconomics* (New York: Norton, 1983).

3. United Nations, *Reexamination*, table III-10, p. 213.

4. Ibid., table III-33, p. 237; and table III-47, p. 254.

5. Peter Drucker, "Multinationals and Developing Countries: Myths and Realities," *Foreign Affairs* 53, No. 1 (October 1974): 121–34.

6. For the six companies intensively studied in this research project, approval from the home office was needed before disbursement of allocations ranging from $1,000 in the lowest case to $2,500 in the highest; approval from the board of directors was needed for disbursements ranging from $50,000 in the lowest case to $200,000 in the highest case. Departures from standard operating procedures included such decisions as amendments to labor agreements, experimentation with new technologies, and compliance with new host country regulations on foreign business.

7. For discussions of the nature of headquarters–subsidiary relations in transnational corporations, with special emphasis on the issue of centralized control versus subsidiary autonomy, see Michael Z. Brooke and H. Lee Remmers, *The Strategy of Multinational Enterprise: Organization and Finance* (London: Longman, 1970), especially chap. 3 and 4; and Ronald E. Berenbeim, *Operating Foreign Subsidiaries: How Independent Can They Be?* (New York: Conference Board, 1983).

8. Fritz Machlup, "Theories of the Firm: Marginalist, Behavioral, Managerial," *American Economic Review* 57 (Mar. 1967): 9.

9. Michael A. Crew, *Theory of the Firm* (New York: Longman, 1975), p. 2

10. Yair Aharoni, *The Foreign Investment Decision Process* (Boston: Harvard Business School, 1966), p. 246. This quote prefaces Aharoni's critique of neoclassical theory.

11. These nine assumptions are presented in an attempt to "put flesh on the ghost" of neoclassical theory of the firm. The firm as a resource allocator is such a primitive concept in neoclassical economics that its basic nature is rarely, if ever, spelled out. Such specification was deemed necessary here so that a precise understanding could be achieved regarding which aspects of neoclassical theory are helpful for illuminating the problem at hand and which aspects are obfuscatory.

12. Aharoni, p. 15.

13. When a decision maker is unable to make assumptions about all determinants of possible outcomes and consequently cannot assign probabilities to different outcomes, a situation of uncertainty exists. Risk, on the other hand, is a situation in which the decision maker can assign probabilities to different outcomes. Risk and uncertainty were first distinguished by Frank H. Knight in his *Risk, Uncertainty, and Profit* (Boston: Houghton Mifflin, 1921).

14. Herbert A. Simon, *Models of Men* (New York: Wiley, 1957), pp. 204–5.

15. Adolph A. Berle and Gardiner C. Means, *The Modern Corporation and Private Property* (New York: Macmillan, 1932).

16. Robert A. Gordon, *Business Leadership in the Large Corporation* (Washington, D.C.: Brookings Institution, 1945).

17. Kenneth E. Boulding, "Implications for General Economics of More Realistic Theories of the Firm," *American Economic Review*, 42, No. 2 (May 1952): 30–44.

18. William Baumol, *Business Behavior, Value, and Growth*, 2d. ed. (New York: Harcourt, Brace, & World, 1967).

19. Edith Penrose, *The Theory of the Growth of the Firm* (Oxford: Basil Blackwell, 1959).

20. Ibid., p. 200.

21. Oliver E. Williamson, *Economics of Discretionary Behavior: Managerial Objectives in a Theory of the Firm* (Chicago: Markham, 1967).

22. See Robin A. Marris, *The Economic Theory of "Managerial" Capitalism* (New York: Macmillan, 1964).

23. Piero Sraffa, "The Laws of Return under Competitive Conditions," *Economic Journal* 36, No. 144 (Dec. 1926): 335–50.

24. Joan Robinson, *The Theory of Imperfect Competition* (London: Macmillan, 1933).

25. Edward H. Chamberlin, *The Theory of Monopolistic Competition* (Cambridge: Harvard University Press, 1933).

26. Joe S. Bain, *Barriers to New Competition* (Cambridge: Harvard University Press, 1956).

27. Described by Martin Shubik as "an attractive model to start the analysis" in his "A Curmudgeon's Guide to Microeconomics," *Journal of Economic Literature* 8 (June 1970): 417.

28. United Nations, *Transnational Corporations and World Development: A Reexamination*, (New York: United Nations, 1978), chap. 3.

29. For an excellent discussion of financial control systems in transnational corporations, see Brooke and Remmers, op. cit., chap. 4.

30. Michael G. Duerr and John M. Roach, *Organization and Control of International Relations* (New York: Conference Board, 1973), p. 18. Also see Berenbeim, op. cit.

31. Richard M. Cyert and James G. March, *A Behavioral Theory of the Firm.* (Englewood Cliffs, N.J.: Prentice-Hall, 1963).

32. This critique of the argument of *A Behavioral Theory of the Firm* is based on points originally made by Aharoni in *The Foreign Investment Decision Process*, pp. 266–72.

33. John R. Hicks, "Annual Survey of Economic Theory: The Theory of Monopoly," *Econometrica* 3, no. 1, (Feb. 1935): 8.

34. Oliver E., Williamson, *Corporate Control and Business Behavior* (Englewood Cliffs, N.J.: Prentice-Hall, 1970). Williamson suggests that on-the-job leisure might be considered a component of a firm's utility function "as influenced by the participation of . . . functional division chiefs." He remarks that its importance might vary with circumstances of firms and indicates that it is not normally included in discussions of the theory of the firm, "perhaps attributable to a recognition that on-the-job leisure is a general condition characteristic, to a greater or lesser extent, of every line of human endeavor" (pp. 50–52).

35. This was the case in the situations for which interviews were carried out for the current research (see table 2.3).

5:
Small Nations,
Giant Firms,
Complex Dealings

The idea of a large TNC, such as Anaconda Copper, Unilever, General Motors, Hoechst Pharmaceutical, or Standard Oil, invulnerable in their dealings with third-world host countries, is a thing of the past. With the passage of time, there have been dramatic changes in the objectives and capacities of third-world host country governments, of home country governments, and in the firms themselves. Such changes have been evident in different ways for each of the types of industries in which TNCs operate—raw materials, manufacturing, and service industries.

TRANSNATIONAL CORPORATE POWER IN THE PAST

NATURAL RESOURCE INDUSTRIES

In the past, natural resource companies have been able to derive power by setting terms at the beginning of the investment. This was due to their control over certain production factors—capital and technology—while host country regulators were attending to more mature industries and because critical host country elites derived from their presence. For the firms, it was crucially important to have discretionary control over the conduct of their operations and high returns if investments were successful because the investments were large and made under substantial uncertainty. Early investments by Anaconda and Kennecott in Chile, by the Cerro Corporation in Peru, by Standard Oil and U.S. Steel in Venezuela, and by Alcan in Jamaica each totaled hundreds of millions of dollars in current costs. Uncertainties ranged from the future ability to do business in the host country, to possible production problems, to the vagaries of world markets.[1]

As a result, early raw materials investments in Latin America included such terms as forty year, ninety-nine year, or perpetual rights to exploit minerals; little or no requirements to pay local taxes or share profits; absolute control over setting values on exported mineral products and imported material; and company control over how and where the raw material was processed.

Once the investment was made, however, much of the company's power to protect its investment had been eroded. Its large fixed costs had been sunk, and its technology installed. Furthermore, once uncertainty over the profitability of the investment had been dispelled through a period of successful operation, the original terms often appeared as overgenerous to host country nationalists.[2] Until World War II, however, firms were generally able to continue to operate following the terms of their original agreements with host countries. Three factors were responsible for this: (1) political and military pressure placed by TNC home governments on host governments; (2) the acquiescence of host country leaders to the status quo—as both a result of indifference and private involvement with the companies; and (3) the inability of host country governments to monitor effectively and supervise the firm's operations.

MANUFACTURING INDUSTRIES

While foreign investment in manufacturing industries has a history almost as long as that in raw materials, few industrialized nations' firms had substantial investments in third-world nations until well after World War II.[3] The vast majority of international business in manufacturing was carried out by exporting finished goods from industrialized nations, sometimes with final assembly operations in third-world nations. For example, automobile manufacturing did not begin in Mexico until the early 1960s,[4] and foreign firms did not set up factories to manufacture electrical machinery in Brazil until the late 1950s.[5]

The importance of transnational manufacturing operations in Latin America, for both firms and nations, was quite different from that of raw materials. Contrary to the vision of sophisticated, globally integrated TNCs, natural resource firms sought to do business in Latin America in order to secure access to raw materials for use in operations that were centered primarily in their home countries. Manufacturing firms went abroad largely to hold on to markets for their products that they had formerly served by exporting.[6] Despite the fact that markets in third-world nations have been of only marginal importance to manufacturing firms, in the context of firms' worldwide operations, penetrating these markets was beneficial for a number of reasons: Sales for products could be augmented with little additional startup cost; early market penetration could produce experience valuable when demand for a given product expanded; competitors could be kept in check by matching rivals' patterns of foreign involvements; and hefty profits could be made on minimal investments, due to host countries' inability to monitor investments closely. Despite these advantages, third-world sales for most transnational manufacturing firms in the 1970s were less than those in important home country sales districts.[7]

On the other hand, direct foreign investment in manufacturing has been highly desired by governments of Latin American nations. Substituting locally manufactured goods for foreign imports was desired to improve balance-of-payments accounts. It was hoped that establishing foreign firms would generate links both within the domestic economy and between it and the international economy that would spur national development. And similarly, it was hoped that foreign firms would bring the advanced production and marketing techniques that were scarcely developed in Latin American nations.

In this context, some firms in consumer goods industries made substantial investments in Latin American countries. As in natural resource industries, their power derived from pressure the home country governments exerted on hosts, host country acquiescence to the status quo, and host country inability to monitor investments. However, unlike the TNCs in natural resource industries, their power to set terms was not necessarily at its apex prior to the commitment of the initial capital. Although the power to withhold investment was also a source of initial leverage for these firms, their power from another source often grew with time. As their operations became more and more integrated into the national economy, a growing network of suppliers, workers, and customers came to share the interests of the foreign firms.

Thus, manufacturing firms, although not involved so early as natural resource industries, have lost less relative power in the years since their initial investments. Furthermore, with the growth of certain national markets—most notably those of Mexico, Brazil, and Argentina—some investments in Latin American countries have become of central interest to some TNCs. In 1978, for example,

Mexico was the third most important national market for Coca Cola, and Latin America accounted for more sales of Massey–Ferguson tractors than any other world region, including North America.

SERVICE SECTOR INDUSTRIES

Beginning in the 1970s, service sector industries, such as banking, insurance, tourism, consulting, and transportation followed a pattern similar to that of manufacturing. This is due in part to the fact that these industries established themselves in a particular region in response to the growing presence of transnational manufacturing companies. Manufacturing firms often saw advantages in dealing with the same service organization, be it banker, insurer, hotelier, or accountant, in both home and host countries. Thus, the operations of transnational service corporations have dramatically expanded in the third world since World War II, following the expansion of manufacturing firms. As with manufacturing firms, service organizations have often become increasingly integrated into host economies with the passage of time. They, too, have a source of corporate power not so readily available to natural resource firms.

Among service sector industries, banking has played an especially important role since the mid-1970s, first providing massive capital inflows to third-world nations and later, in the 1980s, causing net capital outflows through interest payments and service fees. This rise in importance of transnational banking was caused by the increase in oil prices in the early 1970s, resulting in capital surpluses among oil exporters, which were then channeled into investment outlets by transnational banks, many in oil-deficit developing nations. From the late 1960s through 1981, the average annual rate of growth of transnational bank lending exceeded 20 percent a year.[8] In 1982, bank lending to developing countries suddenly dropped by 40 percent.[9] The claims of commercial banks on developing countries, which had stood at $89 billion in 1975, reached $362 billion by mid-1982. By the end of 1984, Latin American external debt exceeded $360 billion, and interest payments on this debt exceeded 35 percent of the value of the region's exports.[10] Severe payment and economic growth problems were reflected, in the mid-1970s, in fears of overexposure by certain transnational banking centers, particularly those in the United States. At the end of 1982, outstanding loans to five Latin American countries exceeded 150 percent of the capital of the nine largest U.S. banks.[11]

COMPLEXITY OF THE PRESENT: SIX DIMENSIONS

The vision of firm power in the past is rather straightforward. Encouraged by its home government, a firm would arrange to do business in a host country with the expectation that the arrangement would endure and the firm would exercise discretion over both the costs and the division of profits. International business today is conducted in a far more complex fashion than that suggested by this vision of the past. Both firms and nations are aware of a vast array of possible means for achieving their separate goals. As a result, the specifics of each arrangement are determined by the circumstances of the parties involved. Nevertheless, changes in business relationships between TNCs and host countries are summarized in the six dimensions of these relationships, which are:

1. Identity of the initiator of the relationship
2. Number of parties involved in the relationship
3. Relative permanence of the relationship
4. Nonrevenue contributions of the relationship to host country development
5. Calculation of costs and prices attendant on the relationship
6. Division of profits resulting from the relationship

Most contemporary international business arrangements diverge dramatically from our view of the past along many of these dimensions. The range of this divergence can be sampled by discussing these dimensions.

IDENTITY OF THE INITIATOR

Past operations suggest that early business arrangements between TNCs and host countries were initiated by the foreign firm, sometimes with the encouragement of its home government. For example, U.S.-based firms were generally encouraged to make arrangements either in the United States or abroad that enhanced their earnings. European firms were also encouraged to engage in international business sometimes, however, explicitly limited by concerns of a part-owner home government.[12] Business arrangements today are sometimes initiated by host country governments to further development objectives, sometimes by host country business interests, sometimes by home country governments in search of material or markets, and sometimes by one or more TNCs.

Two aspects of the current situation are particularly important:

(1) The initiative can lie in the hands of a number of parties, not just a single party, such as a TNC; and (2) the initial impetus for exploring a possible interest often results from the convergence of interests among a number of parties, not just one. The notion of a TNC initially seizing an opportunity with unsuspecting host and home governments, as well as domestic and other transnational firms, and making after-the-fact adjustments is scarcely realistic today.

The Peruvian government's 1969 invitation to foreign oil companies to exploit presumed oil reserves according to a formula explicitly linked to Peruvian development priorities is a good example of a host government taking the initiative. Later, solutions to the problem of transporting the limited and inaccessible petroleum produced resulted from the combined efforts of American and Peruvian firms drilling the oil; Japanese, West German, and Peruvian firms building pipelines for its transport; and the Japanese government providing finance in exchange for future production. All of these arrangements were made to pursue specific and separate objectives, and the eyes of all parties were relatively wide open as they worked out arrangements.[13]

NUMBER OF PARTIES INVOLVED

An important element of the present complexity is that many arrangements are being worked out that involve more than one party on one or both sides of the business relationship. In addition to making business arrangements more complex, different types of arrangements often result, depending on the source of the impetus for the arrangement and on the mix of the parties involved.

Syndication: TNCs Working Together

The initiation of a business arrangement by a TNC through the involvement of many firms has been labeled "risk spreading,"[14] but is more often referred to by the term syndication. Risk spreading describes one important aspect of this arrangement—each of the parties involved is less exposed to loss if the arrangement fails than if it had underwritten the entire agreement. In addition, Moran asserts that risk spreading enmeshes the host country in "a web of public and private interest groups" that "magnifies the hazards" of disrupting the original arrangement. Thus, syndication may both spread risk and enhance control for TNCs. In addition to these benefits, syndication can sharpen the partners' skills through a division of labor, and it can increase the stability of the global business environment. In one recent syndicated loan, one U.S. bank drew up the documentation; another U.S. bank kept track of who was participating in the deal and how much each partner had committed; a third wrote the confidential prospectus; one British bank kept track of the money after agreement had been reached and now serves as the continuing information clearinghouse and liaison with the borrower for the six partner banks; a second British bank organized publicity and handled inquiries from nonbankers; and a German bank made arrangements for the signing ceremony.

Syndicated agreements are not restricted to finance. Although U.S. antitrust legislation prevents U.S. firms from acting in concert, European and Japanese companies in many instances have combined to manufacture products ranging from motor vehicles, to electrical machinery, to textiles. Perhaps more important, syndicated agreements can create networks that bind together divergent economic factors or reinforce existing patterns of business relations. For example, an international industry which functions as an oligopoly can incorporate new firms on oligopoly terms by allowing their participation in a syndicated deal. Similarly, existing oligopoly structures can be reinforced if the "majors" in an industry combine among themselves to launch a new operation.

Multiple Sourcing: TNCs involving Many Hosts

Firms have long followed the practice of producing a final product from far-flung inputs. They can also involve numerous host countries in their production processes through multiple sourcing, or using a number of different sources for the same input. For example, Ford Motor Company produces small automobile engines in the United States, the United Kingdom, and Brazil. This not only allows the firm to reduce transportation costs by shipping from the nearest factory, but it also gives the firm the flexibility to switch sources if a given plant is experiencing production difficulties. While syndication enables firms to mobilize a network of allies if a host country wishes to alter the terms of an agreement, multiple sourcing allows a firm to go elsewhere for its product if it encounters difficulties in a given host country.

Unbundling: Host Country involving Many TNCs

Host countries have added complexity to international business arrangements by "unbundling" business agreements. Rather than accept a "package deal" from a single firm, host countries can unbundle the package into a set of components and then negotiate separately with suppliers of each component. For example, in setting up a nationally owned watch factory, the government of Ecuador first contracted with a Swiss consulting firm to carry out a feasibility study and then used results from that study to combine separate inputs for financing factory construction, providing machinery, and supplying intermediate goods for production and management skills to help direct the operation. Similarly, Venezuela's huge national petroleum company, Petroven, has taken over a set of formerly "packaged" direct foreign investments by major oil firms and now contracts drillers to explore and develop wells, purchases and installs technology for its refineries, and manages the operation and markets its product. In the late 1970s, these tasks were accomplished with the help of managers from the former TNC owners, Exxon and Shell, hired through management and service contracts.

While unbundling an agreement may give the host country an opportunity to put together a package more suited to its development objectives than one set up by a foreign firm, not all hosts can unbundle all international business arrangements to their advantage. Knowledge of the various components of a business arrangement, including management skills and the ability to recognize fair prices for goods and services, comes only with experience. As a result, host countries usually do not actively involve themselves in the details of an arrangement until after they have had some relevant experience. Even then, as with Venezuelan oil, they are usually careful to contract for outside assistance while simultaneously developing national skills.

Collective Solutions: Host Countries Working Together

Just as host countries can involve many firms in a particular arrangement by unbundling a business package, so, too, can they involve a number of other nations by working out collective solutions to national development problems. The most ambitious scheme in the third world has been the Andean pact, discussed in Chapter 2. Through its industrial sectoral programs, the Andean group countries attempted to develop schemes for shared production in areas as diverse as metal working, chemicals, glass, automobiles, and fertilizers. Through its Decision 46, the group made provision for the formation of Andean Multinational Enterprises—joint ventures among shareholders in different Andean group nations.[15] However, the experience of the Andean group suggests, even in the words of a sympathetic analyst, that "existing national productive capacities are too far below the financial, technical, and organizational levels required."[16] While the results of this agreement and others in the Caribbean, Africa, and Asia are, at best, ambiguous, the pact has added to the complexity of international business in the region. Firms and nations have simultaneously followed both national and Andean policies, the former focusing on benefits to the nation in question, the latter on the collective solution promoted by the pact. Making these collective solutions work has been exceedingly difficult for these countries due to factors just mentioned, internal political instability, changes in the prices and volume of export commodities, and the fact that individually and collectively, these nations have less to offer international business than nations with more diversified economies.

PERMANENCE OF THE RELATIONSHIP

The inviolability of a signed contract is basic to the legal conception of world order. However, as circumstances bearing on existing international business agreements change, host countries have pressed for contract renegotiations.[17] For example, foreign interests began exploiting Venezuela's oil in the first quarter of the twentieth century. Terms for this exploitation were renegotiated in 1936, 1943, 1955, 1967, and 1971, with Venezuela nationalizing the industry in 1976.[18] Often, firms also decide that terms of initial agreements are inappropriate, given altered economic conditions. Although few firms seek to give up a subsidiary, as did the Cerro Corporation in Peru in 1973, it is not uncommon for a TNC to threaten to close down a subsidiary unless tax rates or other restrictions are altered by national governments.

The pressure of the host country's need for foreign exchange, combined with increased abilities to bargain with foreign firms and to monitor and supervise business operations, has resulted in the pattern of firm–host country relations called "obsolescing bargain."[19] In this pattern, a foreign investor is offered attractive terms to make an investment in a host country. Once the investment becomes profitable, the terms appear overgenerous to the host, which imposes new and stricter terms. The foreign investor, usually after attempting to soften the new terms, decides to accept them rather than withdraw. Although Vernon and others focus on host country pressure to alter terms, the concept applies equally well to firms requesting new terms in the face of cost overruns, changes in

127

the international industry, or alterations in the host's domestic economy.

International business has become more complex today because firms and countries now often expect initial bargains to obsolesce.[20] Firms evaluate the long-term profitability of investments under different patterns of bargain obsolescence. In part to reduce the uncertainty implicit in arrangements that end in obsolescing bargains, some contracts are now written in which it is specified that either party may renegotiate terms under certain conditions. The necessity of continually reassessing costs and benefits of agreements has become another dimension of the complexity of contemporary international business.

NONREVENUE CONTRIBUTIONS TO THE HOST'S DEVELOPMENT

As host countries have become skilled in monitoring the operations of foreign firms, they have also increased their ability to judge whether a particular arrangement makes a sufficiently positive contribution to national development. While the ability to make such judgments varies widely among nations and from arrangement to arrangement, the concerns of host country monitors touch on a number of areas in addition to revenue contributions. Such areas include the amount of employment generated, links to other areas of the nation's economy, consumer and worker protection, efficiency of production processes and technology, and ecological impact.

The importance of adhering to standards in these and other areas increases demands on both national monitors and company managers. It is often difficult for the host country to assess accurately company performance. Furthermore, corporate managers often see such concerns as interfering with their discretion to run their operations efficiently and as wasting valuable time. While these inputs are more difficult to measure than revenue contributions, they are crucially important for realizing national development objectives.

CALCULATING PRICES AND COSTS

The need for revenue and foreign exchange to respond to both national development demands and those of special interest groups has been a primary motivation for host countries both to work out arrangements with TNCs and to renegotiate them. To the extent that such revenues result from the profitability of the arrangement they are, in turn, a function both of the prices that firms can charge for their goods and services and of costs of doing business. This is a particularly complicated calculation when dealing with a complex organization like a TNC because the profitability to a firm of an operation in a given host country can be determined only with reference to its contribution to the global corporation. Furthermore, there is a clear incentive for managers to set prices to service global corporation welfare rather than reflect the costs of production and to include as operating costs items that might more appropriately be considered reinvestment or questionable payments.[21] The problem is additionally complicated for host country regulators who must use social rather than market prices in their analyses.[22]

Prices

Host country concern with price setting has focused on transfer pricing.[23] This involves setting prices for transactions between two related parties, such as two subsidiaries of a TNC. If a subsidiary wishes to send revenue out of a country and/or avoid taxes, it can raise the transfer price on imports or lower it on exports. If the subsidiary wishes to accumulate revenue, it can do the obverse and lower the transfer price on intrafirm imports or raise the price on exports. Countries have attempted to review price levels since the late 1950s but have often been unable to assemble information needed to determine whether a given price makes sense. Progress on this front is the result of both the work of specialized agencies in some countries and, in raw materials industries, information pooled by producer organizations. However, the variety and volatility of pricing decisions occurring in the normal course of doing business has made this an especially complex area for host country negotiators and monitors.

Price setting between unrelated parties is also a subject of concern for the host. Formally unrelated firms have, at times, colluded to affect interfirm transfer pricing or set prices at levels not reflective of market forces.

Costs

Since profits are normally the difference between operating revenues and costs, it is also important for the host to prevent firms from artificially inflating costs. Such practices are at times employed by firms when hosts place restrictions on profit remittances or subsidiaries are not making profits. Cost inflation strategies include subsidiaries assuming unneeded loans or paying inflated rates for loans, licensing agreements, royalties, or service contracts. In addition, it is sometimes advantageous for firms to reduce taxes by listing plants and equipment improvements as operating costs, rather than after-tax reinvestment. While host country scrutiny of costs and prices has received less attention than such issues as nationalization and the division of profits between foreign firms and host governments, it is easy to see that these matters are crucial if a host expects to gain revenue from the operations of a TNC's subsidiary by means of corporate income tax.[24]

THE DIVISION OF PROFITS

How profits from TNC investments are divided between the firm and host country is the result of an intricate conjunction of policies.[25] Among the policies affecting the division of shares is the level of the corporate income tax; limits on profit remittances, royalty, service, and credit payments; and requirements that ownership be shared or transferred to host country hands. Calculations are further complicated by the fact that profit for the firm is measured internally, not merely by the reported profit of the subsidiary in question, but by the effect of that subsidiary's activities on the corporation's global operations. In addition, calculations are complicated when firms sell equity to the host country and receive revenues through a combination of payments from the sale of the subsidiary and payments for services rendered through management contracts.

How a host brings pressure on a firm to continue the operations of its subsidiary, yet allow the host to take a larger share of the profits, can be the result of either pressure from domestic political sources or changes in the structure of an international industry. Domestic political forces, stimulated by either nationalist pride or the need for increased revenues to meet development objectives, can result in a host country taking steps to alter the division of profits in a given industry. Beginning in 1945, for example, nationalist sentiment in Chile resulted in Chile receiving increased revenue from the Chilean copper mining subsidiaries of the Anaconda, Cerro, and Kennecott corporations.[26]

Another, perhaps more frequent, reason for changes in profit shares arise from changes in the structure of an international industry. A host country may desire more favorable terms from the operations of a given type of firm and may be unable to extract such concessions from a major firm in the industry; however, a smaller firm hoping to increase its role in the industry may grant those concessions. The petroleum industry is perhaps the most famous for examples of "minors" accepting conditions unacceptable to "majors," with the result that the power of the minors increases, and the entire industry eventually operates on terms accepted by the minors.[27] However, this is also not unusual in manufacturing industries.

Firms can and do, of course, mount counter strategies designed to increase their earnings. One such strategy is to agree on a smaller share, as long as total profits are increasing sufficiently so that the firm's return on assets or invested capital stays the same or grows.[28] Firms can also attempt to affect host countries through the intervention of their home governments, as was attempted by ITT during the 1970 to 1973 Popular Unity government in Chile and by Standard Oil of New Jersey in the aftermath of the 1938 nationalization of Mexican holdings. Finally, firms can obtain a share of profits through the fees of management and service contracts and the sale of purchased goods. In 1979, for example, oil firms nationalized in Venezuela three years earlier were still reported to earn royalties on 500 million barrels of Venezuelan oil a year and to earn more than $350 million from technical assistance contracts.[29] The possibility of waging battles of this dimension contributes importantly to current negotiation complexities.

SIMPLICITY AMID COMPLEXITY

The current complexity of firm–state bargaining results from the attempt to take into account as many factors as possible when working out business arrangements. However, it is both infeasible and impractical for both parties to ask every question anew and explore each in its entirety when working out a new arrangement. It is infeasible because all information can never be collected and impractical largely because executive time is an especially scarce commodity for both firms and nations. At some point in negotiations, the costs of continuing to use scarce executive time and tolerate start-up delays may exceed gains resulting from complex bargaining.

Apart from these pressures, improvements in the bargaining skill of the parties involved can simplify bargaining. As previously stated, host countries since World War II have been rapidly improving their ability to evaluate and monitor business relationships. The same has been true of TNCs, although, for the most part, they have possessed more highly developed skills for a longer period of time.

One process that substantially simplifies bargaining is the adoption of an arrangement worked out in another context. For example, the 1971 arrangement between the Occidental Petroleum Company and PETROPERU, Peru's national petroleum agency, has been substantially followed in operations contracts concluded by national petroleum or mineral agencies in Bolivia, Brazil, Guatemala, Panama, and Uruguay.[30] Such adoption of the terms of agreements struck elsewhere both simplifies other similar bargaining situations and constitutes the formation of new bases for carrying out firm–state relations.

Another example of a convention that can simplify bargaining involves a country assigning responsibility to a foreign firm for a portion of the business operations, without the country relinquishing control over the operations. For example, the Occidental–PETROPERU agreement just cited involved Occidental providing all necessary funds and technical services for hydrocarbon exploration while acting as contractor for the Peruvian agency. Title to oil or gas discovered and produced remained vested in Peru, with Occidental receiving between 44 and 50 percent of the hydrocarbons extracted, net of Peruvian taxes.[31] This arrangement resembles the unbundling strategy previously discussed, since each aspect of the production process is treated separately. It simplifies the bargaining process because rather than completely unbundling and reassembling the necessary finance, technology, and manpower inputs, PETROPERU assigned responsibility for all of them to a single contractor.

The contracting relationship between PETROPERU and Occidental is paralleled in manufacturing industries by an arrangement in which a firm contracts to build an entire plant for a fixed fee. The firm then delivers the plant to the host country, which assumes ownership and runs the plant itself, sometimes also contracting with the foreign firm to provide management or technological assistance. Such deals are called turnkey arrangements because the contractor builds the plant and then "turns over the keys" to the host government in exchange for the agreed-on fee. Examples of such arrangements are the construction of nuclear power plants for Brazil and Argentina by Siemens's subsidiary, Kraftwerk Union, and the construction of lumber mills, cement factories, and chemical plants by various TNCs for Latin American governments.

Although these devices do away with much of the red tape involved in carefully monitoring every aspect of a business arrangement, they do not equal in simplicity the traditional direct foreign investment concession agreement. As a result, in certain circumstances, a direct foreign investment "package" may be more attractive for a host country than a complex unbundled, multiparty arrangement. This might be the case if the host country is not yet able to monitor the foreign firm or if the firm possesses technological, marketing, or managerial skills lacking in the host country, but a business arrangement is particularly important to the host government. Dealing with a single TNC and accepting a prearranged division-of-profits formula rather than assuming responsibility for assembling a number of inputs and continually monitoring the project may at times save executive time and thereby exceed gains made through more complex bargaining—especially if the host country does not yet have the ability to carry out the bargaining and monitoring processes.

Therefore, despite strong pressures for increasing complexity, counter pressures for simplicity also exist. These counter pressures exist because: (1) Scarce executive time in both firms and nations is consumed by complex bargaining; and (2) while often suggesting new areas for negotiations, learning can also lead to devices that simplify bargaining. There may be other motivations for a host country's use of traditional business agreements; for example, to indicate clearly that a "hospitable environment" for foreign business existed, the post-1973 Chilean military regime attempted to attract foreign investments by offering a package of incentives giving foreign firms wide discretion in managing and profiting from Chilean operations.

SPIN-OFFS FROM COMPLEX BARGAINING

Bargaining between firms and nations goes on, spawning business arrangements of varying complexity. These arrangements are negotiated, however, in continually changing environments that are altered by both forces external to the firm–state bargaining process and by forces intrinsic to it. Although it is difficult to specify aspects of environments exclusively affected by bargaining, it is possible to indicate a variety of circumstances in which new phenonema have been created, at least in part, as a result of newly complex firm–state bargaining. For the sake of crispness, let us refer to these new circumstances as spin-offs, since they exist side by side with the bargaining process. Spin-offs have resulted from two aspects of the bargaining process: (1) the learning that both parties have experienced over time, and (2) the outcomes of the bargining.

SPIN-OFFS FROM LEARNING

Both firms and host countries as well as home countries and other interested observers have had the opportunity to derive lessons from firm–state bargaining and to tailor future practice and policy. This learning has resulted in a number of new developments, among them new goals for both firms and nations, new forms of doing international business, new divisions of activities between firms and nations, new guidelines for links between politics and business, new institutions especially created to service situations resulting from the complexity of firm–state bargaining, and new forms of legislation for international business, enacted by both the host and home countries of TNCs.

NEW GOALS FOR FIRMS AND NATIONS

The continuing struggle between firms and nations over the division of profits from international business has already been discussed and indicates changes in goals. Nations now expect to earn more from international business than one or two decades ago. Firms no longer anticipate that assuming substantial risks entitles investors to unlimited gains. The contributions and objectives of all parties to investment agreements have become increasingly explicit.

However, this is but a part of the picture of changed goals. Host country reassessment of goals—both in the areas of profit division and in other aspects of international business impact—have led to difficulties. There have been periods in which host countries have imposed new conditions, such as high taxation rates, limits on profit remittances, gradual divestments, and total nationalizations. Firms have sometimes reacted to such changes with hostility by "milking" existing investments or curtailing future plans. In other circumstances, firms have evaluated the changed environment of international business and made adaptations that took account of new host country objectives. Attempts at innovation in investment agreements have usually been followed by evaluation of their successes and failures, and policies have been sometimes reformulated to facilitate realizing attainable objectives. Revisions of Peru's petroleum development legislation and the Andean pact's Common Regime for the Treatment of Foreign Capital are examples of host country evaluation and reassessment. The petroleum majors' agreement to take on service and management contracts in the face of OPEC nationalizations and Nestlé's 1979 decision to reduce its exposure in developing countries are examples of reassessments of regional and global strategies by major TNCs.[32]

Finally, critical for understanding the process of nation–firm goal assessment is recognition by both parties that such change must be limited and gradual. Both TNCs and third-world nations expect to be, for the foreseeable future, part of an international order in which the identities of the principal actors will not change overnight. Therefore, while carefully evaluating the appropriateness of a particular arrangement, both firms and nations also take into account the expectation that the other party will continue to exist and have strongly articulated objectives for the life of the agreement in question and beyond. Although it is possible to characterize this as a movement to reduce short-term exploitation of host countries, it is perhaps more important to view this as a profound adjustment of goals consistent with long-term participation in the currently constituted international order.

NEW FORMS OF DOING INTERNATIONAL BUSINESS

The three traditional forms of conducting international business have been the international sales of goods and material by exporting and importing, licensing rights to produce patented products or utilized patented processes, and establishing production subsidiaries in other nations through direct foreign investment. Through the unbundling processes previously described, firms and nations have learned to rely on such once unusual forms as management contracts, service agreements, and technical assistance. To the extent that these new forms have been instituted, they have also meant a change in the exercise of control by TNCs. These forms result when firms give up equity control of operations in host countries but still contribute know-how and technology through formal agreements. Control has thus shifted from equity owners' ability to dominate boards of directors and appoint managers, to influencing the operation of firms by controlling technology, management skills, or marketing. At times, this results in greater host country control, and at others, it merely shifts the form of TNC control.

In order to prevent production and employment losses due to private sector failures and to implement development objectives, the state has recently come to play an increasingly active role in national economies.[33] Operations formerly owned by TNCs have become state firms either because no private sector host nationals can be found to purchase them or because planners judge state control to be in the national interest. Thus, the former Grace sugar plantations in Peru are now state owned, as are the former Reynolds bauxite facilities in Guyana and the former Bethlehem Steel iron and coal mines in Chile.

New business alliances are also cropping up in many Latin Amerian countries. Host governments have learned to go into partnership with varying combinations of transnational and local investors. For example, Brazil has forged agreements with foreign and domestic interests to develop petrochemical facilities in its Northeast.[34] Peru has formed, together with Canadian and Swedish interests, an industrial complex to manufacture tractors and trucks.[35] Bolivian investors have formed a partnership with the Bolivian state development bank and a Brazilian bicycle company to manufacture bicycles for export to the Andean countries.[36] An international reinsurance company has been established in New York with majority shares owned by the Brazilian Reinsurance Institute and various Brazilian insurance companies, in partnership with companies from Argentina, Britain, West Germany, and Venezuela.[37] These new combinations of partners make the ties that bind the international economic order more complex.

A new form that had been hailed as a striking development in international business is the TNC owned by interests in third-world nations.[38] Newly formed TNCs have been established in such resource-rich third-world nations as Chile, such market-rich nations as Brazil, and such labor-rich nations as South Korea. The largest firms in Latin America are state owned, such as Mexico's Petroleos Mexicanos and Brazil's Mendes Junior construction firm, while Bunge & Born, the Argentine export house, is privately owned.[39] The rise of these firms is seen in some quarters as a threat to the dominance of European, Japanese, and North American firms, but Heenan and Keegan suggest that it may be more properly viewed as a force for further integration of the international economic order.[40]

NEW DIVISIONS OF ACTIVITIES BETWEEN
TNCS AND HOST COUNTRIES

An essential component of a nation's development plan is the role it assigns to foreign business and the sectors it reserves for local control. Government planners have concluded that national security and development may sometimes be best promoted if foreign firms are blocked from full participation in certain economic activities. Such sectors as energy, transportation, banking, and natural resource development have been reserved for national interests by most Latin American nations. In addition, some have reserved such industries as textiles and leather goods, where dependence on foreign factors of production is minimal. In a controversial 1984 decision, Brazil decided to severely limit foreign participation in the "informatics" industry because it judged it a matter of national security to develop an internationally competitive domestic capacity. Although these proscribed sectors vary from nation to nation, and also change in particular countries,[41] they indicate the existence of a de facto international division of labor, in part structured by third-world development plans.

This shift in the division of labor is most visible in natural resources industries where TNCs often serve as consultants, final processors, and marketers, with major production and initial processing in the hands of host countries. The shift is not so clear in other sectors, although the Andean Pact's Common Regime for the Treatment of Foreign Capital outlined an ambitious framework for excluding foreign participation in sectors in which domestic firms could compete internationally. Future divisions of labor will be influenced by evolving host country capacities as well as the ability of TNC bargainers to convince host country nationals that the proscription of foreign firms from certain sectors is not basic to national economic security, and may exacerbate global protectionism and slow economic development—a real concern for third-world nations who hope to export manufactured goods.

The evolving international distribution of economic activities is also affected by the extent to which TNCs internalize such flows as direct foreign investment, technology transfer, finance, and trade. To the extent that such flows occur within the transnational frameworks of single firms, both home and host countries lose the ability to control prices, quantities, and location of goods produced.

In the area of technology transfer, 81 percent of the fees and royalties received by U.S. TNCs between 1979 and 1981 were from affiliated firms. Similarly, substantial capital transfers are generated internally by TNCs or provided by affiliated financial institutions.[42]

In the area of trade, intrafirm transfers by TNCs are particularly important. In 1977, TNCs accounted for 90 percent of U.S. trade, and total intrafirm transfers accounted for 39 percent of imports and

36 percent of exports. In the United Kingdom, where TNCs account for 80 percent of trade, intrafirm transfers represented 31 percent of exports in 1980.[43] Since arm's-length prices do not exist for many of the items traded, prices are set in light of considerations internal to the firms involved—considerations on which little research has been done concerning their relevance for home or host country well-being.

Intrafirm transactions are critical if home and host countries hope to plan their economic development strategies according to dynamic comparative advantage or national security considerations. Their ability to separately and jointly shape the evolving international division of economic activities is influenced by their knowledge and control over the large number of economic transactions that take place outside of the "market," within the confines of single firms.

NEW GUIDELINES FOR LINKS BETWEEN POLITICS AND BUSINESS

As bargaining between firms and nations has increased in complexity, both parties have expressed concern over relations between business and politics. Nations have voiced concern over corporate interference in internal political affairs and intergovernmental affairs; firms have worried about political considerations interfering with business objectives. Both parties have learned that the absence of guidelines for separating business and politics results in uncertainty over future business arrangements.

One result of this concern has been the drafting of *international codes* for conducting relations between firms and nations. Over fifty corporations, led initially by the Caterpillar Tractor Company and the OECD, have drafted codes stressing norms of ethical conduct by firms and indicating the importance of corresponding behavior by host governments—including equity in national legal treatment and fair treatment in the event of nationalization.[44] The U.N.'s Commission on TNCs is coordinating an Intergovernmental Working Group that is developing a code of conduct for activities and treatment of TNCS. A draft of this code proscribes firms

> resorting to subversive activities aimed at influencing the political and social systems in . . . countries . . . interfer[ing] in affairs that are properly the concern of government . . . act[ing] as instruments for the advancement of the foreign policy of governments . . . and request[ing] governments to act on their behalf in any manner that exceeds normal

diplomatic representation . . . in particular in any manner that amounts to the use of coercive measures of an economic and political character . . .[45]

It is unlikely that these codes or more grandiose plans for international regulation of TNCs will ever, in themselves, result in a mandatory separation of business and politics. For this to happen, procedures for monitoring firms' conduct, adjudicating complaints, and imposing sanctions would have to be included in an international agreement subscribed to by more- and less-developed capitalist and socialist countries. Since, to date, steps have been taken only to agree on statements of principles, that separation can only result from restraint and regulation by individual firms, host and home countries. However, the salience of codes is a reflection by all parties concerned that clearer understandings must be worked out, and widespread discussion has increased global awareness of the importance of separating politics and business, as well as increased uniformity and nondiscrimination in host country regulation.

Within the United States, the home country of half of the world's TNCs, concern over maintaining such a separation has been expressed on many fronts. To combat direct interference through bribery, the U.S. Congress in 1977 passed the Foreign Corrupt Practices Act. This act makes it a criminal offense for a U.S.-based corporation or its employees to make improper payments to foreigners. On the level of intergovernmental relations, concern has been expressed that the billions of dollars of liability assumed by the U.S. government through the insurance program of its Overseas Private Investment Corporation may cause policies to be instituted in favor of regimes that respect the property of U.S. firms, irrespective of their other qualities. In a similar vein, it has been asserted that U.S. banks are making foreign policy by granting loans to nations without repayment ability and then lobbying the U.S. government to grant these nations favorable commercial treatment. This excessive financial exposure, it is argued, contains a dangerous potential for business interference with political objectives.[46]

Within *host countries*, regulations prohibiting foreign firms from influencing domestic politics are relatively commonplace, although the particulars of statutes and abilities to enforce them very among nations.

Firms have also developed mechanisms for avoiding inappropriate involvement in politics. The boards of directors of firms are charged with ethical oversight of corporations and, in some cases, have established committees to evaluate company actions or worked together with corporate managers to develop mechanisms for assuring proper behavior at all levels of the corporate hierarchy. This is no easy task, since individual managers may be tempted to consider influencing key host country decision makers when their proposals are being evaluated, and high-level executives may be similarly tempted to try to bring home government pressure to bear on host countries from which they feel they do not receive equitable treatment.

Evidence that corporate self-regulation has been effective is difficult to obtain. Media reports that managers are more cautious in their individual operations are available,[47] yet no study has been carried out that documents modified business practices by individual firms. There is, however, evidence of restraint by individual firms. In 1979 the Venezuelan government, for example, withheld payment of a $425 million security deposit made by transnational oil companies in 1976, as guarantee that nationalized plants and equipment would be turned over in good condition. By 1979, final evaluation of plant and equipment had been settled, but Venezuela continued to withhold payment of the $425 million on the grounds that it had neglected to collect $650 million in oil taxes for 1970. Rather than mounting pressure, firms were reported to be biding their time, expecting to find a way of working out an arrangement with Venezuela.[48] This is a far cry from gunboat diplomacy or firms asking the U.S. government to block bilateral and international aid as they did in the late 1960s and early 1970s in response to nationalizations.

On the level of individual employee practice, the following general guidelines were developed by a U.S.-based manufacturing firm in response to corporate discussion of the U.S. Foreign Corrupt Practices Act:

All employees are expected to understand and subscribe to the following general standards of corporate behavior:

1. The Company competes on a straight commercial basis; if something more is required, the Company is not interested.
2. Company employees do nothing in search of business that they should not reveal willingly and publicly to any other member of the Company family or to any government official in any land.
3. The Company neither practices nor condones any activity that will not stand the most rigorous public ethical examination.

4. If an employee has any doubt about the appropriateness or morality of any act, it should not be done. If any employee believes that there is a conflict between what his or her supervisors expect and what corporate ethical standards require, the employee should raise the issue with the Corporate Responsibility Department. The Company is prepared to help any employee resolve a moral dilemma and to ensure that no employee is put at a career disadvantage because of his or her willingness to raise a question about a corporation practice or unwillingness to pursue a course of action that seems inappropriate or morally dubious.[49]

In summary, while a clear separation of politics and business has not been achieved, firms, home, and host countries appear to have learned from the past, as expressed by concern with such issues and also by some limited attempts at developing and enforcing guidelines for appropriate behavior.

NEW INSTITUTIONS

Firms and home and host nations have been involved in creating new institutions. These both enable them to deal with the new complexity more effectively and they also, themselves, contribute to even more complexity.

Firms initially reacted to increased complexity of host country demands with disbelief but soon learned to treat them seriously. Indicative of this shift has been the transformation of the Council of the Americas, a self-proclaimed forum for discussing international business issues in Latin America, supported by more than 300 corporate and organizational members representing 90 percent of U.S. investors in Latin America. In 1971, members of the council wrote to the president of Colombia attempting to prevent Colombia's ratification of the Andean Pact's Decision 24. This was publicly denounced as *terrorismo economico* by Colombia's Minister of Development[50] and served as a stimulus for reorganizing the council. Today the Council serves as a forum where leaders of Latin American nations explain their international business policies to U.S. business people. Among its other functions, it organizes task forces of U.S. executives who visit Latin American countries and then report on business conditions there, and serves as a discussion forum for U.S. companies' problems with home country regulation of international business. The Council of the Americas now attempts to influence the conduct of international business in Latin

America, not through direct pressure on host countries, but by airing disparate viewpoints in an environment supportive of the interests of its corporate members.[51]

While this pattern is more easily observed in a service organization such as the Council of the Americas, complex business arrangements attest to similar learning and transformations within the firms themselves. The "bottom line" of these changes is that corporate managers find it makes better business sense to discuss proposed policies with host country officials, to point out corporate-perceived problems, and make adjustments when necessary, rather than take on the role of adversary and be excluded from business relationships. Particularly important is the growing awareness in the strategic-planning processes of many TNCs that "the degree of responsiveness to host government concerns [is] a strategic variable."[52] Long-term objectives in a given host country are increasingly seen as viable only when they reflect a clear mutuality of interest for the firm and its host. Activities that must be imposed on host countries are not seen as viable.

Home countries have also engaged in institution building in response to demands of the new complexity. Their efforts have not gone so far as to institute the income transfers recommended in the 1969 Pearson Report,[53] or to set up a Marshall Plan for the third world, or to support the stabilization and redistributive measures advocated in studies by the Group of 77 developing nations and the U.N. Commission on Trade and Development. However, task forces and special offices have been established by the U.S. government's Treasury Department Office of Technology Assessment and by other developed countries' governments, as well as by the OECD, to recommend policies for providing third-world countries with flows of capital and technology that more properly correspond to their development objectives.

Host countries have sparked the most visible institutional change, although much of the impetus for creating institutions to restructure the international economic order has been dampened by the turndown in commodity prices following the boom of the mid-1970s. Among the institutions that have been established are those attempting to coordinate the efforts of third-world nations so that their demands might help create a New International Economic Order (the Conference on International Economic Cooperation), to pool knowledge about prices and the availability of international technology (within the Andean group), to facilitate investment and development in third-world nations (the Andean and Caribbean Development corporations), and to provide knowledge about the operations of TNCs that increases the negotiating capacity of host countries (the U.N. Commission on Transnational Corporations).[54]

Although this institution building may constitute a necessary beginning for cooperation among third-world nations, it has not had a strong impact on international business. Its importance lies more in creating longer term competences. International business activity is focused on direct bargaining with particular nations or groups of nations. Trade negotiations, such as those between the United States and Mexico, or the nations of the European Economic Community and the fifty-four former colonies who are signatories of the Lomé Convention, will largely focus on immediate problems and not force major restructuring of international economic relations. Although host countries have learned that individually and collectively they must build new institutions to assist themselves in bargaining with TNCs and more developed nations, with the exception of the early successes of the Organization of Petroleum Exporting Countries and the International Coffee Agreement, the immediate impact of these institutions is likely to be considerably less than that resulting from the creation of new institutions initiated by the needs of the more developed nations.

NEW FORMS OF LEGISLATION FOR INTERNATIONAL BUSINESS

National legislation from both home and host countries sets limits on the bargaining positions adopted by firms and nations. Host country legislation indicates permissible types of foreign investment, terms for technology transfer, forms for labor organization, investment, incentives, tax policy, levels of profit remission, and myriad other details crucial to the operation of business.[55] Home country legislation can limit cooperation between competing national firms, restrict funds available for foreign investment, specify technology allowable for export, and set tax treatment of remitted earnings. The U.S. Congress has passed laws designed to regulate U.S.-based transnationals that include prohibitions on illegal payments and compliance with the Arab boycott of Israel, changing the income tax exclusion for citizens working abroad, and restricting trade with human rights violators.[56]

Latin American nations have been especially active promulgating international-business-related legislation. Enactments include both the regional decisions of the Andean Pact and national legislation. For most countries the enactment of appropriate legislation has been part of the pursuit of new development objectives.

While forming a necessary basis for pursuing national goals, changes and interpretations of national legislation have also worried managers of foreign firms. These concerns stem in part from such regulations as tax increases, which, in themselves, may jeopardize company earning power. However, concerns more frequently reflect the fear that considerable time will have to be expended to understand implications of the new legislation, which could lead to new delays and make business planning difficult. Profit remittances by foreign firms in Colombia, for example, were limited in 1967 to 10 percent of registered capital. This limit was raised to 14 percent in 1970. In 1973, in accord with Andean legislation, an additional 5 percent was allowed to be capitalized, thus raising the amount of permissible remittance. In 1977, following the Andean Pact's Decision 103, these limits were raised to 20 and 7 percent, respectively. In 1979, profits above the 27-percent limit were allowed to be capitalized provided that the firm invested at least 50 percent of the new investment in bonds issued by Colombia's Institute of Industrial Development.[57] Such changes reflect the delicate balance between limiting the operations of foreign firms so that national goals may be pursued, and creating conditions that are attractive for those business arrangements consonant with the pursuit of those goals. In such countries as the United States, the balance is between adopting regulations for firms operating abroad that are consistent with regulations for national firms, while not putting its own firms at a competitive disadvantage with those from other countries. Battles over regulations affecting the operations of TNCs therefore are, and will continue to be, a standard feature of both home and host country politics.

SPIN-OFFS RESULTING FROM BARGAINING

The results of firm-state bargaining have themselves caused changes in international business and politics. These changes are only beginning to be perceived because many third-world nations have only begun pursuing development objectives that are both nationalistic and comprehensive. Furthermore, the uproar surrounding certain bargaining situations, especially those involving the nationalization during the 1970s of raw material properties owned by foreign firms, has sometimes seriously clouded understanding. Three areas in which spin-offs from the bargaining process are currently visible are: (1) the way in which bargaining between firms and host countries now takes place; (2) the emergence of a new pattern of international stratification that corresponds to outcomes of the bargaining process; and (3) the evolution of an international order based less on economic or political principles than commonalties of objective economic and political interests.

NEW BARGAINING CONDUCT

The conduct of both firms and nations has undergone considerable change as a result of the added complexity of bargaining. Firms increasingly seek to identify mutualities between their business objectives and development objectives of host countries, or they are not coming to the bargaining table at all. Similarly, nations are more systematically relating the terms of specific business arrangements to longer term national objectives.

Although firms do not hesitate to push to obtain the best possible terms for an investment, considerable care is now exercised to assure that corporate objectives are not at variance with long-term national goals. This makes sound business sense, since it reduces chances of interrupted operations once an investment is in place.

The uncertainties of operating in situations in which politics and economics can be extremely volatile have resulted in attempts to develop flexible business arrangements that can survive not only changes in ministers and production declines, but also revolutions and massive currency devaluations. When the Peruvian military moved to establish a nationalistic and socialist regime in 1968, a number of foreign firms reacted by removing substantial assets and attempting to close down operations where possible. Those that remained, willingly or unwillingly, learned with the passage of time that it was possible to do business with the new regime, however different it was from its predecessor, and turned their efforts to building longer-term arrangements.[58]

This and similar lessons have not been lost on firms faced with questions of how to deal with dramatically altered circumstances in Latin American nations and elsewhere. "Wait and see" and "build new bridges" are the usual current rules of thumb rather than "write off losses and run." In part, this is based on a desire to minimize losses and in part on a greater understanding of circumstances in host countries by both subsidiary and home office managers.

Nations have also adopted new bargaining practices. Possible arrangements are now often reviewed by a variety of national boards before both discussion with foreign firms and approval by the relevant national authority.[59] These review boards are staffed by professionals with both practical experience and advanced training in planning, finance, law, and economics. When expertise is lacking, outside consultants can be hired or provided by international organizations, such as the U.N. Development Program. Communication among relevant government bodies has also been improved, with standard procedures developed for telephone and telex links, which allow prompt consideration of alternatives, access to relevant data, and confirmation of the status of negotiations. Firms have also improved their bargaining skills. Past firm failures have frequently been due to an inability to understand fully criteria used by host country officials who evaluated their investment proposals. In part, this derived from heavy reliance on engineers and lawyers as negotiators. Improvements have resulted from including on negotiating teams individuals with a mastery of the business, economic, and political data relevant to host country officials and prior political risk assessment.

The stereotype of inexperienced teams of representatives of third-world countries confronted with insensitive negotiators dispatched by home offices of TNCs, backed up by instantaneous telex ties to superiors and massive data banks, has been replaced by a negotiating process in which skills and resources are more suited to the task of setting terms that allow the parties to pursue their joint and separate interests.[60]

A NEW PATTERN OF INTERNATIONAL STRATIFICATION

Outcomes from bargaining between host nations and TNCs have resulted in a pattern of business activity in which some nations are heavily involved with foreign firms and others have worked out few business arrangements other than importing consumer goods and exporting small quantities of traditional raw materials. As discussed in Chapter 1, twenty-six developed countries are most central to TNC operations, a dozen or so third-world nations are of some importance, and the remainder—nearly one hundred nations—are of importance in only special circumstances.[61]

This pattern reflects a division among third-world nations that poses a dilemma for officials in the home countries of many TNCs.

A small number of third-world nations—some of the "newly industrialized countries" previously mentioned, plus some oil-producing
nations—are developing relatively strong, diversified economies and
being incorporated into the core of the world's economy. The dilemma is that while this promises increased trade as well as greater
coincidence of interest between these nations and the industrial
world, a corresponding fear exists that these nations will pose a
challenge for the economies of industrial nations that will necessi-
tate difficult economic adjustments, perhaps requiring a political
will that may be difficult to forge.

While posing a dilemma for officials of developed nations, this
division also reflects the relatively weak position of the remaining
approximately one hundred nations. These one hundred relatively
marginal nations are firmly tied to the international capitalist economic system, while they are not diversifying and growing with a
speed equal to the new industrial countries. They are tied primarily
through debts owed to foreign banks and international lending agencies that totaled over $828 billion in 1984,[62] and through the mate-
rial standard of living of the elite groups that dominate their
national politics. Immediate prospects for development within the
existing structure of the international system are dim due to economic and political obstacles to self-generated growth and lack of
resources or markets attractive to international business. Most of
these nations do earn foreign exchange by exporting one or more
commodities, but the lack of diversification of their economic base
makes them vulnerable to periodic fluctuations in world markets so
that development planning becomes an exercise in hoping and bor-
rowing.

Increasingly complex bargaining between firms and host governments has put these poor third-world nations (sometimes called
fourth-world nations) at a disadvantage. Their abilities to evaluate
alternatives, monitor the progress of existing arrangements, or to
generate resources needed to share risks and responsibilities with
foreign firms are as limited as their short-term development potential. In a sense, the complexities of working out international business arrangements have exacerbated a sink-or-swim situation for
third-world nations. Countries with substantial resources, such as
Brazil, Mexico, and Venezuela, are of sufficient economic interest to
other nations and foreign firms that they, albeit with difficulty, will
be able to work out arrangements that further promote their national development and greater centrality in the international order.

147

Poorer nations that lack resources or markets will be hard pressed to attract beneficial business arrangements and will become further marginalized in the international order.

Thus, the outcomes of increasingly complex bargaining between firms and nations help to strengthen the positions of a few resource- and market-rich third-world nations, but further weaken the position of the remainder. The result is a pattern of international stratification comprised of a first world of industrialized capitalist nations, a second world of less industrialized socialist nations, a third world of new industrialized countries, and a fourth, semi-developed world of marginal interest to TNCs.

TNCS AND THE EVOLVING
INTERNATIONAL ECONOMIC ORDER

A major feature of the 1970s was the weakening of U.S. domination of the international capitalist economic order.[63] The reconstruction and resurgence of the economies of Western European nations and Japan, as well as the leverage exercised by the OPEC countries, have led to increased sharing of power among a number of economic actors. Transnational corporations, in addition to nations, have exercised considerable power over international markets and been an important factor in this sharing of power.

The weakening of U.S. domination was accompanied, in the early 1970s, by a global petroleum and commodities boom. While oil-producing third-world nations were major economic beneficiaries, other third-world nations benefitted from the boom only until a decline in commodity prices occurred in 1975. This brief boom period sparked a third-world nationalist movement for the creation of a New International Economic Order (NIEO). This new order was to reduce inequities both within and between nations and to advance the overall development process of third-world nations. However noble the objectives of this plan, substantial consensus on major issues was short lived even among third-world nations. By the late 1970s, hopes for the creation of such an international order had dimmed,[64] and by the mid-1980s, with continuing declines in the prices of all commodities, including petroleum, developing nations were looking inward to solve problems of development.

Still, a new international economic order has emerged, not fueled by third-world nationalism, but by the economic interests of transnational actors. To a large extent, the new order can be described by the pattern of international stratification previously discussed. The core of the new order is the developed industrialized nations, especially the seven largest national competitive market economies—the United States, Japan, West Germany, the United Kingdom, France, Canada, and Italy. Rather than accepting the post-World War II hegemony of the United States (when it accounted for more than 50 percent of the global product), substantial power sharing and coordination are now required of these nations.

Among developing nations, newly industrialized nations, such as Brazil, Mexico, South Korea, Hong Kong, and Taiwan, are becoming more central to the economic order. The mass of more than one hundred relatively poor nations remains marginal.

Within this order, TNCs continue to be involved in working out business arrangements, but their activities take into account evolving goals for nations and firms and new guidelines for doing business. The bases for the international economic order are the economic and political interests of the nations and firms involved. These bases are new because the order is less shaped by the hegemony of single powers. As in the U.S.-dominated international economic order, TNCs are well suited for turning economic opportunities to their own advantage and reinforcing the basic structure of the original system. In the near term, their bargaining with nations will likely work to facilitate economic cooperation between industrialized nations of the North, the newly industrialized nations of the South, and, to a lesser extent, the more marginal countries with less dynamic economies. The bargains reached between firms and nations will be an important and flexible glue for an evolving order based on the economic and political interests of a varied set of actors.

NOTES

1. For histories of early natural resources investments, see Theodore H. Moran, *Multinational Corporations and the Politics of Dependence: Copper in Chile* (Princeton: Princeton University Press, 1974); Franklin Tugwell, *The Politics of Oil in Venezuela* (Stanford: Stanford University Press, 1975); and Norman Girvan, "Making the Rules of the Game: Country–Company Contracts in the Bauxite Industry," *Social and Economic Studies* 20, no. 4 (Dec. 1971): 378–499.

2. The interaction, resulting in changed investment terms and derived from the host country's need for more revenues and the development of its bargaining skills, has been called "the obsolescing bargain" by Raymond

Vernon in *Sovereignty at Bay: The Multinational Spread of U.S. Enterprises* (New York: Basic Books, 1971), pp. 46–59.

3. Mira Wilkens's two books provide a comprehensive study of U.S.-controlled multinational business; they are *The Emergence of Multinational Enterprise* (Cambridge: Harvard University Press, 1970); and *The Maturing of Multinational Enterprise* (Cambridge: Harvard University Press, 1974).

4. Douglas C. Bennett and Kenneth E. Sharpe, *Transnational Corporations versus the State: Political Economy of the Mexican Auto Industry* (Princeton: Princeton University Press, 1985).

5. Karl Epstein and K. R. V. Miro, "Impact on Developing Nations of Restrictive Business Practice of Transnational Corporations in the Electrical Equipment Industry: A Case Study of Brazil" (New York: United Nations, 1977).

6. The dominant explanation for manufacturing firms going abroad to protect markets serviced by exports is Raymond Vernon's product cycle theory, described in his "International Investment and International Trade in the Product Cycle," *Quarterly Journal of Economics* 80 (May 1966): 190–207.

7. Peter Drucker, "Multinationals and Developing Countries: Myths and Realities," *Foreign Affairs* 53, no. 1 (Oct. 1979): 122.

8. United Nations Centre on Transnational Corporations, *An Update,* p. 13.

9. Organization for Economic Cooperation and Development, *External Debt of Developing Countries* (Paris: OECD, 1982), p. 7.

10. International Monetary Fund, *Balance of Payments Yearbook* (Washington, D.C.: IMF 1984).

11. International Monetary Fund, "Aspects of the International Banking Safety Net," Occasional Paper no. 17, Washington, D.C., Mar. 1983, p. 10.

12. While state participation in European firms was most prevalent in extractive industries (see C. Fred Bergsten, Thomas Horst, and Theodore H. Moran, *American Multinationals and American Interests* [Washington, D.C.: Brookings Institution, 1978], chap. 11]), multinational manufacturing companies, such as British Leyland (U.K.), FIAT (Italy), Pegaso (Spain), and Peugeot (France), also have significant state participation.

13. See Alfred C. Stepan, *The State and Society: Peru in Contemporary Perspective* (Princeton: Princeton University Press, 1978), especially pp. 263–71 for a discussion of the making of Peruvian petroleum policy.

14. See Theodore H. Moran, "Transnational Strategies of Protection and Defense by Multinational Corporations," *International Organization* 27, no. 2 (Spring, 1973).

15. Eduardo White, *Measures Strengthening the Negotiating Capacity of Governments in Their Relations with Transnational Corporations: Joint Ventures among Firms in L.A.* (New York: U.N. Centre on Transnational Corporations, 1983).

16. Ibid., p. 32.

17. Trends in the renegotiation of contracts between TNCs and host countries are discussed in "Transnational Corporations in World Development: A Reexamination," pp. 114–20; and *3d Survey,* pp. 238–72 (chap. 4).

18. For a discussion of how poor nations can gain autonomy by controlling their international economic relationships using the Venezuelan oil industry as a case, see Franklin Tugwell, "Petroleum Policy in Venezuela: Lessons in the Politics of Dependence Management," *Studies in Comparative International Development 9,* no. 1 (Spring 1974).

19. Vernon, op. cit.

20. See David N. Smith and Lewis T. Wells, Jr., *Negotiating Third-World Mineral Agreements* (Cambridge, Mass.: Ballinger, 1975), chap. 1.

21. These issues are discussed in a generally descriptive fashion in Sidney M. Robbins and Robert B. Stobaugh, *Money in the Multinational Enterprise* (New York: Basic Books, 1973). They are also discussed with particular concern for host country regulators in Constantine Vaitsos, *Inter-Country Income Distribution and Transnational Enterprises* (Oxford: Clarendon Press, 1974).

22. Social prices (sometimes known as "shadow prices") measure the scarcity value or opportunity cost to society of the components of a particular project. Social cost–benefit analysis, the methodology of using social costs, is described in Michael Roemer and J. Stern, *The Appraisal of Development Projects* (New York: Praeger, 1975).

23. For an interesting discussion of the impact of transfer pricing on developing nations, see United Nations Conference on Trade and Development Secretariat, *in* "Dominant Positions of Market Power of Transnational Corporations: Use of the Transfer Pricing Mechanism," (New York: United Nations, 1977).

24. Because of these and other difficulties, host country revenues are often fixed to production or sales figures as well as profit. Frustration with monitoring TNC production and profit played an important part in third-world nations' nationalizations of mineral companies and consequently the use of service and management contracts. See Theodore H. Moran, "The Impact of U.S. Direct Investment on Latin American Relations," (Washington, D.C.: Commission on U.S.–Latin American Relations, 1975) for a discussion of these issues.

25. Home country forces have also affected the division of profits in recent years. Concern about tax evasion or avoidance by TNCs has induced a number of home countries to adopt measures aimed at curbing the use of tax havens; at limiting business expense allowances, foreign tax credits, foreign business losses; monitoring transfer pricing; and taxing worldwide, rather than local profits.

26. See Moran, op. cit., chap. 3–5, for a discussion of this episode.

27. See Bergsten, Horst, and Moran, op. cit., pp. 134–36 for examples.

28. An example in the Venezuelan oil industry can be calculated from data in Appendix A in Tugwell, op. cit. Venezuela's share of oil profits increased from 16 percent in the early 1920s to nearly 60 percent in the late

1940s to 90 percent by the time the industry was nationalized in 1976. Despite this, industry profits as a percentage of invested capital increased during the life of the investment and accelerated during the 1970s.

29. *Wall Street Journal*, March 12, 1979, 6.

30. Reported in E. J. Cardenas, "New Characteristics of the Juridical Framework of the Exploitation of Natural Resources in the Latin American Context," United Nations Center on Transnational Corporations, 1977, photocopy.

31. Ibid.

32. Nestlé's decision is described in its 1979 *Annual Report*, Nestlé 1979. The nationalizations of Aramco by Saudi Arabia in 1975 and of Texaco's and Exxon's affiliates in Venezuela in the same year were both accompanied by host countries offering management and service contracts to former TNC equity holders.

33. The essays in William Glade, ed., *State Shrinking: A Comparative Inquiry into Privatization* (Austin: University of Texas, 1985), demonstrate that state participation in Latin American economies has occurred largely in situations where important sources of production or employment were endangered. State participation in Latin American economies grew in the 1960s and 1970s from private sector failure rather than from public sector desire for control. In the wake of the debt crisis, most Latin American governments are searching for ways to stimulate their private sectors and restabilize and dynamize their economies.

34. Described by Peter Evans in *Dependent Development: The Alliance of Multinational, State, and Local Capital in Brazil* (Princeton: Princeton University Press, 1978).

35. *Annual Report*, Massey Ferguson Ltd., 1972.

36. *Boletin sobre inversiones y empresas latino-americanas: INTAL (BIEL)*, no. 2 (Oct. 1978): 4.

37. *BIEL*, no. 1 (Sept. 1978): 2.

38. David A. Heenan and Warren J. Keegan, "The Rise of Third-World Multinationals," *Harvard Business Review* 57, no. 1 (Jan.–Feb. 1979): 101–9. See also Rachelle L. Cherol and José Nuñez del Arco, "Andean Multinational Enterprises: A New Approach to Multinational Investment in the Andean Group." *Journal of Common Market Studies* 21, no. 4, June 1983, pp 409–28. and Eduardo White, *Joint Ventures Among Firms in Latin America* (esp. section 4, The Role of Latin American Joint Ventures and Their Power Relations with TNCs).

39. Reported in *Latin America Economic Report* 6, no. 50 (Dec. 22, 1978): 399.

40. Heenan and Keegan, op. cit.

41. For example, after dropping out of the Andean pact in 1976, Chile has enacted new legislation giving foreign firms access to industries previously proscribed under national legislation. Peru, which after 1968 developed laws regulating foreign investment that were more restrictive than Andean legislation, revised much of this legislation in light of its changed economic and political circumstances.

42. United Nations, *Transnational Corporations in World Development: Third Survey* (New York: United Nations, 1983), p. 6.

43. Ibid.

44. Caterpillar Tractor Company, *A Code of Worldwide Business Conduct* (Peoria, Ill.: Caterpillar Tractor Company, Oct. 1974. Organization for Economic Cooperation and Development, "Declaration by the Government of OECD Member Countries and Decisions of the OECD Council on Guidelines for Multinational Enterprises, National Treatment, International Investment Incentives and Disincentives, and Consultation Procedures. (Paris: OECD, 1976). Also see *OECD Observer*, July 1976, p. 9.

45. United Nations Commission on Transnational Corporations, "Transnational Corporations: Code of Conduct," formulations by the chairman, Dec. 1978, paragraphs 10–14.

46. Jack Zwick and Richard G. Goeltz, "U.S. Banks Are Making Foreign Policy," *New York Times*, Mar. 18, 1979, D16.

47. See *Business Week*'s Mar. 12, 1979 discussion of the multinationals, in their special issue on the decline of U.S. power, especially p. 76, "How the Multinationals Are Reined in."

48. Discussed, for example, in *Wall Street Journal*, Mar. 12, 1979, 6.

49. The Company, "Confidential Memorandum on 'Ethical Standards'", Oct. 1980, pp. 2–3.

50. Discussed in Miguel S. Wionczek, "La Reacción norteamericana ante el tratado común a los capitales extranjeros en el grupo andino," *Comercio exterior*, May 1971, 406–8.

51. Current Council of the Americas activities are reported in its *Annual Report* and the monthly newsletter of its present parent organization, the Americas Society.

52. Michael E. Porter, *Competitive Strategy: Techniques for Analyzing Industries and Competitors* (New York: Free Press, 1980), p. 293.

53. See Lester B. Pearson's report to the World Bank published as *Partners in Development* (New York: Praeger, 1969). This report recommended a 1-percent transfer of the gross national product of developed nations to developing nations through private investments, loads, and grants by 1975 and official development assistance equal to 0.7 percent of GNP by 1980 (p. 152).

54. For a general analysis of host country efforts at cooperation, see Fernando Fajnzylber, "Las Empresas transnacionales y el "collective self-reliance," *Trimestre Economico* 43, no. 172 (Oct.–Dec. 1976): 879–921.

55. A summary of host country legislation is provided in *National Legislation and Regulations Relating to Transnational Corporations* (New York: U.N. Center on Transnational Corporations, 1978).

56. *Business Week*, Mar. 12, 1979, 76. See also Lars Schoultz's *Human Rights and U.S. Policy toward Latin America* (Princeton: Princeton University Press, 1981), pp. 88–90.

57. *Latin America Economic Report* 8, No. 11 (Mar. 16, 1979): 84.

58. Reported in Shane Hunt, "Direct Foreign Investment in Peru: New Rules for Old Game," in Abraham F. Lowenthal, ed., *The Peruvian Experi-*

ment: Continuity and Change under a Military Regime (Princeton: Princeton University Press, 1975).

59. For a summary of national review processes, see United Nations Centre on Transnational Corporations, *National Legislation and Regulations Relating to Transnational Corporations.* (New York: United Nations, various years).

60. Improvements in organizing for negotiation are described in chap. 6 of Smith and Wells, Jr., *Negotiating Third-World Mineral Agreements.*

61. Data from United Nations Centre on Transnational Corporations, *Transnational Corporations in World Development: Third Survey,* (New York: United Nations, 1983). Also found in United States Department of Commerce, *International Direct Investment* (Washington, D.C.: U.S. International Trade Administration, Aug. 1984), p. 8.

62. International Monetary Fund, *World Economic Outlook: 1985* (Washinton, D.C.: IMF, 1985).

63. For a critical analysis of literature on the dynamics of the erosion of hegemonic control of the international capitalist economic order, see Arthur A. Stein, "The Hegemon's Dilemma: Great Britain, the United States, and the International Economic Order," *International Organization* 38, no. 2 (Spring 1984); 355–86.

64. For an excellent concise summary of third-world demands for a New International Economic Order, see Donald J. Puchala, ed., *Issues before the 35th General Assembly of the United Nations, 1980–1981* (New York: U.N. Association of the United States, 1980), pp. 73–104; as well as Geoffrey Barraclough's provocative articles "Waiting for the New Order," *New York Review of Books,* Oct. 26, 1978; and "The Struggle for the Third World," *New York Review of Books,* Nov. 9, 1978.

6:
The Injuries
of
Marginality

Both small third-world nations and giant TNCs sustain injuries because of the marginality of their TNC operations. If outside the main focus of TNC activity, small nations lose development opportunities and compete less effectively in the global industries in which TNCs are at the cutting edge. Giant firms, unable to fine tune their operations to small-nation business environments, lose opportunities for market expansion as well as additional loci for global sourcing and international integration of production.

The injuries of marginality for small third-world nations are more obvious than those for giant firms. Detrimental terms of trade for primary products, international commercial banks reluctant to grant additional credit, crushing interest and fees on existing debt, and the specter of worldwide protectionism have caused opinion leaders in both developing and industrialized nations to suggest, in the words of a *Wall Street Journal* editorial, "Foreign direct investment constitutes the ideal solution for debtor nations . . . it generates well-paying jobs, new technologies, and a flow of fresh capital."[1] To date, however, such urgings have not been reflected in increased investment flows.[2] With few exceptions, small third-world nations worldwide remain marginal to TNC operations.

Giant firms also sustain injuries from the marginality of their operations in small third-world nations. As suggested by the discussion in Chapter 2 of subsidiaries of four firms that flourished in the difficult business environments of Chile and Peru in 1973, additional growth and earnings can be realized if giant firms adapt their practices to small-nation business conditions without exhausting their scarcest resource—managerial time.

While neither small nations nor giant firms can easily redress these injuries, with effort, fewer opportunities need be lost. This concluding chapter suggests some steps that can be taken by both small nations and giant firms to reduce such marginality and its attendant injuries.

GIANT FIRMS AND THE INJURIES OF MARGINALITY

Transnational corporate managers have good reasons for focusing attention on the industrialized nations and a handful of developing countries, including Brazil. Furthermore, publicly owned U.S.-based firms have especially good reasons: Their share prices (affecting the cost of an unfriendly takeover) and business performance (affecting management evaluations and rewards) are heavily influenced by quarterly or even shorter term results. This makes managerial attention to the most unambiguous immediately productive elements of these firms essential and continuous.

However, such firms do pay for disregarding seemingly marginal concerns. For example, U.S. auto makers' focus on their apparently successful sales of large fuel-inefficient automobiles in the 1960s resulted in a costly scramble for survival and reorganization in the 1970s and 1980s. This was precipitated by foreign competitors' attention to the previously seemingly marginal concerns of fuel efficiency and quality control that resulted in huge inroads into U.S. firms' traditional markets. More dramatic damage to giant firms has resulted from the Hooker Chemical Company's marginal attention to the effects of dumping toxic chemicals in Love Canal and other sites; from A. H. Robbins's focus on the effectiveness of its contraceptive Dalkon shield and its marginal attention to the device's facilitation of uterine infection; and from Union Carbide's lack of safety and security controls in its Bhopal, India, and Institute, West Virginia, pesticide plants. All of these examples of inattention resulted in serious financial damage to the corporations involved. Finally, ITT's pressure on the staff of its Chilean subsidiary to manage firm–host country relations as effectively as had their counterparts in neighboring Peru, plus the company's marginal attention to these managers' involvement with anti-government forces during the 1970 to 1973 Popular Unity government of Salvador Allende, severely tainted that giant firm's reputation as a corporate citizen.

These are cases of massive corporate loss due to inattention to seemingly marginal concerns. In Chapter 2 it was reported that the home offices of firms in the study sample rejected more than twice as high a percentage of capital allocation requests from their Andean subsidiaries as from their Brazilian subsidiaries. Furthermore, these rejections took place despite high profitability of the Andean subsidiaries and recommendations from subsidiary managers. It was also noted that four firms whose home office staff had recent experience in the most difficult 1970 to 1973 Andean business environments found ways of bringing these subsidiaries to the attention of their home office colleagues, with resulting expanded operations. While the size of the earnings lost or gained by these acts was small within the context of these firms' overall operations, there was an economic impact in each case. Furthermore, where opportunities were foregone, one could say that the firms sustained injuries.

How can a firm be managed so that seemingly marginal concerns do not drive it into bankruptcy, as happened with the A. H. Robbins Company, and so that full earnings can be gained from all of its subsidiary activities? Findings from the previous chapters offer no magic solution. Devices for focusing home office decision makers on issues that are not central but may make a difference was an important concern of all top managers interviewed in the course of this research. The solutions firms have developed include special regional managers housed in the home office, corporate offices in charge of "international integration" who serve as ombudsmen identifying issues and raising them at headquarters, and innovative formats for reporting and reviewing subsidiary activity. The increasing complexity of the world of international business, however, poses a continuing challenge to managers of giant firms.

SMALL NATIONS AND THE INJURIES OF MARGINALITY

A greater challenge exists for public officials in small nations wishing to reap public benefit from involvement with TNCs. The desirability of working with these giant firms is always hotly debated, especially in Latin America.[3] Problems of negative impact on national balance of payments due to the importation of intermediate goods; overinvoicing and transfer pricing; and dividend, royalty, and interest payment remittances are routinely cited as economic dangers of small-nation involvement. On the other hand, a number of small- and medium-sized nations have, during the 1970s and 1980s, promoted extensive involvement with TNCs, while experiencing substantial economic growth. These countries include Malaysia,

Singapore, South Korea, and Taiwan. Their pattern of involvement with U.S. TNCs and their average annual GDP growth rates are presented in Table 6.1. These rates of increased foreign investment and GDP growth are among the highest in the world. During that same period, the five countries constituting the Andean group exhibited markedly less acceptance of direct foreign investment and much lower GDP growth; this is shown in Table 6.2.

Increases in TNC involvement among the four Southeast Asian countries, their rapid GDP growth, and the opposite pattern among the Andean countries suggest cause and effect. However, that is clearly not the case. Both sets of statistics are separately affected by a range of political and economic factors that make comparison difficult. Furthermore, differences between the politics, cultures, histories, resource endowments, and levels of development in the two sets of countries are so strong that cloning lessons or strategies from one region to another would be highly inappropriate. However, the dramatic growth in TNC investment in Malaysia, Singapore, South Korea, and Taiwan in the 1970s and early 1980s merits analysis. Some of the techniques officials used to make their nations central rather than marginal to a number of TNCs may be relevant for public policy in other small and midsized developing countries, such as those in the Andean group.[4]

The strategy followed by these four countries is derived from the key finding reported in Chapter 2—business opportunities are best presented to TNC managers in a manner that makes it clear that inordinate executive time will not be expended evaluating and managing a prospective project. This and three other elements of public policy were closely coordinated in Malaysia, Singapore, South Korea, and Taiwan to successfully generate the flows of foreign investment reported in Table 6.1. These elements are:

1. Analyzing evolving changes in the world's industrial structure, paying particular attention to industries with high-growth prospects and those in which the analyst's country has a comparative advantage or a historically strong position.
2. Developing an industrial development plan—including clear specification of priority industries for TNC involvement.
3. Upgrading local technology capacity to assure skilled labor for industries with TNC involvement and local technological sophistication to monitor, complement, and compete with TNCs.
4. Saving executive time by streamlining and centralizing foreign investment promotion, permissions, entry, and ongoing negotiations with the host country.

TABLE 6.1

U.S. Direct Foreign Investment[1]
and Gross Domestic Product (GDP) Growth:[2]
Malaysia, Singapore, South Korea, and Taiwan[3]

	U.S. Investment*			Average Annual GDP Growth	
	1966	1982	1982/1966	1965–1973	1973–1983
MALAYSIA	$57	$1031	18.01	6.7%	7.3%
SINGAPORE	30	1,803	60.10	13.0	8.2
SOUTH KOREA	42	817	19.45	10.0	7.3
TAIWAN	58	620	10.09	11.3	7.5

SOURCES:
1. U.S. Dept of Commerce, *International Direct Investment: Global Trends and U.S. Role* (Washington, D.C.: GPO, 1984), table 8.
2. World Bank, *World Bank Development Report 1985,* (New York: Oxford University Press, 1985), table 2.
3. Taiwan growth data from Council for Economic Planning and Development, Executive Yuan, *Taiwan Economic Statistics* (Taipei: Overall Planning Dept., 1985).

*Millions of U.S. dollars.

TABLE 6.2

U.S. Direct Foreign Investment[1]
and Gross Domestic Product (GDP) Growth:[2]
Bolivia,[3] Colombia, Ecuador,[3] Peru, and Venezuela

	U.S. Investment*			Average Annual GDP Growth	
	1966	1982	1982/1966	1965–1973	1973–1983
BOLIVIA	$82	$209	2.55	4.4%	1.5%
COLOMBIA	459	1,655	3.61	6.4	3.9
ECUADOR	40	366	9.15	7.2	5.2
PERU	651	2262	3.47	3.5	1.8
VENEZUELA	2,136	2,371	1.11	5.1	2.5

SOURCES:
1. U.S. Dept of Commerce, *International Direct Investment: Global Trends and U.S. Role* (Washington, D.C.: GPO, 1984), table 8.
2. World Bank, *World Bank Development Report 1985,* (New York: Oxford University Press, 1985), table 2.
3. Bolivia and Ecuador investment data from U.S. Dept. of Commerce, Bureau of Economic Analysis, unpublished data.

*Millions of U.S. dollars.

For example, beginning in the early 1970s, Malaysia, a leading producer of rubber, palm oil, tin, and timber, and a new oil and gas exporter, aimed to involve TNCs both in the development of re-source-based industries and in two new industries in which it antic-ipated a changing worldwide structure—electronics and automo-biles. In natural resource-based industries, Malaysia wished to in-crease its one-half of 1 percent of global manufactured rubber products to more closely approximate its 40-percent share of world natural rubber production. Malaysia also wished to establish facto-ries to transform its timber into semi-finished furniture for pro-jected growing North American and European home improvement markets and to process its palm oil and integrate this with chemical production used to produce soaps and perfumes. Malaysia had begun to produce tin plate for export.

In electronics, Malaysia developed plans that resulted in that industry becoming the country's largest by the early 1980s. By 1983, it was the largest exporter of semiconductors to the United States, and it had nearly one hundred electronics plants, mainly labor-intensive assembly operations located in planned export-oriented "industrial estates."[5] In addition, the Malaysian government planned to increase both local ownership and technological sophis-tication in this industry.

Local ownership was also a priority in Malaysia's automotive industry. A 70/30 joint venture was established between Heavy Industries of Malaysia (HICOM) and Mitsubishi to produce a car with initial local content of 40 percent.[6] In addition, the Malaysian government has signed a marketing agreement with a British firm and has sought British investors for local parts supply companies.

Clear in the behavior of the Malaysian government is its selec-tively interventionist role and its attempt to compensate for an uneven indigenous business base by targeting TNCs for involve-ment in industrial development. While the Malaysian Economic Development Board, its coordinating body, has not gone so far as Singapore's similarly named agency—which has established offices in Boston's and San Jose, California's high-technology areas to monitor emerging technology and seek new investors—Malaysia's board does seek specific prospective foreign investors for particular projects.

Technological upgrading is also part of Malaysia's strategy for attracting TNCs. While its focus has been on working with foreign firms to establish training programs to assure the skilled labor needed for TNC operations, its Southeast Asian neighbors have taken additional steps. South Korea has invested intensively in technology development. Nearly 1 percent of its GNP is spent on research and development, ranking it with such countries as Austria, Denmark, and Italy.[7] South Korean government and private-sector technology investment has now moved to the stage where four Korean electronic conglomerates—Samsung, Daewoo, Lucky-Gold Star, and Hyundai—have established subsidiaries in the United States, both to expand their own technological base and attract trained South Korean and Korean-American engineers to participate in their projects.[8] Singapore is also a heavy technology investor and stresses continual industrial modernization and skill training through government loans, grants, and training centers. Its domestic skills development has been so successful that local capital increased its share of Singapore manufacturing from 5.7 percent in 1978 to 31.9 percent in 1982.[9] Taiwan has linked technology to industry by locating high-level academic science and technology institutions in a science-based industrial park, as well as stressing training and industrial modernization.

The Malaysian approach to saving managerial time has been to establish a one-stop center to speed up processing foreign and domestic investment applications and business requests in its Malaysian Industrial Development Authority (MIDA). Organized on an industry basis since 1978, MIDA handles inquiries from prospective manufacturing investors, advises investors on feasibility and technicalities of locating projects in Malaysia, provides postinvestment follow-up advice, and maintains a registry of potential investors for the possible establishment of new projects. Similar agencies in the other Southeast Asian countries are South Korea's Foreign Investment Promotion Division of its Finance Ministry, Singapore's Economic Development Board, and Taiwan's Joint Industrial Investment Service Center.

The strategies of these Southeast Asian countries are extremely aggressive and competitive. To combat the injuries of marginality, they have taken stock of their places in the international economic system and launched campaigns to gain greater centrality, gambling that TNCs will provide them with scarce capital, technology, and marketing networks in exchange for providing skilled and disciplined labor, economic infrastructures attuned to their needs, and export platforms permitting free financial flows.

The practices of these four neighboring countries are sufficiently dissimilar that the idea of other developing nations precisely imitating them is out of the question. Their examples must be carefully filtered through local circumstances if other nations are to make progress on these fronts. Furthermore, outright rejection of decision 24 or other local schemes, such as that implied by Colombian ex-President Misael Pastrana Borrego's quip, "The Andean countries signed Decision 24, and all foreign capital went to Southeast Asia,"[10] is counterproductively simplistic.

Some observations can, however, be made regarding ANCOM's Decision 24 as an attempt to constructively involve TNCs in the development plans of its small and midsized nations. The objectives of ANCOM, summarized here, and in Chapter 2, resemble those of the Southeast Asian countries: (1) promote efficiency and self-sufficiency in traditional industries; (2) spur regional development through the use of economies of scale; (3) facilitate intraregional investment; (4) provide capital for investments contributing to regional integration; and (5) regulate the role of foreign investment in the development process.

The interviews with TNC managers and host country officials described in Chapter 2 revealed two crucial differences between the implementation of these objectives and the strategies used by the Southeast Asian countries. Curiously, despite widespread criticism of Decision 24, its provisions were not the issue. Subsidiary managers of TNCs in the Andean group generally felt that the clear mutuality of interest between their business objectives and their host country's development plans would result in few changes in their operations. These responses mirrored the reports of other studies carried out in the 1970s.[11] Managers expected little difficulty continuing operations in the Andean group, using appropriate technology or earning reasonable profits.

The two crucial differences were: (1) While capable of flexible interpretations of regulations, neither the Andean group nor its six member countries possessed the *administrative capacity* to streamline investment permissions and regulations so that TNC management time could be used effectively: (2) TNC regulation, stressed by Decision 24, is only one side of the coin employed by Southeast Asian countries. In addition to regulating TNCs, Southeast Asian countries *aggressively devised means to attract particular TNCs* to invest in their nations' economies.

The ANCOM countries lack of individual and collective administrative capacity led to both frustration and uncertainty in TNCs, especially in home offices. In the words of one TNC manager interviewed in 1981:

Behind our initial skepticism regarding the Andean group, we were hoping that it would develop new opportunities for our business. We found we could cope with the letter of Decision 24, but we were constantly frustrated by the changes in its interpretation and, more importantly, the endless inefficiency of host country officials implementing both the general provisions and their own national regulations. We are very disappointed in what we have seen so far.

(WASHINGTON, 1981)

There is no doubt that ANCOM was an attempt to strengthen the positions of small nations and to involve them in the world economy and to provide incentives for constructive TNC investment there. However, by failing to recognize that a lack of administrative capacity and aggressive promotion would limit constructive TNC involvement, the Andean group may have adopted a plan that was at best neutral in redressing the injuries of marginality.

Since home office perceptions that managerial time will be used effectively are crucial for expanding TNC activities in small nations, one would hope that steps might be taken both to compete forcefully for TNC involvement that facilitates national development objectives and to create effective and streamlined administrative capacity to monitor and advance that involvement. Whether or not such changes are possible in the Andean group or other marginal developing nations is, of course, another matter. In the final analysis, streamlined aggressive development planning depends on domestic politics effectively pursuing those objectives.

SOCIAL SCIENCE THEORY AND MARGINALITY

As discussed in Chapter 4, the neoclassical vision of instantaneous, centralized, and unitary decisions based on perfect knowledge of markets and alternatives for the firm, taking place in an environment of perfect competition, and rationally motivated to maximize profits so that shareholders' interests are satisfied bears little resemblance to the decision processes described above. Similarly, revisions of the neoclassical approach, suggesting that decisions in the firm are consensual rather than unitary, or that profit maximization does not fully reflect the decision criteria used by managers have not paid sufficient attention to the asymmetric relationship between headquarters and subsidiary in terms of power; the different values placed on earnings and executive time in evaluating different types of opportunities; managers' concern with advancing their own careers; and the complications posed for decision makers by oligopolistic competitors and the conflicting objectives of home and host country regulators.

These considerations were central to the decision processes examined in this study. Of particular importance were differences in the way home office managers reported handling capital allocation decisions involving a centrally important subsidiary (Brazil), compared with less important marginal subsidiaries (ANCOM). The size of the Brazilian operations made home office managers much more willing to invest time and energy adjusting to changes in the Brazilian business environment than in smaller Andean operations.

The immediate implication of this finding is that different conceptual models should be employed for considering decisions central to the operations of a firm than for those that are marginal. Neoclassical theory and its most widely discussed revisions implicitly focus attention on decision processes central to a firm's overall operations. Little concern is expressed for the great diversity of situations that are the daily fare of most firms, especially large complex ones, such as TNCs. The argument has been made that it is not necessary to discuss this diversity when developing theoretical understandings of economic processes because firms (in microeconomics) and economies (in macroeconomics), taken as a whole, behave "as if" unitary, equilibrated, homogenous processes were at work.[12]

While such a view may be useful for examining general trends in economic or social units, it leads to serious problems when it is important to be sensitive to deviations from the norm or to activities removed from the main thrust of corporate activity. The importance of such sensitivity is most evident when one considers lost opportunities. Firms continually evolve and change as their internal capacities develop and they respond to changes in environments in which they operate. A firm's direction of change is determined by the opportunities it seizes and develops. New opportunities can appear from unexpected sources. The capacity to take advantage of opportunities, be they in the form of capital allocation requests from subsidiaries or other initiatives, is critical to the healthy growth of a firm. Too many lost opportunities can weaken a firm's competitive position and imperil its very survival.

Viewing all decisions as if they were similar may simplify certain decision processes and conserve executive time in the short run but seriously undermines a firm's ability to identify and seize opportunities important for its future growth.

Too much attention to extraneous detail, on the other hand, can sap the creative power of a healthy enterprise. This was often suggested by home office managers interviewed for this study. They felt that it was more important to pay close attention to activities they were relatively certain would be important for their company's growth (for example, capital allocation requests from Brazil) than to items of less obvious import (for example, similar requests from ANCOM). Perhaps they were correct. Since those interviews were held, TNC activity in Brazil has continued to outpace that in AN-COM. However, the general point for firms is that a balance must be struck between an all-absorbing corporate focus and a too widely stretched net.

From the point of view of developing theories of decision making in the firm, the recognition of different decision processes for different types of decisions is important because firms change. Sensitivity to the direction of change is essential to understanding the firm as a dynamic entity. Equally important for theory building is the recognition that firms do many things and decision processes used to describe some activities are not useful in describing others. In the present study, decision processes pertaining to Brazil and ANCOM involved markedly different evaluations of the importance of earnings relative to the use of executive time. Understanding these differences helps illuminate TNC behavior in both business environments. If managers make correct decisions for their firms, this becomes important for understanding the bases of successful corporate practices; if judgements are incorrect, this becomes helpful for explaining where managers went wrong.

The diversity of corporate activity does, indeed, provide many opportunities for "going wrong." In masking the diversity of decision processes, unitary theory building prevents easy understanding of how a decision process has gone wrong—especially when it is in an area that was, at one time, of marginal concern to the firm in question. On the other hand, the message of this book is that there are also many overlooked opportunities for "going right." Both small nations and giant firms can adopt new strategies to redress the injuries of marginality and further the objectives both of corporate growth and national development.

NOTES

1. *Wall Street Journal,* Jan. 21, 1985, 18, in an editorial agreeing with recommendations by the IMF and Ottawa Summit that foreign investment be increased in the third world.

2. *Business Week,* Mar. 22, 1985, 155.

3. See, for example, Gabriel Misas, op. cit., and Instituto Colombiano de Comercio Exterior, *Capital extranjero, balanza de pagos y exportaciones,* (Bogota: Incomex, June 1983).

4. The section that follows draws on Ronald E. Müller, Arthur L. Domike, and Joseph Holtzman, *Trends in Foreign Investment in Developing Countries* (Washington, D.C.: Economic Development Group, 1985), photocopy.

5. *Business Week,* Aug. 6, 1985.

6. "Making a Malaysian Car," *Business Asia,* Feb. 18, 1983.

7. Kenneth Flamm, "Technology Policy in International Perspective," in *Policies for Industrial Growth in a Competitive World* (Washington, D.C.: Overseas Development Council, 1984).

8. "South Korea," *Financial Times Survey,* July 12, 1984.

9. Singapore Economic Development Board, cited in Müller, Domike, and Holtzman, op. cit., p. 48.

10. *Business Week,* Aug. 17, 1984, 42.

11. See "How Will Multinational Firms React to the Andean Pact's Decision 24?" *Inter-American Economic Affairs,* Autumn 1971; Michael Aho and Nuñez de Arco, "U.S. Direct Foreign Investment in Latin America, 1966–1976: An Empirical Analysis of the Impact of the Andean Code (Decision 24)," *Latin American Integration,* Apr. 1981, and Jürgen Riedel, "Attitude of the Federal Republic of Germany toward the Policies of Developing Countries regarding Foreign Investors," *Industry and Development,* no. 13 (1985).

12. The classic statement of this view is expressed in Milton Friedman's *Essays in Positive Economics* (Chicago: University of Chicago Press, 1953).

Bibliography

AHARONI, YAIR. *The Foreign Investment Decision Process.* Boston: Harvard Business School, 1966.

AHO, MICHAEL C., and JOSE NUÑEZ DEL ARCO. "U.S. Direct Foreign Investment in Latin America, 1966–1976: An Empirical Analysis of the Impact of the Andean Code (Decision 24)." *Latin American Integration,* Apr. 1981.

ANINAT, AUGUSTO, RICARDO FFRENCH–DAVIS, and PATRICIO LEIVA, "La Integracion andina en el nuevo escenario de los años ochenta." *Apuntes CIEPLAN,* no. 52 (Oct. 1984).

APTER, DAVID E., and LOUIS W. GOODMAN, ed. *The Multinational Corporation and Social Change.* New York: Praeger, 1976.

BAIN, JOE S. *Barriers to New Competition.* Cambridge: Harvard University Press, 1956.

BARNET, RICHARD J., and RONALD E. MULLER, *Global Reach.* New York: Simon & Schuster, 1979.

BARRACLOUGH, GEOFFREY. "Waiting for the New Order." *New York Review of Books,* 26, Oct. 1978.

———. "The Struggle for the Third World." *New York Review of Books,* 9, Nov. 1978.

BAUMOL, WILLIAM. *Business Behavior, Value, and Growth.* 2d ed. New York: Harcourt, Brace, & World, 1967.

BENNETT, DOUGLAS C., AND and KENNETH E. SHARPE, *Transnational Corporations versus the State: Political Economy of the Mexican Auto Industry.* Princeton: Princeton University Press, 1985.

BERENBEIM, RONALD E. *Operating Foreign Subsidiaries: How Independent Can They Be?* New York: Conference Board, 1983.

BERGSTEN, C. FRED, THOMAS HORST, and THEODORE H. MORAN, *American Multinationals and American Interests.* Washington, D.C.: Brookings Institution, 1978.

BERLE, ADOLPH A.; and GARDINER C. MEANS. *The Modern Corporation and Private Property.* New York: Macmillan, 1932.

BLANCHARD, OLIVER, and LAWRENCE SUMMERS. "Perspectives on High World Real Interest Rates." *Brookings Papers on Economic Activity,* no. 2, (1984): 273-324.

BLANK, STEPHEN, JOHN BASEK, STEPHEN J. KOBRIN, and JOSEPH LAPALOMBARA. *Assessing the Political Environment: An Emerging Function in International Companies.* Report no. 794. New York: Conference Board, 1980.

Boletin sobre inversiones y empresas latino-americanas: INTAL (BIEL), no. 1 (Sept. 1978): 2; and no. 2 (Oct. 1978): 4.

BOULDING, KENNETH E. "Implications for General Economics of More Realistic Theories of the Firm." *American Economic Review* 42, no. 2 (May 1952): 30–44.

Brazil em exame. São Paulo. Editora Abril: Sept. 1974.

BROEHL, WAYNE. *The International Basic Economy Corporation.* Washington, D. C.: National Planning Assoc., 1968.

BROOKE, MICHAEL Z., and H. LEE REMMERS. *The Strategy of Multinational Enterprise: Organization and Finance.* London: Longman, 1970.

Business Asia, "Making a Malaysian Car." 18 Feb. 1983.

Business Latin America, "Betancour Gets Serious about Proposals to Ease Foreign Investment Rules." 29 May 1985.

CARDENAS, E. J. "New Characteristics of the Juridical Framework of the Exploitation of Natural Resources in the Latin American Context." United Nations Center on Transnational Corporations, 1977. Photocopy.

Caterpillar Tractor Company. *A Code of Worldwide Business Conduct.* Peoria, Ill.: Caterpillar Tractor Company, Oct. 1974.

CHAMBERLIN, EDWARD H. *The Theory of Monopolistic Competition.* Cambridge: Harvard University Press, 1933.

CHEROL, RACHELLE L., and JOSE NUÑEZ DEL ARCO. "Andean Multinational Enterprises: A New Approach to Multinational Investment in the Andean Group." *Journal of Common Market Studies* 21, no. 4, June 1983, pp. 409-28.

CONNER, JOHN M., and WILLARD F. MUELLER. *Market Power and Profitability of Multinational Corporations in Brazil and Mexico.* Washington, D.C.: GPO, 1977.

The Continental Group. *Annual Report for 1977.* New York: The Continental Group, 1978.

Council of the Americas. *Toward Realism in Western Hemisphere Relations.* New York: Council of the Americas, July 1980.

CREW, MICHAEL A. *Theory of the Firm.* New York: Longman, 1975.

CURHAN, JOAN P., WILLIAM DAVIDSON, and RAJAN SURI. *Tracing the Multinationals.* Cambridge, Mass.: Ballinger, 1977.

CYERT, RICHARD M., and JAMES G. MARCH. *A Behavioral Theory of the Firm.* Englewood Cliffs, N.J.: Prentice-Hall, 1963.

DOS SANTOS, TEOTONIO. "The Structure of Dependence." *American Economic Review* 60, no. 5 (1970): 235–46.

"Drastic New Strategies to Keep U.S. Multinationals Competitive." *Business Week*, 8 Oct. 1984, 168–72.

DRUCKER, PETER. "Multinationals and Developing Countries: Myths and Realities." *Foreign Affairs* 53, no. 1 (Oct. 1974): 121–34.

DUERR, MICHAEL G., and JOHN M. ROACH. *Organization and Control of International Relations.* New York: Conference Board, 1973.

EASTERLIN, RICHARD A. "Economic Growth." In David L. Sills, ed., *International Encyclopedia of the Social Sciences.* New York: Macmillan, 1968.

Economic Commission for Latin America and the Caribbean. "Preliminary Overview of the Latin American Economy during 1984." *Notas sobre la economía y el desarollo* 409, no. 10 (Jan. 1985).

EPSTEIN, KARL, and K. R. V. MIRO, *Impact on Developing Nations of Restrictive Business Practice of Transnational Corporations in the Electrical Equipment Industry: A Case Study of Brazil.* New York: United Nations, 1977.

EVANS, PETER. *Dependent Development: The Alliance of Multinational, State, and Local Capital in Brazil.* Princeton: Princeton University Press, 1978.

FAJNZYLBER, FERNANDO. "Las Empresas transnacionales y el "collective self-reliance." *Trimestre Economico* 43, no. 172 (Oct.–Dec. 1976): 879–921.

Financial Times Survey, "South Korea." 12, July 1984.

First National City Bank, "Brazil." New York: First National City Bank, 1974.

FLAMM, KENNETH. "Technology Policy in International Perspective." In *Policies for Industrial Growth in a Competitive World.* Washington, D.C.: Overseas Development Council, 1984.

FRIEDMAN, MILTON. *Essays in Positive Economics.* Chicago: University of Chicago Press, 1953.

GEREFFI, GARY: *The Pharmaceutical Industry and Dependency in the Third World.* Princeton: Princeton University Press, 1983.

GIRVAN, NORMAN, "Making the Rules of the Game: Country–Company Contracts in the Bauxite Industry." *Social and Economic Studies.* 20, no. 4 (Dec. 6, 1971): 378–449.

GLADE, WILLIAM, ed. *State Shrinking: A Comparative Inquiry into Privatization.* Austin: University of Texas, 1985.

GOODMAN, LOUIS W. "Prospects for Investment in the Andean Group." In Council of the Americas, *Andean Pact: Definition, Design, and Analysis.* New York: Council of the Americas, 1973.

―――. "The Decision Process in the Firm: Theoretical Underpinnings of How Power Is Exercised in Complex Organizations." New York: Wenner–Gren Foundation, 1980.

GORDON, ROBERT A. *Business Leadership in the Large Corporation.* Washington, D.C.: Brookings Institution, 1945.

Grace, W. R., and Company. Internal Documents.

HEENAN, DAVID A., and WARREN J. KEEGAN,. "The Rise of Third-World Multinationals." *Harvard Business Review* 57, no. 1 (Jan.–Feb. 1979): 101–9.

HENDERSON, JAMES, and RICHARD QUANDT. *Microeconomic Theory.* New York: McGraw-Hill, 1971.

HICKS, JOHN R. "Annual Survey of Economic Theory: The Theory of Monopoly." *Econometrics* 3, no. 1 (Feb. 1935): 8.

"How the Multinationals are Reined In." *Business Week,* 8. Oct. 1984, 168–72.

"How Will Multinational Firms React to the Andean Pact's Decision 24?" *Inter-American Economic Affairs,* Autumn 1971.

HUNT, SHANE. "Direct Foreign Investment in Peru: New Rules for Old Game." In Abraham F. Lowenthal, ed. *The Peruvian Experiment: Continuity and Change under a Military Regime.* Princeton: Princeton University Press, 1975.

IANNI, OCTAVIO. *A formacão do estado populista na america latina.* Rio de Janeiro: Editora Civilizacão Brazilien, 1975.

INGRAM, GEORGE M. *Expropriation of U.S. Property in South America.* New York: Praeger, 1974.

Instituto Colombiano de Comercio Exterior. *Capital extranjero, balanza de pagos y expantaciones.* Bogota: INCOMEX, June 1983.

INTAL. "The Andean Group: Fifteen Years Later." *Integracion latinoamericana,* Jan.–Feb., 1985.

Inter-American Development Bank. *Economic and Social Progress in Latin America, 1977 Report.* Washington, D.C.: IADB, 1977. Pp. 170–81, 391–404.

———. *Economic and Social Progress in Latin America, 1984 Report.* "Economic Integration in Latin America." Washington, D.C.: IADB, 1984.

International Bank for Reconstruction and Development (IBRD). *World Development Report, 1984.* Washington, D.C.: IBRD 1984.

———. *Balance of Payments Yearbook.* Washington, D.C., IBRD, 1984.

———. *World Economic Outlook: 1985.* Washington D.C., IBRD. 1985.

International Monetary Fund. "Aspects of the International Banking Safety Net." Occasional paper 17. Washington, D.C., Mar. 1983.

KINDLEBERGER, CHARLES. *Economic Development.* New York: McGraw-Hill, 1965.

———. *American Business Abroad.* New Haven: Yale University Press, 1969.

KNIGHT, FRANK H. *Risk, Uncertainty, and Profit.* Boston: Houghton Mifflin, 1921.

LALL, SANJAYA. "Less-Developed Countries and Private Foreign Direct Investment, A Review Article." *World Development* 2, nos. 4 & 5 (Apr.–May 1974): 43–48.

LITVAK, ISIAH A.; and CHRISTOPHER J. MAULE,. "Nationalism in the Caribbean Bauxite Industry." *International Affairs* 51 (June 1975): 43–59.

MACHLUP, FRITZ. "Theories of the Firm: Marginalist, Behavioral, Managerial." *American Economic Review* 57 (Mar. 1967): 1–33.

MANSFIELD, EDWIN. *Principles of Microeconomics.* New York: Norton, 1983.

MARRIS, ROBIN A. *The Economic Theory of "Managerial" Capitalism.* New York: Macmillan, 1964.

Massey Ferguson Ltd. *Annual Report,* 1972.

MIKESELL, RAYMOND, ed. *Foreign Investment in the Petroleum and Mineral Industries: Case Studies in Investor–Host Country Relations.* Baltimore: Johns Hopkins Press, 1971.

MISAS ARANGO GABRIEL, *Empresas Multinacionales y pacto andino.* Bogota: Oveja Negra, 1983.

MITTENDORF, J. WILLIAM. "Free Enterprise: Key to Latin American Economic Revival." *Current Policy,* no. 692. Washington, D.C.: United States Department of State, Feb. 22, 1985.

MORAN, THEODORE H. *Multinational Corporations and the Politics of Dependence: Copper in Chile.* Princeton: Princeton University Press, 1974.

————. "Transnational Strategies of Protection and Defense by Multinational Corporations." *International Organization* 27, no. 2 (Spring 1973).

————. "The Impact of U.S. Direct Investment on Latin American Relations." Washington, D.C.: Commission on U.S.–Latin American Relations, June 1974.

MORAWETZ, DAVID. *Integration among Developing Countries.* Cambridge: MIT Press, 1974.

MÜLLER, RONALD E., ARTHUR L. DOMIKE, and JOSEPH HOLTZMAN. *Trends in Foreign Investment in Developing Countries.* Washington, D.C.: Economic Development Group, 1985. Photocopy.

MUELLER, WILLARD F. *A Primer in Monopoly and Competition.* New York: Random House, 1970.

MYTELKA, LYNN K. *Regional Development in a Global Economy: The Multinational Corporation, Technology, and Andean Integration.* New Haven: Yale University Press, 1979.

NEWFARMER, RICHARD S. *Transnational Conglomerates and the Economics of Dependent Development.* Greenwich, Conn: JAI Press, 1980.

NEWFARMER, RICHARD S., and WILLARD F. MUELLER. *Multinational Corporations in Brazil and Mexico: Structural Sources of Econmic and Noneconomic Power.* Washington, D.C.: GPO, 1975.

Organization for Economic Cooperation and Development. "Declaration by the Governments of OECD Member Countries and Decisions of the OECD Council on Guidelines for Multinational Enterprises, National Treatment, International Investment Incentives and Disincentives, and Consultation Procedures." Paris: OECD, 1976.

————. *External Debt of Developing Countries.* Paris: OECD, 1982.

————. *Interfutures.* Paris: OECD, 1979.

————. *Investing in Developing Countries.* 4th rev. ed. Paris: OECD, Sept. 1978.

PEAR, ROBERT. "Corrupt Practices Dispute." *New York Times,* International Financial Survey, Feb. 8, 1981.

PEARSON, LESTER B. *Partners in Development.* New York: Praeger, 1969.

PENNAR, KAREN, JEFFREY RYSER, RONALD BUCHANAN, LYNN CURRY, and LAXMI NAKARNI. "Solving the Third World's Growth Crisis." *Business Week,* 12 Aug. 1985, 36–38.

PENROSE, EDITH T. *The Theory of the Growth of the Firm.* Oxford: Basil Blackwell, 1959.

POLK, JUDD. "The International Corporation." Hearings before the Subcommittee on Foreign Economic Policy of the Joint Economic Committee, Congress of the United States, 27–30 July 1970.

POLK, JUDD, and HOWARD V. PERLMUTTER. "Super-Giant Firms in the Future." *Wharton Quarterly* (Winter 1968).

PORTER, MICHAEL E. *Competitive Strategy: Techniques for Analyzing Industries and Competitors.* New York: Free Press, 1980.

PUCHALA, DONALD J., ed. *Issues before the 35th General Assembly of the United Nations, 1980–1981.* New York: U.N. Association of the United States, 1980.

RIEDEL, JÜRGEN. "Attitude of the Federal Republic of Germany toward the Policies of Developing Countries regarding Foreign Investors." *Industry and Development,* no. 13 (1985).

ROBBINS, SYDNEY M., and ROBERT B. STOBAUGH. *Money in the Multinational Enterprise.* New York: Basic Books, 1973.

ROBINSON, JOAN. *The Theory of Imperfect Competition.* London: Macmillan, 1933.

ROEMER, MICHAEL; and J. STERN. *The Appraisal of Development Projects.* New York: Praeger, 1975.

RUMMEL, R. J., and DAVID A. HEENAN. "How Multinationals Analyze Political Risk." *Harvard Business Review,* (Jan.–Feb. 1978), vol. 56, no. 1.

SCHELLING, THOMAS. *The Strategy of Conflict.* London: Oxford University Press, 1963.

SCHOULTZ, LARS. *Human Rights and U.S. Policy toward Latin America.* Princeton: Princeton University Press, 1981.

Security and Exchange Commission, Form 10-K; KMI Continental, Inc. Washington, D.C.: SEC, 1985.

SHUBIK, MARTIN. "A Curmudgeon's Guide to Microeconomics." *Journal of Economic Literature* 8 (June 1970).

SIGMUND, PAUL. *Multinationals in Latin America.* Madison: University of Wisconsin Press, 1980.

SIMON, HERBERT A. *Models of Men.* New York: Wiley, 1957.

SMITH, DAVID N.; and LEWIS T. WELLS, JR. *Negotiating Third-World Mineral Agreements.* Cambridge, Mass.: Ballinger, 1975.

SRAFFA, PIERO. "The Laws of Return under Competitive Conditions." *Economic Journal* 36, no. 144 (Dec. 1926): 335–50.

STEIN, ARTHUR A. "The Hegemon's Dilemma: Great Britain, the United States, and the International Economic Order." *International Organization* 38, no. 2 (Spring 1984).

STEPAN, ALFRED C. *The Military in Politics: Changing Patterns in Brazil.* Princeton: Princeton University Press, 1971.

———, ed. *Authoritarian Brazil: Origins, Policies, and Future.* New Haven: Yale University Press, 1973.

———, ed. *The State and Society: Peru in Comparative Perspective.* Princeton: Princeton University Press, 1978.

STIGLER, GEORGE. *The Theory of Price.* New York: Macmillan, 1961.

STOBAUGH, ROBERT B. "How to Analyze Foreign Investment Climates." *Harvard Business Review* 47, no. 5 (Sept.–Oct. 1969): 43–59.

TUCKER, STUART K. "Update: Costs to the United States of the Recession in Developing Countries." *Overseas Development Council,* working paper no. 10, Jan. 1986.

TUGWELL, FRANKLIN. *The Politics of Oil in Venezuela.* Stanford: Stanford University Press, 1975.

———. "Petroleum Policy in Venezuela: Lessons in the Politics of Dependence Management." *Studies in Comparative International Development* 9, no. 1 (Spring 1974).

TURNER, LOUIS, COLIN BRADFORD, and NEIL MCMULLEN. *The Newly Industrializing Countries, Trade and Adjustment.* London: George Allen & Unwin Ltd., 1983.

United Nations. *Economic Survey of Latin America and the Caribbean.* Vol. I. New York: United Nations, 1982.

———. *World Economic Survey 1985.* New York: United Nations, 1985.

United Nations Centre on Transnational Corporations. *National Legislation and Regulations Relating to Transnational Corporations,* Parts I–IV. New York: United Nations, 1978–83.

———. *Transnational Corporations in World Development: A Reexamination.* New York: United Nations, 1978.

———. *Transnational Corporations in World Development: An Update.* New York: United Nations, 1984.

———. *Transnational Corporations in World Development: Third Survey.* New York: United Nations, 1983.

United Nations Commission on Transnational Corporations. "Transnational Corporations: Code of Conduct." Formulations by the chairman. Dec. New York: United Nations, 1978.

United Nations Conference on Trade and Development Secretariat. "Dominant Positions of Market Power of Transnational Corporations: Use of the Transfer Pricing Mechanism." New York: United Nations, 1977.

United States Department of Commerce. *International Direct Investment: Global Trends and the U.S. Role.* Washington, D.C.: International Trade Administration, Aug. 1984.

United States Federal Trade Commission. *Report on International Electronic Equipment Cartels.* Washington, D.C.: GPO, 1948.

United States House of Representatives, Committee on Interstate and Foreign Commerce. *International Electrical Association: A Continuing Cartel.* Washington, D.C.: GPO, 1980.

VAITSOS, CONSTANTINE. *Intercountry Income Distribution and Transnational Enterprises.* Oxford: Clarendon Press, 1974.

VERNON, RAYMOND. "International Investment and International Trade in the Product Cycle." *Quarterly Journal of Economics* 80 (May 1966): 190–207.

———. *Sovereignty at Bay: The Multinational Spread of U.S. Enterprises.* New York: Basic Books, 1971.

———, and LOUIS T. WELLS, JR. *Manager in the International Economy.* Englewood Cliffs, N.J.: Prentice-Hall, 1981.

WALTERS, KENNETH D., and JOSEPH R. MONSEN. "State-Owned Business Abroad: New Competitive Threat." *Harvard Business Review* (Mar.–Apr. 1979) vol. 57, no. 2: 160–70.

WARDLAW, ANDREW B. *The Andean Integration Movement.* Washington, D.C.: U.S. Dept. of State, 1973.

WEINERT, RICHARD. "Why the Banks Did It." *Foreign Policy,* no. 30 (Spring 1978): 143–48.

WHITE, EDUARDO. *Evolution and Recent Trends in Host Developing Countries vis-à-vis TNCs.* Buenos Aires: Centro de Estudios Juridicos–Economicos Internationales, Dec. 1982.

———. *Measures Strengthening the Negotiating Capacity of Governments in Their Relations with Transnational Corporations: Joint Ventures among Firms in Latin America.* New York: United Nations Center on Transnational Corporations, 1983.

WILKENS, MIRA. *The Emergence of Multinational Enterprise.* Cambridge: Harvard University Press, 1970.

———. *The Maturing of Multinational Enterprise.* Cambridge: Harvard University Press, 1974.

WILLIAMSON, OLIVER E. *Economics of Discretionary Behavior: Managerial Objectives in a Theory of the Firm.* Chicago: Markham, 1967.

———. *Corporate Control and Business Behavior.* Englewood Cliffs, N.J.: Prentice-Hall, 1970.

WIONCZEK, MIGUEL S. "La Reacción norteamericana ante el trato comun a los capitales extranjeros en el grupo andino" *Comercio exterior* (June 1971): 27–30.

ZWICK, JACK, and RICHARD G. GOELTZ. "U.S. Banks Are Making Foreign Policy." *New York Times.* 18 Mar. 1979.

Index

Page numbers followed by "t" refer to tables; by "f", to figures.

IN MY PRAYERS WITH MY LEGS WIDE OPEN

IN MY PRAYERS WITH MY LEGS WIDE OPEN

JATANA ANITA WILLIAMS

ASTA PUBLICATIONS

Stockbridge, GA 30281
www.astapublications.com

Jatana Anita Williams
www.msthangwrites.com

Library of Congress Cataloging-in Publication Data
Williams, Jatana
In My Prayers With My Legs Wide Open/Jatana Williams
p. cm.
Includes index
ISBN: 1-934947-08-3
ISBN 13: 978-1-934947-08-1
LCCN: 2008925410

First Asta Publications trade paperback edition April 2008.

1. Urban-Fiction. 2. African-American Contemporary. 3. Relationships-Fiction. I. Title

Editor: Windy Goodloe
Cover Art: Gallery By DZINE
www.gallerybydzine.com
Cover Design:
Text and Composition: Asta Publications

All Scripture quotations are taken from the King James Version of the Bible.

Printed in the United States of America

I pray for healing and if healing is not in God's plan, then strength!

DEDICATION

With this book, I dedicate my heart to my four handsome sons; Devon, Ken, Joe and Markus. I couldn't have been blessed with better! God blessed me with each of you. You all have given me strength each and every day. Thank you for your patience so many nights. Thank you Markus for the peanut butter and jelly sandwiches!

To my mother—thank you for giving me my wonderful imagination and the attitude of moving forward. Thanks for showing me how to smile no matter what is going on in my life.

To my father—thank you for helping me make this dream come true and for standing by my side. You taught me not to take no for an answer and that I can do anything I put my mind to.

To my sister, Lessie—thank you for always being my number one fan. I bet you didn't know I knew!

To my sister, Amanda—thank you for holding on to God's Promises and reminding me of them.

To my brother, Big T-thanks for showing me how to be a go getter!

To my brother, Joe—thank you for telling me, "You can do it, Sissy!"

To my Papa—thank you for the talk in the rain under the gazebo! It changed my life! I have no regrets!

To my friend, Jason Stuckey—thank you for making me pick up the pen. I am free again!

Sid- thank you for telling me to "Keep my notebook close."

ACKNOWLEDGMENTS

The Lord- Without you, I can do nothing. Thank you for not denying me.

Derrick- My book is blessed by your gifted artwork.

Tania-Your talent is blessed by God. Keep trusting in him.

INTRO

Lord, I don't know why I GIVE INTO TEMPTATION? WHY DID YOU GIVE ME THESE DESIRES?

When it comes to matters of love and life, the heart can be the most deceitful device we use. Our hearts takes us to places we wish we had never journeyed; but, without struggle in our lives, we would not evolve. We would not have a testimony for the person behind us, next to us, and in front of us.

Most of us reach out to others and look for love during difficult situations. Physical love cannot replace the yearning many of us have inside for true love. These situations test whether or not someone truly cares. When it comes to the Lord, these situations are nothing but a grain of salt. Call on the Lord. And He will blow them away as such.

Try the Lord when no one else is listening. Call out to the Lord and put your trust in Him. The journey of life without faith can be trying but reliance on the Lord will make your journey ever so sweet. In My Prayers with My Legs Wide Open chronicles one woman's spiritual journey as she struggles with the desire to give into her flesh, love the man God has given to her, and let go of the people and the mistakes from her past.

CHAPTER ONE

"LORD, HELP ME. You said before I even say my prayers you will answer. HELP ME!"

I'm standing in the mirror wearing my Sunday best for what I feel is going to be my last time. The tears coming down my face are no longer made of saltwater but of blood. The face that I've been so proud of and quick to brag about is now bruised. I should've taken my ass straight to church and not to Mr. Dress Shop's crib. This is one time I needed to pass on getting to know a brotha better...

I'm sitting in this oversized burgundy sofa chair wearing a black lace corset, crotchless panties, lacey thigh highs, and a pair of hooker shoes from a Halloween costume from years ago. The clothes I wore to meet him are thrown around the hotel room as if a hurricane just hit. I was on my way to my church's weekly bible study meeting when he sent me a text to come see him tonight. Bible study is always held on Thursdays. For the last few weeks, I haven't missed once; and I wasn't planning on missing it tonight. I agreed to this last minute plan and told him I'd see him after nine. Usually when I meet up with a man, I'm already prepared. I'm already dressed in my seductive lingerie and leave straight from my house. Tonight, I had to stop off the freeway to change clothes in a gas station restroom. Good thing I left some of my 'sexies' in the trunk of my car from another meet and greet session. I never hook up with someone unless it's a Friday or Saturday night, but he said this was all he had open for weeks. I didn't want to pass up on the opportunity of getting to know a brotha better.

Hmm...looking around I have to say this is one of the most stylish hotel rooms I've been in recently. It has Asian color palettes with 1940's inspired cherry wood furniture and floor to ceiling windows. The city light shining through the windows makes the room luminous and gives it a romantic feeling. I guess reading all those damn home decorator magazines taught me a little something. His choice of rendezvous location proves to me that he's got good taste. Really the fact I'm here proves he has excellent taste. That's not a conceited statement; I just know I'm the shit! I can tell he took time preparing for my arrival. He's got a tea light and votive candle on each nightstand and the room is filled with the scent of jasmine. There's a bottle of Cabernet Sauvignon with two wines glasses on the table in the sitting area.

JATANA WILLIAMS

I look into the bathroom and admire his naked body. He stands in front of the Spanish marble sink with his dick rock hard, shaving and singing "PYT." This man can't hold a note to save his life but it doesn't matter. I didn't come here tonight to hold talent auditions. Hell, if I did, I'm not looking for that kinda talent. He notices me in the mirror staring at him and gives me a smile. A man with a nice smile and big lips is a natural aphrodisiac for me. His smile is what caught my attention in the first place...

It was Monday morning around 7:30. We were both waiting for our orders at the local coffee house. I saw him standing by the table of discounted coffee mugs texting on his cell phone. He looked up at me and there it was...a smile sent down from the Greek gods! I remember feeling a twitch between my legs when he did it. I stood straight and fixed my hair. I wondered if he noticed me foaming at the mouth over the pastries. I was talking myself out of buying a piece of lemon pound cake when he walked up behind me and told me to go ahead and have one. "I'll treat you," he said. That was how our conversation started.

I explained to him why I was on a diet and all about how my battle with being overweight had begun in my childhood. He explained to me why he always loved big women; he considers them to be sexy. He told me his mother raised him by herself and she was a big woman. I never considered myself to be big, but I rolled with it. I didn't want this to be our first and last conversation. When the guy behind the counter called out "J" we both walked up to grab the coffee cup. We laughed and stood in the way of others trying to get their orders as we exchanged phone numbers. He ended up walking me out to my car. We talked and sipped on our coffee. He told me he works for a marketing firm in their IT department. He does side work designing web sites for small black businesses. He has plans of going to Africa for six months to teach a school how to do computer programming. Not only was he sexy, but he was smart. I found him to be very interesting and became attracted to his personality as much as I was to his body. The conversation was so good before we knew it we had drank up our coffee and he was late to work...

He turns around to look at me, "I hope you like the scent of jasmine? I sprayed a little bit on the bed."

"Yeah, it smells good."

I'm rubbing my hand up and down my thighs. Besides trying to look sexy, I'm rubbing trying to remember his name. I always forget names. I never let on to men that I don't remember. It's better not to know a brotha's name then to get names mixed up. There's nothing worse then calling out the wrong name during an orgasm. I always give men nicknames according to how I met them. My name for him is Mr. Coffee. Of course, I don't tell the men this. Their nicknames are just for me to know. If people were to look at my cell phone address book it would trip them out. I have names like Mr. Gym Parking Lot, Mr. Grocery Store Bread Aisle, and Mr. Gas Pump. These men don't matter to me so why should I learn names anyway.

He looks back into the mirror and continues shaving. "Jasmine with JJ, together they stimulate my mind and you're sure to stimulate my body."

His comment sounds like some shit said in a Harlequin novel. But his effort to be romantic is cute and I make note of it. It actually reminds me of when I first met my husband Darius. He was so cute. Damn...speaking of my husband I said I wasn't going to do this again. I told myself the last time I cheated...was the last time, but here I am again and I can't wait for it! I'm feeling inpatient so I get out of the chair, walk into the bathroom, and stand behind him. He knows I'm up to something because his smile got bigger. I start stroking his dick and kissing him on his back. Mr. Coffee's feeling me because he can't stop flashing those pearly whites. I stand in front of him so I can kiss those luscious lips. I have to get on my tippy toes because he stands about 6'4 and I'm only 5'5.

His dark, smooth skin makes my mouth water. He reminds me of the fudge topping I put on my ice cream. I bet he tastes just as good. He's powerfully built and by the story in his eyes he's nothing to be played with. I better come with it or he might split me in half. I'll make sure I take my time and not get him too excited. I don't want him pulling my hair or smacking my ass too hard. Don't get me wrong, I like a good freak every now and then, but getting my ass whooped while trying to bust one is not on my To Do list. I wonder if I'm even gonna be able to handle this man. He looks like he's been in the desert for weeks without water. I know he's strong so I have to make sure I'm in control. I always have to be in control anyway. I can feel his body tensing up. I need to get him relaxed. Hmm... How can I take his mind where I want it to go? I take the razor out of his hand and place it on the sink. I wipe what's left of the shaving cream off of his face. I put one of the bath towels over the toilet seat.

"Sit down," I demand.

"Right here?" he asks.

I push him down on the toilet.

"Yeah, right here!"

I grab the condom from on top of the sink, unwrap it and place it on top of a wash cloth so I can have quick access. I'm not trying to be unprepared. That's what gets folks caught up. Trying to un-wrap these child proof wrappers is enough to make me say fuck it! But I have too much to lose by not protecting myself. 'Wrap it up' is my motto. I gained this motto from learning some tough ass life lessons. When I was younger all I cared about was feeling a raw dick. Butt-naked was my motto back then. Now, I know better.

I get on my knees and spread his legs apart. I take the tip of my tongue and run it up and down the shaft of his dick. I suck the head into my mouth then take it out just to tease him. I start stroking it with the palms of both hands. I look up at him, watching as he leans his head back and moans. Now, he's relaxed. Ooh, his moaning is exciting me! I feel the wetness from my pussy form a stream in between my thighs. I can't wait to feel him inside of me. I start sucking his dick. The harder I suck the more he moans and the more I get excited! I start sucking so damn good he can't do nothing but grab for shit in the air that don't even exist and smile big!

Mr. Coffee knocks over the complimentary toiletries and pulls the towels down from the rack behind his head. His smile is different from a few minutes ago. It's a smile of exhilaration and of pleasure. I take pride in knowing he's enjoying himself. It makes me want to please him more. I want to keep going until he cums. Suddenly, he grabs me by the shoulders.

"Get up!" He demands.

I'm confused.

"What?"

"Get up and sit on my dick!"

I quickly grab the condom and put it on him.

He laughs, "You makin' sure I don't give you nothin'!"

I respond with sassiness, "You don't know me and I don't know you."

"Well, babe. I hate to tell you, but you can catch shit in your mouth!

I make sure the condom is on good.

"Don't fuck up the moment!"

"Nah, I ain't doing that one. Do what you do, ma."

He shows off how strong he is by bending over and putting his hands around my waist. He pulls me up on top of him. I'm no small female, so this move turns me on! I'm riding his dick like he's a black stallion horse and I'm his jockey. I'm digging into his back with my nails and he's softly biting me on the neck and sucking my titties.

He yells, "Ride it, babe! Yeah, that's what I'm talkin' bout!"

I love when a man talks to me. Letting me know I'm handling my business. I want to take this to the next level of ecstasy. So, I tighten up my pussy muscles and rotate my waist like a belly dancer. That's too much for him to take.

"Ah shit, I'm cumin'!" He shouts.

He cums so hard. It's like a pipe busted! We sit in each other's arms silent. For a moment, I think about how much he reminds me of my husband Darius, but only for a moment. Feeling his dick throb makes me want some more. I'm ready for round two, but he still wants to sit here. I'm frustrated, so I get up and wash myself off. He's sitting on the toilet with his eyes closed and rubbing his hands through his thick, beautiful, salt-n-pepper dreads. I pull him by the arms.

"Let's take this to the bed."

"That sounds good. I'm ready for a nap."

A nap! Ah, hell no! I guess I'm gonna have to remind Mr. Coffee that I didn't get mine and that's the point of me bringing my ass here. Before I can say anything, he stands up, picks me up and carries me over to the bed. He's standing over me and his dick is hard again. I look up at him and wet my lips.

"Now, that's what I'm talkin' bout!"

Mr. Coffee walks over to his pants and pulls a handful of condoms out of the pocket. "I'm prepared!"

I give out a little laugh. "Damn, I guess so!"

He slowly puts the tip of his dick inside of me. That's all he puts in at first is the tip. He's teasing me. "This is pay back for earlier." He states while showing his beautiful smile.

Before I know it Mr. Coffee starts turning me out. He strokes my pussy in rhythm like he's on the dance floor. Damn, this man knows what he's doing! He's not just the average in and out brotha. He's making circular motions and moving his waist from side to side. He's hittin' the corners of my pussy I forgot I had! Now, I understand how women get caught up stalking men. If they're putting it down like this all the time, it's like giving crack heads one hit and then telling 'em to go away. It's not gonna happen like that. They're coming back until they get another hit. Shit, I knew he was going to be good, but I didn't know this damn good! It's so good I lost count of how many times we came. All I know is there's a sea of condoms on the floor.

"You gonna pick those up?" I ask him laughing.

He pulls out another condom. "Right after I hit it again."

"Ooh, go ahead and make me a crack FIEND!"

"What was that babe?"

"Nothing, do what you do!"

I wake up to find Mr. Coffee is gone. The bottle of wine is still sitting there and a cart with breakfast and a white carnation. I find a note on the table in the middle of the room. I get up and stumble over. My legs are still weak from last night. It's been a long time since a man has made my legs weak. I'm looking at what's on the cart trying to see if there's anything good. It was nice of him to make sure I ate. That must be part of his liking big girls—keep 'em big! Let me stop. How sweet. The note is sitting on a piece of lemon pound cake. Huh, I might have to remember his name. I pour myself a cup of coffee and read the note written on the hotel stationery.

Hey Jasmine,

I enjoyed last night. If we were not already married, I'd ask you to be my wife. That's how good it was! Holla atcha later!

Big J

Hmm...now he's gone to far with shit! Dude reminds me a lot of my husband, but not that much to be my husband! Hell, I can't see myself married to nobody but Darius; but because his dick was so damn good, I'm gonna have a hard time shaking thoughts of this brotha. He made my legs shake! Let me get my mind right. Mr. Coffee was just another piece for me. I can't be catching feelings for a man just because he laid the pipe right. I throw the note in a wastebasket and grab a piece of toast. I take a bite. It's hard and dry as hell with no damn butter!

"Must be white folks cookin' in this hotel!"

I throw the toast down and finish up my coffee. I walk into the bathroom and start running the shower. I stand in the mirror. "Damn, what's wrong with you? Look at yourself Jasmine James-Brooks!"

I've always had this fear of losing who I was once I got married; even though, I wasn't exactly sure who I was. So when I finally did jump the broom, I thought it was a good idea to hyphenate my last name. The idea of no longer being referred to as 'JJ' wasn't working for me. My dumb ass didn't know marrying somebody wasn't going to change what people have been calling me for years. JJ is my nickname from childhood and hearing it helps me keep it real. Just because I'm livin' the good life doesn't mean I have to change. Even if I wanted to I couldn't, regardless of what name I carry around. The scars and beauty marks of my past are what made me. Not a name.

Hell, it's easy to drop off a brotha's last name but hard to get rid of them bastards. Right now I'm not trippin' 'bout that. My life with Darius is sweet. We have our ups and downs, but we're good for each other. He shows me how folks with money live and I show him how to BYOB at a garden party. Ha ha, for those of you who don't know, a garden party is what rich white folks call a BBQ! Sometimes I forget I don't have to be ghetto about everything I do. Yeah, I'm not the best person in the world, but I'm not the worst either. Darius is not perfect. He has his little evil ways. But one thing I do know, he'd never put a hand on me or try to hurt me in any other way. Yeah, I make mistakes, but the Lord always forgives me and so does Darius.

The Lord already knows I'm hardheaded. I try to fix my wrongs by giving more then ten percent in tithes. I show up early to church for Sunday school and help clean up after service. I don't know what else I should be doing. I'm a good person, but I'm still young. Only old folks close to dying worry about their walk with God. At least I'm working on my walk with Him now and not waiting until I'm on my death bed. I still have time to get it right. I'm only thirty-eight years old.

I'm still trying to figure out what I want to do when I grow up. Darius is very supportive of me. He's put me in different courses and certificate programs over the years. I've never finished any of them, because in the middle I found out I didn't like none of them. My husband doesn't get upset. He makes real good money, so it's not as if he's trying to get me a job. When I'm not in class, I end up having too much time on my hands. I try to keep myself occupied with activities while my husband is gone on business trips; but the PTA isn't as exciting as forbidden sex in a five star hotel on a Friday night. I try to go to the gym a couple of times a month. All that does is give me more opportunities to meet other men. I get on a couple of machines and work up a sweat, but I have a short attention span. I end up standing by the water fountain collecting phone numbers. I used to be self-conscious about the scar on my neck and my kangaroo pouch stomach. I would go to the gym all covered up in sweats. Once I started reflecting on the things my grandma used to teach me and realized how fine in the face I am and that I have a stop traffic ass and thighs. Huh, nobody could tell me shit! Hell, I'm too damn fine for men to pass me by. They can't help but want to try and hit this at least once. So I don't have to explain how the gym is not the best place for me to go.

And I don't like hanging with a bunch of females, so girl's night out is not happening. Shit, I'm no longer a girl; I'm a grown ass woman. I don't have time to play on the playground. Anyway, females are too busy being in your business or trying to be in the bed with your man. I only have one close friend and she knows a lot of dirt on me. I never trip about her telling it, because her dirt is mud. There's a reason for only having one close friend. The fewer witnesses I have, the better.

I've also tried doing volunteer work for different shelters, but even that doesn't keep me from feeling lonely for a man's touch. My husband doesn't go on these trips often. He's not gone for weeks at a time. At the most, he's away from home four days; but those four days are so long, I can't stand it. I thank the Lord I'm not married to a military man. They're away from home too much. I have to get mine on the regular. I'd completely lose my mind if I had to wait for six months or longer. Then again, I wouldn't wait. I'd be doing the same thing I'm doing right now—taking care of getting me some dick. You see, my sexual desires overtake me on a daily. Having sex for me is just like eating breakfast everyday. I need it to get me going and it's the most important meal of the day. Look, I'm trying to fight these desires; but, so far, I'm losing the battle.

When I was a teenager, my grandma warned me, 'JJ, baby, when you hit your mid-thirties, you gonna get excited by looking at the shape of a lamp post!'

My grandma swore there was some crazy sexual curse put on all the women in our family. Supposedly it hits us when we reach our thirties. I used to laugh it off because she was known for her exaggerations. I'm sure if she was around today, she'd have some new crazy ass story to tell.

I wish grandma was around. I need someone to talk to about what's been going on with me. I'm having this uninvited battle between doing right and wrong. Between loving the man God has given me and not loving him.

I want to be faithful, and then again, I don't. I'm sure it has something to do with me going to church and studying the bible. That's why I waited so manyyears to start going to church faithfully. Don't trip, I went to church growing up, but nothing ever stuck. That's because I never wanted to have a conscious. Now that I'm getting one, everything looks and feels different. Being sexually promiscuous or, in layman's terms, a ho is starting to bother me, but I have this thing about fucking other man that excites me and I can't control it.

Don't get it twisted. My husband is a real good man. They're hard to find these days. He's also a good lover. Nobody can kiss me the way he does. Matter of fact, nobody can lick the kitty the way he does. When he's home, he definitely takes care of business. I love the hell outta my husband. I love who he is and what he stands for. The truth is, besides the Lord, my husband is the only other reason I keep it pushing everyday. Darius came into my life and brought stability and a comfortable lifestyle.

I know you're wondering why I just fucked Mr. Coffee if my life is so sweet with my husband. Hell, I don't know! Maybe you can tell me what's going on. Yeah, I've heard it all before from my girl about how my husband must not be fulfilling my needs. Yeah, I've watched Oprah, Montel, and even sat through ten minutes of Dr. Phil. What is the problem? None of these shows helped me to find out why I cheat on such a good man. I know I should find a way to figure this out, but I'll be damned if I go talk to some psychiatrist or therapist who don't know shit about us and tell all my business. I'm gonna have to do what my pastor always says and take it to the Lord.

CHAPTER TWO

So much for taking it to the Lord! It's Friday night and I'm in another hotel room with another fine ass brotha! This hotel is a step down from where I was last night, but it's not cheap. I made my usual move by sitting in the hotel room chair. I didn't bother with getting dressed up as much for this one. He'd probably be happy if I wore a potato sack. I did decide to put on a sexy red silk camisole and g-string. He walks over to the bed in a poetic motion and lays his fine body down.

"Hey, sexy, you ready for this good lovin' that's comin' your way?" he asks.

Ooh wee! He has the sexist voice I've ever heard. I thought nobody could top my husband's voice, but this man's voice is hypnotic! His voice is what made me take notice in the first place. If I can even call him a man...hmm...hell, he might be old enough to buy a beer. What is his damn name? Bobby, Robby... hmm something like that. Doesn't matter, like I said before, I'm not one to pass on the opportunity of getting to know a brotha better. I never know what tricks I can learn. I don't go out hunting for brothas. I meet them going about my own damn business just like I met Mr. Coffee. This dude right here was delivering some packages to my house yesterday when I heard his sexy voice. It reminded me of Barry White in the song "Secret Garden." Yeah, it was sexy like that. When I heard his voice I was upstairs using the bathroom. I cut my business short just so I could peek downstairs and see what he look like. I was glad he didn't look like Barry White, although Barry wasn't a bad looking brotha.

Okay, it's Bobby...hmm...fuck it. I can't remember his name right now. His nickname will be Mr. UPS. Yeah, that will work. Mr. UPS is short about 5'5, shorter than what I usually go for. I don't like looking a man straight in the eyes. That's too personal. Plus, I don't think short men have much to offer in the dick department. I remember in high school how all the girls used to think by looking at boys' height, shoe size, and how big their hands were would tell us how big their dicks were. I've slept with enough men to know you can't judge a book by its cover, but a short man I've never read before. I hope he proves the theory wrong, 'cuz I really need to bust one right now.

He has honey brown skin with big round midnight color eyes. His eyes are so big it seems he's always surprised by something. He has a sexy bald head, a bomb ass body with a strong ass. When he gets on top, I'm gonna grab tight and not let go! It's easy to tell I wasn't disappointed at what I saw yesterday. The more I stare at him the better he looks. I know what you're probably thinking—you about to sleep with the boy. Now, don't get self-righteous on a sistah! Don't act like you've never been tempted by the mailman, water deliveryman, or the guy who stocks groceries at the store. These men have muscles and they're sweaty!

Yeah, I said sweaty! Not that nasty funky sweat. I'm talking about the sensual running from the top of a bald head sweat. I'm talking about the kind of sweat that drips down your breasts while he's on top hittin' the pussy real good. It's the kind that smells like sugar water. Damn, sorry about that. Sometimes I get distracted when I think about how blessed women are with the variety of men the Lord has put on this earth. I mean who can blame me for admiring all the fine ass men walking around. Whatever your definition of fine is, you can't help yourself for taking notice.

Now, let me get back to what I was saying. Oh yeah, getting to know a brotha better. Well, I wasn't going to let his sexy ass get away. I ran back into the bathroom and took a bird bath. I'm not a nasty ho. Everybody has taken a bird bath at least once in their life. When you don't have time for a shower or a tub bath, wiping your stuff down with a wash cloth, soap, and water is good. Hell, I was already clean, but I ate Manny's killer guacamole and spicy tomato salsa during lunch. Only Darius knows what that shit does to my stomach. There are some things only a person who truly loves you understands.

I sprayed on some Perry Ellis 360 because old school perfume has never failed me. I greased my legs and thighs with some baby oil and slid on a tight pair of jeans. My plus size hips and thighs look good in tight jeans. I put on my favorite red silk low cut blouse to show off my big breasts. Shit, before this man could get a leg off my doorstep, I was in his face. I engaged him in some small talk and slipped my cell phone number in his pocket. It was just my luck he called me today. Or should I say, it was just his luck...

"Come here, girl. Don't make me have to come over and take it!"
He runs his hands across his muscular chest and licks his lips.

His lips are watering like I'm a piece of his favorite cake. Damn, he looks good! I know he's gonna break me off. So, why am I hesitating? My body won't move from this chair. This is new for me. I've never hesitated before when I'm about to get mines. What's going on? My body is ready for this. I can feel the wetness from my pussy run down my inner thighs, but I'm hesitating. I can tell by the look on his face he knows something is wrong with me. He puts his hand out to get me to come to him. He offers in such an attractive tone. "Tell you what. I'll give you a back rub to calm your nerves."

I'm a pro at this. I don't need my nerves calmed the fuck down! I know he can't tell by the way I'm acting. He puts his hand down since I couldn't move from the chair and walk over to him. I know he's ready to do this. He keeps rubbing his chest and slightly closes his eyes. He must be imagining what it feels like to fuck me because he's all into his thoughts. Mr. UPS comes out of his meditation. "Damn, I got it. You're one of those females that like music and wine and shit like that to get you in the mood. Let me see if this place has a radio, CD player or something." He looks around and notices the room's TV has a CD/DVD combo. He's excited by the discovery. "Hell yeah, that's what I'm talkin' 'bout. Let me put some good music on. Will that get you in the mood?"

My response is dry. "Yeah, that will work."

For a minute his thoughtfulness took me out of this unfamiliar cloud of guilt I was in. His eagerness to please turns me on a little bit. I'm finally able to move. Before he can get up from the bed and walk over to the TV, I get out of the chair. I walk over to him and, in a seductive voice, tell him that I'll be right back. I walk into the bathroom and close the door. I splash some water on my face and stare into the mirror. I'm trying to convince myself that it's only sex like all the times before, but my mind is working overtime. I start thinking about last night and how good it was. Maybe it was only that good to me because Mr. Coffee reminds me of Darius. Maybe I couldn't feel guilty last night because of that. I'm focusing on my reflection in the mirror. My thoughts are on Darius telling me how much he loves me. His feelings would be so hurt if he knew what I've been doing. My thoughts are interrupted by what's happening on the other side of this door. I can hear Mr. UPS searching in his bag for something.

"Hey sexy, I think you'll like this CD," he yells through the door.

When I first started cheating years ago, I didn't care about my husband's feelings. I used to think it was his fault for not giving me what I wanted. This was always a good enough reason to step out on him, but what I want is unreasonable. If Darius gave me what I wanted, he'd never be able to go to work. He'd be too busy having his dick up in me to do anything else. I'm selfish. My husband loves me and provides for me and all I can focus on is one stupid ass thing.

"Hey, sexy. Are you comin' out?" Mr. UPS asked with serious sexiness.

"Yeah, give me a minute!"

Back in the day, I would've smoked a joint to relax, but that kinda shit is in my past. Darius upgraded me from doing shit like that. I don't forget the old me, but I don't want to go back to being that person. The old JJ worked from the bottom of the bottom to survive. The old JJ had distrust for people. It was all for a good reason. I was mistreated and taken advantage of by family and men. But once I started putting into action what my grandma taught me, it was on!

Yeah, I regret some of the things I did. Those things fuck with my mind to this day, but everything I did was for a reason. When I took something from someone, it was because I needed to eat. When I hurt someone, it was because that someone tried to hurt me first. Most of the things I went through I brought on myself. I made bad decisions and I still do. The difference is now I'm more careful in choosing the things I get involved in. Just because it's all good doesn't mean I can't get thrown back into being the old JJ.

I'm not trying to mess up what I have going on, so I'm very cautious. I'm better at livin' the good life then tryin' to find a place to sleep and eat. That's why over time my feelings for Darius have grown. He took me away from all the bullshit and made me better. It's not like he didn't accept me for who I was, he just knew I could be better than that. Even though I never finished high school or held a job for long, he sees potential in me. After all the courses I've dropped out of and all the changes my career path has gone through, he still loves me.

I wanted to be a guidance counselor for teens, but didn't want to go back to get my high school diploma. I wanted to be a fashion designer, but I couldn't sew the patterns right. Right now, when I'm not fucking around and getting into something, I'm being supportive of his business by attending different functions and stuff. He knows that one day I'm gonna figure out what I wanna do with myself. Watching him with his career inspires me to reach higher. I'm starting to love him deeper. Maybe that's why I'm feeling hesitation with Mr. UPS.

Don't get the wrong impression. I loved Darius when we first got married. Things were different then. We were both thirty years old and trying to learn each other's ways. We both had baggage to deal with and worked hard to make things comfortable for each other. Darius was growing his consulting firm and I was dealing with the kids. There wasn't time for holding on to the fire that made us get married, but it's all good. I think it was better for us to go through tough times in the beginning so we can live out the rest of our lives being happy. I know I'm happy. I cheat, but that doesn't mean I'm not happy. I didn't love him as much then as I do now. I know it doesn't seem like it. I shouldn't even be trippin' like this. I should be strong enough to walk outta this room and not do this shit again. As much love as I have for Darius, there's still this part of me that likes fucking other men. There's this part of me that keeps struggling to do what is right and I don't understand it. I take for granted that no matter what I do, Darius will love me. If I were ever asked whether or not Darius is happy, my answer is he's happy. Why else would he love me the way he does?

So, could my hesitation be a feeling of guilt? Hell no! My body is running this show not my mind. Hesitation is a damn wet dream killer. I'm not known for being one to let anyone's dreams die. So, I'm gonna do the damn thang and stop thinking so much! I'm making a simple physical transaction difficult. Let me stop! I put on some fresh strawberry/melon lip gloss to make my lips look extra seductive.

I hear the music playing. What the hell is he playing? It sounds like...no...I know his ass isn't playing 'Baby Got Back' to get me in the mood! I crack open the door and tell him to find another CD. I hear him blow hard and talk underneath his breath. This confirms it—he's young! A grown ass man would've known what music to play and damn sure wouldn't be blowing hard acting like a child. Well, I'm gonna have to break his ass in on how grown folks play this game. First, I need to act like I know how to play. Shit, my ass is sweating like a ho in church. Maybe because I am the ho that be sitting up in the church clapping and singing like I ain't did a damn thing wrong all week!

I look back in the mirror. "Pull it together, girl. You 'bout to take advantage of a young man. You like young men!"

I adjust my titties in the cami and picture his mouth all over them to distract my mind. That doesn't work. My guilty thoughts get worse. Thinking about church reminds me of a sermon my pastor gives when he knows half the church was at the club getting drunk the night before. Pastor Jones be breathing hard and waving his handkerchief in the air yelling, 'The bible says in John 15:10 that If ye keep my commandments, ye shall abide in my love.' He'll pause to wipe the sweat off his face. 'You see, CHURCH, it's not that hard to do what the Lord wants you to do. It's not hard for you to get to work on time to make that money. It's not hard for you to get in that fancy car of yours and drive to your favorite restaurant. It's not that hard for you to drink down all that devil's water and drop it likes it's hot on the dance floor. You just make it hard to obey the Lord. Ask yourself, why you don't obey a God that loves you so much?'

Damn, if I'm imagining my crispy black, eight-months-pregnant-looking pastor instead of this fine young man in the room next door, I know I'm trippin'! Usually when I hear this sermon, I'm sitting in the back pew making excuses as to why I don't obey. Since I'm hearing this in my head, while in a hotel room wearing a "cum and get it" outfit, I know God is trying to tell me something. I open up the bathroom door and he's lying on the bed looking so young and so sexy. Damn, he deserves first place in a Mr. Black Pageant contest.

I ask him, "How old are you?" For some reason I need to know.

"Old enough," he smiles with white teeth that belong in a Crest commercial.

I look back into the mirror. "What the hell am I doing this for?"

"What did you say, sexy?" He sits up on the bed.

I don't recognize the woman looking back at me in the mirror. This woman I'm looking at wants to do right by her man and doesn't want to lose him. I don't understand why this is happening to me right now; but if I don't stop cheating now, I never will. "Lord, help me have strength right now!"

He smiles with confidence. "Sexy, you don't have to pray for strength, you just relax. I'll do all the work."

I walk out of the bathroom and start putting on my clothes. No words come from his mouth. He's sitting on the bed giving me a confused look. Then, all of a sudden, as if some spark of genius hits him, he stands up with his hard dick in his hand. He's just standing there smiling at me, as if I was supposed to be turned on. Hell yeah he's sexy and he turns me on, but that move he just made damn sure wasn't. I'm breathing hard, grabbing my stuff, frantically digging in my purse trying to find my wallet. I throw a hundred dollar bill on the bed. "Sorry, I have to go; this should help take care of the bill." I'm almost out of the room when suddenly it hit me that he was just about to get some of the best coochie of his life. I walk back over to the bed and grab my money. Then I lean into his ear "For what you was 'bout to get, you should be giving me your whole damn paycheck and then some."

I wink and head for the door. He jumps up, throws on the hotel robe, and follows me. I pause for a moment to see what move he's gonna make now. He stands behind me and opens the door. I don't want to say a thing. I rush out of the room, but half way toward the elevator I take a quick glance over my shoulder at him. I'm close to the elevator when he finally says something. "Give me a call!"

It is at this moment I realize his voice doesn't sound so sexy to me after all. A grown ass man would've told me I wasn't going anywhere. I shouldn't be messing with young men anyways. But when I turn around to give him one more look, my body takes over my mind. Juicy is throbbing as if she's knocking to say wake up! Yeah, I said Juicy. That's the name I've given my pussy. Women talk about men because they name their dicks, but women do the same thing. We take pride in how good our stuff is. There's no better way to show pride then by giving it a sensual name.

I stood at the elevator for a minute trying to decide whether or not I was actually going back to fuck him. He's still standing there, leaning back against the door smiling and rubbing his sexy chest. His nipples are hard. Ooh, I want to kiss 'em. The only thoughts I have now is satisfying my needs. Darius, who? I walk back over to Mr. UPS. He flashes he's commercial smile. "I knew you wasn't gonna leave a brotha hangin'."

I pull up my skirt and move my g-string to the side. I grab his right hand and put it between my thighs. I shove his middle finger up into my pussy. His voice is filled with so much excitement. He seductively shouts, "Damn, girl. You are so wet!"

For a moment, it seems his eyes are going to pop out. I open up his robe, grab his dick and feel how hard it is. Only a young, strong dick feels this good in my hand. I look down at it because a nice looking dick is a wonderful sight. It's so hard I could trace with a marker all the veins popping out. The head is perfectly shaped like a large mushroom. I can see the eagerness in his face like a lion about to pounce on his prey. Now, don't misunderstand when I talk about having sex with younger men. Of course, I've had older dick. I just had some yesterday, and it was all good. Experience counts for something, but young dick aims to please. It has something to prove. It has to challenge a woman in order to show who is boss. And that is a challenge I love to take on! So, how could I pass on such a good looking challenger? I couldn't. I push him back into the room, pull off his robe, get down on my knees and start sucking his dick. The hotel room door is wide open. I'm so into what I'm doing, I don't even bother to take my clothes off. I don't even notice if people are walking by. I don't care and, apparently, he doesn't either. He tries to tell me something, "Sexy, we need to cloooooooossseee the...ahhhh shit." I thought I heard voices at the door but didn't look to see if people were watching. After about ten minutes into it, Mr. UPS busts a nut all in my mouth. I get up and run for the bathroom and spit into the toilet. I only swallow my husband.

He sits on the bed and shakes his head. "Damn girl, that shit felt good as hell!"

He stands up, fixes the bedspread and fluffs the pillows. "Now it's your turn, you sexy ass bitch!" He's waiting like a little boy for his mommy to give him another scoop of ice cream. I enjoy making him wait for it. I walk outta the bathroom shaking my hips from side to side giving him a mini striptease. I slowly peel off my blouse and skirt to reshow my simple but sexy outfit. He keeps patting the pillows and bed signaling for me to hurry up. He's enjoying my show but wants to get busy. "Lay down, I wanna taste it!" His mouth is watering again.

I look into his big sexy eyes and kiss him on the lips. That shit is against the rules! I like it and so does he. Oh damn, here it comes again that overwhelming feeling of guilt. How come, all of a sudden, I start having a guilty consequence? Very convenient for guilt to hit right after he got his nut! I try to pretend I don't hear the guilt trip ticket being brought inside my head. Mr. UPS is giving me that look again. The look of what the hell is wrong with her now?

"What do I need to do to make you comfortable wit me?" His voice is so sincere.

"You good, I just need to rinse my mouth out." I walk back into the bathroom.

"Damn, you the kinda woman a brotha wants to make his wifey!"

I rinse my mouth with the hotel provided mouthwash and spit into the sink. I grab a towel to dry my mouth and wipe some of the sweat off my forehead. I turn toward him and catch my breath so I can deliver the bad news. "Look, I need to tell you something important." I pause. "I'm a married woman!"

He laughs and starts telling me why he's so damn tickled. "I knew that shit. Damn, the package I delivered to your spot yesterday had a man's name on it and your housekeeper said the man of the house wasn't home. I knew then what was goin' down when you slid your number in my pocket. I'm no dumb ass!"

Wow, I thought me telling him I was married was gonna mess his world up! I guess I'm the dumb ass. He walks over to me with cum from his dick dripping on the carpet. I'm not feeling his cockiness. It's turning me off. He grabs a hand towel and wets it in the sink. He stands behind me wiping his dick off, cheesing from ear to ear, and staring at me in the mirror.

"Look, Ms. Thang. You don't have to worry 'bout me tellin' anyone 'bout this. You givin' me exactly what I want. Older, married women know what the hell they doin'. I don't have to tell ya'll what, where, when, and how."

His statement pisses me off. I think it's because he's calling me old, not because I feel used. I can't even say used.

The CD stops. He walks outta the bathroom and digs in his bag for another CD. His back is turned to me. I should walk up behind his ass, knock the shit outta him, and leave, but I won't do that. I'm gonna get what I came back for. I know all I want is to get some satisfaction. That's my only reason for being here. I'm not looking for love in a one night stand. There is no love to find in that. Hell, I've got love at home. No, what I'm looking for tonight is something different and I need to show him what that is. I take my cami and g-string off and lay down on the bed. Mr. UPS puts in another CD. This time he put in a good one without me telling him. Prince, now that's it right there. If Prince's sexual lyrics can't get a person in the mood, then we done! It didn't matter anymore, anyways. I don't need it to get me in the mood now. Once I put my mind there, it's on and crackin'. Shit! All the music is gonna do for me now is cover all the noise I'm 'bout to make. With legs wide open, I point downward and command, "Eat Juicy like your life depends on it!"

He smiles. "Juicy, huh? I'll see 'bout that. Not a problem!" He licks his lips and claps his hands together. From the look on his face, you'd think he arrived at his favorite soul food buffet. I relax in anticipation for what he's 'bout to do to me. Mr. UPS doesn't hesitate in diving right in.

CHAPTER THREE

So much for my anticipation, it's been at least 15 minutes and I'm bored. He hasn't come up for air and it doesn't seem like he's planning to anytime soon. I have to do something to get this brotha to stop, so I tap him on the head. He's still going at it like this is his last meal. Hell, if he don't get his ass up it just might be his last meal! I'm gonna shut these big thighs on him and kill his ass! I stop tapping and hit him hard right on the top of his head.

He jumps up and yells, "What the hell is wrong with you?"

He looks possessed and I'm lying on the bed wondering if I'm gonna have to cut his ass to get up out of here. I think of a lie to tell him so I can leave without catching hell. I sit up against the headboard and strike a sexy, but innocent pose.

"Look, baby. I need to get home before my husband. He gets back in town tonight. You don't mind if I catch up to you another time?" I can see all over his face that he's upset at the thought of not fucking me all night, but I don't care. I should've kept walking in the first place. Matter of fact, I should've kept my ass on the damn toilet yesterday.

"So you gonna stop me in the middle of eating you out and tell me you need to go home? Your husband ain't comin' home tonight, but it's cool. You got kids to get home to. I'm a real niggah, I understand that shit! I'll have another chance to hit it." He's licking his lips again.

I only know of one man on this earth who can constantly lick his lips and get away with it and that is LL Cool J. This boy needs to stop! This shit is annoying me, especially since he's not good at eating pussy! I get up from the bed and put my clothes on. I brush my hair back into my hair clip and take my compact out to fix my make-up. I'm wondering how he knew my husband wasn't coming home. He's guessing. I don't remember even telling him about the kids. And I don't remember them being around when he delivered the package neither. Who gives a shit! I don't want to get into a conversation and have to deal with him licking his lips for another five minutes. As I'm gathering my stuff to leave, Mr. UPS grabs the back of my neck and gives me a strong and forceful kiss.

He slaps me on my ass and walks away laughing. "Oh, yeah. Juicy is very juicy."

I know my thoughts are demented or the so called curse is kicking back in because what he just did turned me on. But he probably can't deliver in the fucking department. So trying to find out if the dick is good would be a waste of time. What a waste of such a beautiful body. Mr. UPS is still young, he's got time to learn how to lay the pipe like Mr. Coffee.

He lies back on the bed and prompts himself up on the pillows. His dick is hard again and he is making it wave at me. "Say hello to the sexy ass bitch." That is some old high school shit but he looks good doing it. He asks, "Hey, what do you think I should call him?"

I nod like I've not a clue in the world. "I don't know, what do you think you should call him?"

He grabs his dick with both of his hands and starts talking to it. "What should I call you?" Now if this man's dick answers back, I'm not walking outta here; I'm running out! His voice gets serious. "When I see you again, I want you to have a name for him."

Who does he think I am? The Dick Whisperer. This dude has solved my career struggle for me. Oh yeah, that's what I'm gonna do with my life. Run around and give niggahs names for their dicks. I can see it now. My husband will be my marketing manager. I'll have a web site with pictures and the names I've given them to show how good I am at it. His ass must be crazy!

I can tell he's going to get on my last nerve and be a pain in the ass. I have to let him know this isn't going to be a regular thing between us. "Look, I don't care what you name your dick. It's yours, attached to your body. You know your dick better than anyone, right?"

He stops grabbing himself, sits up in the bed, and gives me this crazed look. "Ok then, I got you. After me, you're going to be the next in line for knowing my dick well. So, come and put your mouth on your new best friend!"

I rolled my eyes and put up my right hand to signal 'whatever' to him like a true Cali girl. He doesn't like my gesture because he jumps out the bed and starts ranting and raving. "You know I'm sick of you type bitches. The type that thinks you can just use a brotha like me one night and not have to deal wit me again. Your type sees a fine-ass brotha like me and can't wait for me to hit it! You kick it wit me for a couple of hours. Get treated the way you can't by him. Then, you go home, take a shower, get in the bed and think it's all good! You don't call me again until you want some mo' good dick. Bitch, it doesn't work like that. You see, I can blow your shit right out the water if I want to, but I'm not gonna do that. Nah, because when I call your ass again, you'll come running until I've had enough and don't call your ass no mo'."

I'm standing there looking at him with my arms crossed. He sits back and calms down. In a calm and serene tone, he starts to tell me what he thinks my problem is. "You see your problem is that you don't appreciate the man you have at home. I can tell you don't give a shit 'bout how hard he works to take care of your ass! That big ass house and fine car, I bet you didn't work a lick for shit. No, you don't appreciate the shit you have. I'm sure I'm not the only other niggah you done fucked. I feel sorry for that niggah!"

I'm getting pissed now. Nobody calls my husband a niggah. Nobody! Mr. UPS is the one who is a niggah! He thinks he knows what's going on in my damn house. His childish outburst shows how unstable he is. He's the type to inspire Hollywood to write a Fatal Attraction Part II – the Crazy Ass Black Man version. Oh, I see he wants to play mind fuck games with me and I don't play that. He's messing with a grown ass woman right here. I'm not going to be seeing his crazy ass again. I regret that he knows where I live.

He's wiping his mouth off with a towel. All that yelling made him foam at the mouth. He makes it clear to me his reason for letting me leave. "I'm gonna let you walk out that door tonight because I'm gonna get sum of dat later this weekend. You gonna make time for me or I'll come knocking. You got that, sexy ass bitch?"

I don't have a blade on me so I'm feeling nervous 'bout how he shifts his tone so easily. I smile and give him a kiss. I don't want his crazy ass flipping out on me again. "Yeah, baby. You're the first thing I'm gonna do this weekend."

He starts laughing again. "You know, I've changed my mind. I'm not gonna let you leave and ruin us having such a beautiful room. Before you go, you gonna suck my dick again!"

I know this niggah ain't serious. I run this shit, not him! "No, I ain't sucking shit. I'm going the fuck home!"

He grabs his cell phone from off the dresser. "Aiight then, I'm gonna call another triflin' ass bitch to come take your place. I'm done with your fake wanna be freak ass. You ain't gettin' a call from me no mo'! Bitch, as the Don puts it—YOU'RE FIRED!"

This niggah is psychotic! I run out of the room before he starts some more shit. By time I make it to the elevator, my heart is pounding fast. The fear of what just took place getting back to Darius overwhelms me. I can't let this type of shit happen anymore. I've got to stop messing around with other dudes. I'm digging in my bag desperately trying to find a piece of gum to chew on. I need to calm my nerves. What I wouldn't do for a piece of my grandma's pie right now. That's how most of my childhood issues were settled. I'd be talking to my grandma and eating a piece of her famous pecan pie. She'd give me the advice I needed no matter what the situation. Since I can't get a pie fix or talk to my grandma, I need a substitute. Soon as I get home, I'm having a glass of wine.

I step on the elevator and there is a young couple hugged up in the corner passionately kissing. Watching them makes me feel even more ashamed of my actions. I bet they are so in love. I bet they wouldn't cheat on each other. They are looking into each other's eyes smiling. The young gentleman looks over and gives me a sexy smile. Hmm...then again, I could be wrong. What looks good on the outside, isn't always the way it is on the inside. I need to stop being so jaded in my thinking. Not everyone does what I do. I decide to return the smile. The young lady holds up her hand to show off her wedding ring. Her voice is filled with joy as she shares her good news. "We just got married yesterday!"

I feel the need to give some encouragement. "Congratulations!"

She buries her head into his chest, smells his shirt, and rubs his back. Their laughter fills the elevator. I listen to their conversation as they talk about going to their room to start making ten kids. He goes into detail about her becoming a team mom for their sons' football team. Ah, they're so cute. I'm happy for them and, at the same time, I'm jealous. I don't know why. I have a good husband, two beautiful kids, an outstanding home, and everything money can buy. I shouldn't feel jealous of anyone; but the more I listen to them, I can't seem to help myself from being jealous. Maybe because I started my life off on the wrong foot. I didn't start off being in love, getting married, and then having kids. I did everything ass backwards. Hmm...I didn't do everything the right way then, but I have a chance to do it now. What's my problem? The elevator stops. I snap out of my jealousy. Before I know it, I am speaking out loud. "Oh, thank goodness!"

I see the reaction of the young couple. I'm embarrassed for allowing those words to come from my mouth. I don't want them to think the love they show for each other in public is wrong.

I look at them both and apologize, "Sorry, I'm just a little cranky."

I straighten my clothes to show them I've had a tough night. I get off the elevator and head toward the valet. I'm feeling antsy. I try handing my ticket to the valet guy and end up dropping it. He picks it up, smiles, and looks me in my face. Did I have something on my face? What the hell is he looking at? I pull out my compact to take a look.

"You look wonderful, Miss."

Wonderful! He must be high off something. I'm all sweaty and my clothes are half put on. I have an overpowering smell of mouthwash oozing from my mouth. It goes to show how men can't help but to want me.

"I'm in a rush, so could you hurry up and get my car!"

I was rude. I act like his compliment didn't matter to me, as if he was nobody. I know that's not right. I hate when people treat me that way.

"Of course, I apologize," he says and quickly walks away.

Usually I'd jump at the opportunity to flirt with a younger man with a great smile, if for no other reason then to make myself feel twenty years old again, but I'm not in the mood. I'm still shaken up by Mr. UPS. I need to stay away from young dudes. I need to roll with the current focus on my husband before my attention span moves from it. My feet feel cold. I left the room so fast that I forgot to grab my shoes, so that's why the couple kept looking down and laughing. Damn, those were Jimmy Choos! It isn't like I don't have another pair at home. It could have been worse. I could have left that money with his crazy ass.

It seems like I've been standing here damn near all night. I wish he'd hurry up. Oh, here he comes. I give him a tip, jump in and throw my Louis bag on the passenger side of my black Cadillac XLR. Yeah, I had to have one. It reminds me of a strong, sophisticated black man with style and power. Just like working hard to get one of these, you have to work just as hard to find a stylish and powerful black man. I'm blessed. I already have both. I need to focus on doing right by my man. I treat this car better than I do him. Let me go home and get it together.

I pull out from the parking lot. I don't know why I am rushing. My husband isn't home and Eva is watching the kids. I already know the Lord sees what is going on. I can't hide so He won't see me. Getting in an accident isn't going to help! I slow down and reach over into the glove compartment to find a piece of gum. I always keep a pack of gum in the car. I put a piece in my mouth and head down the street. Why can't I be satisfied with just one man? I start thinking about the story of the curse my grandma always talked about when she was alive. She called it Un peu plus (a little more).

This curse was supposedly placed on our family generations ago by a woman named Dominique Bernard. She was the beautiful daughter of a plantation owner and his housekeeper. She was fair skinned with gray-blue eyes and reddish brown hair. Although she was beautiful beyond anything that could be painted on canvas, she was still a bastard child. Because she was rejected by the plantation owner's family and her mother had died during childbirth, she was raised down in the center bayous of New Orleans by a Creole woman named Lissette.

Lissette practiced voodoo and Dominque became her number one pupil. As Dominque came into womanhood, she also came into being very good at her craft. She soon was given the name Mistress of the Loa Spirits, and became renowned for her ability to heal. Although she conjured up many spells for others, she could not make them for herself. Even when Dominque had fallen in love, she could not make the man she loved, love her. The man she desired was Baptiste Trudeau. He was the target of many women's affections and the husband of my great-great-great grandmother Sophie Trudeau.

Baptiste was a handsome, tall, muscular, dark-skinned man who catered to Sophie's every want and need. He worked hard tending to rich white folks' horses to provide a magnificent home for them and their children. Sophie was a beautiful, majestic woman with sexual charms, and enough mystery about her to leave men wanting to know more. Sophie and Dominique were the finest women in town. Growing up, there had always been an unspoken competition between them. Grandma always retold the events of Baptiste and Sophie as if she had been there herself. She told me that what caused the curse was Dominique's infatuated rage. She had seen Sophie in town flirting with another man. Dominique was outraged! She never believed Sophie deserved to be Baptiste's wife in the first place. So she thought what she had seen was her opportunity to take Baptiste from her. She decided to go pay him a visit.

Dominique had taken extra care in putting on her make-up and dressing in her special homespun full skirt and tight bodice with several pieces of expensive jewelry. She felt sure Baptiste would see the passion and concern she had for him and fall in love with her. When she went to tell Baptiste, he was furious. Instead of her gaining his heart, he told her to go to hell and take her lies with her! Dominique's heart was broken and she had vowed to show Baptiste that he had married a common whore. She placed a curse on Sophie. Sophie would never be sexually satisfied by just one man, and all of her female off-spring would also be cursed.

The way the story goes is that Baptiste had taken their children out for a walk one afternoon. On the path back to their home from a distance, he saw Sophie on their porch having sex with another man. He quickly covered their children's faces and turned them around. He told them to go run and hide for a game of hide-n-seek. Baptiste turned back around and watched his wife. He stood still, unable to move. Sophie did not see her husband standing by the magnolia trees watching as she wrapped her legs around her lover's waist, scratching his back, and moaning in a way she never did with him. Baptiste did not confront her right away. Instead, he took the children to a family member's house. No one would've ever known what was going on because Baptiste acted as if nothing was wrong. He went back home to deal with Sophie. She and her lover had already left. So he sat on the porch, where it still had the stench of musk, sweat, and her perfume, and waited for her. When she returned home, it was late into the night. Sophie didn't care about his feelings. She saw Baptiste sitting on the porch bench, walked right passed him, and into the house. He followed her inside. She went into the kitchen to get a glass of water.

My grandma told me that our family believed the curse made Sophie mistreat Baptiste. That the spell Dominique placed had an extra dosage of spitefulness. I remember my grandma acting out the story. She said that Sophie stood by the sink sipping on water and said nothing to Baptiste. His anger grew as thoughts of how long he sat and waited for her to come home raced in his mind. All she could do was drink water and not say a word to him! He was trying to keep the jealous rage from building up inside of him, but her cold-hearted attitude didn't help. Sophie rolled her eyes at him and turned to leave the kitchen. Before she could take a step out, he grabbed her arm and stabbed her twenty times. He stood over her body and watched her bleed to death...

This story haunted me as a teenager. My grandma didn't start telling me this story until I had my first period. She said all of the women in the family were told this story once they reached womanhood. I got tired of her telling me this story all the damn time. I told myself that if I ever got married I wasn't going to cheat. And if I did, I damn sure wasn't going to get caught. I used to think the point of my grandma telling me this story so many times was to keep me from growing up and becoming a cheating wife. Now I think the point was not to get caught. My grandma was no saint. She was quick to give it up. She was the last person on earth that could tell somebody not to cheat. She must have been crazy to think folks was going to believe this story. Who in the hell is going to believe in a sexual curse? Then again, thinking about how whorish my grandma was, maybe she was right about the curse. Look at what happened tonight. I couldn't do the right thing even when I was so close to walking away.

Maybe the curse is an explanation for my high sexual nature. My sexual peak hit me with a vengeance when I turned thirty-two. I couldn't get enough. Yeah, thirty-two was the beginning of wanting it more than a couple of times a week, which was our normal routine. I started asking Darius for sex several times a day. He's such a submissive husband, he never denied my wishes. He did fine with the early morning requests. He enjoyed early morning fucking most of all. When I'd ask him to eat my pussy after getting out of the shower first thing in the morning, he'd be on his knees before I could step out. At first coming home for lunch to dick me down was fun for him. Then he started booking client appointments during lunch time. Our before dinner quickies would hold me until bedtime, but then he started spending extra time helping the kids with homework. I could tell he was getting tired because when I turned thirty-four, he started bringing home new toys for me to try with a super pack of batteries. I took the hint, but I couldn't seem to satisfy myself.

Now I'm thirty-eight, and it seems to have only gotten worse. I think of sex all the time. My life is a constant replay of Jamie's song "Three Letter Word". I find myself thinking of sex when I'm driving on the freeway. I think of sex when I put on my lip gloss. I think of sex when I watch television, when I take a bath, and when I'm eating breakfast. Hell, a damn banana turns me on! I don't know what is happening to me. I'm completely out of control. No matter how hard I try, I can't wait for my husband to come home to get some. Shit, I'm starting to think there is some truth to this sexual appetite curse!

My best and only female friend Eva tells me that I'm just a nasty freak. I think she's just a hater because the last time she got fucked was when America was bent over for the first George Bush. And I'm not talking about an intern, but I'm not mad at her. We still have freedom of speech left in this country, so she can say whatever she wants to about me. This is my body and I can do what the hell I want, as long as I play it safe. "Wrap it up baby!" Yeah, that's my motto!

I play it safe not getting caught up with any one particular man. I always pick men who are only looking for a piece of ass for a couple of hours. I have to admit sometimes I've been in such a big rush I didn't screen 'em well enough. I should've checked Mr. UPS out some more. Then I would've found out he was crazy as hell, but my ass wanted to fuck. I didn't think dude would flip out like that. I just wanted to take some of the edge off before Darius got back from his trip. I believe I'm doing my man a favor. I don't want him thinking I only want his dick and nothing else. I let other brothas feel like that. Although Darius wouldn't care much if the first words out of my mouth when he got home were 'Fuck Me.' No, I don't think it would bother him, but I do think he would get tired of it after awhile. He has a lot on his plate. No, the truth is I don't want my high class man to think he got hold of a low class ho.

My car starts slowing down. "What the hell?"

The gas light comes on. Damn, I meant to get gas yesterday before going to the hotel, but I was in a hurry. I regret getting up this morning!

CHAPTER FOUR

I pull into a gas station. It's twenty minutes till midnight. The station should be closing in a few. Looking in my purse, I forgot to bring a credit card with me. Good thing I took my money back. I hurry and run up to pay the gas attendant. I don't see anyone at the window.

"Hello!" I'm yelling through the glass window. Hmm, thought I made it in enough time before closing. I was just about to walk away when suddenly I see two figures moving in the back office area. "Hello, can you hear me?"

I know they hear me yelling. You would think I was a Jehovah's Witness around this joint. I press my face up against the window so I can get a closer look. It looks as if two people are having sex on the office desk. Now I've got an attitude. I don't want anyone else getting it if I can't get mine. My voice sounds like a bullhorn.

"Hello. Can I get some damn gas, please?"

I hear moans, sounds of relief, and laughter. I guess they both got theirs. A man comes walking out of the office. He's Hispanic, about 6'2, and with a body like he stepped from Men's Health Magazine. His black wavy hair is shining and he is wiping sweat from his face. Yes, I said sweat and I can smell it. Ooh, it smells like sugar water!

"Si, Senorita. How may I help you?" He asks while flirting with his eyes.

The question came from his lips like a sweet song of seduction. I almost forgot what I'm here for.

I try to sound hard. "I know you heard me yelling a minute ago, but you're too busy playing executive producer in the back."

Then the woman comes out of the office. She's a sistah! I'm thinking to myself—go, girl! Get your caliente on!

"This is none of yo' business. Do you want some gas or not?" Her voice sounds heavy, as if she smokes a pack of cigarettes a day. That's a shame, especially since she's a fine looking sistah. I sense she has an attitude with me. "We 'bout to close in five, so yo' ass gotta hurry up!"

She buttons up her Baby Phat jeans and pulls her blouse together. She has beautiful dark ebony skin, with round full lips, and a body like a brick house. Mr. UPS needs to be singing 'Baby Got Back' to her! She looks young enough, maybe I'll introduce them. Then again, Mr. UPS wants women my age. Let me stop trippin'. I don't need to help anyone else burn in hell with me. I notice she has a large tattoo on the left side of her neck. It's an eagle or dove. I can't really tell. Personally, I think she should take her good looks and make some money on a runway instead of fucking some dude at a gas station. I should tell her what is on my mind. What good would it do? I don't know her and she doesn't know me.

She doesn't strike me as being the type of woman who gives a damn what others think. I like that. Doesn't matter. I don't have the right to judge her, especially since I just sucked a man's dick who is too young for me and crazy as hell!

"I need forty dollars of supreme gas if you don't mind." I put my money in the window slot, look her man dead in his face, and smile.

He's so sexy that I can't help myself. "Did I see you in a magazine ad awhile back?"

This sistah opens her mouth again. "Damn, girl. Do yo' ass think he'd have his ass in here selling gas if he was in a magazine? Get yo' gas and go, it's dangerous to be out late at night by yo' sef."

I take that as a big hint. Hell, I'm not fighting over some dick I didn't get or don't plan on getting. If I wanted to, I'd take his ass from her. She better be glad I'm tired and ready to go home and hit the sheets. I walk to my car, pump my gas, and jump back in. I glance back at the attendant booth through my rearview mirror. I'm acting like Lot's wife in the story of Sodom and Gomorrah, except the Lord has mercy on me and doesn't turn me into a pillar of salt. Despite feeling sinful and guilty, I continue to look in my rearview mirror. I notice sistah girl watching me. It's funny how she makes a point of pressing her breast against the window as he walks up behind her. She pulls him closer. I see him grab her breasts then put her in the doggie style position. She's smiling and looking in my direction.

I open my legs and rub my inner thighs. Ooh, I can just imagine myself having sex with Mr. Caliente. Just as I'm about to get into my fantasy, the station's lights go out. I stop imagining and pull my thighs together. "Damn, I'm missing a good peep show."

What is wrong with me? Why am I taking the Lord's mercy for granted? I've been learning in Sunday school about sinful natures. I know my sinful nature wants me to believe they're doing something exciting and that I'm missing out. I damn sure want to blame the curse for my out of control hormones, but I know better. It's just my sinful thinking. If I focus on the Lord's words, I can overcome these desires. It all starts with the mind. I know the strength to be faithful to my husband is inside of me. Right now, it doesn't matter. I won't be able to figure out all my issues tonight.

Before I pull off from the station, I let my drop top down. I take the huge clip out of my hair and run my fingers through it. I look into the mirror so I can get a better look. Darius makes sure that I keep my hair done. He says there's nothing worse than a woman with a nappy ass kitchen. He's so serious about it. He has his secretary book my hair appointments to make sure I go. My hair is past my shoulders, dark, and silky like a black cat. It looks sexy against my milk chocolate skin. Especially when it's wet! He loves to run his hands through my hair when we are in the shower together. Sometimes he'll pull my hair while kissing me passionately.

Damn, a shower with him sounds so good right now. When I get home tonight I'll imagine him in the shower with me. I do that when I miss him real hard. I take a handful of soap and imagine my hands are his and touch all over my body. I'll stand under the showerhead and allow the hot water to run down my soapy body. I play with my large, dark brown nipples. I picture him on his knees putting his tongue inside of my pussy, allowing the water to run from the top of his head down his backside. I run my fingers over my clit in a slow circular motion until I climax. It doesn't feel as good as when Darius does it to me, but it damn sure does the trick on the nights he's away and I'm not being bothered with another man. Just sitting and thinking about it is making me wet. It's getting late; I need to get home. I speed out of the station. You'd think I was in the Indy 500!

I finally pull up in front of the house. All the lights are on. Eva knows I'll spend money on clothes and getting my hair done, but I don't like spending money on a high ass electric bill! I get out of my car and stomp inside. Eva is passed out on the couch. There's a couple of empty forty bottles on the floor. The music system is loud and the TV is on BET music videos. I turn everything off and throw a blanket over Eva. I walk upstairs to check on the kids. I stop at my daughter's room first. As usual my son is in the bed with her. They are passed out. I check the floor to make sure they don't have empty forty bottles. How else could they sleep with all that noise and all the lights on? The kids are so sweet wrapped up together. I cover them up with the comforter, kiss them both on the forehead, and whisper 'I love you' in their ears. I can't help but stand at the door and admire how precious they are. "This is what life is all about."

I walk out and head toward my bedroom. There's a pathway of toys for me to follow. I start throwing them in the hallway toy box. These kids still play with toys as if they're three years old. My body feels tired and my throat is dry. I make a U-turn and go back downstairs to get a drink. I owe myself a glass of wine but grab water instead. I stand in the kitchen looking into the living room at Eva asleep on the couch. We've been friends for along time. I don't know what I'd do without her in my life. She's always here for me and the kids no matter what. Even when Eva gets her drank on, I know the kids are safe. I trust her before I trust anyone in my blood family. She will give her life to protect them if she has to. Hmm... it's a trip how neither one of us never thought we'd be living large. We've come a long way from when we first met twenty-one years ago, when we had to fuck strangers for a hot meal.

I go back upstairs and into my room. I run a hot tub of water instead of taking a shower. The steam from the Jacuzzi tub fills the air like a thick fog in London. I change my mind. I don't want to imagine being with my husband. Matter of fact, I don't want to think about sex anymore tonight. I turn on some jazz. I love listening to Norman Brown while the bubbles surround my body. I light a lavender candle and I step in...mmm, the water feels so good. I lean back and relax; my thoughts are none for a moment. Then, my mind starts up again. I should've known better than to believe I could keep my mind off sex for longer than ten minutes.

The last time I was in a Jacuzzi hot tub with someone, it was Reggie Wilson, number nine on my cell phone's speed dial. I know you're trippin' off me remembering a brotha's name. Of course, this brotha is special. He gives me something I can feel. Some real magical shit happens when I have sex with Reggie. He is the only one who is not a one night stand. I tried to make it that way. I tried to keep my policy of only fucking men who want a booty call, but he's different. He's a true gentleman and sexy as he wanna be. Not only is he pleasing to my eyes and to my body but also to my mind. He's passionate! No, he's not the one I call when I want a night of raw fucking. No, I call Reggie when I want to be massaged, caressed, and kissed from my head to my toes. He should be the poster child for a foreplay campaign and help some of these other brothas out. Don't get it twisted now; he had a nickname in the beginning—Mr. Dress Shop.

I was at the La Jolla Village Square inside of a dress shop when he walked by. He came back and stood in the window and stared at me. At first, I thought he was some thug and that he was gonna jack me once I left the shop. When I took a good look at him, however, I knew something else was up. He had on a black fedora and a black slim fit shirt—which I usually think looks gay—but, it fit him just right and showed off his cut body. When I looked at his manicured hands, I thought he was gay for sure and was just admiring something I had on, but he was giving me a seductive look. He was letting me know he wanted me. When he walked away from the window, I felt disappointed. At the time, I immediately thought he probably didn't want a thick sized sistah like me. He's shopping in La Jolla, girl. He probably dates skinny white girls.

I was at the cash register paying for my dress when he walked up behind me with a huge cookie in his hand. "I didn't want to take the chance of looking for a flower shop and you'd be gone. The closest place was the cookie shop!"

I remember telling him, "You better be glad you explained yourself or you was gonna get your ass whooped with that cookie in front of all these white folks!"

Reggie and I burst out laughing while everyone in the store looked at us like we were crazy. We spent that afternoon together. We walked around shopping and harassing salespeople in the jewelry stores, making them think a big commission was coming their way. It was a beautiful sunny summer afternoon, so we sat at one of the outside restaurants. We didn't order anything to eat. The restaurant workers quickly grew tired of us. They kept coming over asking if we needed anything. Reggie told them we were reviewing the menu and to bring us fresh water. We ate the cookie, sipped on water, laughed and talked until they closed. That was one of the best times I have had in California since I first met Darius. We used to have fun like that all the time. Now, our marriage is about taking care of business, no time for fun. It's all good because I'm lucky to even have Darius as my husband.

Now when I think about who I would marry if I was single, it would be Reggie. Let me stop trippin'. Like I said before, I can't imagine being married to anyone other than Darius. Don't get it twisted; but if something happened where I couldn't live my life with Darius, I'd take Reggie in a hot minute! I haven't been able to find anything wrong with him yet. I like everything about Reggie—from his huge hands and thick fingers to his stylish goatee. My first impression of him was right, except for the gay part; he always keeps his fingernails manicured. I don't give a damn what people say, a metro-sexual man is the shit! He knows how to pick a great bottle of wine and he knows how to play the right song at the right time. Hey, I'm still getting to know a brotha better, so no telling what bones are in his closet.

The water is getting cold. I turn on the hot water faucet to warm it up some. I lean back so I can think about Reggie some more. Ah, that feels good. Huh, when I'm in his presence, I feel like a queen. He opens doors, pulls back chairs, kisses my hands and shoulders, and tells me how sexy I look all the time. He's not worried about my body's flaws so he holds nothing back when touching me. He's a passionate lover and he comes correct when it's time to eat Juicy. Reggie is the only man I've ever known that can make me cum by sucking on my nipples. It's not just the sex with him that keeps me going back. It's the things he does to make me feel like more than just a booty call. Wherever we meet, he always has a dozen red roses waiting on me. He reads me poetry and sings Vandross songs like Luther resides in his soul. He orders in some of the town's best restaurant menu items for us to snack on. He tickles my body, he makes me laugh...he makes me laugh...he makes me happy.

Don't misunderstand when I talk about how good Reggie is. He still can't out do my Darius. When it comes to a man being a good provider and father, Darius has it on lock! It's hard to believe Reggie isn't doing the damn thang like Darius. He has a great career as a financial advisor for a top firm. He said he loves children. I don't understand why he's never been married and doesn't have kids. That's a shame! He'd be a bomb ass husband and father. Maybe he's a lying ass and does have a family. Now that I'm thinking about it, I haven't been to his crib. He hasn't invited me, but I'm sure he will. If he never does I can deal with that. I'm not looking for love. I have that at home. But I wouldn't mind if Reggie fell in love with me. Yeah, when I need more than sexual healing, I press nine on my cell phone's speed dial.

I've been in the water for over thirty minutes. I step out and the cold air surrounds my body. I quickly grab my towel, wipe the mirror and stand in front of it. I look worse than a raisin. I turn my body from side to side, noticing every imperfection. I've never been a skinny girl. I'm what some folks call thick. These days I wear a size sixteen and that's only because Eva hasn't been on her cooking game lately. Usually, I'm a size eighteen. The smallest I've ever been is a size ten and I think I was ten years old at the time. Growing up, my Grandma Pauline, used to say I was just big boned. I've never seen a big boned skeleton! But I let her roll with that one, it made her feel good. Hell, it made me feel good, too! She even had a funny nickname for me...hambones. I wasn't enthusiastic about being compared to a chunk of fat on a bone; but it was cute how she said it, so I never tripped on her. She'd say, 'There's nothing fat about you, baby. You're a fox!'

Grandma Pauline always told me I was pretty. She had a thing for women to have thick legs. In her thinking, men didn't want chicken legged women. She would laugh. "If a man wants skinny legs, he can go out to the chicken coop and sleep with my chicken, Esther!" She'd grab the back of my legs. "Look at those big pretty legs!" She'd be happy to see they're still the same, just a lot more of them.

Grandma Pauline helped my father raise me and my older brother Francis in Louisiana. She was a big, pretty, high yellow woman with large dimples and pearly white teeth. Her eyes were hazel and she had long curly eyelashes. She loved to drink moonshine and talked more mess then any man could. Grandma Pauline always wore a loud pinkish flower-print housecoat and a bandana tied around her head. She had so many different colors you'd think she owned stock in a bandana company. I never understood why she didn't style her hair. It was a beautiful light brown color, very thick, and hung down her back.

I remember my father saying she didn't comb her hair because she was very tender headed. He told me that when he was seven years old he brought her a comb for Christmas. The thought of combing her hair made her so mad she whipped him with it. She felt so bad about it that she allowed him to stay up all night to listen to the radio and eat bags of pecans. She might not have cared whether or not her clothes matched or whether or not her hair was done, but one thing was guaranteed. She wasn't going to be caught without wearing her bright fuchsia lipstick.

Although grandma couldn't read or write, she was a successful businesswoman. She owned a small roadside café where she sold the best pecan pie in the world. I can picture her right now sitting in her rocking chair in front of the café, patting her feet, and listening to Al Green. She enjoyed talking about how she almost had his love child. She swore up and down that she had sex with him behind the café when he came through on tour. I think I got my imagination and my love of men from her. Ha, but according to her, the love of men is a curse! Grandma Pauline would flirt with every male customer who came into her café. If she thought a man was good looking and he ordered a slice of pie, he would get a discount. If she thought he was worthy of her time, he would give a slice of Pauline.

She did things her way. She was a woman who believed in being in control no matter if she was wrong or right. She ran her business the way she wanted to. Her idea of an accounting system was keeping twenty dollar bills in the red socks, ten dollar bills in the blue socks, five dollar bills in the white socks, and one dollar bills in her bra. She didn't trust banks because, in her mind, the white man was going to keep her money. When she passed away from a heart attack at the age of sixty-eight, my father and I had to go through her dresser drawers, underneath her bed, and in the cabinets to sort out all of the socks. It took us a couple of days, but, in the end, she had saved thousands of dollars in those socks.

Yeah, my grandma was something else! When she passed away she had everything in place. She had a will and all of her burial and memorial plans together. Grandma didn't want to have a gravesite service or anything to take place inside of a church. She wasn't a religious woman. I think she wanted to believe, but so much shit had happened in her life that it made it difficult for her. Once in awhile, I'd catch her talking to the Lord while she was outside hanging clothes on the clothesline. She insisted that she was talking to herself when I would say something about it. Her thing was that no Lord would allow colored folks to be hung by trees and burned to death if He loved 'em. Grandma would lock the door to the café on Sunday evenings when she saw church women coming her way. She would wave her rolling pin in the air and say, 'I'm not 'bout to be hearing those old buzzards preach to me!'

The reading of her Last Will and Testament took place at her café. Everything was done in Pauline fashion. It seemed more like a holiday gathering than a memorial service. There were mason jars and tubs of moonshine just as she requested. She wanted everyone in attendance to wear something with her favorite colors, red or pink. She also asked for everyone to receive a slice of pie. My father, my brother, and I cooked pies for two days before the service!

My grandma requested to have me read the will at the memorial service. I remember as if it happened yesterday. I was standing in front of a room full of people. Many of them I'd never seen before that day. I didn't know she knew so many people. I was nervous. The paper shook in my hands. My father walked up to me and steadied them. 'Don't be afraid. Your grandma trusted you to handle this. Be a big girl.'

At the time, I was only sixteen years old! When I looked at my father's face, I knew I could handle it. Grandma always had faith in me. I stopped shaking, stood up straight, cleared my throat, and spoke out loud.

"I, Pauline James, being of sound body and mind, leave my home which includes six bedrooms and five acres to my one and only son, Cedric James. Cedric, you were there with momma from the start. Your little hands helped me bake pies when no one else would help me. I leave all of my socks to my sexy granddaughter, Jasmine James. JJ, don't ever let anyone take away who you are and remember you run shit! To my grandson, Francis James, I leave my recipe book and all my special cooking stuff because your gay ass loves cooking." I stopped reading the paper and looked around the room. My grandma had written. Hey Jasmine, is everybody looking funny? Tell them this...Don't ya'll being acting like ya'll didn't know that boy is gay. He's gay as those male dancers in tights.

I couldn't say my grandma's little nasty comment out loud. It wasn't right. Folks in the room were already looking at Francis. He didn't care. Francis was eighteen and flaming. When I think about who honored her wishes, Francis sure did. He had on a black suit with a pink shirt and fuchsia lipstick on. Nothing was subtle about his dress and he was secure in his sexuality. He ate right and kept himself in shape. He was all about keeping himself groomed. His midnight black curly long hair was kept in a ponytail. Francis was always one of the tallest boys of his class. He was fine as hell! If he wasn't my brother and gay, I'd holla at him. Females would ask me to give him their phone numbers in the hopes of making him change teams. I tried to tell them it was a waste of time. Francis didn't want to be bothered with a girl unless they went shopping or cooked something together.

Ever since he was fifteen, I knew what was up. I remember the day he came home from the neighborhood recreation center. He fell to the ground in front of me crying because some boys beat his ass in the locker room. I can still picture the look on his face when he stopped crying. He stood up straight, dusted his clothes off, and declared he would never cry again because someone called him gay, faggot, or queer! To this day I don't believe the ass whopping hurt him. It was the reason he got the beating that bothered him most. He didn't understand why he couldn't just be who he was and have everyone accept him. Shit, he took that ass whopping better than any straight man I know. Francis was tough! He refused to let those boys keep him from going back to that recreation center. He loved sports and he loved being around other people. The very next day, he went back to play basketball with his friends and they jumped him again. This went on for weeks until that group of boys realized they weren't going to win.

I believe Francis got his fighting spirit from grandma. They were very close. He spent a lot of time with her cooking and listening to the oldies. Sometimes my father would get jealous because Francis would chose spending time with grandma over him. The two of them would go for secret shopping trips and go to the salon and get their eyebrows waxed. Back then, I wasn't into all of that. In many ways, Francis was her granddaughter for all the girly things she liked to do.

Once when she was down with pneumonia, Francis stayed out of school for an entire week to care for her. It was his senior year of high school. He missed out on a lot, but he put her first. Despite her telling him he wasn't a real man and that the Lord we believed in made a mistake, he still loved her to death. I don't believe the Lord made a mistake. To this day when I look at my brother all I see is a real man. I don't see nothing else.

Regardless of how secure I knew he was, I remember standing there feeling bad for him. For those folks who didn't know he was gay. This was no way for him to be outted to everyone. I remember wanting to grab him and walk out, but I had to finish reading. 'Now for the big shit ya'll no good ass black folks showed up for. Pauline's Pies! You think I'm leaving it to Cedric? Well no! As much as he helped me, he hated cooking pies all the time. He hates the smell of vanilla. So, I ain't leaving it to him. I'm leaving it to one of the other important men in my life.'

I remember hearing the water running in the underground pipes it was so quite. Everyone's face looked confused, especially my father. None of us knew she had anyone special in her life. My grandma loved men in general, so the thought of her having a favorite was too hard to believe. She sure was good at keeping a secret, because nobody knew these "important" men she was talking about. I felt happiness in my heart because I just knew she had to be talking about Francis. It only made sense that if daddy didn't get the café, Francis would.

I continued to read. "I leave my café, Pauline's Pies, to Raheem James."

My father jumped up. "Why and the hell did she leave the business to a dead man?"

He wiped sweat from his forehead. Everyone in the room whispered to each other. A couple of folks refilled their mason jars and laughed. I continued on with what my grandma had her lawyer write down. "Raheem James is the only man I've ever loved. He's the man who told me my pies were the best in the world; but, more important, he made me believe in myself. When I felt like I couldn't do anything else but wipe old white people's asses, cook their food, and wash their clothes, he helped me to find my calling. He helped me to find Pauline's Pies. We built the café with our hands, nails and hammers, and hearts. And he's the only man in the world that could make my toes curl."

The entire room got loud as everyone discussed what I had read. My father paced around the room, gulping down moonshine like it was water. My father pulled grandma's lawyer, Mr. Reynolds, to the side and asked him what to do. When my father got the lawyer's response, he threw the Mason jar he was holding up against the wall. It was funny how the room cleared out like roaches running from light. This was when we found out who cared about my father and who didn't. Only a few folks stayed. Then again, maybe they waited to see if they'd get something. My father was so angry. Mr. Reynolds told my father he'd give Mr. James a call first thing in the morning. So of course, that pissed daddy off. He hadn't seen or heard from his father since he was five years old. He was confused. Why was he told his father was dead? What really got him was how the lawyer had easy access to my grandfather.

"He's alive and you know where he is?" My father asked as he grabbed onto Mr. Reynolds's shoulders as if he was a slave pleading for his freedom.

Mr. Reynolds was a funny looking white man in the face. He had big front teeth, pretty blue eyes, and stringy blonde hair that was bald at the top. For an older man, he had a nice body which made him look funny. Nothing matched together. He always spoke softly which made it difficult to hear him.

"Well, of course, young man, I have been taking care of legal correspondences between your parents for years." Mr. Reynolds answered as if my father should've known what had been going on.

That was it! My father completely broke down. I never thought black folks had breakdowns until that day. He sat on the bench and cried. I understood where my father was coming from. I never knew my mother. She died while giving birth to me. If someone told me she was still alive after forty years of my life had gone by, I'd be hurt and pissed off, too! Daddy had every right to react the way he did. I ran over to my father to hold him in my arms. He was always there for me, even when he didn't know how to handle girl problems. I had every bit of respect for him. He took care of us and my grandma when most men would've found a reason to walk away. I had to be strong for him. I had to be the big girl he told me I was.

Francis, on the other hand, didn't give a damn. He had no sympathy for our father. Their relationship wasn't very tight anyway. My father knew Francis was gay and had a hard time dealing with it. My father never said anything, but you could see the pain he felt in his eyes when he looked at Francis. Even though my brother did the typical son activities like playing sports, my father couldn't stand who Francis was. So, by the time of our grandma's death, they had moved even further apart emotionally. Francis saw me holding our father in my arms, but that didn't stop him from coming over to ask if we could go home because he was bored. That upset me. How could he be so hardhearted towards our father?

"Francis, please. Daddy is upset. Go sit down until it's time to go." I told him as if he was five years old.

He was older than me, but I was always the boss. Francis had this strange look on his face, like he could care less how daddy felt. He bent over and whispered in my ear. "I've known where Grandpa Raheem was all this time. Grandma Pauline took me to see him once a month."

"What!" Immediately, I let go of my father and stood up to deal with Francis.

I grabbed his wrist and demanded an answer, "How come you didn't tell us?"

Francis had a smug look on his face. "Girl, you crazy. Did you really think we did that much shopping?"

My father was still crying, but looked up at both of us. "Tell us what, JJ?" He asked, "What shopping?"

I don't remember why I decided it was best for my father not to know what Francis had told me. All I knew was I had to come up with something good.

"Oh, daddy, you know how Francis is...he's not feeling so good and needs to go lay down. Right, Francis?"

I gave Francis the look. He knew whenever I gave him the look, he had better go along with what I said or it was his ass! Francis and I both knew I couldn't beat him physically, but I would fuck him up mentally.

Francis held his head down and answered, "Yeah, I don't feel so good."

My father pulled himself together and got up from the wooden picnic table bench. Grandma Pauline had her store decorated with a large counter to take pie and lemonade orders and picnic tables with red and white checkered tablecloths for people to sit and wait. Many nights the café stayed opened late so people could play cards, dominoes, and have a little moonshine. I remember looking around the room and thinking of how much my grandma accomplished in her life with no education. She made her mark in life and now, with all of the drama, she also made her mark in death. I wish I had known that my grandmother's death wouldn't be the last funeral I'd see for awhile, but I was about to encounter death in ways I could have never imagined.

CHAPTER FIVE

I finish drying off and start putting lotion all over my body. As I sit thinking over my childhood, I really can't be upset with my grandma for doing things the way she did. Back then I thought she was messed up for leaving the business to my grandfather and not my father, especially since he wasn't around for her and my father the way he should've been. I know she had her reasons, but what the hell were they. She always told me, 'Whatever you earn in life gives you the right to do whatever you want with it because it's yours.'

Hell, she believed in what she preached. She did what she wanted. Still, after all was said and done my father ended up with the café. My grandfather couldn't meet the obligations of running the café. After all the help Mr. Reynolds gave him, it was still too much for him to handle.

Mr. Reynolds hired employees, helped with ordering supplies, and bookkeeping. I remember him even getting in the kitchen to bake pies when one of the cooks he hired walked out. That day Mr. Reynolds and Grandfather Raheem got cursed out by everybody who ate some pie. Gossip started that Mr. Reynolds and Raheem were sleeping together. I asked Francis if he knew anything and he got pissed. He told me just because he was gay didn't mean he knew if other people were. I knew his ass was a liar, but I let it go.

After three months of running the café, my grandfather disappeared. He didn't leave a note or ever try to contact any of us. Mr. Reynolds even lost touch with him. Mr. Reynolds visited his home several times to attempt to ask him what to do with the café with no success. It was sad how Mr. Reynolds fell into a deep depression. He started drinking moonshine on the regular and let his law practice fall apart. Everybody said his behavior was proof that something more had gone on between the two.

Raheem's disappearance didn't surprise my father. Come to find out this was my grandfather's usual behavior. Disappearing was what he had been doing to my grandma and my father for years. He'd be gone for days at a time and then return home as if nothing happened. My father was only five years old when my grandma got tired and told him to leave for good. I never found out why she thought telling my father he was dead was a good idea; but with everything she did, it was the way she wanted it to be.

Needless to say, my father didn't want anything to do with my grandfather when he returned to run the café. Before his disappearance, all they did was yell and curse at each other. My father's last words to him were 'You should have stayed dead to me!' I was feeling what my father felt. I didn't want Raheem to cause anymore pain to our family. He had done enough. He really did need to go, so it was a blessing when he left—until the family found out his disappearance wasn't his usual skipping outta town, he was dead!

Authorities found my grandfather's body in a back swamp outhouse. The autopsy report stated he'd been dead for approximately a month. He was still sitting upright on the toilet with a bullet hole in his forehead. The investigation into his death moved slowly. The police department didn't work hard to find the killer. Folks in town didn't cooperate with the investigation. No one was concerned about who killed Raheem James. I guess my father and grandma weren't the only ones in town he did wrong. There wasn't a funeral or memorial service. My father had his body buried next to my grandma's. Nobody in the family talked about it anymore.

My father sold the café a year after my grandfather's body was discovered. The little roadside café where folks enjoyed the best pie, moonshine, and gossip in town was torn down and turned into a service station. Francis never did forgive my father for selling the café. Francis's dream of putting grandma's pies in grocery stores across the states was killed. I think the guilt of selling it killed my father inside. Daddy became deeply involved in his church to keep his mind off what he did. He had always been a church-going person; but after selling the café, you could hardly find him any place else. He was there six days a week, sitting as chairperson for one committee after another. He was hardly at home in the evenings. This left me and my brother to fend for ourselves. I didn't give a shit because we were old enough to take care of ourselves. My father seemed to be happy as hell and his lack of parental guidance gave me time to really fuck up.

My brother got over his anger and continued doing his thing. He became a freshman at LSU and kept up a 3.8 grade point average. He took business and marketing courses for the purpose of expanding the café. Since it was gone, he decided to focus his education on something else. Francis didn't like how a couple of his "close" friends were not ready to come out of the closet because of fear of being beat down. So, he became involved in human rights groups and the student council. Francis found his calling in life and decided to study law.

I wasn't doing as good as my older brother. I was in my senior year of high school and bored with the prospects for my future. College was the furthest thing from my mind. I was glad my father sold the café so I wouldn't have to cook pies for the rest of my life. The only thing that kept my interest was boys. By the time I was a senior in high school, boys no longer would do. I wanted men...grown ass men. I wasn't allowed to wear makeup and spandex shorts. So I packed my war paint and cum and get it shorts in my backpack. When I got to school, I'd change my clothes and put on my game face in the girl's locker room. I'd go into class for roll call and then step out to the girls' restroom and leave school. In the middle of my senior year, I stopped playing the damn games with my teachers and didn't bother with roll call. Instead of going to class, I'd go kick it at the local motorcycle club so I could take rides with men. That's when I discovered getting high and fucking on a bike was more exciting then sitting in history class. That proves my grandma was wrong about the curse. I was fast before my mid- thirties.

Damn, I miss Grandma Pauline. I wish she was here to meet my family and see how I'm livin' the good life. She would be so proud of me. She always said if I put my mind to it I could have anything I want in life. Hmm...she was all about teaching life lessons. One of her favorite lessons was Womanhood 101. Whenever she'd get a new tube of fuchsia lipstick, she'd sit me next to her at the vanity. The only time I'd see her comb out her hair was when she wanted to put on her new lipstick. She'd put it on real thick and then kiss me on my cheeks. 'Listen here, hambones, you was born into this world a woman, so you might as well use what a woman's got to get what you want in life. This world is hard on women but we's lucky, we sum foxy thangs!'

That night, Grandma Pauline drank too much moonshine and talked more than usual. She told me how she got the land she built the café and house on. "Hambones, sum mens in this world don't think with the head on top of their shoulders. Sum of 'em think that us women don't know that, but oh yes we do! But don't ever let 'em know you know. They like feeling smarter than us. But they ass is as dumb as a blonde chicken!"

All these years I've tried to figure out where the hell she got a blonde chicken from. But she was drunk and I've been there a few times in my life. There have been times I thought I had conversations with blonde chickens!

My grandma stood up from the vanity and danced across the room. I asked her why she was dancing without music. She replied. "Never let life take away your music. If you don't have it playing on the radio, let it play inside your head. Life can be an evil thing. Music can fight evil."

All I was thinking then was how the only evil going on was that moonshine. Once my grandma was done dancing across the room she sat back down in her chair at the vanity. She continued to comb out her hair and look at me in the mirror. "JJ, a mirror can tell you a lot about yourself. It helps you look deep into your soul. It helps you face troubles. 'Cuz you are the reason you have troubles in your life. When something isn't going right look at what is causing it."

With my grandma being such a damn control freak, she believed that we controlled everything that happened to us. If something didn't go right, look at what you did for it to get that way. The life lessons taught to me while looking in the mirror are why I stare in the mirror when faced with something hard to deal with. I can look deep into my soul and talk to the Lord. I can look my troubles right in the eyes.

I wasn't ready to learn the next lesson my grandma wanted to teach me that night. She continued, "Your grandfather Raheem told me I had the best pecan pie recipe in the world. He told me I needed to use my womanhood to make a better living for us. We knew that having a café would be a good way to make money, but didn't have money to get started. I was working at this old white folks' retirement home in town. I worked long hours for a little bit of nothing. There was an old fool that liked to grab my ass when I'd go in his room to bathe him. That old man had lots of money, but his family left him there to die. They said there wasn't enough money in the world for 'em to put up with his bullshit! After dealin' wit him for years, I knew what they was talking 'bout. One day I heard him on the phone talkin' 'bout some land he wanted to get rid of. I asked him how much he'd sell it to me for. He laughed at me and said niggers would never have enough money to buy his land, but there was something else he was willing to accept. And that was your Grandma Pauline; old dumb ass fool!" She was so damn drunk she fell outta her chair laughing until she cried. Her crying wasn't from the joy of laughter it was from the pain of selling herself. I believe that night my grandma didn't like what she saw in the mirror. No matter what she told me about using my womanhood to get what I wanted, I believe she hated doing so herself.

Her mirror lessons were every once in awhile, but she never passed on an opportunity to teach me something daily. From the time I was a little girl, there wasn't a day that went by she didn't tell me how pretty I was. She would say. "Love yourself when nobody else does." As I grew older, she told me I wasn't pretty anymore. She said I was foxy. I couldn't understand how a woman who didn't want to put fancy clothes on or comb her hair could put so much value on looks. Grandma dogged men who liked skinny women. She said they are fake because every REAL man wants a woman with meat on her bones. She'd tell me not to be intimidated by what I saw on television or in the magazines. She taught me how to walk with style and grace and to be happy with being me.

She'd have me walk across the café and repeat these words, "My curves make me foxy. I have something for men to hold onto and every inch of me feels good to a man. I really don't care what people think."

My father would get mad at her for teaching me shit like that. He said she was trying to make a ho outta me. He resented her for being the way she was. I think that's because she was what he wasn't—so confident and in control of her life. My grandma said she tried to teach him to love himself, but he was too busy hating her for not having his father there for him. She told me after awhile she got fed up with trying to explain why Raheem wasn't around. Sometimes when my father would come into the café, she taunted him. She'd stand at the counter mixing up her secret ingredients and roll her eyes at him. I guess women in my family are good with that one. She'd run her tongue across her gums and start talking shit to him. 'You know Cedric, yous funny lookin' just like your daddy. And yous act just like him. Got your ass up on your shoulders like you better than everybody else. You think you know everything when you don't know shit! You think your sorry ass daddy left because I was cheatin'. Well, yous don't know shit!'

My father would throw pie pans around the kitchen and yell that the only reason he bothered with her was because of me and Francis. Otherwise, he'd be gone. How in the hell could two people be there for each other one minute and then hate each other the next. I bet it had something to do with my father not having a real childhood. He didn't go to school all the time like other kids. He was busy at the café helping Grandma Pauline cook pies. He was twenty years old and bitter by the time he finally finished high school.

Many days, I'd sit and watch daddy in the kitchen standing beside my grandma cooking. I'd notice how handsome and impressive he was. He stood 6'3, deep chocolate with such a strong essence of loyalty coming from his pours that it would make folks want to be just like him. I'd think about how he'd laugh out loud and everyone else couldn't help but to laugh with him. I'd think about how my grandma would get so damn drunk that she'd fall out in front of the café. He'd pick her up, take her in the house, wash her up, and put her to bed. Hmm...I'd think about what he'd do if he didn't have his mother in his life anymore. You see as much as they fought, they were also best of friends. When Grandma Pauline died, so did my father's best friend. Things changed for him and so did his relationship with his children.

My father was not the same man I'd sit and stare at for hours. He became selfish and cold-hearted. I needed him to know that I noticed he'd changed. I stopped calling him daddy, he was Cedric. "Cedric. Hey, Cedric!" I'd call across our living room. Sometimes he wouldn't even answer me or look in my direction. I was pissed when he decided to abandon me emotionally after grandma was gone. When I needed him most, he didn't give a damn! I tried hard to get him to change back into the man I admired, back into the man who made me believe I could do anything, back into the man who steadied my hands and told me to be a big girl. I tried everything to get his attention. I'd stay out all night knowing he would come looking for me. Sometimes when I would see his car coming down the street, I'd hide on purpose. I wanted to put him through the hell I felt inside. When I realized that wasn't working, I focused on getting other men's attention.

Yeah, getting men's attention became a full-time gig for me. I would put on tight leather mini-skirts, fish-net stockings, and stilettos. I really did the damn thing when I put on false eyelashes. I walked around smacking on gum, blowing bubbles, and yelling "Hey, baby" to men passing by on the streets! Shit, since I no longer had the love of my father, I looked for love other places. I was seeking love when there was no love to be found in one night stands.

No, I wasn't a prostitute. Hell, I should've been! At least I would've been paid for all the times I was on my back or on my knees. I was so pitiful. It didn't take long for Cedric to completely give up on me. When he married the church ho, she persuaded him to move on with his life and he did. He stopped trying to keep up with me.

The last time I saw my father alive, I was standing outside of the main entrance of Major Mart. I was flirting with some biker who told me my ass was the shit. Cedric was holding hands with his ho ass wife walking toward the store from the parking lot. He saw me and was about to run toward me when the bitch held him back! I was hurt that he allowed her to stop him. I told the biker to take me for a ride. Of course, he wasn't going to let a young thang like me down. As I jumped on the motorcycle I looked back at Cedric. He stood still and watched as we rode off. I kept looking back at him. He had the same look on his face the day he put his mother in the ground.

CHAPTER SIX

Ah... that's enough lotion. Let me put a little moisturizer on my face. I'm getting older and I have to take good care of my skin. Black don't crack, but it sure does get dry! Damn, instead of looking in the mirror at my troubles, I need to start looking to pluck some of these gray hairs out. Francis and I both have gray hair in our eyebrows. He tried to give me a tip on how to color them. I tried it once and almost made myself blind from all the dye that got in my eyes. I have the money to get them done professionally, but it's not that serious for me. Darius only cares about the hair on my head and I don't give a shit what booty calls think. I'll just keep plucking them out.

If my grandma were alive today, she'd probably make a lesson out of me having gray hairs. She'd probably tell me how much control I have over the gray hairs. I can hear it now. 'You pluck them bastards out. You don't have to deal wit that, JJ. You run shit!' She called the shots and everyone who met her knew it. If they didn't know within the first few minutes of talking to her, they'd soon find out. She was known for kicking folks out of the café for being what she called 'disrespectful'.

One night, my grandma had a group of folks at the café playing cards and drinking. She was sitting back and relaxing in her rocking chair. One of the men playing cards told her to get her ass up and get him another sip of moonshine. She acted like she didn't hear him. Then, he made the mistake of getting loud with her.

"Bitch, get me some mo' drank!" Grandma stopped rocking back and forth in her chair. Everyone in the room got silent and stared at him. "What the hell wrong wit ya'll niggahs?" he asked.

Before anyone could answer him, Grandma Pauline knocked his ass over the head with a damn firewood log! She stood over his limp body. "I run shit here and don't ever call a lady a bitch!" Everyone fell out laughing. "Ya'll stop all that damn laughing and drag this disrespectful ass outta here!" Yeah, my grandma didn't play.

When she wanted something, she got it! She never did something for nothing—not even having sex. To her, that was a bad business transaction unless she just wanted to get hers and I remember that was a hell of a lot! Every man who got a slice of Pauline gave up a slice of himself one way or another. She had a drawer filled with men's rings, watches, and a box filled with shirts. What the hell did they give her their shirts for? I wonder how she even asked for them. I know she didn't always feel good inside about being that way, but that's how she rolled.

My grandma would jump out of her grave and slap the shit outta me if she knew how many times I didn't get a damn thing from having sex but a nut! If she was still alive and knew what went down tonight, it would have killed her. Her philosophy was a man can use his hand or you. It's his choice and if he chooses you, he has to pay for it one way or another. If you don't get money, a dress, or at least a meal then sex is nothing but a waste of energy. Grandma loved to lean back in her chair and talk loud. 'JJ, don't let dem niggahs sweat all over you wit theys stank breath breathing hard and makin' noises for nut'n!'

I believe my grandma had a reason for the way she thought. Something must have happened for her to feel the way she did. I don't think giving that old white man pussy for the land was her reason for her ways. One incident just doesn't make a person as controlling as she was. Plus, she had a serious sex drive. That was a whole other issue. I know she'd blame it on the curse, but she was just a horny old woman. It's too late for me to ask her about all this shit now. All I know is I'm grateful for her. When I ended up living on the streets with no place to go, I had no choice but to get something for my time. I wasn't stupid like I had been in the past—having sex with grown men to get my father's attention. I've heard people say sexually promiscuous women are crying out for help. I was crying out then; but, now, I'm crying out for dick. When I was on the streets, it became about survival. If a brotha wanted to holla at me, I made sure he was hollering while we sat in somebody's restaurant eating a meal. If a brotha wanted to touch all over my body, he had to be touching me while we lay in a warm or air conditioned hotel room. Nowadays when I fuck men, I don't worry about whether or not they have something to give me. The way I see things is if I get satisfied then I did get something. If a man makes my body feel the way I need it to, I'm good.

Sex is a two way street. Women are getting theirs just like men are. I know some women are being left unsatisfied, like I was tonight with Mr. UPS. If that is the case then, ladies, don't never go back to those men for seconds. In these cases, sex should be chalked up as a waste of energy. On the other hand, if a woman is getting satisfaction and she's happy with the man in her life, why should she make him pay for it? It's a matter of perspective. Right now, my reward is to get an orgasm and keep it moving. No attachments and no promises. Don't get it twisted. If you need to get the car note taken care of and a brotha is willing to handle that, than work yo' pussy on his ass!

With Darius, it's different. It's a matter of connecting. When I have sex with him, it's more than sex; it's a time for us to bond on a higher level. It's a powerful event. It's just these events don't take place often enough. When I fuck other men, I don't allow them to be on top. I don't allow them to kiss me, and I damn sure don't allow them to look me straight in my face. We have to be in positions where none of these things takes place. I have to be in a position of control or think I am or else it won't work. I will lose my wetness and desire to fuck a man until his eyes roll back in his head. I know you're thinking, "Hold up, sistah. You didn't talk that shit about Mr. Dress Shop!" Yeah, he's different. I don't mind him having a little bit of control. You see, I'm allowing him to do what he does. Just thinking about him excites me! Let me not put too much into that niggah. Men, in general, excite me! After tonight, I might need to change my thinking on that one!

Yeah, I need to change my thinking. I could be up in a hotel room with some dude—hell, the wrong dude and end up dead! Tonight was dangerous! Mr. UPS scared me. It wasn't the fear of being hurt physically, but of what might happen next.

Tears start to roll down my face. My vision is so blurry I can't even see good enough to get in touch with my soul. I grab my towel and wipe the tears. I enjoy sex...I enjoy sex with men who are not my husband. Damn, my grandma was right. When I look in the mirror I do see the problem.

I don't know. This is something the Lord is gonna have to work with me on. The Lord is gonna have to break me down and rebuild me into an entirely new person. I don't think this temple is worth renovation. He shouldn't even waste His grace on me. There is no hope for me. There's no fixin' this mess called JJ. I know I shouldn't doubt what the Lord can do. Maybe that's why I haven't been able to stop. I'm just playin' myself. I haven't been able to stop because I enjoy having sexual control over men. I'm losing my touch. You see how well shit went tonight! I lost control of the situation. I should've knocked his ass out! Huh, all this going to church with Darius and the kids for the past year and trying to live a decent life is getting to me. Trying to live in the light is making me crazier than sitting my ass in the dark!

This is gonna trip you out. For the past few months, the Sunday school focus has been on purity! I need some prayer because stuff isn't sticking to me. I've been trying hard to think the way the Lord does when it comes to my body. I know the Lord is trippin' off me! He's up in heaven telling his angels to watch over me because He can't stand to see me do what I do. Pastor says that kinda stuff breaks His heart. He is our Heavenly Father, we're His children and He hates to see us go through shit. Pastor says that His love is triple what our earthly fathers have for us. I damn sure hope so. My father didn't hurt when he saw me fucking up! Hmm...let me find my notes from Sunday. I know I put them somewhere over here on the dresser. Okay, here it is. Last Sunday's memory scripture was from Romans 8:6. To be carnally minded is death, but to be spiritually minded is life and peace. I would've never been at a hotel with Mr. Coffee or Mr. UPS if I kept this scripture in my head. My mind was wondering at the gas station tonight because I was not spiritually focused. I thank the Lord for His grace and mercy. After what happened tonight, I need to pray. I get on my knees in front of the dresser.

Father God, I know in order for me to change, I need to walk a different path. Grandma Pauline taught me a lot of things, but following your path wasn't one of them. I'm on a path that I am not happy with but struggling to give up. I don't know why I'm having such a struggle; but, at some point, in order for me to be the woman you want me to be, I have to walk the path you are directing me in. I know you are using my husband as my guide and I'm struggling with the walk. I am in the midst of change. I can feel it. Tonight, I felt it or else I wouldn't have hesitated the way I did. Help me, Lord. Help me to want to do what's right. Amen!

Woo, I need to finish what I was doing and get in the bed. I reapply my moisturizer because I wiped it off, along with my tears, with the towel. I turn around in circles in front of the mirror. Around and around, I turn. I wish that in one single turn something would change. I wish that I would be the woman my husband deserves. The woman the children can admire. I wish that all of my stretch marks would disappear, that the extra fat on my stomach would disappear, that the scar on the right side of my neck would disappear, that my sin from tonight would disappear. I'm making myself dizzy—dizzy with the hope of making my past disappear, but I know better than that. If I wouldn't have gone through certain things in my life, I wouldn't be as strong as I am. I turn to take a good look at the scar on my neck. Hmm... the Lord mapped out my life a long time ago. He is in control, not me. I stop reviewing the scars of my past. I throw my wet bath towel in the dirty clothes basket and sit down on the edge of my bed. I need to get some sleep. This has been one unnecessarily stressful day. And tomorrow doesn't look any better.

CHAPTER SEVEN

I take the pillow off my head. The sun is shining bright...what the hell! I'm lying on the bed and my body feels like a ton of bricks. I need to get up, but I don't want to. Damn, somebody opened the curtains in my bedroom! I guess somebody wants me to bite. I don't know why I'm a vampire in the mornings. It doesn't matter. It's time to get my ass up. I'm just about to jump from my bed when I realize I went to sleep naked. This is something I never do at home. The kids are good at running in my room and jumping on my head in the morning. That didn't happen this morning, maybe it did and I was too exhausted to move. No those kids are probably still in the bed. They're all partied out.

Somebody opened those damn curtains. If it wasn't the kids, who did it? Darius isn't home and Eva doesn't give a damn what time I get up. If grandma was still alive, I'd say it was her. She used to open my curtains every morning and shout, "It's Pie Time!" I hated that shit. That's probably the reason I hate mornings! I roll out of bed and grab my red kimono and slide it over my silky soft skin. At least I still have good skin. My stomach might have train track marks, but they're soft as hell. I walk over to the bathroom. It's still here! Damn mirror, the damn thing didn't go no fucking place! I wipe the mirror with my hand as if to slap it. I pause for a second. *"Lord, please help me not to have a mouth like a sailor today or a mind like one."*

I need to start this day off right. Pastor Jones always tells his congregation that the first thing we should do when we wake up is meet with God. I have circles under my eyes and they're puffy. Why would the Lord want to look at me first thing in the morning? I splash a little water on my face to get the crust out of the corners of my big light brown eyes. I walk over to the dresser and pick up my bible. I look at an old church program that's tucked inside. It has notes written all over it. This belongs to Darius. He's so good at taking notes during church. Hmm... what have we got going on here? Jeremiah 31:3 was the theme scripture for that Sunday. *Yea, I have loved thee with an everlasting love: therefore with loving kindness have I drawn thee.*

What a trip, the Lord just answered my question. Okay, I'm feeling it this morning. The Lord has everlasting love for me! The kinda love that looks at my eye boogers and pillow dents on the face first thing in the morning and still thinks I'm beautiful! He can look at me because He loves me, plain and simple. I can roll with that today! Yeah, my pastor is right. How could I not want to do right by the Lord? Whether I deserve it or not, I get his love on a daily. He doesn't think the way I do. He has forgiven me for last night and is giving me another chance. I hope I don't fuck it up! Damn, oh see, I messed up already! Forgive me, Lord. Let's start over.

I say a prayer. I brush my teeth, then go downstairs for a cup of coffee. As I'm heading down, I hear voices coming from the family room. The kids are up watching Saturday morning cartoons. I thought they were still sleeping. They didn't come and jump on me and say good morning. Or did they? I wasn't drinking last night, so why I am so forgetful this morning? Both of the kids are so into the show, you'd think they were hypnotized. How can they watch the stuff that's on TV these days? They have no idea about what a good cartoon is—like Tom and Jerry, Transformers, and The Smurfs. They're so into TV, they don't even notice I'm standing behind them. I don't bother them. I just grab my coffee. I'm looking around to see where Eva is at. She was torn down last night. I'd be surprised if she was able to get up by herself this morning.

On the kitchen counter, there's a copy of my agenda for the weekend. I guess she's not too hung over. She managed to remind me of what I've got going on or she's just rubbing my face in it. I have another boring ass dinner party on my calendar for tonight. You know what kind of dinner I'm talking about. The kind where you are obligated to laugh at jokes that aren't even close to being funny. The kind where all the ladies have nothing to talk about but who did their hair and who designed their dresses and how they've hired new help because the help they had before had no green card. Hell, I always laugh. Like they didn't know their employees were illegal when they hired them. I'm not tripping. I'm determined to not get caught up in gossip tonight.

Is it obvious I don't like attending these snooty ass fundraisers? Doesn't matter how I feel about it. These dinners are a big part of my life now. I do it for the social responsibility of my husband's business. Darius sent me to one of those uppity charm schools so I wouldn't act ghetto. If I had it my way, I'd walk into the joint with a bucket of fried chicken in one hand and hot sauce in the other. Don't get it twisted. These dinners raise money for good causes. It's just sometimes the focus is not there. That's because most of the women who attend were born into the money and then married it. They don't know what it feels like to be homeless or work from paycheck to paycheck and still not be able to pay all the bills. They don't know what it feels like to fuck for a hot meal, or do they?

I put my agenda back down on the counter. Sipping on my cup of coffee, I watch the kids, look around my beautiful home, glance out of the kitchen window at the gardener cutting the rose bushes, and review how sweet my life is. I mentioned before how I'm livin' the good life and it's hard for me to believe. The only way I can try to explain it is by saying how sweet it is! Yeah, my life is ever so sweet. Sweet is not even a good enough word to describe my life now. Have you ever heard surfers say the phrase 'sweet in excitement'? Maybe not, it's more of a Cali thing. When they say it, it's said with so much enthusiasm it makes you excited. SWEET! SWEET! No, sweet sounds good, but not good enough. Here's something everyone can relate to. Have you heard a rapper say THAT'S THE SHIT! No, even that is not good enough to describe how good things are money wise right now. I know you might have a hard time believing my life is sweet and the shit since I cheat on my husband. I would be confused if I were you; but when I stop focusing on my selfish needs, I can clearly see how truly blessed I am.

I'm married to Darius Brooks. You already know a little something about him. He's so damn fine and one of the most giving men on earth. My husband is 6 feet, 4 inches tall. He has dark brown eyes with dark brown skin. He's so dark chocolate sweet that I sometimes wonder if Hersey didn't get the candy bar idea from looking at him. His eye lashes are so thick and long you would think he wears fake ones. He has soup cooler lips and they are yummy. Yeah, I said yummy. I know at this point you wish you knew just how yummy. Well, have you ever heated up some honey butter and dipped your finger in it and licked it off ever so slowly? Yeah, that kind of yummy!

Now back to what I was saying, hmm...his body is chiseled to perfection. He believes in eating healthy and keeping himself in perfect shape. Ooh and his smile... it is my flashlight in times of darkness. Boy, does this man have a smile that lights up my world! Umm umm, his smile is what first caught my attention! Ooh and his hands are as strong as titanium, yet they are softer than my 600 thread count sheets.

I often think to myself that he's the modern day black Superman. Okay, you are thinking I'm crazy to compare my husband to a brotha that flies through the sky and leaps tall buildings; but, he's one of the strongest men I know. I don't know how else to describe his strength to you. I see it on a daily. It's the strength of his getting up at 3 am everyday to go on a prayer walk, then to the gym, then come home and make love to me. Afterwards, he walks our dog Buster, wakes the kids and then goes to the office. I'm talking about the strength of running his own consulting firm; but everyday at 6 pm, regardless of what is going on, he's home for dinner. He helps the kids with their homework, puts them to bed, and then goes back to the office to take care of unfinished work.

Yeah, my husband is Superman to me. Not only is he Superman, he's a modern day Moses. He leads this family into freedom everyday. He makes the kids focus on their education and teaches them to obey the Lord's word. That is only because the Lord is his first love. Church isn't something he just started doing recently. He has always had a relationship with the Lord. He pulls from the strength and power of the Almighty. His love for the Lord is what makes him the sexiest man ever to me.

So, why do I still sleep around with other men? Am I sick in the head? What else can you say about it? I have what other women dream about. I have what other women would kill for. I'm just an ungrateful, selfish ho who needs to repent. I'm glad none of your asses is God or I would probably be on fire right now. I have to say, last night was a start to repentance. I'm going to put my Superman where he belongs and that is being the only man between my legs, my heart, and in my soul. Is this really any of your business, huh? I sound like ole girl at the gas station last night.

Damn, you see how easily I can get off track. I was telling you why my life was so sweet. Anyway, Darius is not the only joy in my life. I have the two of the sweetest step-children, Allen and Jayne. I love my step-children for real. I'm honored they call me mother. I gave up my children years ago when I was nineteen years old. I had twins, two beautiful little girls. I didn't get to hold them when they were born. Before my delivery, I signed paperwork agreeing to give them up for adoption. I couldn't keep them. I had no money and no man for them to call daddy. I think I know who their daddy is, but I am not for sure. This is one of my reasons for my motto.

Sometimes when I look in the mirror, I wonder if they look like me. Do they have big light brown eyes and soft milk chocolate skin? I wonder where they are and how they are living. I wish I could have them here with me. They would be so happy to be with Allen and Jayne and have a step-father like Darius. Let me stop. I have to focus on how good my life is right in this moment. Yeah, let's see. Allen is ten and has a big imagination. I can't count how many imaginary friends he's had over the past couple of years. Each friend always gets him into trouble. One time when Allen was six, I caught him throwing eggs out of his bedroom window. I walked in and asked him what he was doing. He responded by saying, 'I'm not throwing eggs out of the window. It's Billy. See he's standing right here.'

I had to let him know I was going to mess him up if he didn't stop. 'Well, you need to tell Billy, who looks a lot like you, to stop throwing eggs or else he is not gonna have hands to throw anything anymore!' From what I recall that was the last imaginary friend Allen had. I can't tell you how grateful everybody was. We saved a lot of money on eggs and a whole lotta other shit!

Jayne is about to turn eight. Sometimes, I think she's fifty years old. I know she can be smarter than all of us grown-ups put together. She's my eyes and ears when I'm not around. Sometimes, she's my therapist. I never thought a damn seven year old girl could tell me so much about relationships. Jayne broke it down for me one night. She explained to me how I should be obedient to her father. I remember this as if it were yesterday. She was sitting on the kitchen counter, swinging her legs, and sucking on a blow pop. 'Mother, you don't really have to obey Daddy. Just make him think you're doing what he asks. He's too busy to remember what he asks you to do in the first place. Then, daddy will feel like you love him a whole lot. That's what I do.' Who would have guessed this little bit of advice would keep me and Darius out of so many disagreements? You know she reminds me of a younger version of my grandma. Jayne runs shit! Allen and Jayne, you can't keep them apart. They both have a big room of their own with a huge bed, but they have to sleep together every night in Jayne's bed. I don't deny them that since they're still small. I'll try and break it up as they grow older. I didn't have that when I was young so why keep them from it. I would have loved to cuddle up with my brother. Francis and I didn't show affection to each other like we should have. No, we were too busy cleaning and baking pies.

Ah, here comes Eva. She looks terrible! "Good morning, Eva!" I say it loud and clear with a smirk on my face.

Eva's angry. "Don't say nothing to me and I won't say nothing to you!" I love this trick's accent.

I try to sound like her and say with confidence, "You can't say nothing to me anyway, I'm the boss around here and my business is my business."

Eva starts throwing dishes in the sink. "If I didn't have a banging ass headache right now, I would put my foot up your!"

I interrupt her. "Hey, I prayed for God to help me with my potty mouth and forgot to pray for you. Try not to curse. The kids are sitting right here."

"Those kids can't hear shit when watching those stupid ass cartoons!"

"Yes, we can!" yells Jayne.

"Of course, Little Miss Thang hears everything," Eva states with bitterness.

I pull on her dress. "Okay, what's up? Do you wanna talk?"

She grabs a cup of coffee, walks away from me, and goes outside. I have no idea what's going on with Eva. Usually when she gets drunk like she did last night, she's thinking about the family she left behind. She's thinking about how to get her family into the United States. Eva is half black and Puerto Rican. I was always jealous of her beautiful curly hair and warm brown colored skin. She has a coca-cola bottle shape. Because of her accent, men love to hear her talk dirty. Just like I didn't know my mother, she never knew her father. All she knows is he was in the military, maybe...

Her mother was a waitress for some small raggedy bar military guys would hit up while in port. Most likely her father was military since her mother slept with military men for extra money. When Eva was seventeen, she found her mother outside of the bar dead with her clothes ripped off and a rope around her neck. From what Eva told me, she had been brutally gang raped. She left Puerto Rico a year later with a promise to go back for her sisters, brothers, and grandparents. Eva is almost forty and I believe her broken promise haunts her at night like the story of Sophie and Baptiste haunted me as a teen.

I know it was our broken hearts that bound the two of us together. I was on the run from the Louisiana authorities when I met Eva in front of a night club in New York. I was new in town and trying to find my way. She hooked me up and let me stay at her crib. Even though I was only in New York for eight months, she and I became like sisters. I never thought I would allow myself to become so close to another woman in my lifetime. I knocked down all of my walls and allowed her to know the real me. Eva is the only person, besides Darius, that knows I have night-mares! I have these nightmares of being surrounded by a black cloud and suffo-cated by these huge black hands coming from the cloud. She knows I'm afraid of my own shadow and of the sound of crickets at night. She knows I get sick at the sight of pecan pies and the smell of turnip greens. She knows that I am afraid of dying and going to hell. She knows why I was running from the police.

I kept in touch with her when I left New York for California. I couldn't stand that cold ass weather. Money was tight for the both of us so we talked on the phone only once a week. That was all I could afford, but we made the most of those calls. One promise we made to each other that wasn't broken was the Take Care promise. We made this promise one night when we were on the phone with our stomachs growling. We told each other whoever made it big first— meaning if you got a husband and had kids or lots of money—would take care of the other one. But the one being taken care of would watch the kids! You can't just trust anyone with your kids, Eva would always say...

"Okay, enough of the boob tube," I turn the TV off. "It's time to do chores, take a bath, and get ready for golf lessons." I sound like a real mother.

I hate that Darius makes the kids take golf lessons instead of what they want. He always tells me how some of the biggest deals for his firm happens on the golf course. He wants his children to be well-rounded, and I'm not gonna stand in the way of that. Darius was raised in a different world then I was. He went to school everyday, graduated, and headed to college to make something of his life. A big accomplishment for my family was the girls not getting pregnant before eighteen and the boys staying outta prison. So who am I to tell him what is right for his children? Hell, I really don't know how to raise kids. I go off what I remember seeing on The Cosby Show, and by a few things my grandma and father did for me and Francis.

Allen stands up and stomps his feet. "I don't like golf, I want to play football!"

I grab Allen and sit him on the couch and try to explain why he has to learn golf. I don't think I'm doing a good job at it because he starts crying. Jayne is feeling left out and starts fussing about taking golf lessons, too. I'm trying to get control of the situation when Eva walks over. "Nobody wants to hear this shit early in the morning. Get up stairs and clean your rooms!" The kids run upstairs.

At this point, I'm pissed she fronted me with them. I have to let her know. "Damn, Eva. I don't know what the fuck is going on with you, but I'm those kids' mother and I need to get them to listen to what the fuck I say!" My prayer went right out the window.

"Is that right?" Eva laughs. "I thought you wasn't going to curse today?"

I'm getting pissed with her now. "It's just us right now, Eva!"

Eva is standing at the sink rinsing off dishes. I can tell by the look on her face she is debating whether or not she is going to talk with me. "If you're their mama, then you need to stop letting them get over on you. These are black kids, girl. You have to be strong with them 'cuz this world isn't going to be kind."

I sit on the couch and think about what I just heard. I understand where she's coming from; but, at the same time, if they don't get love and understanding at home, how will they know what love looks like when time comes to have their own families? I'll be damned before I let either one of these kids end up like me—all fucked up about what love is. Before I can speak my mind, she starts up again.

"You need to have them kids call you Mama like black people are supposed to. I don't know why we having this conversation anyways, you not they Mama." Eva finishes the dishes and runs upstairs.

She knows that hurt. Just like she has pain from her past, so do I. She didn't have to go there with me, but she did. My stomach hurts when I think about how I don't have my daughters with me. Allen and Jayne didn't come from my womb, but I still love them. I'm these kids mother, mama or whatever you wanna fucking call it! You see, I wasn't going to be talking like this but sometimes folks just take a person there! I get up from the couch and head upstairs behind Eva. Suddenly, I change my mind. Instead, I turn around and go outside to sit by our lagoon-style pool. I remember when Darius and I fought about what type of pool to build. It was Eva who came to us with this beautiful solution. She knows how to address everyone's needs. I know something is messing with her, but I can't go trying to fix her. I'm all messed up myself right now. I can't be selfish! I get up and run upstairs to Eva's bedroom. I lightly knock on the door. "Come in, girl." Eva says while opening the door.

"Look Eva, I know you're having a hard time with something. Talk to me." I sit on the bed.

Eva sits next to me and looks me in the face. "We've been through some shit together. We've always had each others' backs. I appreciate you keeping our promise, but...I need to move out."

At first, I don't know what to say. If everything is all good, why does she want to leave? I'm silent for a moment as I try to think of the words to say. I know Eva keeps a bottle of rum in her nightstand, so I get up and take it out. "Hey girl, let's make us a special cup of coffee and talk about this."

Eva looks at me and grabs the bottle. "I don't want a special cup of coffee. I want you to give me the money to move out!"

I snatch the bottle back from her. "Okay, what the fuck is wrong with you?"

"I can't be your nanny, housekeeper, or damn cook anymore!" Eva shouts. "I need to find a man of my own, have kids of my own, get my own damn life!"

Wow, I didn't know she was feeling this way. She never talked about getting married and having kids before. She told me she never wanted to have stretch marks or morning sickness. She told me she never wanted to answer to any man. Eva told me she was happy living with us and being here for the kids. A part of me wants to handcuff her to the bed and the other part wants to write her a big ass check. I walk out of her room without saying a word. I come back in and hand her an envelope. Eva looks at me and starts to cry. "Take the damn envelope!" I want to leave the room, so I don't have to see her cry. She doesn't grab it, so I throw it on the bed and walk out. I head for my bedroom. The kids are standing in the hallway.

"What's wrong, Mother?" Jayne asks.

"Nothing, baby. Go in your room. I'll be in there to help you get dressed." I wipe the tears from my face.

She puts her little hands on her waist. "Okay, if you think I don't know something is wrong you're funny, mother. I'm gonna be eight, remember?"

Her little gesture makes me laugh. She's so grown. "Jayne, call me Mama, okay?"

"Mama, that's ghetto." She walks back into her room.

Allen is standing with a towel around his waist looking just like his daddy. Allen asks, "Eva's tired of taking care of us?"

I lean over and kiss him on the forehead. "No, sweetheart, she loves all of us. She's ready to have Allens and Jaynes of her own."

Allen put his head down. "Is father going to give them to her?"

"What?" I was confused by his question. "Repeat what you asked!"

"Father and Eva spend a lot of time together. I thought he was going to give her a family like he told her?"

My heart almost stopped. I hope this little boy is starting up with his imagination again. I know Eva and Darius are not fucking each other. When do they have time to be alone with each other? I try to hide my surprise and anger. I know Allen must be making this up. "Allen, this isn't funny. You shouldn't be saying stuff that isn't true!"

Allen lifts his head up to look at me. "I'm not making this up. He kissed her and said he was gonna give her a family!"

"Take your ass in that room and finish getting ready to go right now, boy!" I hit him on the ass and direct him to his room.

I need to find out the truth from Eva. I go back to her bedroom and stand at the door for a moment. How do I ask her about this without her being suspicious?

I hear her on the phone talking. I can't help but eavesdrop. I put my right ear closer to the door. It sounds like she's trying to keep her voice down. She whispers, "Yes, I told her I want to move out. She did just like you said she would, she gave me a big ass check! I'm going to have Manny help me pack my stuff today and I should be out of your house by Monday."

Was this bitch talking to my damn husband? What the hell is going on? Instead of me talking to her to get answers I go to my room. I start throwing clothes around. I know this niggah ain't cheating on my ass! He must be out of his fuckin' mind! I stop to look at the mess I made and begin to cry. It's not Darius cheating that hurts; it's who he's cheating with that feels like a knife in my heart. Let me stop. Before I jump to conclusions, I don't know if they're sleeping together. I need to talk to Darius. He'd never lie to me, never! I dig through the mess to find my cell phone. I think I programmed the hotel's phone number where he's staying at into my phone.

Here's my damn phone! "Okay, get it together, girl. Call your husband and find out what's going on. Be yourself. Don't sound funny." I look on my cell phone and find the number. I take a deep breath and dial. The operator answers, I ask.

"Yeah, may I speak to Darius Brooks?" The operator tells me to wait a minute while she connects me. I catch my breath to slow my heart beat. He picks up the phone, "Hello."

At first, I can't say anything. He repeats, "Hello? Is anyone there?"

I use my sexy phone voice. "Yeah, it's me, babe."

My voice surprises him. "Hey, JJ, what's up? You never call me at the hotel. Is everything alright with you and the kids?"

I think of something quick. "Yeah, I was just missing you. That's all."

"You should've called me on my cell phone. You know we have the family plan, right?" Listen to Darius always thinking of how to save a penny. "Call me back on my cell. We can talk without getting charged for using a land line."

It pisses me off that he's not excited to talk to me regardless of how I called his ass. "Darius, talk to me now. How are you?"

"Baby, you sound funny. Are you sure you're alright?"

The part of me that was taught to be in control starts losing it. "Look, Darius. Nothing is wrong with me except...I need to know if you're fucking Eva?" I ask without any hesitation.

Darius's voice changes, he sounds angry. "I can't believe you asked me that. Eva is fam. She's like your sister. Hell, she's like my sister!" Darius hardly ever curses and he just said hell. I know he's pissed. I don't give a shit! I have my own agenda. "Were you on the phone talking to her today?" Darius gets quiet. I wonder if he's trying to think of a good answer. Then, I hear him coughing. He better be choking and not stalling. I ask the question again to make sure he heard me. "Were you on the phone talking with Eva earlier today?"

He answers with an attitude. "Yes, so does that mean we're fucking?"

He didn't say having sex. He said fucking. Yeah, he's pissed. "No, that doesn't mean you're fucking. Kissing her and telling her you gonna give her a family does!"

He starts to laugh. "Jasmine, you can't be serious about this? You got jokes now, right?" He hardly ever calls me Jasmine and I don't see what is so damn funny.

"Niggah, I'm not joking!"

"Jasmine, you know I don't like using that word. You know better than to act like this. Use your head, baby. Think. I have nothing but love for you. I only want to be with you. You're the woman God gave to me. When I thought I couldn't love again, he sent me you! Come on, baby. Stop being so emotional and think." His voice sounds so loving. I'm embarrassed for steppin' to him like this. Darius has been nothing but good to me.

"I'm sorry, baby. I didn't mean to act like a crazy bitch. I love you so much I can't picture you leaving me." I sound so pitiful.

Darius goes into explaining their conversation. "It's fine, baby. Just let me tell you what we talked about. Eva told me before I left town that she wanted to move out, but was worried about how you were going to feel about it. I told her knowing JJ, she's not going to express feelings one way or the other and that you'd probably just write her a check and not talk about it."

Now, I feel even worse. I don't have the right to be upset about Darius if he was cheating. I'm the one with my legs up in the air for other men. If I was a good wife, I'd be bringing the pussy home to him. Reality sets in on how my husband would feel if he found out about me. Damn, this shit hurts. I don't want him feeling this! He doesn't deserve nothing close to the feelings I'm having right now. I turn on my sexy phone voice again. "When you get home, baby, I'm going to make this all up to you. I promise."

"That's alright, baby. You can keep your promises. Look, I need to head out to a meeting. I'll talk to you later. Love you!" He hangs up.

What kinda shit is that! He hangs up on me without letting me say goodbye! What did he mean by keep my promises, like I'm writing him a bad check! Oh, I know I need to pray now! *Father God, please help me not to choke the shit out of my man when he gets home. Amen!*

Fuck all this! I better get these kids ready for their golf lessons. Hell, I'm going with them so I can learn how to swing a golf club. I might need to whoop some asses up in here! He better be telling me the truth! Eva needs to hurry up and move the hell outta my house. This kinda shit is why I don't hang with females; but, Eva is not just any female. Darius was on point when he said sister because that is what she is to me. I hear Jayne pulling stuff down from her closet. I better get her dressed before she comes out looking like Rainbow Brite. I go to Jayne's room and get her dressed. Allen has already gotten himself together. I throw on my clothes and call Manny on his cell phone. "Manny, it's time to take the kids to their lessons. Can you meet us out front with the car?"

Manny is always on top of things. "I'm already out here, Ms. Lady."

"Thanks, Manny. We'll be right out."

I see Eva through the crack in her door. She's packing stuff in boxes. I want to say something to her, but I can't. Too much is going on in my head right now and I have to sort it all out before I cut somebody! The kids and I get outside and Manny is standing by the car with the doors open. "Hello, my little bambinos!" The kids start laughing and jump in. I get in on the other side of the car, put on my sunglasses, and lay back to enjoy the ride...

My mind wanders to when I started dating Darius. He was very open and honest about his life. He told me what happened to his wife, Shelia. She died because of medical problems. She acquired a bad heart condition after giving birth to Jayne. He told me how Shelia would hold the kids in her arms for hours thinking that might be the last time she'd hold them. It broke his heart knowing the love of his life was going to die. Jayne was only three months old when Shelia passed. Darius's family said he couldn't even stand up at the funeral he was in so much pain. They had to wheel him in a wheelchair to the limo because he wouldn't walk. I don't think he would've gotten married again if it weren't for his family. He was under pressure from his parents to find a mother for his children. So, it didn't take him long to start dating.

I met Darius at the movie theater when he was out on a date with this chick younger than him. She worked for Darius's father answering the phones. His father was trying to live through his son when he fixed them up. Mr. Brooks knew he wanted to fuck that young girl! He might be fucking her now, she still works for him and don't know shit.

Darius was walking out from seeing a movie and I was arguing with the ticket guy that I left my ticket in my jacket. I had to go to the restroom bad and forgot I left it. Dude didn't want to let me back inside. I saw Darius watching our argument. He flashed his phenomenal smile and I had to pause my yelling for a moment to take notice. He walked over and talked dude into letting me in. It felt like I was struck by lighting when Darius spoke to me.

"You're too fine to put up with being harassed. You should tell your man to come out the theater and handle him." Darius's voice was so deep and sexy. It still is. He thought he was slick trying to find out if I was with someone.

"I'm here with my girlfriend." I wanted his question to be answered. "Thank you for getting me back in. I appreciate it." I started to walk away.

He softly grabbed me by the wrist. "You can repay me by coming to the movies with me next time instead of your girlfriend." He placed his business card in the palm of my hand. "Please call me. I think you are my blessing."

Because I didn't know how to respond, a smart ass question came out. "Do you like grown women or you like playing house with little girls?"

He was puzzled until he realized I was talking about his date. "Oh, her. She works for my father. She's a nice person."

I couldn't believe he didn't go off on me. I thought he would've said a little something smart back to me, but he didn't. "You enjoy the rest of your movie."

I watched him walk back over to the little girl he was with. During all of this, she stood in the corner watching like her ass was in timeout. I went back inside the theater and told Eva what had happened. Eva tried to read the business card in the dark. She hated on me. "You lucky ass ho, how come you get the men with a good job and I get the ones on food stamps!" We both laughed until folks told us to hush! Of course, I called his fine ass the very next day. I wasn't about to let the opportunity of getting to know a brotha better pass me by. Darius was slick with his. I didn't know until years after we were married that he slipped the ticket dude a twenty dollar bill.

At the time I met him; Eva and I were still working minimum wage jobs and sharing a studio apartment in southeast Diego. I grew tired of the LA life and moved to San Diego for a change. Eva was tired of the hustle of New York and took a bus down to stay with me. We loved taking trips to the other side of town to watch movies. I don't know why but movies were cheaper and the popcorn boxes were bigger. I believe we took the trip more so for the ideal of feeling rich, not just the great theater experience...

We finally arrive at the golf course. I try to force the kids to get out of the car. Manny has a better plan. He promises to take them for ice cream if they do a great job. They jumped out the car and run toward their instructor without looking back. I hop in the front side passenger seat and look in the glove compartment for some gum. There's one pack left. I open three pieces and shove them in my mouth. I lean the seat back and close my eyes.

Hmm...the fact Darius took me into his heart and home and made me his wife is an honor for me Even though I didn't have a high school education; he fell in love with me anyways. Sometimes in the back of my mind, I wonder if he didn't settle. His mother tells me all the time I remind her of Shelia. I wonder if Darius feels the same and that's why he married me. I've seen her photographs. We look alike, especially our hair. An oil painting of her is still in his office. It never bothered me before. I've always been secure in how much he loves me, until today.

I open my eyes and watch Manny walk around. He's so protective of us. Or just paranoid as hell! I dig in the glove compartment to grab a piece of tissue to spit my gum out. It doesn't taste good anymore. Instead, I find a wallet size family photo of Darius, Shelia and Allen. I can't be mad at him for holding on to her. She was his high school sweetheart. He told me he knew he was going to marry her when they were in the 8th grade. He fell in love and couldn't do a thing about it. It happened the day she poured milk all over his backpack. Shelia was mad because someone told her he said she was nappy headed. It was true. She was nappy headed, but Darius didn't care. I guess he always knew he was going to make money and pay to get her hair done. He told me that from that day forward no one could separate them. They graduated together, went to college together, and then got married. Darius has a degree in international business and Shelia's was in business administration. She helped him to start his consulting firm.

You see, Black on Black Consulting wouldn't be here today if it weren't for Shelia. In their first year of marriage, Darius was fired from the company he worked for. Their reasoning was he wasn't being productive enough. He started looking for another job but Shelia encouraged him to start his own business and that his focus should be on helping blacks get into the game of international business and trade. So I understand why he still has love for the woman. She was a big portion of his life. Well, sometimes I understand. This thing with Eva, however, I don't understand.

I put the photo back in the glove compartment and put a piece of fresh gum in my mouth. Instead of putting the pack of gum back, I squeeze it in my hand. I look up and see that Manny has stopped making his rounds around the golf course. You'd think he was a bodyguard the way he carries on. He gets back into the car and messes with me. "You're chewing gum, what's wrong?"

Damn, I was in the middle of going back into a deep meditation. Manny is my close friend and personal driver. He's not closer to me than Eva, but he's always been there for me during some tough times in my life. Just like Eva, I met Manny years before I met my husband. He's one of those people I never want angry with me. He knows some of my darkest secrets.

He pats me on the shoulder. "Poor Ms. Lady, you live in a million dollar home in one of the most beautiful seaside communities in California. You don't have to cook, clean, go grocery shopping, or even deal with the kids. Hey, you don't have to drive if you don't want to. Yet, you're still so unhappy."

I take my shades off and turn to look at Manny. His face is sometimes so expressionless it's hard to tell what he's thinking. This time I know what he's thinking because he had to say something to me. I'm not in the mood for his 'you should be happy no matter what' philosophy.

"Manny, I know you like reminding me where I've come from and of what I've got. But I'm not in the mood right now."

Manny takes the pack of gum out of my hand. He puts the last piece in his mouth. "Yum. You know, Ms. Lady, when people get ungrateful for things, those things are often taken away from them. I hope you change your heart soon." He gets out of the car and walks toward the kids and their instructor. I see their faces light up with laughter when Manny tries to take a swing at a golf ball. Shit, why can't I be happy right now! I pull my cell phone out of my jean pocket and press nine on my speed dial.

CHAPTER EIGHT

I pull up in front of the house. Oh shit! Look at the time. I better move my ass quick! I run into the house and up the stairs into my room. Manny, Eva, and the kids are sitting down having dinner.

Jayne yells, "Mother, you gonna eat dinner before you go? You know you don't like those white folks' nasty food!"

I can hear Manny telling her to sit still and eat her vegetables. I walk into my bathroom and turn on the shower. I pull out my floor length cocktail dress and try to figure out what shoes to wear. Those Jimmy Choos I left at the hotel yesterday would have been tight. Where did I put my control top pantyhose? I'm fumbling through all of my pairs of pantyhose and none of them will work. This is the problem when you have too much of everything. I didn't always have this problem. I remember having one pair of hose and when it had a run, I would put clear fingernail polish on it to keep it from getting worse. I had one good pair of black leather shoes that I wore so much I can't count how many times I super glued the right heel.

I'm yelling like a crazy bitch locked in a nut house "Eva, Eva, please come here and help me find my control top pantyhose. Eva !"

Eva is my bloodline. This is not just about our promise. Without her, I'm gonna be fucked up! Eva cares for the kids, keeps the house clean, and—as you can tell—helps me get dressed. I didn't want to talk to her tonight, but I need her help right now. I'm looking through all my drawers trying to get shit together. "Eva!"

"Yes, JJ? I'm standing right here." She's out of breath from running up the stairs. "I was trying to have dinner with your kids since you decided to leave the house without telling us. Sorry if I didn't move fast enough for you. I'm a little tired from cooking and cleaning all day." She has to be a smart ass. Her attitude pisses me off. I know what she's trying to say and I don't like that shit.

"No worries. I found the pair I was looking for." I shoo her away as if she was a servant. I know it makes her upset. "You shouldn't have run up the stairs because you need your energy. Go back down the stairs to make sure the kids are good."

"Sometimes you're a WITCH, this is another reason I'm getting the hell outta here! I'm not your fucking slave!" Eva yells while walking away.

"As long as you don't say Bitch, we're good!" Just to get under her skin, I walk to the top of the stairs and yell down to her. "You don't want me cancelling that check do you?"

I shouldn't be acting this way with my friend, but the bitch has gone too far with things today. All she had to do is let me know a long time ago how she felt about shit. Instead, she goes to my husband and confides in him. Then, she wanna make me feel guilty about making a run to see Reggie. She's bringing the old JJ out! Before I really have to go there, let me get my ass ready for this benefit dinner. I put my shower cap on and jump in the shower to take a quick one. When I step out, I try not to look in the mirror. I don't have time for that. I don't need to reflect on anything, but it happens anyway. I look in the mirror.

Hmm...Who would've ever thought poor little JJ would live a life like this? I never thought it myself, but here I am living it! Shit, Reggie's got me feeling high as celebrities in rehab. I rush to get dressed. I stop to look in the mirror once more. Well, I'm not looking too shabby. Damn, I'm fly! This satin red gown was meant for me! I love red and I love silks and satins. I'm about to head downstairs when I remember I need a necklace that will cover this scar on my neck. I buy all of my jewelry custom made because of this scar. My scar is a constant reminder of my past...

When I headed out to Los Angeles from New York, I had to find a means to support myself. I ended up working at this restaurant as a waitress and weekend fry cook. Since I didn't have family in LA, I slept at different shelters and hotel rooms for a few months. I finally found a raggedy hotel room that rented to me on a weekly basis. I felt like I made a step forward. Then all of a sudden, I was taken several steps back. I ended up meeting one of the biggest nightmares of my life—a pimp who went by the name of Juice. He was the ugliest, tackiest dressed, funky breath pimp that ever walked the streets of LA. I know what you're thinking... I thought she said she wasn't a prostitute? I wasn't. That was the problem! He wanted me to be his.

One night after work, I got a ride from a popular businessman who would come into the restaurant for a cup of coffee every night. He was known for going down to Pussy Alley for a good time. My hotel happened to be near Pussy Alley, so why not get the ride? Juice saw me getting out of the businessman's car and assumed I was tricking. From that night on, he wanted to make me his ho. He sent one of his nasty ass bitches over to me to find out what was up. She tried the girlfriend approach like she wanted to be my friend. I stood there listening to her questions and gave her no answers. I wasn't about to give her any information. She got pissed so she tried another tactic. She hemmed me up against the ice machine in front of the hotel. She slightly dug her nails in my neck and put her forehead up on mine.

"Check this out. Juice likes a bitch that knows how to go for the big money. Why don't you walk that big pretty ass across the street and talk to him." Her breath smelled like she'd been sucking his asshole.

I was never the fighting type of female, but that night I was gonna fuck her up! I pushed her outta my face. "Check this out. Take your booty hole breath ass back across the street and tell what's his face to fuck off!"

She was walking backwards, laughing. "Little girl, you don't know who you saying no to. It was nice meeting you!" Juice watched every move I made from across the street. He saw that I wasn't walking back with his girl.

"Ruby, hurry the fuck up and get yo dumb ass over here!" Juice was trippin'. Soon as she reached him he slapped her to the ground. I wasn't going to keep watching that awful shit. I went into my room and hit the sheets.

The next night when I got off work, Juice approached me outside of the restaurant. His voice scared me so bad I dropped my purse. He unbuttoned his pants and took his dick out. "'Bout time, I'm done wit you little girl. You gonna change yo' mind and be my bitch."

I picked up my purse and swung it at him. I told him I wasn't down and for him to leave me the hell alone! He didn't like my attitude. He grabbed me and put me in a position to be slapped! Luckily, I got rides from Mr. Businessman every night. He walked out of the restaurant right before Juice was about to hit me.

"What the fuck are you doing?" Mr. Businessman yelled.

Mr. Businessman was no bitch. He was around 6'6. He didn't have a lot of muscles, but he had big arms and hands. He was one of those corn-fed white men. I don't believe Juice was scared of him, he just didn't want trouble. Juice backed up off me, put his dick back in his pants, buttoned up, and walked away. I thought that was the last time I would have to deal with his nasty pimp ass; but, nope, that was wishful thinking. Juice would walk up to me every night and ask me to be his bitch. Each time Mr. Businessman walked out of the restaurant, Juice walked away.

Mr. Businessman was so kind. He'd tell me to never get into the kind of lifestyle like the women he paid for was in. On the rides to my room, he would tell me how I reminded him of his daughter. He was divorced and wasn't allowed to see his daughter anymore. He never told me why, but I really didn't give a damn anyways. Well, I didn't until the night everyone saw his face plastered all over the news. Mr. Businessman shot his ex-wife and daughter. Then he shot himself in the head. Everyone talked about how I was riding around with a crazy man and didn't even know it. Wow, all those nights of him talking about stuff and reaching out and I didn't even notice. If I had a relationship with the Lord back then, I might have been able to help him. But then again, if you crazy enough to shoot yourself, can't nobody help you. I remember shedding a couple of tears. Yeah, I was sad for a moment only because I knew I was gonna have to start walking to my hotel room alone at night.

That night of the tragic news, I asked everyone to give me a ride. No one was driving in my direction and wasn't about to go out of their way for me. I still remember the chill I got when I saw Juice through the glass windows of the restaurant waiting on me. I knew I was about to go through hell! Strangely, when I got ready to leave, he wasn't standing outside anymore. I quickly walked to my hotel room. I had no idea he was behind me until I opened the door to my room. I heard this voice behind me. "Check this out, little girl. When Juice gives you the honor of being one of his bitches, you best take him up on the offer!"

His voice was raspy. If I knew what the devil sounded like, I would have thought he was Lucifer himself. That was the beginning of Juice enjoying his harassment. Every night when I arrived at my room, he was standing outside of my door. Juice would laugh and then yell, "I'm givin' yo ass one mo' chance bitch!" I'd just run into the room and lock the door. I should have called someone, my father, my brother, Eva, but I didn't.

I really couldn't call my father. I didn't have his phone number anymore. And I hadn't talked to Francis since leaving New York. Every once in a while I hinted to Eva about what was going on, but didn't give her details. I wanted to prove to everyone I could make it on my own. Eva's advice was to cut him with a blade. I should've listened to her, but I was already in trouble with Louisiana authorities. I didn't want California on my ass. Although I didn't let my family know what was going on, I made friends with this Hispanic man who started coming into the restaurant everyday for lunch. He would always call me Ms. Lady. I'm sure you guessed that man is Manny. He sat in my service area of the restaurant everyday. We talked all the time. At first, I thought he was hitting on me, waiting for a chance to get some. He never made a move. Manny had nothing but respect for me.

On my eighteenth birthday, I was lonely. I don't remember telling Manny it was my birthday, but somehow he knew. He walked into the restaurant with a bouquet of balloons and a large card. It was one of the biggest birthday cards I had ever seen. Everyone in the restaurant sang "Happy Birthday". I felt so special. Manny has a way of making everyone he meets feel special. That is one of his special gifts plus making the best damn guacamole and tomato salsa.

As the weeks went by, Manny noticed how on edge I had become and asked me why. By this time, I had endured a month of Juice's harassment. I told Manny what had been going on. Thinking about it now, that was one of the smartest decisions I ever made in my life. The night I confided in him was like taking a pound of bricks off my back. Manny knew who Juice was. Growing up, they didn't live too far from each other. Manny told me that Juice's real name was Nathan Walker. Nathan was very popular when he was in high school. He was on top of the drug game back then. He gradually moved into pimping. Nathan would talk freshman girls into selling their pussy to football and basketball players after the games. He groomed young girls into serious money makers. His star performers were called the Chocolate Donut Club. Nathan promoted their pussy as being so good that men felt like they were sticking their dicks inside a sweet creamy hole. It's a shame he didn't use his marketing skills for something positive!

Manny said Juice was making so much money that he purposely kept failing classes to keep from graduating. It was rumored that Nathan had something to do with several young girls who came up missing. Yeah, Manny knew the deal so he was quick to protect me. He gave me a ride home every night after work. Despite Manny's protective efforts, he couldn't keep that sick minded pimp from trying to kill me. Juice was determined to have me work for him or die. Looking back on it now, I know his wanting me to be one of his bitches was all about recreating his money making days. He wasn't on top like back in high school. He never had a bitch tell him no before either. It was a matter of pride more than him thinking I'd make him money.

He wanted me so bad that he conned the front office person into letting him in my room one night. I should have known something was wrong when he wasn't standing outside my door as usual. I remember sitting in Manny's car looking at my hotel room door wondering what was up. I should've listened to my instinct telling me something was wrong. Manny also thought it was strange for Juice not to be up to his normal routine. He offered to walk me inside, but I told him no. I remember telling Manny, "Maybe Juice is tired. Anyways, he knows you be watching him." I gave Manny a kiss on the cheek and got out of the car. Once

Manny pulled off, I opened the door and tried to turn on the light. It wouldn't come on. When I walked over to turn on the bathroom light, Juice was sitting on my bed smiling with his fake gold front teeth. I should've been able to smell his funky ass when I opened the door.

Juice took a deep breath and put a toothpick in his mouth. "Now bitch, this is the last time I'm gonna ask yo ass!"

He always looked evil, but that night he looked like he called upon all the evil in this world. When I tried to run past him to get out the room, he got up from the bed, grabbed my arm, and cut the side of my neck. I knew he was trying to kill me but didn't hit the right spot. The room was so dark I tripped over a chair and fell to the floor. I was holding onto my neck. I felt a hot burning sensation as the blood oozed out. Not knowing if he was going to cut me again, I crawled toward the door and tried to get away. Juice stood over me laughing. "Bitch, I bet yo ass won't work for nobody now!" He kicked me in the head and walked out the room. He had left me for dead. Thank the Lord I was always forgetful. I left my purse in Manny's car and he came back to give it to me. Manny walked in my room and saw me lying in a pool of blood. He rushed me to the hospital. The doctors stitched me up and told me how lucky I was he didn't cut deep enough or with accuracy. I was blessed to be alive...

"Damn, baby girl. Whoever cut you didn't want you dead, but he or she damn sure wanted to teach you a lesson," the hospital nurse stated.

The nurse who cared for me was an older black woman who always had something to say. Everyday when making her notes in my chart, she would stand at the foot of my bed chewing gum and blowing bubbles. I think that was when I realized chewing gum wasn't a sexy thing to do. Let me think...hmm...oh yeah, her name was Martha.

I sat up in my hospital bed. "So, you think he didn't want me dead?"

"Hell no! Whatever you did, if I was you, I wouldn't do it anymore." Martha was always so loud with her comments.

"I didn't do anything but decide not to be a prostitute." I sounded like a five year old.

Martha stopped charting and frowned up at me. "Baby girl, if a pimp wants you dead, you gonna be dead. No doubt!"

She was a big woman with yellow and green highlights in a hairstyle that reminded me of Tina Turner when she was still with Ike. Martha always walked into my hospital room singing 'Amazing Grace'. I thought that was funny since she cursed like a sailor. She taught me words I never heard before. It didn't matter. She took good care of me for three days. The hospital didn't want to keep me any longer since I didn't have insurance. The day I was discharged Martha walked into my room with a white gift bag. It had rainbow tissue paper inside of it. I remember feeling like it was my birthday again.

"This is for you, baby girl," she handed it to me and smiled, "You pay close attention to what is in this bag. If you do, you will find strength and power in times of trouble."

She turned around to walk out of the room then paused. "I lost my baby girl when she was your age to her boyfriend. He's in prison because of it and will probably get out one day. But my baby girl...well her ashes are in a porcelain container and she will never feel sunshine upon her skin again," Martha turned and looked at me. "I've forgiven him for what he took away from me. I had to learn the healing power of forgiveness. It didn't come easy but knowing that the Lord is taking care of her now makes it a little bit easier." I could tell she was trying to keep from crying. "Do me a favor, watch yourself, and call your family." Then, she walked out.

I opened the bag and pulled out one of the most beautiful bibles I'd ever seen. It was white with rainbow colored writing. Inside she wrote, Do not walk around in fear. God is protecting you. You have a reason for still being alive. I broke down in tears. I always felt like I was living someone else's life. Like I was supposed to be doing something different from what I was doing. I just never knew what. I still use that bible to this day.

I have a very deep love for Manny and it has nothing to do with sex. He saved my life. I have love for Martha. She helped me to explore God's word more by giving me a bible. I even have love for Juice. If it weren't for what he put me through my heart wouldn't had been open to explore God's word. I just wish I would have kept on exploring. I know I'd be in a better place mentally, but everything happens for a reason. The struggles I'm having right now are for a reason. Maybe I'm supposed to help other women with their struggles. Wouldn't that be a trip if I ended up inspiring young women? Maybe I should tell Darius to send me to school for public speaking? Let me stop. Hell, I'd be lucky if they let me call out bingo numbers at the senior center.

CHAPTER NINE

When I think back on the time I was released from the hospital, I can't help but be grateful. Manny took me into his home during my recovery. He never asked me for a dime. Never! He didn't know much about me but he cared. It was as if he took the role of being my father, but never asked for a blood test. I still don't know why Manny did everything he did for me. I asked him one day and he smiled and put his head down and walked away. I used to think he was religious, but I've never seen him read a bible or pray. When I bring up the subject of going to church, he disappears.

So, I don't even know if he believes in God. I guess that's just between Manny and the Lord. I'm sure Manny is just like everyone else. He has demons to fight or mistakes he wishes he could erase. Not long after my release from the hospital, Juice was found lying in a pool of piss and blood in an alley behind this sleazy strip club with his dick in his mouth. I don't have proof, but I believe Manny is the one who killed Juice. Manny would talk about how Juice didn't deserve to be walking the earth after what he did to me. While I'd be sitting in his living room on the couch watching TV, Manny would be walking around the house outside talking to himself. Shit, nobody is exempt from being a little crazy! One of my co-workers at the restaurant told me Manny's little sister was one of the girls who came up missing when Juice was pimping in high school. Huh, that's enough to make a man nut up and kill somebody. I never asked him about it. In my heart, I really don't want to know.

Oh shit! Here I go again getting off track. There we go; this necklace will work just right. Okay, earrings, handbag, and shoes. Now, I'm ready. I hope I don't fall down these stairs. I should probably walk down barefoot but knowing Eva, she's standing at the bottom of the stairs with that damn video camera of hers. I wish I didn't buy it. I sometimes feel like I'm on a reality TV show with her following me around with that thing! I walk out of my room. Damn, there she is with tape rolling! I walk down the stairs. My face is all frowned up.

"Oh, JJ. You need to smile while you walk down. Stop looking like the evil cow that you are!" Eva laughs as she almost drops the camera. I know there's still tension between the two of us. We're gonna have to try and work through it. I'll roll with this for a moment and joke around with her.

"Now, Eva. If I didn't know you loved me, I would have to kick your ass!"

Eva stops laughing. "You don't want none of this HOT Latina whipping your fat ass!"

If only she knew how much the HOT Latina comment is fucking with me right now. Manny walks in and interrupts, "Your hooptie awaits."

"Thanks, Manny. You are just in time. I was just about to take my earrings off, kick my shoes off, and show Eva what's up!"

"Don't go there, Ms. Lady. Remember you don't have to fight anymore." Manny puts out his hand for me.

"Yeah, you're right. I'm not going to jail for kicking a Mexican, no green card having, black lip liner wearing, bean burrito cooking bitch."

Eva yells out the door as I get into the car. "I got yo' Mexican...I'm Puerto Rican and black, you stank bitch!"

I'm about to stick my middle finger up at her when I feel this cool breeze come from nowhere. I have to stand still for a moment before stepping into the car. It was so calming. For a moment I didn't want to get into the car. I step into the car and Manny pulls out of the driveway. He adjusts the rearview mirror. "You two are acting like stupid little children. Grow up. Life is too short for this shit!"

I roll my eyes. "Mind your business, Manny!"

He's driving too fast. I'm feeling frightened and I usually feel comfortable with him behind the wheel. "Slow down, Manny. I'm in no big ass rush to deal with these boring white folks!"

"I'm not rushing, but I am in a time crunch. I have to pick up Darius in about 30 minutes from the airport. He will be kickin' it with you tonight." Manny stated with nervousness in his voice.

"For real, he didn't tell me he was coming home tonight. What a sneaky ass." I faked the joy in my voice for sure. He wasn't supposed to be home until next week. But it's all good. We need to talk about how he hung up on me earlier today.

"JJ, I think you're slipping, girlfriend," Manny laughs. "Tonight is your wedding anniversary and he believes you're the one being a sneaky ass. He thinks you're trying to surprise him with something."

"You're full of shit. Aren't you, Manny?" I pull out my cell phone to look at my calendar.

"No, I am not." Manny responds with seriousness.

He's right and so is my calendar. Why didn't Eva have it written down on my agenda? She always writes down birthdays and my anniversary. Something is up with that. "Okay Manny, don't make me feel guilty. Give me a minute to think!" I lean back in the seat, close my eyes, and try to think of a way out of this mess. With everything that happened today, I forgot our anniversary. I don't see how I could. Becoming Darius's wife was something out of a fairy tale book. Even better was the way he proposed to me. It was one of the most wonderful evenings I've ever had in my life...

Darius and I were both born in October; we fall under the sign of Libra. We are described as being diplomatic, romantic, charming, easygoing and sociable. Hell, he definitely used his romantic and charming Libra powers to pop the question. He proposed to me on a Halloween night. I know it's strange to think of Halloween as being romantic, but it was. Darius had taken me to a costume party earlier that evening. He was dressed as Prince Chocolate and I was Chocorella. It was one of those fancy parties with champagne fountains, caviar, and three different dance floors. We danced until we couldn't dance anymore. My feet hurt so bad I sat down to rest. There he was standing over me with that bomb ass smile of his. He handed me a piece of paper and walked away. It read, Would you like to get a room instead of going back to my house like usual? If so, meet me out front in ten minutes for the ride of your life. I was up for whatever. I was so damn excited that I couldn't wait for the time to pass. I was out front within six minutes.

Darius was standing in front of a horse and carriage. It was beautiful! He was beautiful! I remember him saying, "Only the best in the world, for the best woman in the world."

We road through the city for hours. We sipped on champagne and talked about all the plans he had for the future of his firm. We stopped in front of The Chateau, one of the most expensive places in town. When I entered the suite, there were dozens of long stemmed roses everywhere. I had never seen a rose that wasn't a solid color red, yellow or white. These were multi-colored roses. I learned that they are called Romance Roses. I didn't care what they were called; they gave the suite a sweet smell and made it beautiful! The suite had a huge Jacuzzi. He put floating candles in it. My favorite singer, Luther Vandross, was playing!

Ooh, I couldn't have asked for more, but there was more. On the bed, there was some sexy black lingerie from Victoria's Secret. On the balcony, there was a table set with Fine Bone China and a bottle of KRUG champagne. We sat together in the Jacuzzi and sang to one another. When we got out, I put on the lingerie. We sat on the balcony and ate dinner. Once the bottle of champagne was empty and the food was gone, we started eating each other and made love into the morning hours. I was exhausted. Only a few moments after I closed my eyes, I was wakened by a loud noise. I called out to Darius, but he didn't respond. I got out of the bed and went looking for him. He was out on the balcony.

"Darius, why aren't you sleeping?" I put my hand on his back. "Didn't I put it on you?" I laughed a little, kissed him on the cheek and was about to go back to bed. He grabbed me by the wrist the way he did when we first met.

Darius cleared his throat "JJ, for the past couple of months having you in my life has been like paradise. I never thought I would be this comfortable or this happy with anyone ever again." Darius looked deep into my eyes. "You are a reminder of why God created me and I want to spend the rest of my life loving you." Darius pulled out the most beautiful engagement ring. It was made with platinum gold and our opal birthstone...

"We're here, JJ," Manny called out from the front of the car. I wake up from my reminiscing. I sit for a moment and watch people walk inside. I need to find a way to make this evening special for Darius. I already started things off wrong by accusing him of having an affair with Eva. Once, when my grandma was thinking about Raheem, she told me the women in our family only find true love once in our lives, but, because of the curse, we end up losing our true love. I'm set on breaking this curse if there is such a thing. My life is in the midst of change. I can feel it. Just like tonight, when I walked outside and felt the wind blow. It reminded me of a cool breeze toward the end of spring time. Just like when tree leaves change color in the fall and the wind blows them to the ground. I know a change is about to come. In the meantime, I have to think fast.

With desperation in my voice, I ask Manny for a favor. "Manny, when you pick up Darius try to stall getting here. Can you do that for me?"

Manny's answer sounds reluctant. "I don't know how I'm going to do that one."

I'm surprised at his answer. "Why, Manny? I know you can come up with something!"

Manny is looking toward the front of the hotel entrance. "I wish I could, Ms. Lady, but Darius is already here!"

I turn to see what Manny is staring at and it's Darius! He's standing in the doorway talking to the doorman. He has a corsage in his hand like it's our prom or some shit.

I should be happy to see my husband, but I'm sick to my stomach instead. "Damn, Manny. What am I gonna do now?"

Manny starts to laugh. "I think the first thing to do is to get out of the car, Ms. Lady, because he sees us sitting here."

Darius looks so damn good in his tux, standing there, and being friendly. He's laughing and smiling as everyone walks by. Watching him, I can't help but to think what a great guy he is and always has been. He stops talking to the doorman, shakes his hand, and walks over to the car. I'm sitting with a dumb ass smile on my face. Darius looks in front of the car. "Hey, Manny, good to see you man!" He opens my door to let me out. "Well, don't you look like my Chocorella tonight!" Now, I really feel like shit. He's reflecting back on the night he proposed to me. How can I make this up to him? Manny jumps out of the car. He gives me a weird look and I don't know what it means.

"I'm going to go pick up the THING you need for tonight." Manny hates to lie so I figure he has a good plan.

Darius starts grinning big time. He puts the corsage on my wrist and gives Manny a handshake. "We'll see you later, Manny." He probably thinks we have this big special THING planned for him. I sure hope we do. As he leads me up to the entrance, I turn to look at Manny. Manny signals for me to keep moving and gives me the 'it's gonna be okay' look.

I stop Darius before we reach the entrance. "You look good, babe!"

He doesn't respond verbally. Instead, he grabs me and starts kissing me passionately the way he does when we're in the shower. I can hear people making sounds as if they're disgusted by our display of affection. For the first time in a long time, I look Darius in the eyes. I form my mouth to tell him how much I love him when his cell phone rings.

He kisses me on the lips. "Hold on, babe. I have to take this call."

While I'm staring at Darius, Juicy starts getting wet. She's more than wet, she's leaking! My nipples are getting hard. If I could, I'd fuck him right here in the front entrance. My mouth is starting to water, so I lick my lips. I'm behaving the way Mr. UPS was yesterday. Darius is walking around in circles while having his deep conversation. Ooh, look at the ass on him. You'd think this was my first time noticing it. "Baby got back!"

He turns to look at me and so does the doorman. I didn't realize I said it out loud. Damn, I keep doing stuff like that. He hangs up his phone, turns the ringer off, and takes me by the hand. "I want us to enjoy ourselves tonight, JJ."

Now, I'm feeling much better. He called me JJ and not Jasmine. We walk inside the foyer. It's draped with gold and silver lame fabrics tied with Jacquard ribbons. I point out the decorations to Darius.

"JJ, I'm impressed with how much you know about decorating, fabrics, flowers, ribbons, and stuff," He's smiling at me and laughs. "You should go to Making Stuff Pretty School."

I start laughing with him. "You crazy. It's called Interior Design."

"See you know what the schooling is called. Do it, babe!"

I put my head down. He's always so supportive of me and I always seem to let him down. I don't want to set him up for another disappointment. "Let me think about it later, okay?"

He's excited at the possibility of me trying another career path. "Great, you let me know what school and I'll have them the check soon as their doors open!"

Our conversation is interrupted by a flash in our faces. A photographer is running around taking pictures of everyone. He tells us to smile. The photographer is fine for a white boy! He looks young so I better keep my distance.

"You're a lucky man. She's fine!" the photographer tells Darius while giving him five.

Darius looks at me with pride. "I know!"

The look he just gave me makes me want him so bad right now. I pull him by the arm to get him to go for a walk with me. I start kissing him on the side of his neck "Come on, babe. Let's go find a hidden corner and fuck!"

Darius stops walking with me. He stands looking at me. It's no longer with pride but disgust. "Damn, Jasmine!" Oh, I know it's on now he went back to calling me Jasmine and another curse word. "Is that all you think about—fucking? I mean I love making love to you, but this is not the time or the place!" He keeps the smile on his face the entire time he's fussing at me. He looks around to make sure these white folks don't notice us disagreeing. I feel like a little girl being scolded by my father in the grocery store for pulling something down off the shelves. "Now if you need to, I suggest you go into the ladies room, splash some cold water on your face and chill out, or better yet, say a prayer while you're in there!"

I want to say something back to him, but it's our anniversary and I did enough for the day. I walk to the ladies room like he told me to. Again, here I am standing in a mirror. This time I don't feel the need to look deep inside of myself. All I am trying to do is make this evening exciting for us. Put some fire into the relationship! I sit down on one of the lounge chairs. I'm in here all by myself. Damn, I wish I still smoked! The lights start clicking on and off. It scares me! I've seen too many horror flicks where dumb bitches get cut up in the restroom. "Hello, is somebody there?" I don't get an answer. Then suddenly a flash goes off! "What the hell!" I scream. It's the fucking photographer.

"Sorry, I didn't mean to scare you." He sounds so goofy.

I wish I could run his ass over with a car right about now. "What do you mean, you didn't mean to scare me?' What the hell are you trying to do then?"

He walks over to the door and hangs an OUT OF ORDER sign up, he locks it. Damn, I just know I'm 'bout to end up a dead bitch! He walks toward me and I'm really afraid now. I don't have anything in my purse to cut him with. I forgot my cell phone in the car with Manny.

He starts biting on his lips "I heard you talking to your husband. Sorry, he turned you down. I want to make it up for him."

I look around the restroom to see if cameras are around. "Is this some sick ass joke my husband is playing on me?" That didn't even sound right coming out of my mouth. Darius couldn't come up with something like this. The photographer sets his camera up on the counter. The flash is going off. The camera is automatically taking photos. "What are you doing?" I ask him but, at the same time I already know Juicy is throbbing. This is exciting to me!

"Well, I'm going to eat your pussy and then I'm going to fuck you! And you're going to enjoy every minute of it." He's rubbing on his crotch area. I can see his dick is hard. His answer sounds like the kinda shit those dumb bitches in the movies get told right before they get cut up.

"Look, I don't know you and I don't feel safe in here with you!" I start walking toward the door. He pulls his pants down and this white boy got a big ass dick! Juicy starts clapping! I don't know why, but I walk back to sit down on the lounge chair. I don't know him! He might try to kill me! Still, I chance it. Why? He gets down on his knees and pulls my panties down to my ankles. He starts eating my pussy and it feels good! I need to get his phone number so he can give Mr. UPS some lessons.

I'm moaning in ecstasy. "Ah, oooh, ah, shit...ah!" I couldn't make words come out of my mouth. He looks up at me with his mouth all glazed up. "I want you to cum!"

Cum! The way he's eating it I'm gonna piss on myself. This boy has got superior tongue skills. Right after I bust one, I'm gonna have to let him know he's the bomb—just in case, he's never been told. "Ah, shit, I'm cuming, I'm cuming!" He starts eating me faster. I'm starting to feel dizzy! "Here I cum!" Before I could cum, he sticks his dick in my pussy. He's fucking me so good my eyes are rolling back in my head. I try to see if he put a condom on. Juicy is telling me not to give a fuck and sit back and enjoy. I put my hand on his dick to see if I can feel a condom. I'm so wet it's hard to tell. His dick is so big and hard. I feel it all up in my stomach. I'm yelling, "Wrap it up! Wrap it up!" It feels so good. I don't want him to stop even if he doesn't have a condom on. I start getting more into it. "Come on, white boy. Fuck me!" He's pulling at the top of my dress trying to grab my titties. He manages to pull my left tit out of my strapless bra. He's sucking on my nipple and stroking my pussy with his hard ass dick. His face starts to turn red. He announces, "I'm cuming inside of you!"

"What?" Now, I know he's not wrapped up! I try to push him off of me but he clamps down on my nipple with his teeth. It hurts but feels good at the same time! He's fucking me harder and harder. It feels good to me, but I keep trying to push him off anyway. After a couple of minutes, I finally say fuck it and give in. I lean back and enjoy every stroke he's giving me.

"You got some good pussy. I'm cuming inside you!" He announced that shit about five minutes ago. He better go head and cum before I find the strength to push him off.

"Yes, oh yes, here it comes!" He sounds like he's singing. Hell, I don't care. I'm 'bout to sing right along with him. And I do! We both came at the same time! I hear knocking at the door. He covers my mouth. This is it, he got what he wanted now he's gonna kill my ass! The person at the door leaves.

"I didn't mean to cover your mouth like that. It might have been your husband looking for you." He gets off of me and pulls me up. I see he does have a condom on, thank goodness. "You better freshen up. You look like you've been fucked!"

I look in the mirror and he's right. Luckily we're in a fancy hotel because instead of paper towels they have real wash cloths in the ladies room. I clean myself off as best I can and fix my make-up. At least, I should be a little polite. "What's your name?"

"Ooh, ah, ooh!" He thinks he's funny.

I don't think he should quit his photography job anytime soon for comedy.

"Okay, Ooh ah ooh, what do you plan on doing with the film?" I start getting a little worried about this getting out to anyone, that anyone being Darius.

He grabs his camera and pulls out the film and hands it to me. "If you ever need to give proof that white boys got big dicks and can fuck, here it is."

I give him a half cocked smile "Thanks!"

He finishes wiping his face off. "I think you better walk out before me. I'll stand back for awhile or wait for the next woman to come in so I can fuck her good, too."

Now that joke I thought was a little funny, so I laugh and kiss him on the cheek. He helps to brush my hair back out of my face. I stand at the door peeking out to make sure everything was clear.

"You need to get a new husband. The one you got is lame! If you were my wife asking me to do what we just did, I'd never leave your side!" He's all red in the face and giving me a goofy grin.

"You wouldn't understand. I'm lucky to have him. He loves me." I walk out ...

I walk around looking for Darius and don't see him anywhere. I decide to get a drink at the bar. It's going to be another twenty minutes before they allow us into the ballroom for dinner. My stomach is growling. I sweated out my meal from earlier in the bathroom. I tell the bartender to put another olive in my martini. "Hungry?" he asks. I put the two olives in my mouth. He laughs. "I guess that is a yes." I turn around to resume my search for Darius. There he is! He's in the corner with some people I've seen at his office before. I push my way through the crowd to get to him.

I put my hand on his back. "Babe, I've been looking all over for you!"

The two ladies and the gentleman he is talking to look straight at me like I have dirt on my face. One of the ladies looks down at my dress. "Did you spill something on your dress?"

I look down to see what she is talking about. Damn, that white boy got his shit all over me! How did that happen? He had on a condom, maybe when he was taking it off. Darius looks down and pulls on my dress. Now, all three of them are looking down at it. He whispers in my ear. "Did you make a run to the donut shop and eat some glazed donuts or something?" I move away from his mouth and roll my eyes at him. He was not being funny.

I'm good at thinking quick on my feet; but, damn, this is pressure. "The soap dispenser in the ladies room fell on the floor and busted open, soap went flying everywhere, mainly on my dress!"

The gentleman responds with sternness. "If I were you, I would let the hotel management know about this. They should compensate you for the dry cleaning."

The entire gang agrees with him and you know Darius does. Saving money on a dry cleaning bill is right up his alley. Darius holds me by my hand. "You should go ahead and take care of that, baby, before dinner starts. Go talk to the hotel management."

If only he knew what happened the last time he sent me away, he wouldn't be pressuring me like this. "Sounds like a great plan, sweetheart. It was a pleasure seeing everyone again." I shake everyone's hand and walk away.

CHAPTER TEN

We're sitting at the table watching all the white folks get their boogie on. The band is playing Rick James's "Super Freak" and it seems like everybody is dancing off beat. I pour myself another glass of wine. These folks should've known better than to leave the bottle on the table in front of me. I'm about to take a sip when Darius signals me to go on the dance floor with him. I take a big gulp and follow behind him. The song ends and everyone clears the dance floor. A spotlight is put on us. "Darius, what is going on?" I'm covering my face with my hand. I wish I could cover my dress!

"Chill, JJ. You'll like this." Darius is smiling big time. Music starts playing and this guy walks out on stage singing Luther Vandross's "A House is not a Home". I can't see who is singing, but the voice sounds so familiar. "JJ, I know how much you love Luther so I thought I would have you serenaded by someone who can actually sing." All the people are clapping their hands and watching us as he rocks me back and fourth. The gentleman singing comes off the stage and walks toward us. Oh, shit! It's Reggie! I knew that voice sounded familiar. I turn away to keep Reggie from looking at me. I can tell by the way he is walking around us that he is trying to get a good look at my face. Darius holds my head up to kiss me. I see the reaction on Reggie's face, but he doesn't miss a note. The song ends and Reggie hands Darius the microphone and walks away. Damn, why does fucked up shit always happen to me!

Darius takes out his handkerchief to wipe the sweat off his forehead. "Thank you for allowing me this moment to celebrate my wedding anniversary. This woman has been a blessing to my life and I can't imagine living without her." I can see Reggie standing by the stage looking straight at me. I'm gonna need a handkerchief in a minute to wipe my ass up off this ballroom dance floor. Darius continues with his speech. "I also want to take this time to share some good news with my wife and everyone else. Black on Black Consulting has been doing so well that I'm opening another location in Los Angeles!"

The room gets loud with celebration. All these white folks love Darius. Many of them have helped him to grow his business. Although his focus is on helping black businesses, they've always had his back. He's just one of those types you can't help but want to help out. I hug him to show my love and support. People come walking out on the ballroom floor to congratulate us. I see Reggie walk out of the ballroom. For some reason, I want to run after him. I want to get an answer for him being here. He told me he works for a financial firm. Why would he be playing the role of a wedding singer? This is why men need to be a piece of dick and nothing else. They're always two-faced and up to no good!

Wait a minute, I got my nerves. I'm a married woman sitting up here angry about a booty call telling me lies! I need to focus on my husband. Darius is talking with different people and I'm getting antsy. I want to go home. The band starts playing music again and folks get their boogie on off beat! I pull Darius to walk with me back to the table. "The firm is doing real good. Another location. Wow!" I want to show him I'm excited, but inside I'm feeling sick. I know all this means is more time away from home. We sit down and I quickly grab my glass of wine. I ask Darius if he wants a glass, but people keep coming by the table to congratulate him. He can't pay me any attention. The photographer walks over to the table. My heart is racing!

"Let me give you congrats on having a GOOD thing!" The photographer's voice is cocky. He shakes Darius's hand. "Allow me to take another picture of the accomplished couple. Not only do you have success, but you also have love." He takes our photograph, winks, and turns to take pictures of the people at the next table.

"He's interesting." Darius states as he sits down next to me.

I rub on his back. "Yeah, white boys are weird." I lean in to kiss him on the neck. I see Reggie standing over us. I almost fell out of my chair! Darius stands up to talk with him.

"Brotha, you put it on with that song. You sound just like Luther!" Darius digs in his pocket and tries to hand him a couple benjamins to show his appreciation. Reggie won't take them out of his hand.

He pushes Darius's hand back. "Nah, man. When my baby sister told me you was looking for someone to sing Luther to your wife for your anniversary, I had to jump all over it! Any brotha willing to do something like this for his lady is aiight wit me."

Darius turns to introduce me to Reggie. "Hey, baby, this is my father's secretary's brother, Reggie."

I reach up and shake his hand. He kisses it instead. I feel Juicy getting excited. I try to sound polite. "A pleasure to meet you."

"Nah, the pleasure is all mine."

Damn, why does Reggie's ass have to look better in a tux than Darius? He's messing with my mind. I need to focus on my husband. Lord, please help me focus on my husband. Nothing has been going the way it should've today. I hope Manny has something good going on to turn this night around. Reggie tries to excuse himself. "Well, I hate to run but I have a busy day tomorrow."

Darius has to talk some more. He couldn't let the brotha walk the hell out.

"Hey, your sister told me that you are single, is that right?"

Reggie looks at me briefly "Unfortunately, I'm not blessed to have the woman I want. So, yes, I am single."

Darius acts like he's in high school helping somebody get a date for the dance. "Cool, my wife's best friend has a fine face and body. She's got these eyes that will knock you off your feet. She's fun to be around and has a great sense of humor. Hey, man, she's got a good head on her shoulders too! Maybe you should come by our house one night for drinks and I'll hook you two up. Here's my business card. Give me a call."

Well, damn. Is that how a brother should be thinking of a sister? Darius did say Eva is like a sister to him. He sure was descriptive about her ass to be a BROTHER. Reggie notices me rolling my eyes. He has to dig this entire situation into my skin. He sits in the chair next to me.

"Is that right? You have a fine ass best friend?" Reggie is being a smart ass.

"I guess she's fine. Hell, I don't look at her ass like that!"

"Come on, women know whether or not their friends are fine. Tell me. Does she have a big, JUICY....booty?"

I know his ass is trying to be funny. He is making reference to Juicy and I know it. I'm gonna go head and play this game with him. I have no choice. My husband is looking at us funny! "Darius baby, do you think Eva has a JUICY booty like mine?"

Darius knows the correct answer "No, baby, not at all!"

Reggie stands up from the chair. "Well, I'd like to be the judge on that if you don't mind. I'll be giving you call Mr. Brooks."

"Call me D man!" Darius demands. They shake hands and Reggie walks away.

My husband turns to smile at me and gives me a big kiss on the lips. "See, baby, that's how I'm going to help Eva out. Get her a good man."

I want to address how he described her ass, but I'm gonna let it go tonight. I will put this in my memory bank to be used at a later time if necessary. As for Reggie, Mr. Dress Shop has really pissed me off. How could he even think about coming over to my house to meet Eva? Is he trying to make me jealous? I always told him I don't have feelings for him and that we are strictly sexual. He told me he understood. I got the feeling tonight that he doesn't understand. I guess it could have been worse. It could have been Mr. UPS up in here singing!

I yawn a little bit to try and get Darius to go home. "Babe, can we go?"

"Sure thing. Let me say bye to a couple of people and I'll come back to get you. I know you have a surprise for me and I can't wait to see it!"

The sick feeling in my stomach is getting worse. I don't have my cell phone to call Manny to find out what he's up to. Darius is acting like a kid on Christmas Eve. I hope I don't let him down. Shit, I hope Manny doesn't let him down. I'm not doing a damn thing. It feels like an hour before Darius comes back to the table. He's all excited to go. "Let's go, JJ!" We walk toward the exit. Before we get outside I can see a white horse and a carriage through the glass doors! The doorman opens the door for us. Manny is standing there dressed in a tux with a top hat on! I owe him big time for this one!

Manny shouts. "I thought you were never going to get him out here, JJ!"

Darius turns to look at me. I can see his eyes get full of tears. Is he going to cry on me? I've never seen him cry before. He grabs my hand and we walk down to get in the carriage. I kiss Manny on the cheek and he gives me that 'it's going to be okay' look. Darius and I get in and cuddle up. I couldn't have asked God for a better California evening. The sky is beautiful with the stars glowing. The night is so clear even the air smells different. Ah, I feel that same breeze from earlier tonight. This time it isn't as comforting. It gives me a little chill.

Darius wraps his arms around me. "Baby, you cold?"

"With your arms around me, I'm not."

"This reminds me of the night I proposed to you. Remember on the carriage ride we talked about the future of the firm. Well look, the firm has reached our goal!"

Damn, he's right. That evening we talked about him having offices throughout California. He is on his way! I can see in his face how proud he feels right now. I'm proud of him. How he manages to do it all and take care of us, I'll never know. Yeah, I know. He trusts in God. He's never made a business decision without praying on it. He's never gone into a meeting with a client without praying first. I can say one thing about Darius; he is in true alignment with what the Lord wants. That's why he keeps getting the blessings he does. Funny how he believes I'm one of his blessings. Hell, I'm nothing but a curse...hmm or just cursed!

Darius has joy in his voice. "Baby, look at the sky! The Lord is looking down at us and He's so pleased right now. You know the promises of God are always kept when it comes to us, JJ. He's never let me down, never! He's given me two beautiful children, a beautiful wife, a successful business. There's nothing more a man could want!"

I guess he could ask for a faithful marriage. He has no idea what I've been doing. If he does, he sure is good at hiding it. What did I do to deserve such a good man? All of the shit I've done and still do. I must be dreaming. "I need to wake my ass up!"

"You need to wake up?" Darius questions.

I did it again. I spoke out loud without knowing it. I need to get a grip on that before I say the wrong thing at the wrong time.

"Oh, babe, it's been a full night with so much going on. I'm feeling tired and I thought I was falling asleep a minute ago." I got out of that one.

"We can end the night. It's all good."

"Let's at least keep holding each other and finish the ride." I grab him tighter.

"Sounds good, baby." Darius gets Manny's attention. "Manny, my man, drop us off at the house. JJ is tired and I had a long flight back. We need to get some rest."

"Sure thing!" Manny yells.

We get to the house and all the lights are on. "Oh, no! Eva must be drinking again!"

Darius gives me this confused look. I jump out of the carriage and head for the door. I don't have my house key so I have to wait on Darius. He gets to the door and looks me in the face with a frown. "What do you mean drinking again?" He asks like he really didn't know.

"Babe, you know your wonderful Eva—that you described tonight—gets drunk as a wino sleeping in front of a liquor store."

"JJ, you not mad about how I described Eva to Reggie are you? Baby, don't start this up again. We've had a good time tonight." He's scratching his head with the keys.

I grab them out of his hand. "Let me open the damn door. I need to make sure your kids are alright!" I know the kids are fine with Eva. And I know I shouldn't have said YOUR kids. Pastor always says nasty comments come for the devil. Well, I'm letting the devil get in our marriage tonight. We walk into the house and there are flowers everywhere. Eva and the kids jump out from behind the couch. "Happy Anniversary!"

Eva walks over to Darius. "Good to see you home. Happy Anniversary!" She kisses him on the cheek. She then walks over to me and whispers, "Happy Anniversary, bitch!"

I see things are gonna be interesting until she moves out. The kids jump all over their daddy. They are so happy to see him. Allen starts telling him all about the golf lessons today and how Manny took them for ice cream afterwards. Jayne starts telling him about how she went the entire day without eating a lollipop so she could save room for anniversary cake! Darius is kissing all over them and blowing bubbles on their tummies. He's so happy to be a father. Sometimes I wish he would've allowed me to have a baby by him. He was too afraid something would happen and he'd lose another wife. So, in our second year of marriage, he got a vasectomy. I still take birth control pills. He doesn't know. I put them in a women's vitamin bottle. I can't risk a condom coming off or breaking and then I'd have to come home and explain myself—like what happened tonight. That shit was risky! I wonder how many other women Mr. Photographer has fucked at social events?

The thought of tonight makes me stressed and hungry. I head for the kitchen to find something to eat. Darius and the kids are rolling around on the floor. I look over toward the glass sliding doors and notice Eva watching them. She doesn't look herself. She doesn't look sick, but she looks angry. Why is she looking at them like that? I go talk to her. "Eva girl, let's stop trippin.'" I use our argument as an excuse to find out why she's looking the way she is. "You got a lot on your mind, I can tell. We need to squash this beef between us. Let me be there for whatever you're going through." She doesn't give me any response. She walks out to the pool. I follow behind her because I want to see what's going on in her head.

Eva's standing over the pool with her arms folded. Tears are rolling down her face. I stand next to her to see if she'll allow me to put my arms around her. She does. "Eva, talk to me, girl. This is not like you to be trippin' with me this way." Eva releases herself from my arms, sits down, and puts her feet in the pool. I can feel we're making progress so I do the same.

Her tears start to flow harder. "JJ, I'm so jealous of what you have. I can't even be a good friend to you right now."

I'm not sure what to tell her. I have to think quickly. "Girl, I know you not jealous of those kids that ain't mine and a husband who is nothing but a big nerd!"

Eva wipes the tears from her face "Yes, I am. I take care of those kids everyday. I've fallen in love with them. When I'm around Darius, he makes me feel like I'm more than your flunky. And... I've fallen in love with him, too."

Oh hell, I don't know what the fuck to say! There's not enough thinking quick on my feet left in the world for me at this moment. This is my best friend, huh, my only girlfriend and she's telling me she's in love with my husband. The kids I understand but my husband! Has she slept with him? If she gives me the wrong answer, I might drown her ass in this pool! "Eva, this love you have for Darius, has it ever made you trip and fall on his dick?"

Eva thinks I'm funny because she burst out laughing and falls in the pool. Darius and the kids hear the splash and come running outside. Eva waves for them to jump in the water. "Pool party!" All three of them are down. The kids take their shoes off and jump in. Darius strips down to his underwear. He gives me a look. "I don't want to mess up the tux!"

I watch as they're having too much fun for me to handle. I stand up to walk back into the house. Darius yells out "Baby, you not jumping in, come on. Pool party!"

"No, I got my hair done yesterday." He should know since he makes sure the damn appointments are booked. He shrugs his shoulders as if to say whatever. I don't care about their pool party. But what I do care about is Eva not answering me. Her laughter better be because she thinks I've lost my mind and she could never do that to me. It better not be because she thinks I am a fool, or because she's been fucking him since she's been living with us. I stand at the sliding glass doors and watch. Darius is throwing them all around the pool. Everyone is enjoying themselves. I would get in the pool but I'm more of a Jacuzzi person and my hairdo is looking much too good to mess up. Plus, I don't want to accidentally drown somebody! "I'm going in the house to change clothes." They don't even hear me.

When I walk inside, Manny's standing in the kitchen eating crackers and cheese. It looks good to me. I didn't eat much. I should've had some dinner before I left like Jayne asked me to. I stand next to Manny and help myself to his snack. Manny sleeps in the pool house during the weekends. I guess they were making too much noise for him to relax. "Were they getting on your nerves?" For sure his answer is going to be yes.

"No!" He pushes the plate closer to me "I enjoy the laughter. I just wish some of the laughter belonged to you."

Here he goes again. I don't want to hear this tonight. It's late and I've got a lot on my mind. He must lurk the corners waiting for the opportunity to mess with me. Manny slices some more cheese since I'm putting it down like I never had cheese in my life before. Manny doesn't give up trying to tell me something. "You know lots of things can be going on around us and we won't notice because we are in our own world."

See I wish folks were like my grandma. When she had something to say or something to tell you, she just said it! No bullshitting around, no playing guessing games! I'm frustrated with Manny. I push the plate back toward him. He digs in his pocket and hands me my cell phone. "You left it in the car. It has been ringing constantly for two hours. Tell Mr. Dress Shop he needs to get a life!" I felt a huge rush of happiness go through my body. Reggie has been blowing up my phone. I knew that niggah has feelings for me. I know I have feelings for him. It's just the wrong timing for me. I should've met him years ago.

Manny is frowning up at me. He sees the joy on my face. I guess I should've faked it, but Manny knows how I do. Manny goes over to sit at the breakfast table. He takes the plate of snacks with him so I follow even though I pretended I didn't want anymore. I sit down next to him and take a cracker. He stops eating to take a good look at me.

"Do you remember when your father died from a heart attack?" Manny asks.

I don't want to answer. I don't want to think about painful events tonight. I shove more crackers in my mouth. "Well, I know you remember. Ms. Lady, you were stressed about getting the money to go to his funeral. You worked double shifts and still didn't have enough money. Well, I know you remember what you did to get the rest of the money for the plane ticket. When I saw you the next day you told me you never wanted to feel like that ever again. Remember?"

I'm still chewing on crackers. My throat is getting dry. I get up and grab a bottle of wine from the fridge. I use a big plastic cup instead of my tiny wine glass. If nothing else goes down tonight, one thing is for sure, I'll be drunk. Manny is waiting for me to take a sip so I can answer, but I guess I'm moving too slow because he starts back up again. "Ms. Lady, you're allowing yourself to be lower than low by sleeping with all these different men. They're using up your body and you're getting nothing out of it, but some used up pussy. If you don't watch yourself, you're going to lose everything and everyone around you, Darius, the kids, Eva, and me!"

Manny's little talk reminds me of my grandma. She would be upset to about me giving pussy up for nothing, but Manny's talk has a different angle. He wants me to pay attention to this family and not these niggahs. I get what he's saying. What he doesn't understand is...I can't stop!

CHAPTER ELEVEN

I didn't have a response to Manny and wasn't going to think of one. He brought back memories of my father's funeral, so he could make a point I didn't want to hear. I drink my wine, turning the plastic cup upside down to make sure I don't miss a drop. I go upstairs to my room and change into my bed T-shirt. I stand in the mirror thinking about how certain things went down between me and my father. It was tough as hell for me to get through all the bullshit. I never got to say goodbye to my daddy before he died, but I did get to say good-bye to my grandfather...

I remember when my grandfather Raheem took over the café. My father was very resentful toward him for not bowing out and handing everything over to him. It was a constant battle for control between them. My father was still dealing with his childhood abandonment issues and had a difficult time working side by side with the man who caused those issues. One night, my father, Raheem, and I were working late at the café. Francis left early to work on his homework because of a big exam he had coming up. Since grandma was his only distraction, there was nothing or nobody that could keep him from hitting those books. That was the first night I heard Raheem and my father try to discuss what happened with grandfather leaving my father and grandma all the time. My father was wiping down the tables and humming to himself. Raheem joined in on the humming. I giggled inside wondering if this was a start to them becoming friends.

Raheem stopped humming to make a comment. "You know you have good lungs like your mother. She used to sing to you all the time when you were a baby."

Cedric stopped wiping the tables and stood up straight to look at Raheem. "My mother was blessed with a voice from heaven. Too bad she was always angry at you, she couldn't use those lungs for good. She was too busy fussing and hollering all the damn time!"

Raheem sounded surprised. "You trying to say I made your mother a bitter woman?"

"What else could her problem have been? She worked herself to the bone to keep this place running. She had no help from you. The only time you bothered to come around is to get some money and ass!" Cedric threw the towel on top of the counter.

Raheem stepped from behind the counter and put his hand on Cedric's shoulder. "Son, I don't know what your mother told you about me, but I think it's time you know why I was running away so much."

Cedric pushed Raheem's hand off his shoulder and raised his voice, "There's nothing you can tell me now that can change things. I grew up without a father. Everything I learned about being a man, I learned from the streets. The only thing that kept me out of jail or the morgue was this damn café and you can't even let me have it!"

"I can explain. Things are not as they seem!" Raheem's accented voice was thick with the fear of losing what he never had.

Raheem was raised in Trinidad and came to the United States when he was a teenager. He was tall and very thin; he didn't have much of a body. He had these strange marble blue eyes with dark olive colored skin and curly but nappy brown hair. It gave him an exotic but awkward look. He did not want the spotlight or much attention. I felt he was putting on a front. It was the way he carried himself and the way his hand gestures were that gave me a reason to feel the way I did. I'm sure in his younger years he was something to deal with.

Cedric walked away from him and grabbed his jacket and keys, so he could leave. Raheem stood in front of the doorway. "Son, you're not going to leave until you hear the truth!"

"Stop calling me son!" Cedric pushed him out of the doorway and left.

Raheem sat on one of the table benches with his head down. I really didn't know him so wasn't sure if I should say anything. I walked over and sat next to him. I put my hand on his back. I didn't say a word, but he did. "That feels good. Pauline used to do the same thing to me. Sometimes you don't need words to let a person know how you feel. A simple touch means so much to a man." I was proud to know I was helping him feel better. So I continued rubbing his back. He wanted to get to know me better. "You're a beautiful flower just like your grandma was. Are you very sensual like your grandma?" I was confused by his question. I wasn't sure if I was supposed to answer him.

"What do you mean?" I asked.

He turned to look at me eye to eye. "Well, all of the women in your family are very sensual. They love to have sex! Are you having sex yet?"

I stopped rubbing his back. I didn't feel comfortable with him anymore. I walked back behind the counter and started putting stuff away and cleaning up. He came behind the counter and stood there staring at me. He smiled. "It's okay. You can talk to me. I'm your grandfather. I understand more than you think." I moved faster to finish so I could get the hell out of there. Raheem wanted to tell me about himself. "You may feel uncomfortable because you don't really know much about me. Well, I never had a curse placed on me, but I'm very sensual myself. I enjoy having sex with women and men. We're all God's creatures placed on this earth to love one another."

How dare he use God to condone his actions? My stomach instantly be~ sick. I turned around and threw up in the sink. He walked over to help ~ my face off. While he was squeezing the towel out, he was also sque~ ass. It made me jump. I felt afraid. He stepped toward me. "I kn~ curse! Let me help you take some of the edge off. I will make~ father must have felt my fear because he walked back ~

something wasn't right by the look on my face.

"What the hell is going on?" He threw his keys on the counter and started taking his jacket off.

I ran over to my father and he held me in his arms. "Daddy, he touched me! He grabbed my behind." I told him as I started to cry.

Raheem had an innocent look on his face "I was helping to clean the girl's face. She threw up! Probably that pot of turnip greens you left on the stove. They stink real bad when you leave them out like that."

My father knew Raheem was full of shit! "You get the hell out of here. You get out and don't bring your Soca music playing, dick sucking ass around here no mo'!"

At that moment I was surprised by two things. One, that my father was cursing as much as he was; and two, that he knew Raheem liked men! Raheem had a smirk on his face. "Well, my son. It is you that must get out. This is my café and don't you forget it!"

My father was furious! He pulled me out of the café and into the car. He sped off and drove angrily. I was so afraid. "Daddy, please!"

He kept looking over at me. "Did you try to fuck him, JJ?"

"What?" I was hurt by his question.

He was swerving all over the road. "You're a ho just like your grandma, aren't you? She taught you to be just like her, didn't she?"

My tears kept flowing down my face. "Daddy, no! I didn't do anything wrong. Please believe me!"

He pulled the car over to the side of the road and turned it off. He gripped the steering wheel so tight I thought he was going to pull it off! "JJ, you better tell me the truth. Do you want Raheem to face a horrible punishment if you aren't telling the truth?"

I put my hands up over my face and cried out. "Yes, daddy, he touched me!"

"Then, that niggah's got to die!" He started the car and pulled off...

I wash the make-up off my face and put my moisturizer on. I roll up under my king size satin comforter and relax my body. Darius comes walking into the room soaking wet. He's panting because he's out of breath from having fun at their so-called pool party. He didn't say a word to me when he walked in the room. Now that he's jumped his ass in the shower, he wants to have a full blown conversation.

"Hey, babe, you should've jumped in the pool to have a little fun with us tonight. The kids would've loved to see you whaling around with your no swimming behind!" He's gurgling in the shower. I hate when he does that shit! I answer him, but he can't hear me. He keeps saying huh over and over. It's irritating me, so I get out the bed and go stand by the shower.

"I said that I didn't feel like getting my hair done again sooner than my next appointment so I didn't jump in. I'm glad you had fun with the kids. They needed that."

He pokes his head out of the shower. "They need time like that with you, too, JJ." He puts his head back in the shower. "You should know better than anybody how it feels to not have parents around. You grew up without a mom and you lost your father when you were pretty young, so you know how important it is to get fun time in with the kids."

I contemplate my response. I want to sound sophisticated with my answer. I think of all the lessons I've learned from charm school but I couldn't be Ms. Lady. I'm frustrated that everyone has attacked me today about my mothering skills. Not only am I frustrated but I'm feeling defensive. "What the fuck are you trying to say, you think I'm not a good enough mother for your kids?" The water stops running and I hear a sigh. I'm waiting for Darius to step out, but it takes a minute. I guess he's contemplating his response.

"Could you grab me a towel?" He asks.

I grab a towel and throw it over the shower curtain to him. "Here ya go!"

He steps out and wipes himself down. "You know, JJ. You've been taking stuff too personal lately. I can't seem to say or do anything without you trippin' on me. If you have something to say, say it and let's move on."

My husband is so proper. Sometimes I wish he'd be a hood niggah and curse me out so we could have wild making up sex afterwards! He hands me the lotion so I can start rubbing him down with it. I go ahead and do it even though I don't feel like it.

"JJ, why you rubbing so hard? Baby, be gentle!" He sounds like a big ass baby.

"Alright, I'll be gentle!"

"I've been gone for a few days. It's our anniversary. Let's enjoy each other, okay?"

I rub softer and kiss him on the neck. "Okay."

I rub lotion on his chest and down to his waist. I rub some lotion on his dick. It's hard, ooh, is he going to fuck me tonight? No, knowing Darius he's going to make love to me. He pushes me up against the wall of the bathroom, takes my T-shirt off and starts kissing me on my neck and sucking my titties! He pulls my panties down. Hell, maybe I'm wrong. My husband is on tonight! Darius turns my head toward the bathroom mirror. His voice sounds deeper than usual. "I want you to watch your expressions as I eat your pussy!" Yeah, this is want I'm talkin' 'bout, he's gonna handle his tonight! I'm moaning as he puts his tongue inside of me and moves it around like rhythmic waves. He sucks on my clit just at the tip the way I love him to do! He's holding my head toward the mirror where I can't move to watch him. I can only watch me. I can see my reflection. Damn, I'm enjoying myself.

There's something exciting about him making me watch my expressions. It's as if I'm watching a sexy porn star. He stops eating my pussy, stands up and rubs his dick up against my clit. He's pressing it hard up on the tip, and it feels so good! Darius looks me in the face. "I know tonight is our anniversary. We should probably make love tonight, but all I want to do is fuck the shit out of you!" I can't believe what I hear coming out his mouth. Is my husband trying to get hood on me? Juicy wants to run around in circles. I'm going to be submissive to ' tonight. Whatever he wants, it's on!

"Yeah, that sounds like a good thang!" I kiss him on the lips.

Darius pushes me harder against the wall and grabs my left le~ to spread me wide open. He forcefully sticks his dick inside ~ hard!

He has a passionate frown on his face. "Baby, huh, your pussy is so silky, hot, and wet!"

I can't say a thing it's feeling so good to me. His thick dick is stroking up on the walls of my pussy. He's thrusting himself up against my body. I glance in the mirror and see the sweat roll down his muscular backside. Watching his muscles tighten up with each stroke excites me! I don't know where he got this raging desire to fuck me from, but I'm lovin' this! He strokes me harder then slows down and strokes me soft and slowly. Ah! This feels so damn good. I can tell by the look on his face he's about to cum. I push him back off of me.

He's upset. "JJ, what are you doing?"

I get on my knees and start sucking his dick like it's a drinking straw. He falls back against the other side of the wall of the bathroom.

He's screaming. "JJ, uh, oh, JJ, oh I'm...I'm...oooooh!"

I wipe the corners of my mouth and look up at him. He's looking at something else, so I turn around and Eva is standing there looking at us. I jump up. "What the fuck!" Eva runs out of the room. I turn to look at Darius, he's looks worn out. I've got an attitude "How long was her ass standing there?"

He's breathing hard. "Baby, I don't know. My eyes were closed. Give me a minute. I lost a lot of blood from my brain."

What kinda of nerdy shit is that for him to say? We're not in health class learning about erections. I've had enough of her ass! I throw my T-shirt back on and run to Eva's room. She's not there. I look in the kids' rooms and no luck. I run down stairs and look around. Nothing! I check by the pool and parking garage. "This bitch dun took my fucking car!"

Now I know how my father felt when I took his car for the first and last time...

The day after the incident with my grandfather, my father decided to close the café for the day. Raheem never opened the café. He always came strolling in around one o'clock when the café opened at nine. A few years before my grandma passed, she decided to add breakfast items to her menu. Locals loved to come dine on her catfish and grits. Luckily, she taught all of her recipes to my father and Francis or else business would have dwindled after her death. I remember my father being up extra early that morning. He was sitting at our kitchen table drinking a cup of coffee looking out the window. I don't know how he could have seen anything it was pitch dark. He didn't know I was standing in the hallway watching him. He was talking to himself.

"I'm going to kill that faggot! No good son of a bitch gonna walk up in here and take over my mama's café and touch on my daughter!" He gulped down his coffee. I walked up behind him and he dropped his cup. "What you want, JJ?"

"Daddy, I know you're angry about what Raheem did, but you should let it go. I'm okay!" I tried to convince my father to move on. I didn't want him doing something he'd end up going to jail for.

My father swept up his broken coffee cup and put it in the trash. Francis walked in yawning and rubbing his eyes. He looked at both of us as if we were in the wrong house. Francis asked, "What ya'll black folks doing up so early?" Before his high school graduation, Francis decided to cut his hair and get finger waves. At night, he always wore a headscarf around his head and two rollers in the back to curl his duck tail. My father looked at him and shook his head. He struggled with everything Francis did. He let out a big sigh.

"I'm not opening the café today. I have some stuff I need to take care of."

Francis broke out the pots and pans. "What ya'll want for breakfast?"

My father lifted the coffee pot up in the air . "I ate already, thanks!"

Francis tried to be helpful. "I can run the café until you come back. I don't have any classes until this afternoon."

"No, what I have to take care of might take all day. It won't kill any of these greasy fat folks to miss out on raising their cholesterol for one day." He walked out of the kitchen.

Francis turned and looked at me. "I get the feeling something is up with Pops!"

I had the same feeling and needed to think of something quick. I kissed Francis on the forehead. "Have a good day, big brother. I need to go get ready for school!" I ran out of the kitchen with fire under my feet.

Francis yelled out, "You never get ready for school this early. Hey, are you even still enrolled in school?"

I got dressed and, for the first time without my grandmother, I sat looking at myself in the vanity mirror. I imagined her sitting next to me putting on her fuchsia lipstick. What would Grandma Pauline do in a situation such as this? She would probably knock my father over the head with her black skillet and call him names, but I wasn't down for hurting my father. I knew he had plans to go deal with Raheem, so I had to beat him to it. I wasn't much for praying then, but I knew asking the Lord for guidance was a good idea. I looked in the mirror, put my hands together and cleared my throat.

Dear Lord, no that's not how I start...uh...Father God,

Some pretty bad things are going on with my family. I know you saw what happened yesterday. I don't think grandfather was thinking straight. The devil got in him...he didn't mean to touch me. So I guess I'm praying to have you help my daddy. I think he's going to hurt my grandfather. I can kinda see it in his eyes he's really mad! I don't want daddy to get in trouble so I'm going to warn Raheem so he can leave. He's used to running away so it shouldn't be a problem for him. Help me to have strength. You know those angels you have watching over me all the time, could you make sure they're with me today? Thanks. Amen

I walked out into the hallway to see if my father had left already. I heard the shower running and him singing "Down by the Riverside". I went by the kitchen. I saw Francis passed out over one of his textbooks. I grabbed my father's keys off the key rack by the front door. I headed out to warn Raheem...

I look at the empty space where my car is supposed to be parked and I am pissed like the devil sitting in hell! Darius comes running down the stairs with a towel around his waist. It took him all damn day to get his ass down here. "Thanks for being concerned!" I storm by him and head for the refrigerator. "Not only did the bitch take my car, she must have taken all the damn food because ain't shit in here!"

Darius walks over to me and puts me in a bear hug. I try to get out of it but he's too strong. "Let me go!" I yell.

"No, not until you chill out! I don't think Eva did what she did on purpose. You know she walks around the house freely. She probably didn't know we were in there having sex!"

I keep pulling to free myself from his grip with no luck. "I don't understand why you're making excuses for her. She's never done that shit before. All of these years, she's never walked in on us and now the bitch is going through some shit and she can just walk in and watch. Ain't no voyeur mess going on around here!"

He starts laughing. "I don't know it was kinda interesting!"

I stop trying to break loose and look up at him. "So you knew the bitch was watching?"

"Come on, JJ. Stop trippin'!" He tries to rub our noses together. Whenever he's trying to get me to chill out he always wants to play ring around the nosey. I didn't want play today!

He lets me go. "I can see you want to spend the rest of what's left of our anniversary trippin' off of Eva. That's okay. I understand if you wanna play me like that!"

What the hell is he talking about? Wasn't he in the bathroom with me when all of this took place? He should be mad as hell with me! I had to get a smart mouth with him. "Our anniversary was over two hours ago. It's past two in the morning!"

"There we go! That's the JJ I fell in love with. Smart ass attitude, thinking only of herself, holding on to stuff allowing it to hold her back! Oh, yeaaaaah! That's the woman I married!" Darius puts on a pot of coffee. "Today is Sunday! I'm going to do my regular routine. Let me go change so I can walk the dog. Since Eva's not here, I'm going to make breakfast for everybody and get MY kids ready for church!"

He walks out of the kitchen and leaves me looking stupid. He's been short with me lately. Talking to me out the side of his neck! I know he doesn't think I'm going to church with him today. He tried to hurt me with his little evil comment about the kids. I know I said it myself yesterday, but that's different! Nobody is going to make me look bad today. I can do all the things Eva does around here. Fuck 'em, I can cook! I take out a carton of eggs and a package of bacon. I hear knocking at the sliding glass door, it's Manny. Shit, now I have to deal with his ass! I run and grab my extra robe out of the laundry room and go unlock the door to let him in. He's got Buster on a leash. I laugh and walk back to start cooking.

"What's so funny?" Manny asks.

"You with that dog. I'm surprised he let someone besides Darius put a leash on his little evil ass!"

Manny looks down at Buster. "I had to let the poor thing out of the kennel. The kids don't walk him when Darius is gone. He started barking when he heard YOUR evil ass yelling. He probably senses Darius is home."

I stop beating the eggs and look at Manny. "So, you couldn't sleep with him barking, huh?"

Manny walks Buster over to the kitchen island counter and tells him to sit. "Hell no, or else I'd still be sleep. It's damn near three in the morning! Why you cooking so early, don't you know those eggs are gonna be too cold for the kids when they get up?"

I realize what a good observation he has made. I start putting stuff back. "You right, I'll cook later. I'm upset with some shit that went down last night."

"Oh, like Eva taking your car?"

"Yeah and something else! She better bring her ass back here soon!"

Manny laughs. "No worries, when I heard you yell about her taking your car I called Eva on her cell phone. She's blowing off some steam. She's probably down at the 24-hour coffee house drinking down lattes like water."

"So, did she tell you what happened?" I ask him.

"No, but I don't want you to tell me either. I don't need to know all the crazy stuff that goes on around here!"

Manny is right. He doesn't need to know everything, but I do. I need to find out what is going on with Eva and deal with it. She said she's in love with my husband, but there's more to her actions than what she's telling me. I understand how loving someone can make people do things they wouldn't normally do. It's more complicated when your love is forbidden. I don't want to lose the love of the people so important in my life. I love Eva and she loves me. I love Darius and he loves me. And Darius and Eva...hmm...how much do they love each other?

"I'll be right back Manny." I run into the downstairs bathroom. I look in the mirror to try and get in touch with how I'm feeling. I wish I could call someone. My grandma, Francis, my father...damn...my daddy...

I was headed down the road to see Raheem. I could barely see over the dashboard. My father drove a gas guzzling caddy that always had smoke coming out of the muffler. I pulled in front of my grandfather's house and sat in the car thinking about what I was going to say. I finally figured it out and found the courage to get out of the car. Raheem lived in a secluded area, surrounded by trees and a small swamp in the back. His house was barely standing. The porch creaked as I made my way up the stairs toward the door. The screen door was hanging half way off the hinges. I thought it would fall off if I knocked too hard; so, I knocked softly. I tried to look into the house, but no lights were on. I heard a voice come from inside the house.

"I'll be right out!" It was my grandfather. He walked out of the house with a pink bathrobe on and fuzzy high heel slippers. I knew something was odd about him.

"I've been thinking about you, JJ." His voice was high-pitched.

My voice trembled. "I've been thinking about you too, but not like that!"

"Oh, I see. So what brings you way out here to see me? How did you know where to find me? Are you alone?" He looked behind me to check.

I blurted out my reason for the trip. "I came out here to warn you. Daddy's upset about what you did to me yesterday. If you don't leave town, he's gonna kill you!"

Raheem sat down on the porch swing. It was so rusted it couldn't move back and fourth anymore. He patted the space beside him for me to sit next to him. I didn't go for it.

"Never mind," he said.

I didn't want to be around him longer than I had to. "So, are you leaving or what?"

I remember him taking a comb out of his robe's pocket and combing his hair. I could tell he wanted to irritate me because it took forever for him to answer. "I'm not going anywhere. I'm too old to run. My running days are over. I used to run back then because freedom called me. Freedom to sleep with whom I wanted to, freedom to drink and do drugs, freedom to be me. Back in the day, Pauline was just another pretty face I couldn't say no to. When Pauline found out she was pregnant, she asked me to marry her. I had never slept with your grandma until after she delivered your father. She was in her mid-thirties fucking everyone in town. Pauline had no idea who Cedric's father was. Being the friend that I was, I didn't want anymore shame to come upon her. So I married her, it was a favor. As the years went by, Pauline fell in love with me. She thought with time and the love she gave to me, I'd stop sleeping with men. I wouldn't, so I'd leave to go do what I wanted. I'd be gone for so long and she'd miss me so bad that she'd come visit. We'd have sex over and over again! Sometimes Pauline would allow me to have my friends join in. Your grandmother was a whore from her heart. I would make regular visits back to the café to fuck her. After awhile, she demanded me to stop how I was living or else she wouldn't give me anymore money. I was never one to keep a job. Pauline took care of my bills because the café was making good money. When I told her I wasn't going to do as she asked. She told me to leave and never come back."

I remember standing there with my mouth wide open shocked. Shock turned into anger. "You're a liar. My grandma said you were the reason she decided to open Pauline's Pies. She said you helped her to build it. She said you were her true love and she was yours!"

Raheem stood up from the swing and walked passed me down the stairs of the porch. "Let me tell you why Pauline told you that. Our sexual natures couldn't resist each other. A few months after she told me to never come back, she was back out here to see me. She was ashamed of her behavior because she announced to everyone I was dead when she told me not to come back. Pauline asked me to never come by the café again. I agreed. I didn't care. We continued to have sex and I continued to take her money."

The years went by and Cedric ended up with your brother. Pauline was so committed to being a grandmother. She watched him everyday for your parents, but she couldn't stay away from me, so she brought your brother Francis out here with her. As he grew older he became intrigued by my feminine ways. I'd sometimes be dressed in full drag and he loved it. Once when she left Francis alone with me, I allowed him to watch as I had sex with one of my male companions. Because he was so close to Pauline, he told her."

Raheem stopped in the middle of his story. I didn't know why until I heard my father's voice. "So what happened then?" My father yelled out at Raheem. He had a gun in his hand and it was aimed at my grandfather. "JJ, I want you to get back in my car and go home!" My body was frozen. I wanted to move but I couldn't. My father yelled, "JJ, get your ass back in my car and go home!"

I ran to my father's car and dug in my pockets for the keys. I had so many little trinkets I kept from my grandma Pauline. Each one had a different purpose. My father yelled at me again. "Hurry up!" I found the keys, opened the door, and hopped in. I sat looking at my father hold the gun at who I thought was my grandfather. I started the car and drove away. I cried all the way back to the café.

I remembering running in the back house to look for Francis. I wanted him to be there for me the way I'd been for him so many times before. He was no where to be found. I rolled up in my bed and held on to my teddy bear. I must have fallen asleep because when I woke up I heard people out front in the café. I ran to go see, and, sure enough, the café was open. When I walked inside my father was behind the counter with Francis talking to some customers. I must have slept all day long! I stood looking at my father. I wondered if he did it. I wondered if he shot Raheem! He came from behind the counter and escorted me outside.

"JJ, I want you to know he's still alive and kicking. I told him to pack his stuff and get out of town for good. He agreed." I was so proud of my father for not doing the worst! I hugged him tight.

Francis walked outside. "Black folks always sleeping on the job. I need a little help in here with these pecans!" We all went back inside. The day was going wonderful until the authorities came into the café. There were two officers and ordering a pie or lemonade wasn't on their agendas. One of the officers had a thick beard and a large watermelon-sized stomach. The other one was short and skinny with a big head. He reminded me of someone who should be in a circus act! They were nothing but certified rednecks!

The fat bellied one pounded on the counter. "We stopped by to warn you good citizens that there was a robbery at the Smith's pawn shop early this morning. A gun was stolen as well as cash. Be careful of any suspicious looking people coming through here."

Huh, if they didn't have badges, I would've told them to look in the mirror. They looked pretty damn suspicious. If my grandma was still alive, they would not have walked up in there they way they did. Law enforcement respected Grandma Pauline. They would have waited for her to come outside and then talk to her. No talk would have been done in front of her customers.

My father responded, "No problem, officers. We'll be on the look out."

The officers walked out of the café. As they were leaving, one of Francis's professors came in. Francis tried to run toward the back when she called out to him. "Francis!"

He turned around to look at her. "Yes, Mrs. Merkelson, what would you like to order?"

"I didn't come here to place an order. I came here to find out why you weren't in class today? The test I gave was worth fifty percent of your grade. You're one of the school's top students and you have so much potential. So, I had to stop by to see if you are alright."

Francis replied, "Yes, I'm fine. I stayed up too late studying and overslept."

I looked at my brother as he told his lie. He wasn't at the house when I returned and he told daddy earlier that day he didn't have classes until the afternoon. My father also gave him a stern look because he didn't believe what he was hearing either.

Mrs. Merkelson was old school and didn't believe his story. "Considering class doesn't start until 2pm, I'd have to say that was surely a whole lot of oversleeping. I will allow you to make up the test if you stop by the campus tomorrow morning at 7am."

My brother was grateful. "Thank you, Mrs. Merkelson, I will be there!"

My father offered her free lemonade for driving down to speak with Francis. He felt she went way beyond her duty as his history professor. She graciously accepted the lemonade and went on her way. What was strange to me was that my father didn't yell at my brother. No words were even exchanged. They both continued on with what they were doing as if the professor was never there. I didn't understand it. Being who I was and still am I, I had to make comment.

"Francis, you never miss school, never. What's up with you?"

"Nothing is up with me. I overslept!"

"You liar, I came home and you weren't around. I needed you and you weren't around!" I forgot all about the conversation needing to be about Francis not going to school. I made it all about me needing him.

Francis stopped mixing batter and hugged me. "I was there for you, I promise I was."

He was making me angry because he didn't get that I was looking for him. "I looked all over the house for you. You weren't here!"

Francis looked over at our father then back at me. "I may not have been here at this house, but I was there for you at Raheem's."

The few customers inside walked out shaking their heads. Daddy locked the door and stood by us. He wrapped his arms around us. I knew something serious was up. We had never done the group hug thing ever before in our entire lives. Daddy let go and sat down on a bench. I sat next to him. Francis stood in front of us with his hands semi-shaking. He rocked back and forth for a few seconds then took a deep breath. "JJ, I know about what happened with you and Raheem. The reason I know is because I heard daddy talking to himself early this morning. I cried at first because I felt for you. But I was happy he didn't get a chance to rape you...like he did me!"

I wanted to jump up and hold my brother, but all my aching soul could do was cry out to the Lord. *"Father God, why?"* I looked to my right side and my father was crying. The tears were rolling down his face like a river. My vision became blurry. I thought I was going to faint, but I didn't. Francis continued. "It's not God's fault, JJ. It's grandma's fault. You know how much she needed to be in control of everything and everyone around her. Raheem was the one person she couldn't control. It drove her crazy! All those damn shopping trips were nothing but trips to see him! She would beg him over and over to come back here to the café and stop living as a bisexual but he refused."

Francis paused for a moment. I could tell his mind went back into time. He held back the tears that wanted to be released from his pain. He looked at the ground and then held his head up high. "Grandma didn't like sleeping with a lot of different men. She thought that by having Raheem he could try and satisfy her high sexual nature. She would have given him anything to be with her, even me."

I didn't want to hear anymore. How could Francis say she was willing to do him like that? I didn't care what else he had to say, I wasn't going to believe it. Grandma Pauline was a strong, in control woman. She never wanted to be with one man so bad she'd sacrifice her grandchild. I stood up to leave the room.

My father told me to sit back down. I didn't want to, but I did. Francis got on his knees in front of me. It reminded me of the day he came home from getting his ass beat. "JJ, when I heard daddy this morning I threw on some clothes and went down to the Smith's Pawn Shop. I knew I wanted to take a gun. I only took the money to make it look like a random theft. When you both saw me in the kitchen, I had already returned and put my bed clothes back on so you wouldn't think anything."

I remember feeling chills go up and down my body as my brother told me what he did. Francis got up off his knees. "You thought I was asleep, but I heard you take daddy's keys. I immediately got in my car and followed behind you from far away. When you went into Raheem's driveway I parked down the road. So, JJ, I was there for you today. If he would've put one hand on you while I was there, I was going to blow his brains out!"

I turned to look at my father and asked him, "How did you get to Raheem's house?"

My father wiped his face and replied, "Your grandma's old delivery truck."

"Were you there Francis, when daddy arrived?" I asked.

He sighed. "Yes, I was standing on the opposite side of the house."

I stood up and looked at both of the handsome, loving men in my life and asked, "So you both had guns and you both had intentions to kill Raheem?"

They both answered, "Yes!"

CHAPTER TWELVE

I stop staring in the mirror and go back out to the kitchen. Manny and Buster are still by the kitchen island waiting for me. I look down at Buster, he's so pitiful. Nobody takes good care of him when Darius is away. I wonder if he ate anything in the last few days. I look in the refrigerator to find him a hot dog or sausage.

"Sorry, Buster. Ain't shit in here unless you want some eggs and bacon." Buster barks one time.

Manny rubs him behind his ear. "I think that's a yes!"

I put a piece of bacon in the microwave to cook it up for him. Darius comes down the stairs. He's full of joy to see his childhood friend. You see, Buster is Darius's dog. He's had him since tenth grade. Buster is a funny-looking pit bull. His eyes are different colors. One is brown the other is black. Darius's parents didn't have him clipped when they brought him, so he looks like he should be something other than a pit. Buster is old and doesn't do much, so the kids aren't interested in him. I don't bother with the damn dog at all. He smells funny. You know how old people start smelling funny as they age, like Ben-gay and old powder? Buster has that old dog smell!

Buster breaks the hold Manny has on his leash to run to Darius. "Hey Buster, I missed you, too!"

Darius is on his knees rubbing the dog, letting him lick him all in his face like white people do. Damn, I wish I didn't see that shit! I take the bacon out and blow on it to cool it off for the dog. I put the piece of bacon out for Buster to eat. "Here, Buster!"

Darius snatches the bacon from my hand. "Don't ever give him people food. He's too old! His digestive system can't handle all that grease." He throws it in the trash can. "Poor Buster, JJ's trying to kill you off, isn't she?"

Manny and I look at each other and roll our eyes. We come from the old school where dogs didn't get dog food. They got the leftovers from dinner. I only know of one other man who loved his dog like Darius and that man was my father...

When I left New York for California I called my brother to let him know what I was up to. He was still in school making the grades and loving life. Once I started having steady hours at the restaurant, I decided to get myself a pager so Francis and Eva could reach me. I remember when I got the page from Francis about my father's death. It was a Saturday and I was working as a fry cook. When my pager went off, the restaurant was jam packed with people. The tickets kept coming up and I was frying chicken and French fries like crazy. An hour went by before I had the time to call Francis. I always used the pay phone outside of the restaurant. I didn't want the people I worked with to know too much of my personal life.

Francis's phone kept ringing and ringing. I was about to hang up when he finally answered. "Hello."

"Hello, Francis?" I wasn't sure if it was him. He sounded so different.

"Yes. JJ, what took you so long to call me back?" He asked.

"Sorry, sweetheart. I got busy at work. I only have a five minute break, so what's up?"

The phone line got silent. Then Francis cried out. "Daddy's dead, and those crazy wanna be bitches did it!"

"Francis, what bitches...daddy...daddy is dead?" I dropped the phone for a second. I picked it back up. "What happened to daddy?"

My brother told me what happened to our father. Daddy was out walking his German shepherd, Rex, along one of the back roads. A car load of Raheem's friends were driving down that same road. They were liquored up and dressed like bitches. They had been kicking it at this transsexual/gay bar hidden off in the back woods. Everybody in town knew about the bar, but didn't want to talk about it. Every so often members from different churches would go down there and protest and wave their bibles in folks' faces. My father's church was known for being "regulars" at the bar and trying to convert as my brother put it the wanna be bitches into Christians!

Francis said they pulled my father over and started harassing him. The reasons are not solid. It could have been because of his religious affiliation or because of me. You see, there had been talk around town that I had something to do with Raheem's death. The police found one of the charms Grandma Pauline had given me on the ground in the driveway. Since the authorities were not interested in truly finding out who did it, I was going to be an easy arrest. At the time of the authorities so called investigation, I was running wild sleeping with older men and getting high. Instead of staying to deal with the police, I left for New York with a biker I met in front of Major Mart. Everyone in town assumed I was guilty. My father and Francis were left to deal with the whispers and rumors.

I was holding the phone tightly in my hand feeling guilty as my brother continued to tell me what happened. Francis's voice was trembling. "They took Rex from daddy and tied Rex to a tree!"

Just like Darius and Buster, my father raised Rex from a puppy. My father never missed a day walking that dog, even when he had the damn flu. Francis said two of the men confessed to what they did. They held my father back and made him watch as they tortured Rex. Rex was too old to fight back. He did manage to bite one of the men who confessed. He only confessed because he had to go into the emergency room for his wound. His ass was too drunk to know better than to tell the truth.

"I understand what happened to Rex but what did they do to daddy?" I recall being afraid of what my brother's answer would be.

"Well, JJ, daddy hadn't been feeling so good. All those years of fatty food and moonshine took a toll on his heart. His wife never tried to help matters when the doctors told him to change his lifestyle. She kept feeding him unhealthy food and poured the liquor for him every night." Francis paused. "He had a massive heart attack. They left him right there on the side of the road along with Rex's cut up body!"

Once his words soaked in, I realized his death wouldn't have happened if I had stayed and dealt with things like a big girl. I would have gone to court and the court would've found me not guilty. I didn't kill Raheem, so I wasn't guilty. Then the town would have known the truth, but instead my father had to pay the price of my running!

Francis's voice changed. He sounded like my defense attorney "JJ, I know how you are. Don't you feel guilty; daddy didn't take care of himself. If he did, he wouldn't have had a heart attack. Despite what you believe, you're not in control of everything. You had nothing to do with him having a bad heart, no control what so ever! And what those men did is not your fault either. They probably would've hurt anyone walking along that road. It just happened to be daddy and Rex."

The following week after I had gotten the news, Francis told me how he tried to help my father's wife with the funeral and burial arrangements. The little church ho didn't want to cooperate with him. Before I could get all the money I needed for my plane ticket, the bitch had already buried my father. She didn't even tell Francis about the funeral date. He found out at the last minute from one of our old customers. Francis was able to get down to the graveyard while the funeral was still in progress. Once they put my father in the ground, Francis grabbed the bitch by the throat. He said there was no doubt in his mind that he wanted to put her in the ground with daddy. Francis was blessed that she didn't press charges. Because my father didn't have a will, she was able to fuck both of us by not giving us a single penny...

Manny and I watch Darius as he rolls around with Buster. I hear the garage door open. It better be that damn Eva with my car in good condition. Manny's cell phone rings. It's Eva asking him to come and help her. Manny asks, "JJ, is it okay for me to help her?"

I roll my eyes. "Whatever!"

Manny goes out to help and I think of how I'm going to grab her by the hair soon as she gets close to me. They walk through the door with grocery bags. The bitch stopped at the 24-hour grocery store and the 24-hour coffeehouse and brought cups of gourmet coffee. Darius's eyes light up and he grabs the coffee cup carrier from her. "I'll take that." Manny is helping Eva take groceries out of the bags. I'm standing here looking stupid again. I know she's trying to make me look like shit in my husband's eyes, but why? All these years, I thought she was my girl! I thought no man, no niggah, no dick would ever come between us. I guess I got it twisted.

Eva taps a spoon against a glass and announces "I got each of you your favorite coffee. I want us to make a toast to some wonderful news I got the other day."

We all pick up our coffee cups and give her our full attention. Eva pulls a bottle of milk out of one of the bags. "I'm no longer going to drink coffee because...I'm pregnant!"

"Did this bitch say she's pregnant?" I couldn't help myself and this time I meant to say something out loud. They all turn to give me the evil fucking eye. Huh, I don't care. I want to know who the damn daddy is. "So, who knocked you up?"

Eva takes a sip of milk. "I had a one night stand. You know how that is."

Oh no, she didn't! I know she's not trying to drag my business out in the streets! I pretend I didn't notice her comment. Manny tries to ignore it also. Darius gulped down his coffee and belches. He grins at Eva. "Congratulations, I guess we better marry you off before you start showing!"

I can't help but ask my husband a question, "Babe, who are you going to try and marry Eva off to?"

He looks at me like I'm the crazy one "The dude from yesterday, Reggie. He's a good catch. A good man such as myself can sense another good man. He'll be perfect!"

What he just said sounds so gay to me. If I didn't know him, I'd trip right about now.

Eva punches Darius on his shoulder. "You got jokes!"

"Nah, I'm dead serious! We need to get you a man quick!"

Eva doesn't like his comment. "I thought I had one?"

Manny puts his two cents in. "I thought you said it was a one night stand? If it's somebody you want in the baby's life, you better tell him now and not when the baby is heading to college!"

"The father knows. We just haven't discussed details yet. He's trying to get over the surprise!" Eva folds her arms.

I give Eva a hug and whisper in her ear, "I'm happy for you. I really am happy for you."

Darius grabs Buster and heads for the door. "We'll be back in a few minutes."

Manny leans over and kisses Eva on the forehead. "Congrats! We'll talk later."

He takes his coffee cup and leaves out the sliding glass door.

It's just Eva and me, and it's quiet. This feels strange to me. Throughout our friendship, we've always had something to say to each other. Now within two fucking days, we've become enemies. The incident with her watching us is still on my mind and I'm wondering who the baby's father is. I understand why she's acting up, hormones do some wild shit to us females.

"Eva girl, you know I'm not trying to upset you, but I need to know why you was watching us?" My voice is kind.

She turns her back on me. "I'm not gonna lie to you, JJ. Darius turns me on. I heard ya'll in the bathroom fucking. His moaning was turning me on and I wanted to watch him!"

I don't know whether to feel sorry for her or beat the hell out of her! I ball my hands into fists. "Girl, you taken this love for Darius too far now. Time to come back to reality. He's my husband! Remember, your best friend's husband!"

Eva turns around. "I don't know why you trippin', I've watched you fuck before!"

"Yeah, but we were young back then. And none of those niggahs was my husband!" I'm trying to control myself from knocking her upside the head. "Look, you need to start thinking about this baby you about to bring into this messed up world. What are you going to do for money when you move out?"

"I'm not moving. I've changed my mind. I think it's better for me to stay here, be comfortable. Staying here, I will be eating healthy meals and surrounded by love. There is no better environment for me to be in."

I know after all that's been going on this ho didn't just tell me she's staying in my house. I don't want to kick my friend out, but she's leaving me no choice. I can't have any female living up in here and lusting after my husband. "Look Eva, I can help you go look at apartments today. Once you find something, Manny and Darius will move your stuff. I'll go buy you some things for your new place. You don't have to worry about a job. You can still help with the kids and I'll pay you."

Eva gives me a foul look. "All you want me to do is come over and watch the kids while you go out fucking other dudes, huh?"

"Girl, why you trippin' off what I do?" I'm sick of her sudden self-righteousness.

"I'm sorry, girl. Being pregnant has got me going. I'm just gonna go lay down for awhile. Don't worry about breakfast. I'll get up and cook and get the kids ready to go to church." Eva pats me on the back and walks upstairs.

All of this shit is stressing me out! I need to get some stress released. My haven for relaxation is probably not the same now. I got to find out. I grab my cell phone and dial nine on my speed dial.

Reggie picks up, he's pissed at me. I can hear it in his voice. "It's been hours since I called you and you just now calling me back? Is this how you're going to start treating me?"

I try using my sexy phone voice. "No, baby. I would never mistreat you. I didn't have the opportunity to call you back."

"Give up the voice, Jasmine! I was calling you to say I'm sorry we're not going to work out. I want you to know I enjoyed your company. Good-bye." Reggie is about to hang up the phone I stop him. "Wait!"

"Jasmine, there is nothing to say. I thought the reason we met in hotels is because you didn't want to expose me to your children right away. Not because you are hiding a husband. I'm looking for somebody to love and one day marry. Not a married woman!"

I'm upset about him wanting to put an end to our great sex meetings. I get a little nasty with him. "You got some fucking nerve! I told you it was nothing but sex between us. I told you I couldn't get tied down! Now you wanna act like a bitch!"

His voice sounded hurt. "A bitch, a bitch. I don't know about that one, Jasmine. I can't take your job title away from you, now can I?"

"I'm sorry. I didn't mean to call you a bitch. I wasn't expecting to fall in love with you." I said it before I knew it. I did it again. I let my thoughts out of my mouth.

There's a long pause on the line. Did he hang up on me? "Hello, Reggie. Are you still there?"

The silence breaks. Reggie pleads, "Jasmine, if you really love me, come see me right now. Come to my house, Jasmine, so, I can make love to you!"

There it is...the invite I knew I'd one day get. An invitation to his house! I reach in the kitchen junk drawer for a pen and paper. "Give me your address!" I'm writing down his address when Darius walks through the door with Buster. He smiles at me and walks the dog out back to his kennel. That damn kennel is so big I could make it into an apartment for Eva. Huh, that's what I should do for the bitch. Throw her ass in the kennel!

"I'll see you in one hour!" I hang up and put the paper in the pocket of my robe.

Darius walks back inside and kisses me on the cheek. "What's up with you, babe?"

I have to think of some reason to not go to church with him right away. "You know I've been helping out the PTA, right?"

"Yeah."

"I've been making friends with the different mothers and there's this one mother who's husband has been beating on her ass. She just called me and told me he beat her again! She needs me to come over and take her to the hospital!" It sounds good to me but by the look on Darius's face, I'm not sure if he believes it.

He's concerned. "It's too bad she's going through that. I hope her kids didn't see her get beat. I know for a fact it does damage to a child to see that kind of mess go on. I never could understand what would make a man want to hit a woman." He kisses me on the cheek again. "It's got to be something serious to make a man do that sort of thing."

I respond. "Yeah, something serious."

"Baby, you should call the ambulance. They'll get to her quicker!"

"No, she'll feel better if someone who cares is there with her."

Darius kisses me on my lips this time. "Cares, huh? I'm happy to see you're making more friends. Having only one friend can be stressful, but I wish you wouldn't have picked a needy person. Now, you have two needy friends."

"Damn, baby, I know but what can I do?" I'm walking upstairs so I can get dressed.

Darius answers my question. "You can meet us at church when you're finished, how about that?"

I stop halfway up the stairs. I turn around and Darius is standing at the bottom of the staircase. I need to get out of going to church. "You know how the county emergency rooms are? She doesn't have insurance."

"Then you take her to our hospital emergency room and pay for it. She is your new friend, right? She might as well join the rest in getting the best!"

I'm at a lost for words. "Okay."

"Oh and, baby. Make sure you bring me a receipt so I can use this as a tax deduction." He smiles and walks back in the kitchen. I'm fucked now!

CHAPTER THIRTEEN

I arrive at Reggie's house aka Mr. Dress Shop. He lives on a cute little cul-de-sac with three other houses. His house is right in the middle. Although there is room to park next to his car, I park on the curb. I sit in the car for a few, thinking about how I've never done this before. I've never met a man at his house. I've always kept things impersonal. I'm breaking all of the rules with this dude. At this moment I can sympathize with Eva. She's in love with a man she can never be with and so am I.

I'm dressed up in my Sunday best. I've got my beautiful gray church suit and hat on. I look like I'm married to a preacher. Maybe that's a sign! I should start my car right now and head to the church building and be with my family, but instead I'm taking a chance I shouldn't be. Lord, I don't know why I GIVE INTO TEMPTATION? WHY DID YOU GIVE ME THESE DESIRES? I look toward Reggie's front door and he's standing in the doorway looking at me. He has nothing on but his boxers. Damn, he's sexy as hell! Speaking of hell, that's where I'm headed for eternity! He starts to walk out to my car and my cell phone rings. My caller ID shows that it's Eva. I wave at Reggie for him to go back inside. I hold up my phone to show him I've got a call. I roll down my window and yell, "I'll be right in!"

I answer her call. "What?"

"I'm calling to let you know I got your family off to church. They look beautiful." Eva sounds like she's high off something. The bitch is probably turning up a forty!

I don't want to talk to her ass. "And you're calling to tell me this because of...?"

"I'm wondering where you're at. Darius told me about your friend needing to go to the hospital. Do you need any help with her?"

This bitch knows I'm not at no fucking hospital! Why is she playing games with me. But I am a little glad she called and reminded me about the hospital lie. How am I going to get a hospital receipt for my husband?

"I'm good, Eva. Thanks for the call."

"Hold up," Eva says. "I want you to know something that's been on my heart from the time you met Darius in the movie theater."

I'm beginning to believe she wants to win the award for Cock Blocker of the Year!

"Okay Eva, what the fuck is so heavy on your heart that your ass can't wait till later to tell me?"

Her accent gets thicker. "I never thought yo ho ass deserved him!"

Her comment reminds me of the tension between Sophie and Dominique. I'm Sophie and Eva is Dominique. Except the only witchcraft that's going to be happening here is me pulling her damn hair out. That's it! Baby or no baby, when I see Eva, I'm kicking her ass! I hang up my cell phone. I don't want to play games with her. I want to go inside and fuck Reggie.

I look in my compact mirror and fix my lipstick. "Get 'em girl!" I go up to his door and it's cracked open for me to walk inside. He has a trail of rose petals from the door to his bedroom. I walk inside of his room and I'm impressed with his taste. He has a Cal-King bed with Italian wood posts with a matching chest and dresser. There are silk drapes hanging from the bedposts and the comforter is my favorite color- red! Reggie walks out of his bathroom. He got rid of the boxers, he's butt ass naked! He presses play on his music system. Hmm...it's Luther! He comes over to me singing and takes my hat off and puts it on his head.

He strikes a pose. "How does my outfit look?"

"You're being silly!"

"I'll be anything, as long as I can be with you." He starts unbuttoning my suit.

Now what he said sounds like some shit from a Harlequin novel, but I like it. I stop him from unbuttoning my suit.

"What's wrong?" He asks.

"Nothing, it's just you're always singing to me and now I want to sing to you."

I pull an unlabeled CD out of my purse. "Put it on track number three." He puts the CD in and sits on the edge of the bed. The music starts and he flashes a big smile. Wow, he's got a sexy smile! He snaps his fingers. "It's Anita Baker's 'You Bring Me Joy'." I'm singing along as he leans back and enjoys the show. The song is over and he claps his hands.

"Bravo, baby!" He gets up and turns the CD off. "You did good!"

I'm so proud of myself "Hell yeah, I wanted to show you I can do a little something when I put my mind to it."

He rubs me on my shoulders. "Why don't you put your mind to doing a little something else?" He finishes taking my clothes off. I'm standing here naked and more comfortable then I've ever been. I don't think about running to hide under the bed sheets. I don't want to put anything on to cover my body. I'm happy standing in front of him naked!

"Oh, Reggie baby, now you know your something is not little!"

"Is that right?" He kisses me on my stomach like the stretch marks aren't there.

"Yeah, that's right!" I reply softly. The kisses are so soothing.

Reggie holds my face to look him in the eyes. "Am I ever going to win this prize?"

"Prize, you're still being silly!"

"Even though your body is here with me, I question if your heart is here also, but I don't want to make things complicated for you. I'll take what I can get and every minute I spend with you, I'm going to try and win you over. You'll be my prize."

I'm digging every single romantic word coming from his lips. Usually love is not my thing when it comes to a one night stand or booty call, but Reggie is not a one night stand or a booty call. With every kiss, he gives me, my entire body tingles. We start making love all over his room. We knock shit off the dresser and nightstand. He's got my ass up in the window! The blinds are coming down! We pull the drapes down and throw the comforter, sheets, and pillows all over the damn room!

The next area we hit is the bathroom sink. Reggie's got me sitting on the sink while he's on his knees eating my pussy. I happen to glance at myself in the mirror. Damn, why did I do that!

My mind starts thinking about last night with Darius. Now my mind is thinking about him sitting at church waiting for me.

"Ah, ooh, Reggie stop! I've gotta make a call, ooh!" I'm trying to tell him to stop, it feels so good.

After a couple of minutes of pleading, he grants me my wish and stops. "Soon as you're done, I'm going to make you cum!"

I get on the phone and call Darius's cell phone. I know he won't answer. He's in the middle of church, but, at least, I can leave a message. "Hey baby, I'm running late. See you and the kids soon." I hang up and throw the phone on the floor.

"Make me cum!"

Reggie hugs me tight and kisses me. He's nibbling on my ears and kissing the scar on my neck. My scar has never fazed him at all. Juicy is getting wetter by the second. His dick is standing straight up! He reaches in his medicine cabinet and grabs a condom. I knock it out of his hand.

"Are you sure?" He asks. "I'm not going to pull out!"

I look him eye to eye and hold on to his hard dick and guide it inside of me. "I don't want you to."

CHAPTER FOURTEEN

I'm standing outside the church doors fixing my clothes. I can hear the choir singing. I look up to the sky. *"Well, Lord, I didn't miss too much of service. That should count for something."* I walk into the church wearing a fake smile. I sit next to Darius and the kids. I kiss him on the cheek. He pulls away. That's not like him.

"Nice for you to show up, JJ," Darius says with an attitude. "I'm sure the Lord appreciates you thinking of him today!"

"Baby, I left you a message on your cell phone to let you know I was running late." I respond trying to act like all is good.

Darius asks me a question, "How is your friend doing?"

"Huh?"

"Your new friend, how is she?"

I whisper in his ear. "She's going to be fine."

"Did you get the receipt?"

"Huh?"

"The receipt, JJ. Did you get one?" Darius sounds inpatient. "What are you losing your hearing all of a sudden?"

"Oh, I forgot, baby!"

Jayne looks up at me. "You also forgot your pretty hat!"

I touch the top of my head "Oh, I sure did!"

Darius turns to me and without hesitation presses his lips against mine real hard and looks me straight in my face. "This is one Sunday you better pray hard. You better believe the Lord will answer when you do!"

I sit back in the pew and I feel like I'm going to throw up my insides! During the entire service, Darius acts as if I'm not here. He doesn't hold my hand during prayer. He doesn't tap me on my knee during the choir singing. I'm invisible to him. The children notice something is wrong, but don't say a word. One of the things I've always admired about Darius is he never lets the kids know when things are not right with us. 'Children don't need to be in adults' business,' he says. He believes children should always see a healthy relationship. Darius tells me all the time how there isn't enough black love stories on television for them to see, so they will see it in our home.

I know over the last few days I've been messing up our love story. That's probably why this is the first time I've seen him forget his saying, and I am frightened by it. Although his parents raised him in the church, he saw them fight a lot. From what my mother-in-law tells me things got very violent.

When service is over, I walk outside of the church. Darius and the kids are a few steps behind me. Eva is standing outside with Manny. They never come to church so I know something is going on.

"Hey, Eva! What's up, girl?" I ask trying to seem cool.

She replies, but doesn't look in my direction. She's focusing on the kids. "Nothing much, girl. Darius called us to come pick up the kids. He wants us to take them to Sea World for the rest of the afternoon so he can spend time with you."

"Wow, Sea World...time with me...this is a nice surprise!" I try and act happy about the situation, but I'm worried.

Manny looks worried too and walks over and grabs my hands. "JJ, did you have a good time in church?"

I squeeze his hands, kiss him on the cheek, and whisper in his ear. "Tell me what is wrong, my friend?"

Manny looks down toward the ground and squeezes my hands back. He looks over at Darius and the kids as they walk toward us and whispers in my ear. "He knows, JJ. He knows about Reggie." My mouth drops wide open and I let go of Manny's hands. I step back from him and onto Darius's foot.

"Ouch, baby!" Darius shouts softly.

I continue to look at Manny's face. I know this is his way of trying to protect me in some way, but there is nothing to protect me from. Darius would never hurt me. He loves me too much and if he does know, so what. He'll get over it and we'll be all good.

Darius hugs the kids. "Allen, Jayne, kiss Mommy good-bye."

It sounds so final as if I wasn't going to see them again. I have to point that out to him because I'm suffocating from the serious vibes in the air right now.

"Darius, I'm going to see them later. You act like I'm never seeing them again!" I kiss them both and put them in Manny's car. I give Manny and Eva kisses and walk toward Darius's Expedition. Darius is walking behind me not saying a word. Usually he'll make comments about how good my ass looks in my church suit. He'd joke around saying, "Praise the Lord, Thank Ya Jesus!" Today, he doesn't make one comment. He doesn't even open the car door for me like usual.

"Darius baby, what's wrong?" I ask with a sweet tender tone.

He looks over at me and starts the ignition. He looks forward and starts to pull out of the parking lot when Pastor Jones stops him. Darius rolls down the car window to see what the pastor wants.

"Hey, Mr. Minister, what's up?" Darius sounds like his normal self.

Pastor Jones is breathing hard. The fast pace he had to walk to stop Darius made him out of breath. "Well, young brotha, I wanted to see if you're alright. I looked down from the pulpit and you didn't seem yourself today."

I was glad somebody else was feeling what I was. I knew I wasn't crazy.

I try to laugh things off. "Hmm...Pastor, I'm glad you noticed. I've been wondering if the devil got in him today!"

"I'm fine, Pastor Jones," he responds. "I'm a little tired from all the traveling I've had to do lately. Being away from my loving wife and beautiful kids can weigh heavy on a man."

Pastor Jones laughs out loud and rubs on his pregnant-looking stomach. "Well, you know we appreciate you working so hard. All that money you give to the church is so wonderful!"

Darius looks at me. "Oh, really?" He turns back to the pastor. "Well, I'll make sure I don't skip a beat to keep that money coming into the church!" They shake hands and Darius pulls off. He beats his hand on the steering wheel as if music is playing and beat boxing. I know something is not right with him.

"Baby, you want me to put some music on?"

"No, I got it!" Darius puts a CD in. Usually he tunes into the Sunday Gospel Radio Program but not today.

"Babe, I heard this young cat at work playing this CD when he was pulling out of the parking lot. Since I know you're so into the meaning of words in songs. I couldn't help but ask him to borrow it. Let me know if you like this particular track. It's by Mario and the song is called 'How Could You'?"

I didn't want him to play the song. I've heard it before. I know the exact meaning behind the lyrics. I press the stop button. "I've heard it before. It's a kid's song. You know I'm into old school!"

His voice sounds angry. "I know but this song got my attention. It hit my heart kinda hard but I realized it's just a song. But today, it really has some meaning for me!"

I try to change the subject. "Where are we going? Oh, we should stop at that new seafood restaurant I heard about on the boulevard!"

"No, I'm going to cook for you at home. I want to show you something new I learned while I was on this last business trip."

There's nothing more I can say. He's in control, not me. The rest of the drive there's no conversation and he keeps playing and singing that song over and over.

It's kind of crazy, babe. How I remember things like where you came from and how you had nothing. I went and made you fly, put extras on your ride, hmm...You made it clear to me, you wasn't down for me. Love made me blind, baby, but now I see, hmm...

We get to the house and I'm afraid to get out of the car. He opens the door and pulls me out. Darius has never put a hand on me, so I shouldn't trip. If what Manny told me is true, then so be it. I'll have to pay the price for my sins. At this point I'm tired and don't have the strength to fight. I follow Darius into the kitchen. He sets a bottle of wine on the counter. He pulls out two glasses. "Let's have a drink, while I cook dinner." He opens the wine bottle and pours. "Here, babe, let's make a toast."

I hold up my wine glass. "Sure."

Darius holds his glass up to mine. "To my whorish ass wife, for her being a nasty, malicious bitch for so many years of our marriage!" He drinks his glass of wine and slams the glass down so hard he breaks it! I've never seen him like this before, ever! I notice his hand is bleeding.

"Baby, you cut your hand!" I grab a paper towel and put it on his hand. He pulls away and licks the blood. "Darius, what are you doing? What the hell is wrong with you?"

"You dumb ass bitch! You know what's wrong with me! You've been fucking around on me!" He rinses his hand in the sink and wraps it with paper towels. "It's funny how you thought your girl Eva wouldn't tell me shit. Don't ever believe that people can't be bought in one form or another. Your girl, well she's paid for in full! There are lots of things Eva wants in life and I know how to give it to her. She wants me to help get her family to the United States and I'm making that happen for her. With that, I got her to tell me all about your foul ass ways, which I knew in the first place, but needed some proof. You played yourself that way, Jasmine. I'm a good ass man, but I'm not a mother fuckin' treadmill for you to run all over me! When you thought I wasn't paying attention I was. Let me educate you on something, Jasmine! I knew you wasn't nothing but a low class ho when I met you. But, girl, you can suck a dick better than any high priced ho out there!"

I get in Darius's face allowing him to see the tears flow. "You don't mean that, Darius, you're just hurt right now!"

He walks away from me and paces around the kitchen floor. "Hurt is not the word for what the fuck I'm feeling right now! Jasmine, even though I knew you was a ho, I also knew that you were worth more than what is between your legs. You was the one Jasmine, YOU was the one! Not Shelia! If it was meant for me to be with Shelia for the rest of my life, she'd still be alive! The only reason I keep her portrait is to remind me of who helped me to start Black on Black Consulting! Not because I'm still in love with her! I love you!"

Darius falls to the floor crying. I walk over to try and hold my husband. He pushes me back and I hit the floor. He stands up, wipes his face, and starts pacing again. "You can't seem to realize how good you got it. You don't have to do a damn thing around here. I pay the bills! Eva takes care of my kids! And when I fuck you, all you have to do is lay there! You think you can go out fucking other men, come home, get your ass in the shower, and then lay next to me, and I wouldn't know! Bitch, is you crazy?"

As I watch my husband pacing back and fourth I picture my father at my grandmother's memorial, I picture Mr. UPS when he was ranting and raving. I picture Juice before he kicked me in the head. I know my husband is on the edge. I stand up and move to the other side of the kitchen. Darius stands still. "When Eva first started telling me about all the men, I didn't believe her until she showed me your cell phone. I never knew you had a lock on it because I never ran behind you spying. I guess I should've been spying on you years ago! After she showed me the phone, she told me about Reggie and that you're quick to run and see his ass whenever he calls. Since Eva was so willing to give me all this information, I decided to give her something else she wanted, I fucked her! Hell, yeah. I fucked her! That is why she was watching us yesterday. Her ass was jealous! Oh, and that baby she's carrying is mine!"

I feel my throat get dry as a summer day in the Nevada desert. I grab a cup of water and take a few sips. Wait a minute! This reminds me of something. Sophie! All those years of Grandma Pauline telling me the story of Sophie and Bastista comes down to this. A warning! I know what is going to happen next. I put the glass of water down and start to walk out of the kitchen. He grabs me by the arm!

"Where are you going?"

"I need to go to the bathroom, Darius. Let go of my arm, baby. You're hurting me!"

I can see in his eyes that the hurt he was feeling has turned into evil! "You know when I married you, I said I'd never hurt you. When my father used to beat my mother, I hated him for it. I never understood why he would want to put his hands on her...but I do now!"

I try to get out of his grip. He's too strong for me. He throws me on the kitchen floor and pins me down with his legs. He lifts his right fist and hits me in the mouth. I'm kicking and screaming trying to get up. The more noise I make the more and harder he hits me. I see splashes of my blood on the cabinets. Darius is sweating from all the energy he's using to hit me. After awhile, I stop moving and just let him hit me. He stops and lies on top of me. "You know I love you right, Jasmine?"

If this is love, I don't want no more. He gets up and takes the bloody paper towel off of his hand. He washes his hands in the sink and puts some ice in a Ziplock bag. He shows me his swollen hands. "I made my hands swell up, baby. Look!"

I can't get up. My head feels like a heavy water balloon. He knocked a couple of my teeth out and one of my eyes is swollen shut. I manage to pull myself up and stumble into the downstairs bathroom. I stand in the mirror. I can hardly see out of the one open eye. All I can manage to do is cry and call out to the Lord. "LORD, HELP ME. You said before I even say my prayers you will answer them. HELP ME!" The tears coming down my face are no longer made of water and salt but of blood. The face that I've been so proud of and quick to brag about is now bruised. I should've taken my ass straight to church and not to Mr. Dress Shop's crib. This is one time I needed to pass on getting to know a brotha better...

CHAPTER FIFTEEN

The police officers walk around my house. They take fingerprints and photos. I am answering the investigator's questions. She keeps asking me the same ones over and over again. I was blessed our landscaper, Armando, came by to get his payment today. He usually waits until Monday, but had plans to head to Ensenada to see friends for a week. Lucky for me, he stopped by to lock up his equipment and get his check. He was in the back locking up the shed when he heard me crying out to the Lord. It's amazing how the Lord answered me by sending him! Armando called 911 and sat and prayed with me. Now, I know why every time I offered him a cold beer he didn't accept it. He's an extremely devout Christian.

Eva and Manny walk in the house with the kids. A couple of the officers try to keep them from walking into the living room. I see the shock on their faces. Eva's mouth drops open like she's auditioning for a second-rate soap opera. Manny turns the kids around so they won't see my bruised face. He walks them out back to the pool. I signal for them to allow Eva into the living room. Eva asks the investigator if she can talk to me alone. The investigator agrees, gathers her notes, and walks about five feet away from us, so much for privacy.

Eva sits beside me on the couch. "JJ, what happened? Did you get robbed?"

Even though the paramedics gave me some pain medication, it hurts to talk. I slowly move my swollen lips to answer her. "Darius went off on me."

Eva starts to cry. "This is my fault. I shouldn't have told him about you fucking around!"

Soon as those words came out of her mouth, I want to reach over, throw her on the ground, and stomp her in her head. My head is hurting and so is my heart. My one and only female friend betrayed me as if I was nothing to her. The investigator is taking notes. I guess Eva is going to be in her report. The dumb ho should've kept her mouth shut!

One of the paramedics checks my face. "Mrs. Brooks, are you sure you don't want to go to the hospital?"

"Yes, I'm sure."

My mind is telling me I'm sure, but my head is saying something else. The paramedics told me I was lucky he only hit me in the face and not anywhere else like my chest, ribs, or kidneys. Lucky? I don't see anything lucky about this situation. One of the police officers said they've seen worse. Their team has worked on crime scenes where they could have filled paint cans with the victim's blood. Hmm...thinking about it, I guess I am lucky.

I hear one of the officer's hand radios announce a five-car pile up on Interstate-5, sounds pretty bad. The dispatcher is calling for any available units to assist with traffic control. My head keeps pounding. I need another hit of pain medicine. I'm trying to get the paramedic's attention. He's too busy talking to one of the police officers. Eva's running her mouth apologizing and trying to convince me to go to the hospital. Buster is in the kennel barking as loud as he can. The kids are outside crying. Manny's fussing with a police officer. There is too much damn noise! I feel as if my head is going to explode!

One of the officers walks over to me. "They may have located your husband, Mrs. Brooks. We'll get confirmation in a few minutes."

I try to nod my head. "Thank you."

I see two of the officers in the corner talking to each other. They're looking at me and Eva. Manny tries to walk back into the house and the officers tell him to stay with the kids outside. I hear one of the officers say that someone needs to call a child psychologist to speak with the kids. The officers stop conversing and the female officer walks over to us.

"Mrs. Brooks, are you sure you don't want to lie down or have them take you to the hospital?" She waves for the paramedic to come take another look at me.

"I'll be fine if I can get a little more pain medicine, please!"

The paramedic opens his legalized drug kit and starts fixing me up an IV. He looks at me and says, "I'm going to fix you up right this time. This will make you sleepy."

I hear the female office tell the paramedic that she needs to tell me something before he puts the IV in.

"Tell me what?" I ask.

She sits on the other side of me and puts her hand on my knee. "Mrs. Brooks, I have some bad news. Your husband was in a terrible accident on the freeway. Apparently, he didn't have his seat belt on and when he tried to avoid the other cars in an accident, his car flipped over and his body was flung through driver's seat window. He was pronounced dead on site."

Eva falls out on the floor crying. The female officer drags her into the family room. Manny is looking through the glass sliding doors. He wants to come in, but they won't let him. I can hear him arguing with the police officers. "What is going on? I need to go in there and be with JJ, please!"

I hear the kids screaming for me and Eva. Some lady with a note pad, gray hair, and an orange two-piece suit flies by to go outside with the kids. She must be the child psychologist they called for. Damn, she got here fast!

I'm in too much pain to move. I can hardly talk so trying to tell the police to let Manny inside isn't going to work. I want to cry, but my eyes hurt too bad to produce tears. My cell phone rings. I see on the caller ID that it's Reggie. I can't answer it. I want to but I can't. The room starts to spin around. Before I know it, I black out...

Pastor Jones is sweating and waving his handkerchief. "CHURCH! I want to know if anybody out there knows about a God who is forgiving! CHURCH! I want to know....HA! If anybody out there knows about a God who can make you branddddd NEW! I say CHURCH! I want to know if anybody out there knows about a God who will bring money from out of nowhere to feedddddd your family! If you know who I'm talkin' 'bout can I get an AMEN!"

I excuse myself from my seat and go to the ladies' room. My stomach isn't feeling so good, but that's alright. It's a beautiful Sunday morning! I step inside the ladies' room and it's empty. Thank goodness I don't have to wait for a stall. I wash my hands and take a look in the mirror. Wow, I am so blessed right now!

I don't struggle with going to church anymore. I enjoy hearing the Word and apply it to my life. It's been six months since I was released from the hospital. I ended up staying there for three weeks from the beating Darius put on me. Pastor Jones told me that members of the church took turns sitting at my bedside praying for me around the clock. He said there is no physician on earth better than the Lord at healing somebody. I believe it! My earthly physician said I healed so well it's as if I never got a beating! He was surprised since I've had a couple of head injuries in my life. All the glory is to God!

It's interesting how this beating helped out my mother-in-law. When she came to the hospital to see me, it frightened her to think she could end up fighting for her life some day. So she went home and packed her bags. Nobody knows where she went. My father-in-law has gone on with his life. He moved that little girl, well Reggie's sister into the house with him. I knew he wanted her!

Allen and Jayne are still trying to adjust. They still see the child psychologist who came over to the house that day. That woman loves some loud colored suits! Every time I take the kids to see her, she's got orange, purple, pink or yellow on! Regardless of how she dresses, she is good with the kids. I can see them working on being happy again.

Eva doesn't live with me anymore. After Darius's funeral, she started drinking heavily. I mean heavy like liquor stores were going out of business. Eva drank so much; she ended up losing her baby. Come to find out, she wasn't sure who the father was. She felt so guilty after she slept with Darius that she went to a bar, got drunk, and screwed a couple of guys that night. Eva told me she could have only hoped it was Darius's baby. She decided to give up on bringing her family to the United States and went back to live with them in Puerto Rico. We still talk on the phone once a week. We did make another promises to each other....always be open and honest.

Manny, he's still around and protects me like he's my bodyguard. He lurks around corners waiting for an opportunity to remind me of where I came from. I don't care. He keeps me humble. He got me to sign up for interior design school. I've been going for a month now and loving it. Just like Grandma Pauline found her calling with the pies, I found mine with decorating!

Reggie, he turned out to be my true love. He's sitting in the choir stands right now. He puts a blessing on this congregation every Sunday. That man knows he can sing! You know what else he can do? Huh, you know some of it. He got me pregnant! I guess I should have stuck to my motto 'Wrap It Up'. The pill wasn't strong enough to stop his fish from jumping through the net! I bet it's going to be a big nappy headed boy because I've been showing since I left the hospital. We plan on getting married soon. I called Francis and he agreed to cater the wedding. I always thought he could out cook Grandma Pauline! And he has someone special in his life...her name is Anika! Yeah, I said her name. Francis finally got on the team I knew he belonged on! He was always a happy person, but he is off the chart with happiness now. He's just a Hot Mess!

I walk back into church service and take my seat. I sure wish Grandma Pauline was here to see me now. She'd really be proud of me... I had the courage to do what she couldn't. I decided to change my life and be happy.

Pastor Jones stops preaching loud. "Hallelujah, I want ya'll to turn your bibles to Psalm 32:1. Blessed is he whose transgression is forgiven, whose sin is covered. Can I get an AMEN!

"AMEN!" Jayne shouts.

"AMEN!" Allen shouts.

I shout, "AMEN, Preacher!"

I know you are wondering about the curse.....let me break it down for you like this. Another breeze blew my way. It came when Reggie picked me up from the hospital. I felt it as I walked out of the exit doors. It was a breeze unlike the ones I had felt before. It was a breeze that blew all of my past transgressions away. I took comfort in knowing I didn't have to be in control of everything in my life. God is in control of my life. I handed myself over to Him. You see things and people only have control when you hand over the power. I don't give that curse any power because my legs aren't wide open anymore!

in the United States
RV00002B/259-600/P

9 781934 947081